The Wilmington & Weldon
Railroad Company
in the Civil War

ALSO BY JAMES C. BURKE

The Wilmington & Raleigh Rail Road Company, 1833–1854 (McFarland, 2011)

The Wilmington & Weldon Railroad Company in the Civil War

JAMES C. BURKE

McFarland & Company, Inc., Publishers
Jefferson, North Carolina, and London

LIBRARY OF CONGRESS CATALOGUING-IN-PUBLICATION DATA

Burke, James C., 1958–
    The Wilmington & Weldon Railroad Company in the Civil War / James C. Burke.
    p.   cm.
    Includes bibliographical references and index.

    ISBN 978-0-7864-7154-6
    softcover : acid free paper ∞

    1. Wilmington and Weldon Rail Road — History — 19th century. 2. North Carolina — History — Civil War, 1861–1865 — Transportation. 3. United States — History — Civil War, 1861–1865 — Transportation. 4. Railroads — North Carolina — History — 19th century. I. Title. II. Title: Wilmington and Weldon Railroad Company in the Civil War.
    E545.B87 2013
    385.09756—dc23   2012046613

BRITISH LIBRARY CATALOGUING DATA ARE AVAILABLE

© 2013 James C. Burke. All rights reserved

No part of this book may be reproduced or transmitted in any form or by any means, electronic or mechanical, including photocopying or recording, or by any information storage and retrieval system, without permission in writing from the publisher.

On the cover: *inset* detail of an illustration of the surrender of Fort Hatteras from *The Soldier in Our Civil War* (photograph courtesy New Hanover Public Library, NCD Box 1 019); *background* © 2013 Shutterstock

Manufactured in the United States of America

McFarland & Company, Inc., Publishers
  Box 611, Jefferson, North Carolina 28640
    www.mcfarlandpub.com

In memory of
Dr. W. Frank Ainsley

Table of Contents

Acknowledgments   ix
Preface   1
Introduction   7

I. The Railroads of Wilmington, Before and After the War   13
II. The Events of 1860–1861   35
III. The Freight of War   77
IV. The Enemy, Seen and Unseen   98
V. Demanding the Impossible   134
VI. The Aftermath   146
VII. Rebuilding   158

Appendix A: Locomotives and Inventory of the Company Shops   169
Appendix B: Railroad Employees Living in Wilmington, 1865–1871   176
Appendix C: Freight Shipments for the Confederate Government   204
Chapter Notes   225
Bibliography   250
Index   257

Acknowledgments

Each of the individuals who contributed both time and expertise in bringing this work to fruition is deserving of my sincere gratitude and praise. My colleague Dr. Cyn Johnson enthusiastically accepted the challenge of providing photographs of places of significance mentioned in the text. Determined to anchor the narrative to coordinates on the landscape, she traversed eastern North Carolina from Cape Fear to Roanoke in several trips and repeatedly explored the historic district of Wilmington. Not content merely to document present conditions, she went to great lengths to convey a sense of the tension in images where dramatic events occurred. Her efforts to illustrate concepts pertaining to the nature of Wilmington's urban landscape were executed with the same degree of forethought and repeated experimentation.

For the second year in a row, my friend F. Donald Hickman spent his entire Christmas holidays proofing and editing one of my books. This time, however, he was also battling the flu. Nevertheless, my longtime friend from graduate school days pressed forward, carefully burnishing the rough edges of my prose and correcting more than a few embarrassing spellcheck and typographical errors. I appreciated our frequent meetings to go over the text page by page and the offering of helpful suggestions on ways to make the lines flow. With his constant encouragement throughout the fall of 2011, work progressed rapidly on the text to its completion. From our days in the classroom at the turn of the century to the present, it has been both a pleasure and an honor to work with so dedicated a scholar and gentleman as Mr. Hickman.

Beverly Tetterton, local history librarian at the New Hanover County Library and author, presented me the opportunity to incorporate into my manuscript illustrations from the library's Civil War era publications. After carefully examining and reexamining the contents of three large archival boxes of illustrations over several days, I selected a large number of drawings — far more than would actually be used. Nearly all of these drawing had to be scanned. As a result of her careful attention to this task, I was in many instances able to juxtapose images of a significant scene unfolding on the historic landscape with a modern photograph of the same location.

Jim McKee of the Brunswick Town–Fort Anderson Historic Site shared his extensive knowledge about the Fort Anderson site and other defenses of the Cape Fear River. He also led me to valuable sources that proved essential in determining the nature of the freight shipments carried over the Wilmington & Weldon Railroad during the first year of the Civil War. A brief conversation with Dr. Chris E. Fonvielle of the University of North Carolina at Wilmington before the manuscript was completed shed light upon questions I had about the defense of Fort Fisher and the site of the Wilmington & Manchester Railroad depot on Eagles Island.

I would like to thank John E. Best for his assistance that included providing high-resolution photographic equipment for the field photographs used in this work, solving a host of computer woes that would arise at the most inconvenient moments and generally working behind the scenes to ensure that the progress of this undertaking would not be impeded for want of anything. In addition, our lengthy discussions about the history and economy of Duplin County, North Carolina, and the region proved invaluable when conducting the field study that I considered essential in preparing a work such as this. Most of all, I fully appreciate his friendship.

I would like to thank Victor Galloway for his continued involvement in my field research, particularly ground truthing missions involving daylong treks on the back roads of rural North Carolina. His astute observations, conscientious note taking, and instant recall of details contributed greatly to long term planning and the allocation of resources for most of my research projects.

Finally, I would be remiss in not acknowledging the hospitality and friendship of Almira Johnson and her family — John J. Johnson, Debra Justin, and Dr. Cyn Johnson — throughout my years as a student and continuing to the present.

Preface

The *Wilmington & Weldon Railroad in the Civil War* is a continuation of the history of a corporation that began its existence as the Wilmington & Raleigh Rail Road in the 1830s. The author's previous book, *The Wilmington & Raleigh Rail Road Company, 1833–1854*, chronicled the economic, political, and technical aspects of building what was in its day "the longest railroad in the world." Through a combination of careful planning and managerial genius, the company survived a devastating sequence of setbacks, including political opposition to the decision to change its route from Raleigh to Weldon, the financial downturn brought about by the Panic of 1837, a fire in 1843 that destroyed its Wilmington facilities and equipment, and the enormous cost of replacing its primitive strap-iron wooden rails in the early 1850s. From 1855 through 1860, under its new corporate name, the Wilmington & Weldon Railroad, not only did the company thrive, but so did the entire corridor along which it ran. Wilmington enjoyed its last period of expanding prosperity of the antebellum period as the town became the hub for three great railroads: the Wilmington & Weldon, the Wilmington & Manchester, and the yet to be completed Wilmington, Charlotte & Rutherford.

The history of the Wilmington & Weldon during the Civil War presents a different set of issues from those of the previous period. While the Confederacy ceased to exist in April 1865, the railroads of Wilmington were the product of the antebellum program of internal improvements, and they would play a significant role in building the economy of post–Reconstruction North Carolina. Appropriately, this narrative lends itself to a description of these railroads in the first chapter, both before and after the war. Not only is the function of the rail network defined in advance of describing the events of the war years, but it also frames the conclusion of the work. Supplementing this chapter are Appendices A and B. The first is a compilation of the prewar and postwar material assets of the Wilmington &

Weldon Railroad, including a roster of locomotives and an inventory of machinery, tools, and supplies in the company shops. At a glance, the scope of the industrial operation becomes apparent: the company had the capacity to build and repair its rolling stock and repair locomotives — the shops had even built a couple of locomotives; the rail mending shop reformed damaged and laminated rails; and the machinery was powered by stationary engines. These resources allowed the company to respond to the wear of heavy usage during the war and to resume transportation promptly after Union raids destroyed sections of the railroad.

Appendix B documents the housing patterns of railroad workers in Wilmington from 1865–66 through 1870–71. Compilations of listings in the city directories reveal a pattern of residences over time for the nearly all white wage labor force as they occupied sections of the town. While portions of the workers — particularly those now called blue collar — provided little information other than names and positions, others followed a distinct route to permanent residences by way of hotels, boarding houses, and living with fellow employees or relatives. Unlike the slave labor force of the past, in time the workers established distinct enclaves within sections of the town that would evolve into neighborhoods. The urban form of antebellum Wilmington, dwelling places of wealthy planters, commission merchants, professional men, turpentine distillers, and their slaves, retained much of its preindustrial form. Slaves resided in the households of slaveholders, or in quarters provided for them at their place of work. There wasn't a working class neighborhood, only pockets of outcasts contained at the town margins and at the docks. Postwar Wilmington had a more recognizable form: working class neighborhoods located near their place of work; clerical workers and specialists resided on the opposite side of town — middle class neighborhoods; the company officers and key employees in fashionable new homes and the mansion district; and a distinct commercial district, uninterrupted by residential land usage.

All topics associated with the Civil War tend to excite interest equally in the community of scholars and the general public. The events leading up to the war, the overwhelming scope of its violence, the depth of the human drama that attends its most discrete aspects, and the profundity of its underlying political and moral conflicts justify placing this brief period in American history at the fore as a topic of national introspection. Though its conclusion is removed from present-day life by nearly 150 years, it remains the benchmark from which the survey of the deceptively familiar America must be triangulated. This also holds true for footprints on the cultural and physical landscape. Human history does not unfold in a vacuum; however, a natural but unfortunate tendency exists for the reader to mentally manufacture one when the text neglects or fails to define place.

The author has found that students attain a greater understanding of a historic text if they are provided maps and archival photographs that illustrate past conditions at the place where an historic event occurred; for instance, they better visualize spatial relationships that exist between that place and other elements of its environment. (A site visit further enhances interpretation of a text.) At times, spatial inquiry leads to discovery. Likewise, the method of defining the spatial attributes of the historic narrative employed in this work relies on juxtaposing archival photographs and drawings depicting the locations of significant events with modern photographs portraying the same places: maps establish the wider geographic context. The archival maps, photographs, and line drawings included in this work come from the vast collection of the New Hanover County Library, housed in the North Carolina Room. The field study photographs contributed by Dr. Cyn Johnson highlight elements of the building environment of Wilmington that date to antebellum and postwar periods, as well as the present-day appearance of significant places in the narrative such as the site of political meetings on south side of Wilmington known as the Oaks, and the nearby topographic features associated with the infamous Rouse Pond section where the yellow fever epidemic took hold. Locations outside Wilmington, including the defensive works of the Cape Fear River and sites associated with raids on the railroad, are presented using the same method.

The corporate history of the Wilmington & Weldon Railroad Company during the war is enmeshed thoroughly within the large context of political and economic instabilities, in addition to the demands of servicing the needs of the Confederate military. For this reason, the annual reports of the meeting of stockholders are used as a starting point; primary sources including period newspapers articles, artillery manuals, official reports and communications, annual reports from connecting railroads, first hands accounts from diaries and memoirs, and legislative documents fill out the narrative. Secondary sources, scholarly and professional journals, ranging from period to contemporary, provide the requisite overview of critical issues and events.

Appendix C is a compilation of data derived from transportation vouchers contained in the Confederate Citizens Files (National Archives) that illustrates the nature of freight shipments carried over the Wilmington & Weldon Railroad for the Confederate Government. It is organized into the categories of "Food," "Arms and equipment," and "Other freight" for the months August through October 1861. While the data present only a sample of the shipments, they aid in establishing clear transportation patterns, point data from sources and destinations, identifies specific military units and individuals, and even provides insight into the diet of Confederate soldiers. The Wilmington & Weldon's connection to the Deep South, the Wilmington & Manchester Railroad, appears to be the critical link in the delivery of food to the theater of battle in Virginia, and the amounts of food delivered are impressive. Light arms, tents, blankets, shipments of powder, and medical supplies traveled to destinations north; however, heavy artillery destined for coastal defenses generally was shipped south on the Wilmington & Weldon.

The demands placed upon the Wilmington & Weldon during the Civil War would drive the company to the brink of absolute ruin. While the officers and employees maintained the operations of the railroad with an exemplary level of professional competence, high volumes of military freight wore out rails and rolling stock; occasional Union raids destroyed equipment, bridges, and facilities, disrupting transportation; and the combination of low rates for military shipment and the unstable nature of Confederate currency rendered the profit margin of the company illusory.

The Wilmington & Weldon emerged into the new normal of Reconstruction with 159 bales of cotton, valued at $25,000; the amount of $22,803.86 due on account from the State of North Carolina; and a mountain of worthless Confederate paper with the imaginary value of $1,400,000. From this dismal condition, the company set about resuming service as it rebuilt its railroad; rough and discontinuous operations commenced in August 1865. By 1868, passenger receipts approached 1860 levels with freight receipt increased by $114,436 compared to the same year. The new business model of the railroad would be based upon the transformation of regional agriculture and improved connections south via a bridge over the Cape Fear River. The railroad, once dependent upon slave labor, adapted to wage labor, finding the resulting cost comparable.

Hints of how the company planned to survive and prosper in the postwar socioeconomic environment are evident from a reading of the annual reports of the late 1860s. While the development of new industries would contribute greatly, the company realized the potential for exploiting the diverse agricultural economy that could result from the cheap land prices, small farms, and emigration to the South. In addition to the traditional staple crops, cotton and tobacco, the Wilmington & Weldon would prepare its equipment for the transport of fruits and vegetables. This proved to be timely. An examination of agricultural reports prepared by the State of North Carolina up to the 1920s shows that truck farming and planned agricultural communities along the eastern rail corridor of the state worked well. Statistics from some of these reports are included in the notes.

Since the end of its corporate existence, there has not been a single scholarly work that was entirely devoted to the history of the Wilmington & Weldon Railroad Company, with the exception of the author's previous volume *The Wilmington & Raleigh Rail Road Company, 1833–1854*. The company has usually received attention from books on the Atlantic Coast Line Railroad, of which there are many. As a result, the significance of the earlier railroad might appear to pale in comparison to the grand corporate giant. Nothing could be further from the truth. The antebellum history of the railroad establishes the significance of the history of American railroads, civil engineering, and business. The history of the Wilmington & Weldon Railroad during the Civil War not only establishes its importance during mobilization at the start of the war, but it also served as one of the Confederacy's last channels for supplying the Army of Northern Virginia, earning it a significance within the context of the history of the United States as a whole.

Though this work touches upon material falling within the period of Reconstruction, it was for the purpose, as stated above, of framing the Civil War; and to avoid misleading the reader into assuming the railroad company succumbed during the postwar upheaval. The history of the Wilmington & Weldon Railroad from Reconstruction through the end of the century certainly merits its own volume.

Introduction

The Wilmington & Weldon Railroad in the Civil War is a continuation of the corporate history of a railroad, originally incorporated as the Wilmington & Raleigh Rail Road Company. In its early years, Wilmington's great railroad survived several crises: a trade war between the railroads of the Virginia commercial centers; the national economic upheaval of the late 1830s and early 1840s; a catastrophic fire that destroyed its facilities and equipment in Wilmington; and having to replace iron on the entire length of the system under very difficult circumstances. Under its new corporate name, the Wilmington & Weldon Railroad Company, it would soon be put to the ultimate test, the coming of the Civil War.

From military mobilization in May 1861 to the last effort to supply Confederate troops from the remains of its northern division in April 1865, the company would endure the wearing out of its equipment and rails; the capriciousness and bureaucracy of the Confederate government; sabotage attempts; the gruesome accidental death of its president, William S. Ashe; the yellow fever epidemic in Wilmington; Union raids on its facilities and bridges; the runaway devaluation of Confederate currency; the fall of Fort Fisher and Wilmington; its bisection by forces under General Sherman; and, finally, the unnecessary destruction of locomotives, cars, track, and bridges by retreating Confederate troops. The railroad, unlike the Confederacy, survived, and would eventually transform itself into a powerful regional economic force. However, that is not the whole story.

Unlike the previous volume, *The Wilmington & Raleigh Rail Road Company, 1833–1854*, which focused mainly on the corporation, this work endeavors to describe how the nature of the railroad economy changed the urban form of Wilmington, creating distinct industrial, commercial, and residential districts. It was the end result of free labor dynamics. After the war, the new labor force of the company set about carving out neighborhoods in the hitherto near-homogenous human landscape of the old town of Wilmington.

It would assume the more traditional form of a modern industrial center with districts organized according to socioeconomic classes and ethnic origins. The postwar railroad, deprived of its slave labor force, would rebuild and expand, drawing from a base of displaced and dispossessed indigenous laborers and immigrants as new rail connections were established. When the Cape Fear River was bridged in 1869, the three great railroads that terminated at Wilmington were united within the city limits. From this point forward until the 1950s, the economy of the region would be centered on its rail connections, rather than the railroad merely being an enhancement to the port as it had been during its antebellum history.

Throughout this book, the narrative shifts from an examination of the business of the company, found in the reports of the annual meetings of the stockholders, to the great context of the war raging in the background. For example, the reader is thus given a unique view of the tumultuous political events surrounding the presidential election of 1860 from the perspective of the citizens of Wilmington, juxtaposed with the rather rosy outlook for the company projected in the stockholders meeting, even though, ironically, the election and the meeting occurred within two days of each other. The political activity of some of the railroad's directors is examined as well.

The interpretations of subsequent annual meetings draw upon a host of archival documents and scholarly works to provide a detailed description of the real world context in which the railroad was attempting to maintain efficient and uninterrupted service. These include relevant period documents concerning the secession conventions; Union and Confederate military documents; information from vouchers charged to the Confederate government for transportation on the Wilmington & Weldon and other companies; period newspaper articles, journals, memoirs, and other firsthand accounts of events during the war; treatises on 19th century artillery; and sundry works concerning blockade running, finance, and military theory.

The picture that emerges of the Wilmington & Weldon during the Civil War is that of a critical rail link supplying the Confederate forces in Virginia and a key element in the defense of eastern North Carolina. The "Lifeline of the Confederacy," the moniker given to Wilmington when the port remained the régime's last access to the outside world, was a far more complex supply network than the phrase implies. In addition to blockade runners and inland navigation, the Wilmington & Manchester Railroad, the vital artery through which flowed troops and food from the Deep South. At Goldsboro, where the Wilmington & Weldon formed a junction with the North Carolina Railroad, shipments of supplies continued via the Piedmont Railroad to Virginia after the connection from Weldon to Petersburg was broken by Union troops around Petersburg. Even after the fall of Wilmington, the Wilmington & Weldon continued to serve the Confederacy from its wartime shops at Magnolia and Enfield.

In spite of competent and agile management of the company during the war, the Wilmington & Weldon was flawed in one serious aspect, much in the way most Southern railroads were: they had not been designed for military use on the scale which the war demanded, and wear on their rails and equipment could not easily be remedied without access to iron in quantity. As early as 1861, the enormous volumes of food transported over the railroad to feed the army and urban civilians in Virginia tested the capacity of the corridor as shipments from the Deep South entered the bottleneck between Kingsville, South Carolina, to Petersburg, Virginia. The Confederate government realized as early as late 1862 that the single line traversing the coastal plain of North Carolina could never deliver enough food. However, a combination of political squabbling and commercial resistance slowed the completion of an interior connection between Greensboro and Danville, the Piedmont Railroad, to May 1864. It was late to relieve the stress on the coastal corridor, as access to Petersburg would soon be reduced to the South Side Railroad; and the addition of shipments from Wilmington converged at Greensboro via Goldsboro with those traveling from Charlotte. Then as from early in the war, stores of food piled up at stations, sometime in the open, going to waste as Confederate troops suffered near starvation and the citizens of Richmond faced famine while yet knowing that their land offered plenty.

The combined effects of deflated Confederate currency and of the mischief of profiteers played havoc on the finances of the Wilmington & Weldon. The cost of living in Wilmington was so high that the employees of the company could hardly afford to stay. Employees along the line fared only slightly better. The railroad was a great consumer of wood, oil and grease, and all types of construction material—in addition to iron and other metals—and the price of these items necessary for the operation of the railroad climbed as the value of paper money declined relative to specie. By November 1864, the profits on the books of the company were illusory, and S.L. Fremont, the chief engineer and superintendent of the company, was quick to bring this to the attention of the stockholders. In reality, the railroad was making less than the cost of running it.

The company had other setbacks outside the realm of operations of the railroad and its finances as well. Wilmington had been transformed by the war into something unlike anything before or after. It became the haunt of speculators—domestic and foreign—military men, and every class of criminal and miscreant imaginable. Understandably, town officials were overwhelmed. Into the mix of filth and crime was introduced yellow fever, and during the fall of 1862 it killed 446 out of approximately 3,000 individuals remaining in town. The railroad lost several of its directors to the epidemic. Passenger travel diminished to an occasional handful, and the activity of the port was at a standstill. Only freight shipment connections from the Wilmington & Manchester kept the railroad active on a reduced schedule.

The remarkable fact that the Wilmington & Weldon was not effectively rendered useless until the last days of the war illustrates how well the early decision to locate the railroad more inland (Walter Gwynn's western route) worked. Union forces, well ensconced at Hatteras, Roanoke Island, and New Bern early in the war, were able to make only two cavalry raids on the railroad, and the damage they accomplished then was repaired quickly. The Confederate response to these raids, however, demonstrated the South's inability to mobilize troops and artillery quickly to engage the invaders; having inflicted damage on the railroad, stations, warehouses, and destroyed stores of supplies and arms, Union troops quickly made their way back to the safety of their own lines. Aiding their success was the absence of sufficient Confederate cavalry patrolling the railroad and troops stationed as guards at bridges and stations.

It is generally agreed that the defeat of the Confederate Army can be explained by the fact that the Union Army had the benefit of greater manpower, a strong industrial base for providing the necessities of civilian life in addition to the weapons and equipment of war; the strong support of the United States Navy; and a more unified network of railroads. Knowledge of the wartime history of the Wilmington & Weldon Railroad Company contributes to an understanding of why the war continued as long as it did. In early 1862, Union generals George McClellan and Ambrose Burnside contemplated a plan to launch an ambitious assault on Goldsboro, capturing the railroad with a wing of this invasion force splitting off and attacking Wilmington from the rear by way of the Wilmington & Weldon. The remaining wing would drive on to capture Raleigh. With these objectives accomplished, the supply line to Virginia would be crippled beyond sustainability.

The plan was never implemented, perhaps out of apprehension that Confederate forces would stream along the railroad from Weldon and Wilmington to cut off and surround the advance on Raleigh. Continuing as a bloody stalemate for the next two years, the eastern theater was fueled by the stream of provisions and arms passing through North Carolina on its assailable rail corridors. Given McClellan's timorousness in committing the bulk of his forces, exemplified by the Peninsula Campaign, a bold two-pronged offensive appeared too risky, especially considering the size of Union forces positioned at strongholds on the North Carolina coast. Insomuch as can be said of the military significance of the Wilmington & Weldon Railroad, it appears obvious that the participation of Virginia in the Civil War could not have continued, and perhaps not even commenced, had not the rail corridors of North Carolina been available for logistical support.

In the previous volume, *The Wilmington & Raleigh Rail Road Company, 1833–1854*, the topic of route selection was explored exhaustively. Of the many plans for proposed railroads that were nurtured during the early years of railroad development in North Carolina and of the two that were actually built — the Raleigh & Gaston and the Wilmington & Raleigh — the Wilmington & Raleigh proved to be the more successful. Yet, when considering the performance of the rail network in North Carolina during the Civil War, had the direction of internal improvements for the state followed a different course, the conflict might have been prolonged or fizzled completely. Had the much maligned Metropolitan Route passing through the interior been realized, Virginia would have had an additional connection to the agriculture of the Deep South, providing the Wilmington & Raleigh was not actually built to Raleigh. By contrast, the early construction of great east-to-west railroads, such as Joseph Caldwell's plan for a central railroad or the Cape Fear & Yadkin Rail Road plan, might have, for numerous reasons, made support of the seceded states by North Carolina impractical, if not impossible. While contemplating alternate histories is not particularly productive, modeling of transportation — real and hypothetical — provides some insight into the strengths and weaknesses of any actual network. Even so, the Wilmington & Weldon Railroad, through its connections to the Wilmington & Manchester Railroad and the North Carolina served adequately to prolong the downward trajectory of the Confederate war effort. None of these railroads were designed to handle the frequency of traffic or the volume of freight that prosecuting the war effectively required. Those who thought it a good idea to provoke the United States to take up arms without foreseeing, much less considering, the logistical problems of long-term rail transport, were irresponsible. The critical link in the network was at the junction of railroads at Wilmington, and when Wilmington fell, Richmond was doomed.

In the devastated postwar economic landscape of the South, the Wilmington & Weldon Railroad managed to rebuild in much the same way it had built and rebuilt in antebellum times: through bonds. Within a few years, the profits of the company climbed back to prewar levels. The new labor force, drawing from a now abundant pool of white men, was willing to work cheaply; and in some cases, it cost the company no more to pay wages to laborers than it did to pay slaveholders under the old system. Wilmington's old guard, retreating to the hinterland during the war, filtered back into town to claim their property and reestablish their positions, now it the midst of common whites and emancipated plantation slaves drawn to the town by fear and necessity.

Subjoined to the text of this volume are three useful appendices. Appendix A is an inventory of the equipment belonging to the Wilmington & Weldon Railroad Company prior to the war. It is derived from the annual reports, and details the resources the company had at hand to serve the railroad from the onset of war. Appendix B is a table of company employees residing in Wilmington from 1865 through 1871. It includes the address, job title, and company associated with individual workers — where listed — and the page number of the city directory in which the list can be found. This table illustrates how the number of railroad workers in Wilmington expanded during the postwar years, and in what neighborhoods they resided. Appendix C is a compilation of information derived from freight vouchers showing shipments of food, arms and munitions, and equipment for the Confederate government for 1861. The set of three tables includes the origin of the shipment and its destination, in addition to its weight or quantity, and a description of the load. The date of shipment is also included. This set of tables, providing insight into the nature of freight shipment on the Wilmington & Weldon Railroad, also shows how important its connections via the Wilmington & Manchester Railroad were to the war; and the food shipments, destined for Richmond and the battlefields of Virginia, represented a large portion of the freight volume traveling over the Wilmington & Weldon.

Chapter I

The Railroads of Wilmington, Before and After the War

The history of the Wilmington & Weldon extends back to the early years of railroad development in the United States. Incorporated during the 1833–34 session of the North Carolina General Assembly as the Wilmington & Raleigh Rail Road Company, the railroad was built from Wilmington to the town of Weldon on the Roanoke River. It provided service to Charleston, South Carolina, by way of its own steamboat line.[1] The Wilmington & Manchester Railroad, providing connections to the railroads of South Carolina, brought about the discontinuation of the steamboat line in 1854. By 1860, sections of another railroad, the Wilmington, Charlotte & Rutherford Railroad had been completed, offering the Wilmington port a long anticipated connection through the Cape Fear region westward. Together, these railroads, in part, represented the last phase of what had been known much earlier as a state system of internal improvements. It was brought into being through a remarkable arrangement whereby the State of North Carolina became a shareholder in the railroad companies, backed the railroad's bonds with the good credit of the state, and assumed control in the rare instance of failure. As investments, stock in these companies was hardly an engine for short term gain. Furthermore, most of the shareholders of the Wilmington & Weldon resided within the state and on the route of the railroad.[2] The North Carolina Railroad, extending from Goldsboro to Charlotte, was completed in 1856. In 1858, the Atlantic & North Carolina Railroad was completed from Goldsboro to Beaufort Harbor. At Goldsboro, the Wilmington & Weldon formed a junction with the two railroads. The Tarboro branch of the Wilmington & Weldon went into operation in August 1860, though lacking a permanent bridge over the Tar River. The contractors for the line were Bisset & Birchett.[3] At Weldon, on the Roanoke River, the Wilmington & Weldon

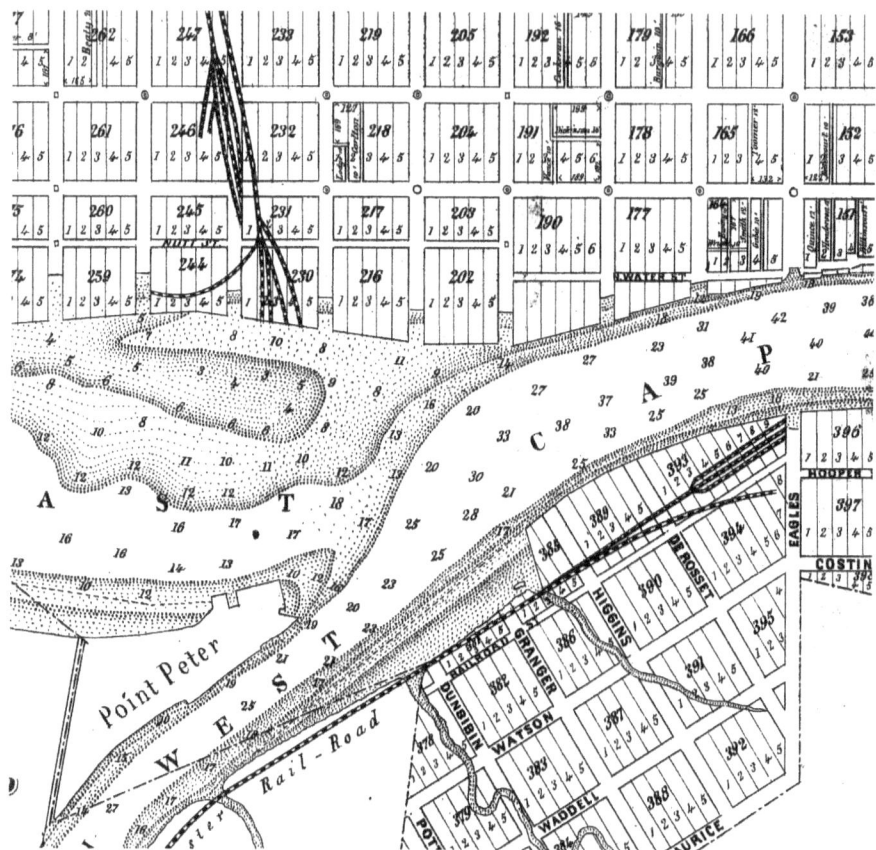

The 1856 Plan of Wilmington, North Carolina, by L.C. Turner shows the locations of the track and depot facilities of the Wilmington & Weldon Railroad and the Wilmington & Manchester Railroad. Transportation across the Cape Fear River between the depots was by steam ferry (courtesy New Hanover Public Library).

formed a junction with the Petersburg Railroad, the Seaboard & Roanoke Railroad, and a branch line of the Raleigh & Gaston Railroad. All the railroads mentioned, with the exception of the Wilmington & Manchester, were built in standard gauge. The Wilmington & Manchester was built in the gauge of the South Carolina Railroad: five-foot gauge. The Cape Fear River presented the greatest obstruction to forming a continuation of the Wilmington & Weldon to the south. The river was not bridged until after the war; a steam ferry was used for the transport of freight and passengers to the Wilmington & Manchester and the Wilmington, Charlotte & Rutherford Railroad until that time.

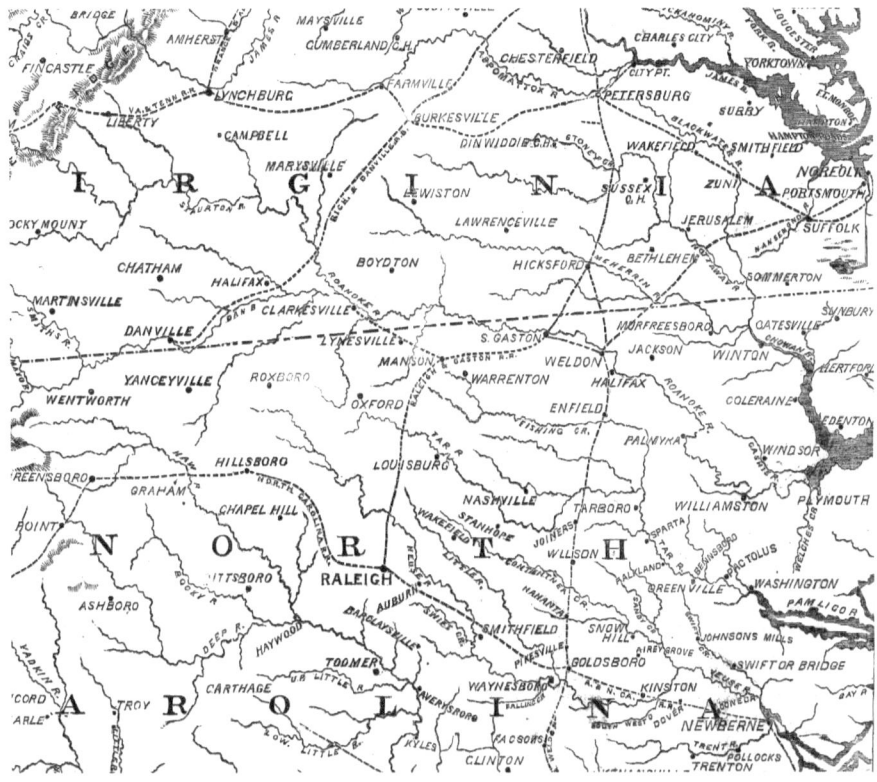

The detailed view of the rail network connecting major urban centers of northeastern North Carolina and southeastern Virginia is taken from a much larger map printed in the February 14, 1863, edition of *Harper's Weekly* (courtesy New Hanover Public Library, NCD Box 1 020).

The Wilmington & Weldon Railroad

From the change of the corporate name of the company from the Wilmington & Raleigh Railroad in early 1855, the Wilmington & Weldon Railroad Company entered a period of consistent profits and improvement of its property. For five fiscal years, from October 1, 1855, through September 30, 1860, the company brought in average annual gross receipts of $479,641.11; the average annual expenses had been $232,785.03, yielding average annual net receipts of $246,856.08. The average annual amount spent on improving the company was $44,302.62, including the building of new buildings, the filling in of the old trestlework, and other construction.[4] The annual reports for the years 1856 through 1859 provide a detailed inventory of the assets of the finishing shop, the foundry, the blacksmith shop, the coppersmith shop, the boiler shop, the carpenter shop, and the paint shop (see Appendix A). On close examination of the inventory, one can realize the scope of this industrial operation. The chief engineer and superintendent of the company, S.L. Fremont, would describe the shops and the needed improvements in his 1860 report.

> The Repair Shops are, with one or two exceptions, now well supplied with good machinery and tools. There has been much delay in completing the arrangements referred to in the two last annual reports, by which we hoped to drive the machinery of all the shops by the new stationary engine, constructed (with abundant power) for the purpose, but in a few weeks these will be completed. The rail-mending shop has been thoroughly rebuilt of bricks, as well as that part of the machine shop now used as an engine house. A good engine house and iron turning table are much needed for our increased stock of engines.[5]

The Wilmington & Weldon, on the eve of the Civil War, was equipped to build and maintain rolling stock, repair rails, cast and mill replacements parts, and rebuild locomotives. The company owned 26 locomotives and 182 coaches and cars.[6] The shops were the critical asset that the company needed to continue its participation in the war. In anticipation of the invasion of Wilmington, the railroad set up shop facilities at Magnolia in 1862.[7] Although the Union Army mounted successful raids at Goldsboro and Rocky Mount and destroyed bridges over the Neuse and Tar, they were not able to cripple the railroad. Even after the capture of Wilmington and Goldsboro, the railroad was marginally functional with its shop facilities at Magnolia and Enfield. Ultimately, Confederate forces, fearful of an offensive that never happened, rendered the Wilmington & Weldon nonfunctional as the war was drawing to a close.

The history of the Wilmington & Weldon did not end with the war, nor did the North Carolina Railroad, Wilmington & Manchester, or the Wilmington, Charlotte & Rutherford. On the contrary, they would prove to be the foundation of a new economy that would revive the state by the 1880s. Not only the railroads of North Carolina, but those of the South as a whole would prove to be the foundation of a new economy that would remain rooted in agriculture, yet expand rapidly in all spheres of manufacturing. Edward L. Ayers, in *The Promise of the New South: Life After Reconstruction*, illustrates in two impressive maps the degree to which railroad construction advanced between 1870 and 1880. Most Southerners lived within a county with a railroad by 1890.[8] The railroads offered the promise of renewal and normalcy, albeit within the context of a society in flux. The companies that survived Reconstruction made the transition from elements in state systems of internal improvements to extensive interstate corporate partnerships. Finally, through mergers, lease agreements, and buyouts, the last vestiges of their provincial antebellum origins disappeared as the great corporate railroad of the early 20th century took form. In 1877, as Reconstruction was drawing to a close, R. R. Bridgers, then president of both the Wilmington & Weldon Railroad and the Wilmington, Columbia & Augusta Railroad, shed light on an important management strategy that had enabled the Wilmington & Weldon to maintain a growth trajectory. Through using its profits for improvements, reducing debt obligations, and increasing its base of shareholders — rather than offering liberal dividends — the company was able to offer satisfying dividends in the long term.[9] The Wilmington, Columbia & Augusta had a lease agreement with the Wilmington & Weldon that commenced during 1873 and was terminated in 1878 when the former failed to comply with its conditions. The accounts of the two companies remained separate during this arrangement.[10] Thus the Wilmington & Weldon emerges, poised for the final decades of its history as an independent corporate entity, before being absorbed into the Atlantic Coast Line Railroad; the latter completed its purchase of the Wilmington & Weldon in 1935.[11]

Almost immediately after the war, black labor was undesirable. S.L. Fremont, chief engineer and superintendent of the Wilmington & Weldon, stated in his report to the stockholders in 1865 that he had authorized the employment of white workers, noting that even though they could be expected to accomplish only three-fourths of work as the former black work force, they would prove to be dependable and cost the company about the same price.[12] His assumption that the former slaves and already established former free blacks would prove less dependable than the itinerate white labor that the company once shunned seems strange: he was the same chief engineer and superintendent who in 1860 noted white labor was "inferior to slaves, or even the free blacks we had heretofore employed."[13] The Freedmen were, in fact, in a desperate state following the conclusion of the Civil War. With slaveholders no longer obliged to provide for them after Emancipation, many were left to their own devices prior to federal intervention.[14] One might expect the railroad to utilize some of its experienced work force on a wage basis, particularly since their prospects for finding employment outside the type of work they had known was limited, and for the time being, their mobility was hindered by the same condition. Yet, at least in Wilmington, all the railroad companies appear to have been avoiding black hires. The 1867 city directory for Wilmington shows only two black employees working for the Wilmington & Weldon: Robert Berry, a mechanic; and Isaac Spicer, a blacksmith.[15] The remaining listed employees for all the other railroads represented in the city are listed in the white section of the directory. The perspective of the antebellum elite, no doubt shared by his audience, which held the notion that the un-propertied classes were not given to industry or sobriety, is also apparent, and as a result, one had to resort to "constant trials" with the better of the white lot to shape them into workers.[16] Though the practice of excluding black labor would abate, the transformation of the railroad labor force from slave based to wage coincides with a reorganization of the urban environment of Wilmington into well-defined districts. As the significance of the railroad economy increases, its impact upon the evolution of the city becomes more pronounced (see Appendix B).

The Wilmington & Manchester Railroad

The Wilmington & Manchester was the second antebellum railroad to terminate at Wilmington. It extended from Kingsville, South Carolina, to its depot on the west side of the Cape Fear River opposite Wilmington. Like its connections in South Carolina, it was a five-foot gauge rail. Because there was no bridge across the Cape Fear, a steam ferry jointly owned by the Wilmington & Manchester and the Wilmington & Raleigh (Weldon) and named for the president of the Wilmington & Manchester, the *W.W. Harlee,* conveyed passengers and freight between the docks of the two railroads. Work commenced on this railroad in January 1849, and by the end of January 1854 it was drawing towards completion as tracks had been laid on both sides of the Pee Dee River.[17] The Pee Dee River bridge, based on an English design, rested on cylinders sunk into the riverbed onto which spans were constructed and would not be ready until October of that year. Walter Gwynn, the chief engineer for the North Carolina Railroad and, before that, the Wilmington & Raleigh, was the consulting engineer on this bridge; he and resident engineer E.J. Flemming were responsible for the design. Each was presented with a gold medal when the first train passed over the bridge.[18] The Wilmington & Manchester was completed, when on October 10, 1854, the first train crossed the Pee Dee River bridge on its way to Wilmington.[19] In January, the stockholders of the Wilmington & Manchester approved a resolution to sell the $200,000 in shares that it held in the Wilmington & Raleigh Rail Road Company in exchange for the $200,000 received from the State of North Carolina, for an equal amount in Wilmington & Manchester shares. Also, income bonds in the amount of $200,000 were approved for the purchase of locomotives and rolling stock, and for the building of workshops and depots.[20] At a meeting of the board of directors for the company held at Marion, South Carolina,

I. The Railroads of Wilmington, Before and After the War

Dr. Chris E. Fonvielle, author and assistant professor in the Department of History at University of North Carolina–Wilmington, recently advised Beverly Tetterton, local history librarian at the New Hanover County Library, that the caption for the line drawing of Union troops crossing the Cape Fear River in the April 1, 1865 for *Frank Leslie's Illustrated Newspaper* was misidentified as Smithville (now Southport). The location was actually the ferry landing at the base of Market Street opposite the river from the Wilmington & Manchester Railroad depot. The present author concurs (courtesy New Hanover Public Library, NCD Box 1 006).

on February 11, Wilmington was selected as the location of the workshops and other buildings.[21] The Wilmington depot facilities of the Wilmington & Manchester Railroad appear in L.C. Turner's *Plan of Wilmington, North Carolina* of 1856. The track follows the bank of the Northwest Cape Fear on Eagles Island to its confluence with the Northeast Cape Fear until the track ends at Eagles Street, opposite the river from Market Street.[22] Today, the site is occupied by the battleship USS *North Carolina* and its visitor parking lot.

In early February 1854, the citizens of Wilmington, North Carolina, witnessed what they supposed was the passing of an age. With the completion of the Wilmington & Manchester Railroad, the steamboat line of the Wilmington & Raleigh Rail Road Company, a fixture of the port that had commenced service years before the railroad was completed in 1840, was no longer necessary. The last steamboat from Charleston swept along the riverfront ringing her bell. The way to Charleston would be by rail

The base of Market Street in Wilmington, photographed from the slip at Eagles Island on the opposite side of the Cape Fear River. Ferries provided transportation across the river from the causeway and the Wilmington & Manchester Railroad depot to the Market Street slip and the wharves at the Wilmington & Weldon Railroad depot. An iron railroad bridge north of the town would not be constructed until after the war (photograph by Dr. Cyn Johnson, 2012).

henceforth, or so it seemed. The beginning of March 1854 brought a remarkable rain event. On March 1 the *Wilmington Journal* reported that at Kingsville, South Carolina, at the southern end of the Wilmington & Manchester, the Congaree River was rising about seven inches per hour. A half mile from the junction, passengers on the Manchester train noticed that 150 to 200 yards of track of the South Carolina Railroad were washed up, and the mails and passengers had to be carried over the breaks on handcars. It was feared that the trestlework of the Wilmington & Manchester on the Wateree River would become unsafe. In fact, a writer for the *Charleston Courier* on February 7 complained that the bridge and trestlework over the Wateree was dangerous, and needed to be rebuilt according to the contract between the two railroad companies. The water, as the Wilmington newspaper reported on March 2, eventually rose four feet above the rails on this four mile trestle. As a result, the steamboat *Gladiator*, belonging to the Wilmington & Raleigh, was put back into

I. The Railroads of Wilmington, Before and After the War 21

The site of the Wilmington & Manchester Railroad depot on Eagles Island as photographed from the base of Market Street (photograph by Dr. Cyn Johnson, 2012).

service, briefly carrying passengers and the mails to Charleston.[23] Upon completion of the Wilmington & Manchester, along with the Wilmington & Raleigh's connection to the North Carolina Railroad, it was hoped that the new rail connection would establish Wilmington as a cotton market, in addition to improving trade in naval stores and lumber. If rates were competitive, the editor of the *Wilmington Journal* stated, "sixty thousand bales will come here annually within the next three years."[24] Even though the railroad was still under construction in 1854, by year's end the Wilmington & Manchester had taken receipts of about $330,000, of which the net profits amounted to approximately $140,000.[25] By the end of 1855, the total receipts were $419,075.22, the total expenses were $211,089.64, leaving $207,985.58 in net profits.[26]

The annual report to the stockholders of the Wilmington & Manchester Railroad Company for the year 1855 was published in detail in the *Wilmington Journal*. Expenses for the fiscal year included a survey for a Wateree & Hamburg Railroad, of which a charter was granted by the State of South Carolina. A report of the survey was prepared by R.H.

Drane, and estimated an 89-mile route from Kingsville, South Carolina, to Hamburg, South Carolina (opposite the Savannah River from Augusta, Georgia). The survey estimate mentions 93 miles of 64 pounds per yard rail for the line and sidings at $9,000 per mile, wire fencing and telegraph at $135,000, and $654,850 for gradation. The total cost estimate for this extension from Kingsville was $2,330,000.[27] This survey suggests that the post–Civil War Wilmington, Columbia, & Augusta Railroad was predated in this plan by the Wilmington & Manchester to establish a corridor from Wilmington to Augusta. In spite of high expectations, the corporation would not enjoy a protracted presence as did the Wilmington & Weldon, nor did the Wilmington, Columbia & Augusta. The railroad would become part of the Atlantic Coast Line Railroad in the late 1890s.

In a letter dated February 26, 1865, Major General J.M. Schofield of the Union forces (Army of the Ohio) occupying Wilmington authorized the superintendent of the Wilmington & Manchester Railroad, Henry M. Drane, to deliver all the company rolling stock and "other movable prop-

This line drawing shows a view of the port of Wilmington from Market Street looking north along Water Street, ca. 1865. The second building on the right, displaying the Stars and Stripes, is the U.S. Customs House that was built in 1844. The Alton Lennon Federal Building that replaced it in 1919, though much larger, mimics the appearance of the Greek Revival building in the façade of its wings (courtesy New Hanover Public Library, NCD Box 1 011).

erty" to his command for use by the United States. It would be returned to the company after it was no longer needed. General Braxton Bragg of the Confederate Army informed General Johnston in Charlotte on February 28 that he had obtained information that the Union forces at Wilmington were repairing the bridge over the Brunswick River on the Wilmington & Manchester.[28] It appeared, however, that the Wilmington terminus of the railroad would not be accessible for some time. When General Grant, traveling in civilian attire, rode on the Wilmington & Manchester in early December 1865, his ferry ride from the wharf at Wilmington to the railroad covered six miles. On that occasion, Grant was on his way to Savannah. The Wilmington & Manchester train had two passenger cars, one for whites and the other for blacks. Among the passengers of the train were stockholders of the railroad.[29] The loyal stockholders — those qualifying under Lincoln's 1863 amnesty proclamation involved taking the oath — were informed in mid–May that the corporation had been returned to their control on the condition that the management was subject to military orders that "have been or may be issued." On May 17, the shareholders elected O.G. Parsley president and set about the effort to raise funds to repair the railroad as far as the Pee Dee River. The company had very little rolling stock remaining, and had requested from the Union forces the release of a contraband locomotive. The company had been severely deprived of locomotives and rolling stock when General Edward Potter and his Union troops had discovered nine locomotives and cars belonging to the Wilmington & Manchester and the South Carolina Railroad near Middleton Depot in the High Hills of Santee, South Carolina. They destroyed them.[30] With the war now concluded, the company strived to resume service. Drane, superintendent of the Wilmington & Manchester, became president of the company at the end of 1865. An announcement in the financial section of the February 7, 1866, edition of the *New York Times* called up all holders of the company's bonds to make themselves known to the company or its agents in New York, M.K. Jesup & Company. Bonds of the Wilmington & Manchester, First Mortgage (tax free 7 percent) bonds and Second Preference Convertible Bonds, were offered for sale by their New York agents in May 1867.[31] The scheduled trains to and from Wilmington, beginning in late 1866, were minimal.[32]

The Wilmington, Charlotte & Rutherford Railroad

The Wilmington, Charlotte & Rutherford Railroad was chartered by the State of North Carolina on February 13, 1855, and a meeting of commissioners was held on March 14 at Wadesboro, North Carolina, for the purpose of organizing the opening of the books for subscriptions. Alexander McRae, former president of the Wilmington & Raleigh (Weldon) Railroad, was appointed chairman. John C. McRae of Wilmington was commissioned to prepare a survey of the route from "from the town of Wilmington, and from Whitesville (Whiteville) to Lumberton.[33] The route from Wilmington to Lumberton via Whiteville was not used; rather a more direct route following the Northwest Cape Fear to present-day Riegelwood, then connecting in a line to Lumberton, was used on the eastern division. Unlike the Wilmington & Manchester, the Wilmington, Charlotte & Rutherford was built in standard gauge. This was a position held by interests in Wilmington that anticipated that the railroad could eventually connect to the French Broad Railroad. Also, with the railroad making a possible connection to Fayetteville, the potential of the setting of conditions for the establishment of the Metropolitan Route, a concept of creating a primary corridor through the Piedmont of the east first proposed in the 1830s, could be avoided. A connection at Whiteville with the Wilmington & Manchester would likely be five-foot gauge. An alternative route, connecting from Marlboro Depot, 11 miles from Wilmington on the Wilmington & Weldon, which would cross the Cape Fear River at Whitehall in Bladen County, was suggested.[34] Either the adoption of five-foot gauge, or a connection off the Wilmington & Weldon to the Wilmington, Charlotte & Rutherford with its bridge at Whitehall, might have changed transportation patterns during the Civil War.

 John McRae completed his survey of the route in July 1856, and many bids on constructing section of the railroad had been taken before the stockholders meeting on October 22, 1856. The first 25 miles of the eastern division were completed on November 30, 1859, at a cost of $243,750. Two days before, Governor John Ellis came to Wilmington to inspect the work. Boarding the steam ferry, the governor took the trip up the Northeast Cape Fear River to Riverside Landing, the terminus of the railroad. Work on the eastern division continued with the second section completed on July 9, 1860, ($237,150), and a third section completed in November 1860 ($238,750), with construction on the fourth section reaching the 81st mile post on Christmas Eve of that year. The first section of the western division, costing approximately $353,000, was completed on January 4, 1861. Seven days before North Carolina seceded, the fourth section of the eastern division had been completed to the 90-mile post at Laurinburg, and the entire fourth section was completed, at a cost of approximately $240,000, to Old Hundred on August 17, 1861. Construction on the second section of the western division managed to proceed only 18 miles to Cherryville before being discontinued in October 1862.[35]

On July 21, 1865, the *New York Times* republished an article from the *Wilmington Herald* stating that repairs on the Wilmington, Charlotte & Rutherford Railroad would be complete, and traffic would resume between Wilmington and the end of the line within, at most, a week's time. Construction recommenced in April 1866, and 112 miles of track from Riverside to Rockingham were completed by October 15, 1868. Work slowed, however, and the four miles to the Pee Dee in this section were not completed, with only grading having been completed from the Pee Dee to Wadesboro by August 31, 1869.[36] Progress on bridging the Cape Fear River at Wilmington offered the promise of a continuous connection between the Wilmington & Weldon and the Wilmington, Charlotte & Rutherford in 1868 and 1869. The Wilmington & Manchester would also benefit from the bridge, because it would be fitted to accommodate the five-foot gauge as well. By early November of 1868, the Railway Bridge Company had accomplished the daunting task of sinking a 14-foot (in diameter) cylinder (caisson) through 63 feet of water, and then 37 feet below the river bed. Two smaller eight-foot cylinders remained. A new iron bridge over the Northeast Cape Fear was completed on November 13, 1868, as work continued on the bridge at Wilmington (at Meare's Bluff). Grading for the new roadbed to bring the Wilmington, Charlotte & Rutherford to the bridge was complete, and two miles of track had been put down by early December. The two iron bridges were open for use in late August 1869, with only a mile and a half of track remaining to connect the Wilmington & Manchester to the bridge at Wilmington.[37] With this improvement, depots and facilities could be located in Wilmington.

In 1866, the State of North Carolina solicited bids for the exchange of the principal on the second bonds secured by the mortgage of the Wilmington, Charlotte & Rutherford it had issued before the state seceded on May 20, 1861; the value was $2,000,000. The stocks held by the Literary Fund (for education) of the state, including stock in the Wilmington & Weldon and the Wilmington & Manchester, were not open for bid. Through several amendments to the charter of the company enacted (and repealed) by the General Assembly of North Carolina in 1868, 1869, and 1870, the management of the company was fully assumed by the stockholders. The securities of the company as of 1869 included the First Mortgage Bond ($500,000 held by the Treasurer of the State of North Carolina, $600,000 held by the company then hypothecated — pledged as collateral — with John F. Pickrell, a New York banker and broker), and North

Carolina bonds held by other financial firms, some of which remained unaccounted for or held as collateral. In 1869, the company received North Carolina Bonds (Special Tax) amounting to $1,500,000 as an appropriation to the railroad, but they had a market value of about 15 cents on the dollar, so the company refrained from offering them. The financial profile of the company is not clear, and for good reason. The Special Tax Bonds were issued by the state in exchange for $4,000,000 in stock. The validity of the bonds issued by North Carolina in 1868 had proven an embarrassment to other companies and financiers.[38] The source of the problems related to state investment in railroads during this period arises from the culture of corruption that had been nurtured in the North Carolina Legislature beginning in 1868. Composed of two-thirds Republicans, with the remainder carpetbag opportunists, the legislature was influenced by lobbyists to pass bills for special tax bonds to aid the completion of unfinished railroads that were actually instruments for the benefit of a ring of bond speculators, notably railroad presidents George W. Swepson, William Sloan, and Andrew J. Jones. Sloan, the shortest serving state treasurer, became president of the Wilmington, Charlotte & Rutherford Railroad. At the 1870 stockholders meeting, he submitted a letter of protest against the resolutions, based upon the repeal of amendments made to the company's charter in 1868 and 1869 which would deny the state the right to appoint directors to the company. The $4,000,000 in state bonds issued to the company proved of negligible benefit, the income having been squandered. When the company was sold by order of the New Hanover County Superior Court and chartered as the Carolina Central Railway Company, the attorney general issued the opinion in 1871 that the state had relinquished its interest in the railroad, and, as a result, of the $3,000,000 of state bonds issued of $4,000,000 authorized, none were ever returned, the stock held by the state being considered worthless. Sloan, along with John F. Pickrell, was later indicted on a charge of conspiracy to defraud the Wilmington, Charlotte and Rutherford, and Sloan on a charge of not accounting (the Supreme Court overturned his conviction on the latter count). The State of North Carolina had $8,878,000 in bond debt before the war; by 1873, it had expanded to $28,772,045; and with wartime bonds included, it was now $29,900,045 with interest due amounting to $6,781,442. The railroad bond debacle not only damaged the credit of the state, but it also left much of the work on the railroad unfinished. After acquiring the Wilmington, Charlotte & Rutherford Railroad at a mortgage sale, the Carolina Central Railway Company had the 60 remaining miles from Wadesboro to Charlotte to complete. In politics, the scandal fueled the revival in the state of the Democratic Party beginning in 1870 and the swelling of membership in the Ku Klux Klan. Investigations held in 1870 and 1871 revealed that large commissions were paid to lawyers and judges while few in the legislature were cognizant of the fraud surrounding the bond legislation. Swepson and Milton S. Littlefield, the New York carpetbagger banker and lobbyist, in Raleigh, would bear the greatest responsibility for the affair. Both would emerge relatively unharmed in the end. When the Democrats finally regained control of the legislature, they repudiated the special tax bonds. The Carolina Central Railway Company was sold on May 31, 1880, and reorganized as the Carolina Central Railroad Company; in 1900, it was merged into the Seaboard Air Line Railway.[39] The railroad, when merged with the Atlantic Coast Line, would become the Seaboard Coast Line, and more recently, a line of CSX Transportation.

Labor, Before and After the War

The antebellum work force of the Southern railroads relied on slave labor, large numbers of whom were secured from legal arrangements with other slaveholders for contracted periods, and a smaller number were owned by the railroad companies. The railroads in Wilmington followed this model. The white railroad personnel, from the board of directors to station agents and engineers, were minimal by comparison and situated in positions of responsibility. Slave labor enclaves for the railroads tended to be concentrated at the railroad facilities and at points along the line. The mechanism for attending to their needs was contained at the work site: provisions, shelter, and medical care were provided by the railroad. Like both the plantation and the mill village, the labor force operated in a work environment that was self-contained. Unlike the urban slave population, it was concentrated rather than dispersed around the community in households, shops, and institutions. The nature of the industrial process shaped this form of slavery: train crews were mobile without freedom of mobility; the pace of work for station crews, dictated by the train schedule, fluctuated; road crews performed different work at different locations along the line, where needed; the shop crews served the unrelenting needs of the locomotives and cars, being the least likely to experience the outside world.

The white salaried employees of the company were less like overseers and more like an officer corps. Given a number of direct and proximate influences, and the nature of railroading as an industrial process, one can draw similarities to a military operation both in construction and operation: most antebellum railroads were designed by West Point trained engineers, for whom military organization and terminology informed their

This two-story brick structure behind the Bellamy Mansion at the northeast corner of Fifth and Market streets is one of the few well-preserved examples of urban slave quarters remaining in Wilmington. Household slaves were housed on the property of the slaveholder. Many residents of Wilmington contracted the services of household slaves on an annual basis. Slaves working on the docks, at industrial sites such as sawmills, turpentine distilleries, and the railroad were housed near or on company property (photograph by Dr. Cyn Johnson).

existence, and the institution of slavery was pliable enough to conform to its uncompromising demands and fluidity. This slave labor system, however, produced only one monolithic consumer: the railroad. The market for a vast range of consumer related goods and services dependent upon wage based labor remained underdeveloped, and as a result, slave labor on the railroad was an economic appendage to the local economy, not a driving force. In a geographic sense, the railroad's slave labor force lacked identity, and thus, had no legitimacy as a community. By contrast, those who earned and spent their own wages had identity and their community had legitimacy; as a result, aspects of their lives entered the historical record, because accounting for the disposition of capital requires identifying the agents of its transfer. Beginning in late 1865, the labor force of the railroads represented at Wilmington acquired — beyond its chief officers — identity and legitimacy; thus, they expressed their economic existence through documented spatial behavior as they pursued their wonted avocation (see Appendix B).

It is difficult to address the topic of slavery as it existed in the United States of the 19th century without encountering the overwhelming social, cultural, and ideological baggage that it has carried into the present, and for the historian, the additional trappings it had acquired before its demise. The history of slavery extends back to antiquity, and, perhaps, to the agricultural revolution of prehistory. Given its enduring presence in human history as an element of culture and social organization, it is somewhat difficult to approach as an economic system subsumed under the aegis of industrial capitalism when the same species of labor system has functioned in economies that were not industrialized or capitalistic. Further, the commoditization of labor in the free market had created, and does create, instances of near-slavery, exemplified by child labor, insufficient wages, credit entrapment mechanisms, sweatshops, disenfranchisement, social marginalization, and actual violent coercion, all of which resemble aspects of the involuntary servitude associated with slavery. Furthermore, the effectiveness of these labor devices to maximize profits and convey a greater portion to a few can present some confusion. Thus one might be led to believe that there are *degrees* of slavery. In all but the special cases, free labor is a commodity that shares the characteristics of other commodities, independent of the person doing the labor; thus, it is subject to the flux of the market. The slave, however, is relegated to the status of property—fixed capital—and his or her efficiency as a laborer is the qualifier that determines the market value of that property. As an economic instrument, a laborer as a commodity (property) displaces labor as a commodity (wages), because the mere act of acquiring the slave implies a purchase of all potential labor and wages from that labor.[40] Labor as fixed capital necessitates the use of the legal and financial instruments of property. To this point, the railroads of the South illustrate the degree to which the institution of slavery and industrial capitalism had become enmeshed; the railroads of Wilmington, with their reliance upon enslaved and free black labor as a matter of preference[41] rather than necessity, provides a telling example of how well the flux of railroads, as an industrial process, embraced the non-autonomous, chattel or disenfranchised. Slave labor was mostly obtained at an annual rate paid to the slave owner, rather than purchased. The 1856 annual report of the Wilmington and Manchester Railroad explains the arrangement in detail.

> At the close of each concurrent year the operation of the Road, especially the repair and freight departments, are much embarrassed, indeed

almost suspended for a period of nearly two weeks, in hiring hands and their re-organization for the ensuing year. This has been severely felt during the past holidays, in consequence of the heavy rains and extremely bad weather, at a time when labor could not be procured.— For this I can see no remedy, except the Company purchase annually a number of negroes until a sufficient force be obtained for the freight trains and repairs of the Road. Viewed as a measure of economy this will be found commendable. For ordinary hands the price range from $150 for road repairs, to $180 per annum for the trains: and, in consequence of the requirements that they periodically be allowed to go home, they do not perform more than 275 days labor. Estimating the interest on the present price of negroes at 7 per cent, and the insurance on their lives at the usual rates, and adding the additional labor that could be obtained from these owned by the company, it will be found that the price of each hand engaged in repairs will be reduced $65, and on the trains $90 per annum.[42]

The legal mechanisms that made this work include the Negro Bonds, and insurance, for both protected the interests of the slaveholder, allowing the responsibility for the productivity and maintenance of their property to be placed upon the railroads. Clothing and subsistence was provided by the company as well as caring for the sick and injured. (The Wilmington & Weldon had its own hospital, and its physician would include his report in the annual report.) The building of the railroads also involved the use of slave labor. The work of clearing land, grading, making crossties and the putting down of rails was accomplished by contractors with gangs of slaves.[43] The labor force responsible for the operation of trains, maintenance of the road, the handling of freight, and work in the company shops consisted of a handful of white employees overseeing black crews that consisted mostly of slaves.

Apart from corporate and legal documents, the black labor was all but invisible to the press, with the exception of accidents. This is the only instance where they emerge as individuals, or there is a hint at their relationship with white employees. A sampling of articles printed in the *Wilmington Journal*, and documents associated with these railroads, from 1854 through 1856, provides a few examples of the dangers these workers faced. The victims of severe injury and death on the Wilmington & Raleigh (Weldon) and the Wilmington & Manchester due to accidents appears not to have been their passengers, though some suffered minor injuries. Member of the train crews, almost always black, were the most frequent casualties while in motion with the train; white men, careless or drunk, constituted the class of individuals accidentally run over by trains[44] during this period. Of the latter, there appears one exception. On August 10,

I. The Railroads of Wilmington, Before and After the War   31

1854, a mail train on the Wilmington & Raleigh (Weldon) ran over a black man. The verdict of the coroner's inquest concluded that the man committed suicide.[45] There were also several accidents involving collisions between trains and those involving farm animals. Some accidents were caused by mechanical failure or human error. An example of the latter is that on the night of November 21, 1854, a northbound passenger train on the Wilmington & Raleigh (Weldon) collided with a sidetracked freight train at Joyner's Depot because the switch was set in the wrong position. A Negro brakeman named Sterling Pontain suffered a fractured leg.[46] Two collisions occurred at Teachey's Depot in less than a year. On October 16, 1854, a southbound passenger train on the Wilmington & Raleigh (Weldon) crashed into a freight train at four o'clock in the morning. A black fireman on the passenger train lost one of his legs in the accident. The fault was placed on the crew of the freight train.[47] In June 1854, a Wilmington & Raleigh (Weldon) freight train ran over a cow about one mile from Wilmington, causing several boxcars to be derailed on a curve. A slave from Halifax on the train crew, who was on one of the boxcars, jumped off, only to be crushed under the falling cars.[48] In August 1855, a slave of a Mrs. White living in the area of Marion, South Carolina, working as a brakeman (presumably on the Wilmington & Manchester) came into contact with the framework of a pen (designed for taking on cattle) while trying to take a look ahead from the platform of a moving car. Unable to maintain his hold from the blow, he fell from the train and broke his skull. This happened at a location called Dickinson's Shantees.[49] There is also an incident reported during this period where the black railroad laborers escaped death, and their careless overseer was killed. There was an accident on the Wilmington & Weldon in January 1856 that claimed the life of Mr. William Gay, the section master for the northern division. Near Rocky Mount, Mr. Gay, along with two Negro laborers, was traveling in a handcar when they encountered a locomotive that had been sent from Goldsboro to Weldon for pulling the mail train. The laborers were able to jump off in time, but Mr. Gay, with his handcar, was thrown off the track by the locomotive. He died instantly from a broken skull.[50] (William S. Ashe, the president of the railroad, would be killed in a similar handcar accident in September 1862.) The most horrific accident of this period occurred on the Seaboard & Roanoke Railroad near a small North Carolina town on the Virginia and North Carolina line called Margarettsville. It was considered one of the worst accidents on an American railroad to date. Around eleven-thirty on the morning of on March 10, 1856, a Seaboard & Roanoke passenger train consisting of an express car, a baggage, mail car, and two passenger cars were crossing trestlework on the south side of the Meherrin River.

The trestlework at this location was about 30 feet high. An axle of the tender of the train failed, causing the train to derail and plunge to the ground. Four men, W.G. Kilkelly, an Adams Express messenger and resident of Goldsboro, William T. Daughtry, the U.S. Mail agent and resident of Norfolk, and two black men from Portsmouth named Cary and Cox were crushed or burned alive when the express car was thrown under the locomotive. Soon, a conflagration raged that consumed all of the cars, the woodwork on the locomotive, and the trestle. Mr. Cary was pulled from the fire but died almost instantly afterward. Mr. Daughtry was reduced to ashes, and was identified only by his watch that was remarkably undamaged and working; Mr. Kilkelly's remains amounted to charred bones. It was presumed Mr. Cox had died instantly; both he and Cary were severely burned and bruised. Cary and Cox had made their living by selling newspapers to passengers on the train. The other fact that emerged about the black men was that they were from Portsmouth.[51] The *Wilmington Journal* and other newspapers of the town were diligent in their reporting of accidents on the region's railroads, and unfortunately, the large free black and slave work force rarely emerged from their nameless void without being dead or wounded; even then, they are without history or familial connection. Even a heroic slave from Marion, South Carolina, who saved a train on the Wilmington & Manchester, remains nameless to both his own time and posterity.[52]

From the *New York Times* correspondent's narrative of the November 30, 1865, trip with General Grant on the Wilmington, it is apparent that the two passenger cars of the train were segregated. The subject of the stockholders traveling that day concerned the solvency of the company and the "negro question." After departing from Florence, South Carolina, Grant took his occasional smoke in the "colored car."[53] Racial tensions were overtly displayed at the railroad facilities. The Wilmington & Weldon had a yard engine named the "Ku Klux" with a large cow skull painted black and mounted on front by 1868.[54] But in the same year, John Divine, master of machinery for the Wilmington & Weldon, had to advertise "Wanted Immediately!!" for machinists and carpenters adding, "None but sober and industrious men and good mechanics will be employed."[55] Except for Robert Berry and Isaac Spicer, evidence of black railroad workers appeared only when they were in an accident. An accident at the Carolina Central depot in early 1874 illustrates changes in reporting these incidents.

> A colored boy by the name of Jacob Ransom was fatally injured yesterday morning by being run over by a car at the Carolina Central Railway depot, in this city. About 9 o'clock, as a freight train was being coupled up, Ransom, after coupling two cars, stepped from between them, they

being in motion at the time. As he did so his coat caught in a spike on the side of the car and he was thrown on the track when the wheels passed over him crushing his left arm at the shoulder and breaking his knee and ankle. Dr. Lane was called in and the injured man was sent by him to the City Hospital where he expired about 12 o'clock, from the effects of the shock to his system. The deceased was originally from Raleigh and is said to have been of very correct habits, and was regarded as one of the very best hands on the yard. Coroner Hewlett will empanel a jury for the inquest this morning.[56]

Unlike the antebellum reports, details of the accident and the response, the victim's name and home town are given as well as the nature of his work and character are given. Death notices, such as those for Abby Dry and Agnes Walker, both dying of natural causes at home, show that an African-American presence existed in the neighborhood on Nutt Street and in the Brooklyn district near the railroad in Wilmington during 1873–1874. In fact, by 1869, the north side of the railroad in Wilmington was beginning to show significant growth, and would become a culturally diverse sub-community where merchants and workers of different ethnic backgrounds lived and worked within the African American core.[57]

The expansion of the white work force in Wilmington for the railroads following the war can be traced through the city directories. By 1871, a distinctive pattern of residence emerges throughout the city that reflects a distribution according to worker class that was not previously in the slave economy. However, it is more indicative of the distribution found in industrial cities in free economies contemporary within the era of slavery.

Salaries listed in the 1866 stockholders report appear to be closer to their 1860 level with the president of the company, R.R. Bridgers, earning $4,500 per year, the chief engineer and superintendent, S.L. Fremont, earning $4,000 per year; and others of the company, from major station agents to the secretary and treasurer, earning from $1,200 to $3,000 per year. Conductors of passenger and freight trains annually earned $1,020 and $720 respectively, first class engineers earned $1,200, and second class engineers earned $900 annually. Other employees worked for daily wages: first class machinists at $3.35, second class machinist at $3.10, first class carpenters at $3.00, and second class carpenters at $2.75.[58] The terms "machinist" and "carpenter" appear to embrace, as new categories of identifiable workers, spatial behavior that would shape previously undefined marginally urban space around road facilities into working class neighborhoods. Conductors and engineers were apt to take up residences in the hotels of the city. The workers of the companies that would be termed today as white collar — clerks, agents, baggage masters — lodged in boarding houses or family homes scattered throughout the town, but trended towards the east and south sections away from the railroad facilities. The chief officers of the companies resided in some of the grander homes located to the east and north of the commercial core and centered on lower Market Street. Some workers took rooms in commercial buildings, and a few are not listed as having any known address. The Wilmington & Weldon employees represent the greater portion of those residing in Wilmington before 1871 (see Appendix B). The completion of the bridge over the Cape Fear River in 1869 allowed the Wilmington & Manchester (soon to be merged into the Wilmington, Columbia & Augusta) and the Wilmington, Charlotte & Rutherford (soon to become the Carolina Central Railway) to move their facilities from Eagle Island and Riverside to Wilmington; this coincided with the expansion of neighborhoods in the railroad district of the city.

Chapter II

The Events of 1860–1861

Until 1875, the large area now known as Pender County was part of New Hanover. The division of the county was a response by the largely rural hinterland of the county to the Reconstruction establishment in Wilmington, perceived to be infested with carpetbaggers. As a result, New Hanover County became a small county and in its present-day form is the Wilmington metropolitan area with its satellite communities and beach towns. In its 1860 form, drawing from county level census data, the total population was 15,429, with 2,258 families; the free population of the county was 8,326 (7,815 native born, 511 foreign born), of which there were 3,129 white males and 3,191 white females. There were 938 slaveholders. The total slave population was given as 7,103 (3,552 males, 3,551 females), and the population of free persons of color in the county was 642. The county had 649 farms, with 57 being between 3 and 9 acres, 97 from 10 to 19 acres, 180 from 20 to 49 acres, 124 from 50 to 99 acres, 177 from 100 to 499 acres, and 15 from 500 to 999 acres. There were no farms of 1,000 acres or more in the county.

The county had 355 manufacturing establishments with 695 males (and no females) employed at an annual cost for labor at $157,416, producing items valued at $1,377,717 annually.[1] Of the 355 industrial establishments in the county, 328 were involved in the preparation of crude turpentine, and there were 4 turpentine distillers. The remaining industries were few. The valuation of estate, real and personal property, for the county was $16, 241,681.[2] The political districts in New Hanover County of 1860 included Wilmington, Federal Point, Masonboro, Middle Sound, Sandy Run, Holly Shelter, Rocky Point, Long Creek, Caintuck, Upper Black River, Moore's Creek, Piney Woods, and South Washington.[3] Figures provided in *Kelly's Wilmington Directory* in June 1860, prior to the publication of the census, predicted the population of the town would be 11,000 (9,552) in 1860, a rise from 4,744 in 1840 and 7,264 in 1850. Wil-

The intersection of Fifth and Castle streets on the original south boundary of Wilmington was once the site of the Oaks, a place where political meetings were held. Political rallies were also held at the nearby Dudley Mill Pond (later known as the infamous Rouse Pond). The area still has an abundance of ancient oaks (photograph by Dr. Cyn Johnson).

mington was the first town in the state to be lit by gas and according to the editor of the directory was the largest naval stores market in the world.[4]

John MacLaurin, in his articles about Wilmington in 1840, placed the boundaries of the old town from the Cape Fear River to Fifth Street going east, and Campbell Street at the north end to what would become Wooster Street to the south. By 1860, Isaac W. Hawkins, a deputy sheriff, and R.M. Lain, a grocer, had their homes at the southern extreme of town at the corner of Fifth and Queen. On the next street north, Castle Street, the Wilmington Gaslight Company was located near the river, the Kordlander Bottling House on Front and Castle, a Baptist church between Fifth and Sixth, and William H. Biddle, a constable, between Sixth and Seventh.[5] At the corner of Fifth and Castle was the Oaks, a gathering place for political meetings before and after the war. The maps on pages 128 through 130 of *The Diary of Nickolas W. Schenck* show Dudley's Mill Pond

II. Events of 1860–1861 from the Wilmington Perspectiver

Both maps contained in *The Diary of Nicholas W. Schenck* and Dr. William G. Thomas's article in the *New York Medical Journal* agree on the location of the Dudley Mill Pond, or Rouse Pond. The dam and outlet was located at the intersection of Front and Queen streets, and it extended to the intersection of Second and Queen streets. By 1862, the millpond appears to have outlived its usefulness, and was being filled in with garbage. The photograph shows the depression at the intersection of Second and Queen streets at the location of the east side of the pond (photograph by Dr. Cyn Johnson).

and dam beyond Front and Castle. Much of the area was vacant, with sscrub oaks and wire grass, except for Negro houses.

Continuing south along the river, there were a few mills, cotton, rice, lumber, turpentine stills, and the Clarendon Iron Works. Schenck notes places in this area to be avoided (B.A.D.)[6] On the north side, beyond the railroad, Owen L. Fillyaw, a cabinetmaker, turpentine distiller, and a director of Oakdale Cemetery Company, lived at Fourth and Bladen. His office was at 10 Front Street, near Market Street. His salesman, J.D. Love, lived at Sixth and Bladen; and his clerk, D.A. Smith, lived at Seventh and Bladen. The lone dwelling listed on the east side of town was that of Captain R.S. Macomber at Thirteenth and Chestnut.[7] Outside the pioneers on the periphery, the boundary of the town containing the heart of the town were the 155 blocks, excluding the wharfs, enclosed by Front, Fifth,

Red Cross, and Castle, and its original central place, Market Street. This was the area that contained the businesses and dwellings of the town merchants, their churches and schools, and the government buildings. On the eve of the presidential election of 1860, the opposing parties held their ritual procession, one to the Oaks, the other to the bridge at Front and Red Cross, leading to the railroad station, and passing each other at Market.

> The turnout last night was an agreeable disappointment to us. The torchlight procession was one of the largest we have ever had here, and the enthusiasm was very great. Our Democratic friends also had a display and seemed to be enjoying themselves. The Union men formed at the head-quarters, and immediately proceeded to the oaks, where they were addressed by Col. John McRae and Mr. John D. Barry. We are unwilling to allow the speech of this young gentleman to pass without especial notice. It was an excellent speech, a speech which surprised, and gratified the whole assemblage, and which gave promise of a bright future for Mr. Barry, as a popular orator. If there was anything which pleased his audience more than another, it was the way in which he skinned those young men who have abandoned the faith of their fathers, and gone over to the camp of the enemy in these latter days. It was done in good taste, without any bitterness, or abuse; but it was well done — it was well seasoned, and was greatly relished by the crowd. After Mr. Barry spoke, the procession formed and marched to the Rail Road bridge, stopping at the corner of Front and Market Streets, for the Democratic procession to pass. Mr. O.P. Meares made a speech at the Rail Road when the procession returned to the Market House, where speeches were made by George Davis Esq., R.H. Cowan Esq., A.M. Waddell, Eugene Martin (another young gentleman who will make his mark) F.D. Poisson, and others whom we did not hear. The best of feeling prevailed — everything is progressing quietly to-day, we believe, at the polls. We hope it will continue so.[8]

This was the report of election eve from the *Wilmington Herald*, the local organ of the Constitutional Union Party, whose candidates were John Bell of Tennessee and Edward Everett of Massachusetts. The *Wilmington Journal*, the Democratic newspaper, would report the night's events with more enthusiasm, and it is worth noting the names of the illustrious speakers: William S. Ashe, president of the Wilmington & Weldon Railroad, S.D. Wallace, assistant secretary and accountant for the Wilmington & Weldon and its future president after Ashe's death, Judge Samuel J. Person, Eli W. Hall, the county sheriff, and attorneys T.W. Brown, E.D. Hall, John L. Holmes, Robert Strange and Julius Wright. The only mention made of an opposition speaker was the address made at Front and Market by George Davis. (In short order, he would be a delegate from the state at the Peace Conference in Washington.) The route of the Democrats' torchlight procession was from Market north on Front to Red Cross, then east to the corner of Fourth, then south on Fourth back to Market, then east on Market to Fifth, continuing south on Fifth to Castle, turning west, the procession stopped at Fourth and Castle, then continued to Front; there, it continued back to Market before ending at Market and Second. At turns in the route, speakers addressed the crowd.[9]

The ritual seemed to the contemporary reader less like a parade, and more like some political variant of the Stations of the Cross. It was the climax of a year of dramatic speeches delivered by the great men of North Carolina politics, and there the editors of Wilmington's newspapers[10] did not demure to journalistic detachment entirely in their coverage. Regardless, there was ample material to work with for both newspaper editors and speechmakers: aside from the Constitutional Union Party, the Democratic Party had split into two wings; the Northern Democrats had their candidates, Stephen A.

The John A. Taylor House at 409 Market Street, with its marble-faced façade, was built in 1847. This house marks a midway turning point of the torchlight procession of the Wilmington Democrats on the election night of 1860. The procession was punctuated by occasional stops where local orators would deliver speeches (photograph by Dr. Cyn Johnson).

The Masonic Hall, built in 1841, is located at the northwest corner of Second and Market street. With its original Gothic Revival façade removed, the structure blends easily into the collection of late-nineteenth and early-twentieth century buildings of Wilmington's old commercial district. The election night procession of Democrats terminated at Second and Market streets where surely they listened to the evening's last round of oratory (photograph by Dr. Cyn Johnson).

Douglas and Herschel V. Johnson, and the Southern Democrats chose John C. Breckinridge, James Buchanan's vice president, and Joseph Lane for their ticket; and the Republican Party candidacy, with Abraham Lincoln and Hannibal Hamlin offered the point of opposition for all the rest. With the Republican Party having selected the moderate Lincoln over the ultra, Seward, their prospects of carrying the election seemed more promising. The mass meeting was a media event by this time.[11] Both Wilmington newspapers covered these meetings and their proceedings in great detail. Meetings of the opposition received detailed coverage as well. Names of speakers, names of important citizens in attendance, and the particulars of the location of the meeting were included.

At a mass meeting in Wilmington in October held by the Constitutional Union Party, ex-governor of North Carolina and ex-senator from North

II. Events of 1860–1861 from the Wilmington Perspectiver   41

Carolina William Alexander Graham gave a speech concerning the Kansas-Nebraska Act. It was covered by the Democratic leaning *Wilmington Journal*, and through that lens, the speech takes on aspects of a debate. The events of the day began at the Bell and Everett headquarters on Front Street where a crowd of about 500 gathered. The procession was organized, and then marched to the hill overlooking Dudley's Mill on the south side of town for the meeting and a barbeque. The speakers platform, decorated with an ornament resembling a bell fashioned from greenery, was erected between two oaks. The editor of the *Journal* remarked that even some Democrats were in attendance, but judged the majority of crowd to be from out of town.[12]

Graham (1804–1875), a Whig, began his career in the United States Senate when Robert Strange (1796–1854), a Jacksonian Democrat, vacated the position in 1840. He served until 1843, and then was governor of North Carolina from 1845 through 1849. During the national elections of 1852, he was an unsuccessful Whig candidate for vice president on the ticket with Winfield Scott. In the Millard Fillmore administration he served as Secretary of the Navy (1850–1852). A section of Graham's speech concerning the presidential candidacy of Martin Van Buren, a former Jacksonian Democrat, for the antislavery Free Soil Party in 1848, termed it a defection. The *Journal* chides that the third party contest allowed the Whig Party candidate, Zachary Taylor, to win the presidency. This, in turn, was a benefit to Graham when after the sudden death of Taylor, Millard Fillmore, rising from the vice presidency, appointed him Secretary of the Navy. The *Journal* at this point countered Graham's claim that Van Buren left the Democrats; rather, the party dumped him on account of his position on Texas (westward expansion — considering the topic of Texas' admission dangerous to the stability of the Union — and having distaste for appeasing slaveholding interests within the party[13]), and the editor continued by stating that Van Buren held considerable influence in the New York Democratic establishment where the Hunker and Barnburner[14] conflict had divided the party. Graham's Whig Party in 1848, the article states, already had some of its New York establishment figures moving towards the Free Soil Party agenda: Thurlow Weed, William Seward, and Horace Greeley.

Aside from its critique of Graham's speech, the details contained in the article exploit the former Whig's knowledge of the political events to explain to the reader of the *Journal* what led to the crisis within the Democratic Party. Buchanan and Douglas had a significant dispute over the power of territorial legislatures to determine the disposition of slavery in their domain. The Supreme Court's ruling in the Dred Scott case early in the Buchanan administration had destabilized the political atmosphere by determining that the Missouri Compromise was unconstitutional. In short,

Congress would have difficulty regulating it in the new territories because the Supreme Court defined a slave as a type of property. Free States, like Wisconsin in the Dred Scott case, might have found some of their anti-slave legislation invalid.

> But Mr. Graham contended that Squatter Sovereignty was contained in the Kansas and Nebraska bill. On the other hand, the Southern and many of the Northern Senators who voted for it, contended that it was not so. The fact is, that in one thing Mr. Douglas has been consistent — in another he has been the reverse. He has consistently adhered to his original idea of the power of a territorial legislature over the question of slavery therein — he has not adhered to his pledge made to his colleagues at the time the bills were passed, to obey and abide by the decision of the Supreme Court with reference to such powers. To all conscientious men the opinion of the Court is as fully expressed as it can be, that neither Congress nor a territorial legislature can intervene for any other purpose than to extend that protection which every citizen has a right to claim for his property. In the face of this and of his pledge to abide by it, Mr. Douglas adheres to his old notion of the power of a territory, and now asserts that no matter what the Court may say, the power of a territorial legislature to abolish slavery in such territory is undoubted.[15]

Graham states that the majority of the Southern people had supported Democrats through two administrations since the Whig Party fell apart and had not managed well, and now was the time to give the Constitutional Union Party a chance. The editor counters, however, that the Constitutional Union Party formed after the short-lived American Party had failed to establish itself as a political presence in the prior election and predicted that the Constitutional Union Party would fail to make any gains over the Democratic Party. Graham concluded with an indictment of disunionist elements within the Democratic Party, and its chief ringleader, the Alabama ultra, William Yancey. The *Wilmington Journal* pointed out to the readers that Breckinridge, not Yancey, was the candidate. Gov. Graham was then criticized for his opposition to reopening the slave trade and his anti–states' rights position. Local politicians Davis and Meares were mentioned to have given speeches at the dinner, and at the Market House, respectively. The content of these speeches was not given. The editor finally concluded that the whole affair was a failure and ends with the line, "Of course, we know our neighbor of the *Herald* will candidly admit the feebleness of the affair."[16] This style of political commentary of a party-biased sort provides the contemporary reader with some insight into the character of political discourse on the eve of the Civil War. Unlike days prior, when on occasions there was one newspaper with a limited distribution, the press

II. Events of 1860–1861 from the Wilmington Perspectiver 43

did not offer an alternative view outside the dominant political element in that community with other political forces always being outside and alien to local sensibilities. In light of the political mirroring, the coverage of William Graham's speech by the *Wilmington Journal* illuminated the entire dialogue.

The Constitutional Union Party was not feeble or composed of outsiders as the *Journal* led its readers to believe, nor was the editor of that paper immune from criticism from the opposition any more than the Democratic candidates. The description of the audience size and response to the speech indicated that there was strong support for the party platform.

This archival photograph is of the Robert H. Cowan house, on North Front Street, taken sometimes prior its demolition in the early twentieth century; it was then the offices of the Seaboard Air Line Railroad. Cowan, who died in 1872, served as president of the Wilmington, Charlotte & Rutherford Railroad (courtesy New Hanover Public Library, Robert M. Fales Collection).

The members of Wilmington's Constitutional Union Party included such community leaders as Gen. James Owen, former president of the Wilmington & Raleigh Rail Road; O.P. Meares, an attorney; James Cassidey, shipyard owner; R.H. Cowen, businessman and an early director of the Wilmington & Raleigh Rail Road; Henry Nutt, commission merchant and turpentine distiller; O.G. Parsley, bank president; and most of the cream of Wilmington's business community.[17] The meeting at the courthouse in Wilmington on October 8, 1860, was not a small matter. This meeting was in preparation to sending delegates to the state convention of "Union Men" at Salisbury. The *Wilmington Herald* opened its article with an account of the procession from the Market House to the courthouse that was accompanied by music from a cornet band. With the meeting called to order in the courthouse, the committee set to work with transportation arrangements to the state convention. Finally, George Davis took the floor amid the cheering of the crowd.

> He began his address — which was one of the best of his life — by stating that it afforded him unfeigned satisfaction to see around him the faces of those with whom he had been associated for years, and with whom he had fought many hardly contested political battles — that he delighted to witness the cordial union of the Whig party for the sake of the Union.[18]

Davis continued by pointing out the causes of political chaos of the nation — largely placing the blame for disunity within the parties on Douglas. He cited the rise of the Republican Party as an ominous event in light of the state of political instability that was prevalent in the country. He then criticized the editor of the *Wilmington Journal*.

> He didn't understand that kind of patriotism, which would prompt gentlemen to appeal to the (Supreme) Court when it decided in their favor, and to ignore its decisions when adverse to them. He well recollected that the editor of the Journal upon his return from the Charleston Convention had written an able article in which he denied as Democratic doctrine the power of the Supreme Court over political questions.[19]

Mr. Davis concluded his speech with praise of Bell and Everett, and made statements asserting the viability of the Constitutional Union Party in the face of charges that it was the "Old gentlemen's party," or worse, the "fossil remains." However, shortly before the election, the Democratic Party held a meeting on November 2. The event, originally planned to take place in Major John Walker's large yard, located between Front, Second, and Princess,[20] was moved to the courthouse when it was learned that a lady of the neighborhood who was sick might have been disturbed by the noise.

II. Events of 1860–1861 from the Wilmington Perspectiver 45

The featured speaker was Robert Strange of Wilmington (not the senator mentioned earlier). The event, like most of the meetings of that election year, was emotionally charged and the issues were the same. But in this case, the Democrats blamed the old Whig Party for the political chaos and accused the Constitutional Union Party of being an extension of the same. The text is worth examining in detail for its historical overview of the political landscape.

> Robert Strange, Esq. (of Wilmington), being loudly called upon, addressed the meeting in a very able speech of about an hour in length. He commenced by referring to the alarming position of affairs — turned to a survey of the parties now appealing to the Southern people for their support. He showed how, under whatever name, the Southern Opposition, now known as the "Union" party, was after all, only another name for the old Whig party. He reviewed the history of that party from the days of 1836 downwards, showing how the abolition element had controlled its action. How the great body of Northern Whigs then voted against the Pinckney resolutions, denying the power of Congress to abolish slavery in the District of Columbia, while nearly all the Northern Democrats had voted for these resolutions. The same with the Atherton resolutions in 1837 or '38. — These resolutions forbade the reception or consideration of the Abolition petitions with which Congress was flooded; the ground taken being that Congress had no Constitutional power over the subject matter — could not grant the prayer of the petitioners without violating the Constitution, and that the right of petition did not extend to the right to ask for a violation of the Constitution. In 1850 the so-called Compromise was passed, including among its measures the Fugitive Slave Law. Mr. Fillmore, after much hesitation and consultation with his Attorney General, signed that bill, and for that he was thrown overboard in 1852, and Gen. Scott put forward, evidently by the influence of Seward and Company. The Southern Whigs squirmed but submitted. Scott was beaten. The Whig party died out, or rather separated. The Northern portion became the Free Soil party, with Seward, Weed, Greely, and all the old Whig leaders, as its leaders. With these facts self-evident — too evident to be gainsaid or disproved — the Democratic party is charged with having brought this Free Soil Republican party into existence, by the repeal of the Missouri Compromise in 1854. How could what was done in 1854 be chargeable with what existed long before. Nay, further, how could 1854 be charged with the acts of 1850? The Territories of Utah and New Mexico, one partly and the other wholly above the Missouri Compromise line, were supplied with governments expressly providing for the right to come into to the Union with or without slavery, as they might select. — The acts of 1854 merely carried out the spirit of the acts of 1850. If any were chargeable, Clay and Webster, and Calhoun and Cass, and all the men of 1850, were chargeable. Mr. Strange examined the doctrine of Squat-

ter Sovereignty, and exposed its falsity. He proceeded to vindicate, in an unanswerable argument, the great Democratic doctrine of the rights of States.[21]

Another Democratic meeting held on November 2 at the Oaks featured speeches other prominent Wilmingtonians including Dr. J.D. Bellamy, C. Allen, Julius W. Wright and John D. Taylor, another bank president. The elite of Wilmington, as their newspapers, were deeply divided along party lines. There was a small number of Douglas Democrats, and they had their own organization. Nobody, including Dr. Keen, the Douglas elector for the sixth district, expected that his candidate had a chance to carry North Carolina, so he planned to cast his vote for Bell and Everett.[22] The residents of New Hanover went to the polls on November 6, 1860.

The Annual Meeting of the Stockholders of the Wilmington & Weldon

On November 8, the Wilmington & Weldon Railroad Company held its 25th annual meeting of the stockholders. The meeting convened at the courthouse, at that time existing on Princess between Second and Third.[23] Mr. R.R. Bridgers, speaking for the subscribers for the Tarboro branch line of the railroad, proposed that the subscribers to that branch who paid in full the entire amount due by November 15, together with interest due up to December 20, 1860, be allowed to receive their shares and participate in any dividends declared after October 1, 1860. A number of the listed subscribers had already paid in full and were now stockholders deserving of its advantages. The board of directors approved the proposal. The directors also approved a swap of 1,000 Wilmington & Manchester Railroad shares held by the company for 1,000 shares of Wilmington & Weldon stock, and the shares should then be cancelled from the company's books. Other items of interest include John McRae's motion that the president and directors of the company had no special rights with regards to the use of the company property, the railroad, or employees of the company other than what had been approved by the stockholders; and a resolution presented by W.A. Wright concerning the issuance of 20 shares of stock, to be placed in trust, for the purpose of providing aid for the widow and children of William H. Laspeyre, an employee killed in the performance of his duties. The meeting continued with the elections of the president and directors. William S. Ashe was elected president, Edward P. Hall, Gilbert Potter, Platt K. Dickinson, William C. Bettencourt, Armand J.

This archival photograph shows the home of P.K. Dickinson, once located at the northeast corner of the intersection of Front and Chestnut streets. Dickinson was one of the founding directors of the Wilmington & Raleigh Rail Road Company, and reportedly one of its most enthusiastic, early promoters. After the fall of Wilmington, Union general Schofield used the house as his headquarters (courtesy New Hanover Public Library, Robert M. Fales Collection).

DeRosset, John D. Bellamy, and Wentworth W. Peirce were elected directors for the stockholders, and L.H.B. Whitaker, W.K. Lane, and W.A. Wright were appointed by the Board of Internal Improvements representing the interests of the state. The next annual meeting was scheduled for the second Thursday of November 1861 in Wilmington.[24] The entire document, containing the various reports on the business of the company, contains nothing to suggest the slightest anticipation of anything beyond the normal for the coming year. The election had taken place, and the results had been published on the day the stockholders convened their meeting. Lincoln had been elected, and the *Wilmington Journal*, citing a pre-election speech by William Seward given at the Cooper Institute in New York City, concluded that after the inauguration, the new president would have a Congress receptive to his views, and the Supreme Court would be "reconstructed — the Constitution interpreted to suit the Black Republicans." The paper recommended that the Southern States, and their statesmen, put aside their political differences and unite for their common defense

The DeRosset House, built for Armand J. DeRosset III in 1842, stands at 23 South Second Street. He and his father were directors of the Wilmington & Raleigh and Wilmington & Weldon Railroad Company; both were physicians, and they were astute in matters of finance and diverse in their business activities (photograph by Dr. Cyn Johnson).

against this threat. As for the great battle between the political camps in Wilmington, Breckinridge received a few more votes than Bell, a mere 26 votes in Wilmington, and Douglas only five votes in the county.[25]

William S. Ashe, in his report to the stockholders of the Wilmington & Weldon, stated that during the fiscal year ending October 1 the receipts had increased $22,654.82 from the previous year due to an increase in freight and way travel. Through travel receipts had diminished by $10,734.39, but he expected an increase after January 1, 1861, when the daily mail would be transported from Charleston to New Orleans via Fernandina and Cedar Key, Florida. Speaking on the condition of the railroad, Ashe reported it was in better shape than in any previous time. Trestlework had been filled in where practical and work had commenced on ditching along the line to keep the road as dry as possible; and a two year project to weld laminated rails was underway. The company planned to begin installing double-lipped chairs on all the rail connections beginning in

This photograph, taken from the rear of the Bellamy mansion, shows a spire from the First Baptist Church rising above the trees. The Bellamy mansion is the most grand of all the antebellum houses in Wilmington, then and now. Architect James F. Post designed the mansion for Dr. John D. Bellamy, a physician, planter, and one of the directors of the Wilmington & Weldon Railroad Company. As in the case of the P. K. Dickinson House, Union officers occupied the mansion after the fall of Wilmington (photograph by Dr. Cyn Johnson).

January. The report of chief engineer and superintendent S.L. Fremont followed closing remarks by Ashe congratulating the stockholders on the prosperity of the company, its improved rolling stock, and the fine state of the road. The company had 26 locomotives and 182 cars and coaches. Two new locomotives, 20 new freight cars, and passenger cars had been added during the year; and a new brick engine house had been built at the Wilmington Depot. The company wharfs at Wilmington were being filled with sand, adding more land near the river. A permanent bridge had been built at Fourth Street over the tracks (certainly, the infamous Boney Bridge that would be replaced in 1876). The streets around the company shops had been graded; two new warehouses had been completed on the wharfs. Under the company assets listed in the depot and shops category were "Eleven Negros — Mechanics and laborers, $13,500." For work on the "permanent way," the cost of "hire of six negroes" was $1,260, or $210 a hand yearly, a price for which Fremont remarks was 15 dollars more than the previous year. Complaining about having to hire unreliable white laborers, he recommended that the company purchase 20 slaves.[26]

The election of Lincoln caused a reader of the *Wilmington Journal*, signing his name "Bilead Cheever," to write a sarcastic letter, appearing in the November 8 issue, concerning the financial cost of ending slavery.

> Why so much excited against the Black Republicans? All they ask of you is to free your slaves, and they will be satisfied. This done and we have everlasting peace. There are but 4,000,000 slaves, and at the outside they are not worth more than $800 each, i.e., three thousand two hundred millions of dollars. Now, can it be that the South, rather than part with this little, pitiful sum will wound the conscience of their Northern brethren and peril this glorious Union! Chivalry of the South, are your hearts set on filthy lucre? Surely not. Then, soon as you gather in your crops (for we are not disposed to precipitate matters) set your Negroes free — and let all be once more knit together as a band of brothers.[27]

On November 8, the *Wilmington Herald* printed dispatches for the Charleston *Mercury* that news of Lincoln's election was met with "long continued cheering for the Southern Confederacy," and the legislature in Columbia was in conference considering a state convention. Two days later, the *Wilmington Journal* downplayed the report printed in the *Herald* about demonstrations in Charleston as "superficial," adding that the cheering was prompted by the resignation of certain local federal officials, not the election of Lincoln.[28] The *Herald* published on November 10 a rather interesting geopolitical scenario where the Cotton States would join together in a southern confederacy and refuse entry of North Carolina and states bordering the North so as to form a buffer between North and South. It also reported that Governor Gist of South Carolina stated in an address to the legislature his intention to see that the state consider secession, and at the same time called for a reorganization of the state's militia: "I am constrained to say, the only alternative left, in my judgment is the secession of South Carolina from the Federal Union."[29] On the same day, the *Wilmington Journal* published an article that attempted to explain what Lincoln's policy might be, quoting from two Northern newspapers, the *New York Courier and Enquirer*, and the *New York Times*: Lincoln considered the institution of slavery to be "a moral, a social and political evil" that should not receive any protection under the Constitution. The *Journal* explained the application of this policy: "Hereafter, it is declared, this Federal agency of ours is to be an anti-slavery government in policy and in principle, and this policy and principle is to be permanent."³⁰ The November 15 edition of the *Wilmington Herald* countered with a strong article attacking the coerciveness of the Cotton States. North Carolina, that article stated, will deal with the situation in ways other than secession.

> North Carolina does not claim to be one of the Cotton States, although her next Cotton crop will, in all probability, be as large as that of "Carolina," but whether her exports are cotton, tar, pitch and turpentine, or corn to feed "Carolina" with, she does not intend now to secede, or to be dragged into secession by that "sovereignty." She will probably impose heavy taxes on the sale of Northern goods, and will prepare herself for any future emergency, but that will be the extent of her actions.³¹

As the atmosphere of uncertainty pervaded public dialogue in Wilmington, the Union Meetings continued and the States Rights faction had their meetings. The *Journal* reported that the lame duck president, James Buchanan, was in favor of calling a convention of all the states so that disunion could be avoided.³² South Carolina held an election for delegates to a state convention on December 6, pursuant to an act of ratified on November 9, and the convention convened on December 17 at the First Baptist Church in Columbia.

The Convention of the People of South Carolina

The *Journal of the Convention of the People of South Carolina, Held in 1860–61, together with the Reports, Resolutions, &c.* is a key document for understanding the complexities of not only the mechanism of secession, but also the attempt to unwind the technical relationships between South Carolina and the United States and the route to conflict. The convention opened on December 17 with an address by the president of the convention, D.F. Jamison, stating the reasons for considering secession. It was an inventory of legislative actions by the United States to limit the expansion of slavery and curtail the political power of the slaveholding states. Beginning with the Missouri Compromise, Jamison asserted that the United States Constitution offered no protection from the "jealousy and aggressions of the North." Of these, he mentioned the petitions from abolitionists to Congress (the cause of the infamous Gag Rule controversy), the complaint that "the South furnished three-fifths of the money, two-thirds of the men, and four-fifths of the graves" in the Mexican War, and California entered the Union as a free state without previous territorial existence, defined boundaries, or a census of its population. The accusations continued with the lack of protection afforded southern settlers in Kansas when a Northern organization called the Emigrant Aid Society, supported by Northern clergymen, contributed firearms to Northern settlers in the territory. Finally, the list of offenses ended with Northern interference with Southern efforts to recover fugitive slaves, supposedly resulting in the loss of millions of dollars in property.[33] By contrast, Alexander H. Stephens gave a speech before the Georgia Convention in January, a month later, portraying the North as willing to compromise with past demands of the South.

> When we of the South demanded the slave trade, or the importation of Africans for the cultivation of our land, did they not yield the right for twenty years? When we asked a three-fifths representation of Congress for our slaves, was it not granted? When we asked and demanded the return of any fugitive from justice, or the recovery of those persons owning labor or allegiance, was it not incorporated in the Constitution? and again ratified and strengthened in the Fugitive Slave Law of 1860? ... Again, gentlemen, look at anther fact: when we have asked that more territory should be added, that we might spread the institution of slavery, have they not yielded to our demands in giving us Louisiana, Florida, and Texas, out of which four States have been carved, and ample territory for four more to be added in due time, if you by this unwise and impolitic act do not destroy this hope, and, perhaps, by it lose all, and have your last slave wrenched from you by stern military rule, as South America and Mexico were; or by the vindictive decree of a universal emancipation, which may reasonably be expected to follow?[34]

When California petitioned for admission to the Union under an anti-slavery constitution in 1848, it set off the first secession crisis that ultimately led to the Compromise of 1850. Stephens, then in Congress, prepared a paper, signed and published by Henry Clay and others, that stated their intention not to support any candidate for office in the state of Georgia who would not support the compromise. The Georgia Convention adopted five resolutions affirming its connection to the Union, and finding the conditions of the compromise, including the enforcement of the Fugitive Slave Law and the termination of the slave trade in the District of Columbia, a resolution to the sectional conflict.[35] Stephens, speaking from experience and his profound understanding of the situation, presented the more reasonable argument than Jamison. Yet, it seems Danton's motto, "To dare! and again to dare," as quoted by Jamison impelled the motives of men, not moderation, reflection, or reason. Under its sway, even men of the composure of Stephens would succumb, he became vice-president of the Confederacy. The opening of the South Carolina convention included an invitation to the delegates to the inauguration of the governor-elect, Francis W. Pickens. The *Journal of the Convention* includes a letter from Governor John J. Pettus of Mississippi dated December 5, 1860, introducing that state's commissioner, C.E. Hooker, to the convention, and a similar letter from Governor A.B. Moore of Alabama dated December 8, 1860, introducing its commissioner, John A. Elmore.[36]

On December 18, the convention convened at Institute Hall in Charleston. This beautiful Italianate style structure located on Meeting Street (destroyed by fire in December 1861) would be the site of the signing of the Ordinance of Secession on December 20 at seven o'clock in the evening. The governor and legislature were invited to be present at the signing. The day before, however, the convention considered a communication received from President James Buchanan.[37]

> That so much of the Message of the President of the United States as relates to what he designates "the property of the United States in South Carolina," be referred to a Committee of ___ to report, of what such property consists; how acquired, can be enjoyed by the United States after the State of South Carolina shall have seceded, consistently with the dignity and safety of the State. And that said committee further report the value of the property of the United States not in South Carolina; and the value of the share thereof to which South Carolina would be entitled upon an equitable division thereof among the United States.[38]

On the same day, the convention resolved to send commissioners to each slaveholding state with a copy of the Ordinance of Secession, and an offer to join South Carolina, with the Constitution of the United States serving as a model for a provisional government after those states seceded, and to send three commissioners to Washington to present to the president and Congress the Ordinance of Secession, and to authorize them to negotiate for the possession of forts, magazines, lighthouses, and other property of the United States in South Carolina up until February 1861. On Christmas Day, a letter from Governor Madison S. Perry of Florida to the convention offered the assurance that after Florida had its convention it would join South Carolina in forming a new confederacy. Mention of North Carolina does not appear until December 26 when the commissioner for Alabama to North Carolina, J.W. Garrett, was invited to the floor. He was not able to come, but on December 26, he sent a communication that was entered into the journal.[39]

> Information, obtained on diligent inquiry in the last few days, justifies me in saying, the gallant sons of North Carolina and Virginia, are now ready to rally around the standard of Southern Rights and Honor, which you have so gloriously reared; and that those two States will also

be members, in all probability, of the Great Southern Confederacy by the 4th of next March.[40]

1861

On January 9, 1861, a large crowd of Wilmingtonians had gathered at the Oaks to hear Senator John J. Crittenden's resolutions[41] read, and to listen to various speakers' discourse on them as a means for preserving the Union. John A. Baker, the key speaker, could not make the meeting, but John McRae, O.G. Parsley, and Fred D. Poisson delivered speeches. The weather was windy that evening, and since the meeting was held out of doors, the speakers struggled to be heard. The meeting was postponed to Friday, January 11, 1861, when the meeting could take place in the theater. The *Wilmington Herald* notes that all were invited, "particularly the ladies," to attend the meeting. In the same issue is an article concerning the firing upon the *Star of the West*, a ship attempting to enter Charleston Harbor, by batteries at Morris Island and Fort Moultrie. The steamer retreated to sea, and the defenses at Fort Sumter withheld their response. At about 11:00 A.M., Lieutenant Hall from Fort Sumter entered

This line drawing from *Frank Leslie's Illustrated Newspaper* shows the earthwork defenses at Fort Johnston at Smithville (Southport). Fort Johnston was constructed during the Colonial Period, and improved in the early-nineteenth century. On January 9, 1861, a group of about twenty local men led by John J. Hedrick of Wilmington took possession of the fort from Sgt. James Reilly of the U.S. Army. The fort was returned to the control of the United States by order of Governor John W. Ellis two days later; and on April 16, 1861, Confederates took possession of the fort again from Sgt. Reilly (courtesy New Hanover Public Library, NCD Box 1 009).

The remains of the Officers' Quarters from Fort Johnston. The portico of the building is a later addition (photograph by Dr. Cyn Johnson).

Charleston under a sflag of truce to speak with Governor Pickens. After conferring with the governor and his council until 2:00 P.M., Hall returned to the fort. While the substance of the meeting was not known at the time, an unnamed individual of authority stated it was "of a most threatening character."[42] Major Robert Anderson, commander of United States forces at the Charleston forts, had consolidated his command by moving the forces of nearby Fort Moultrie to Fort Sumter. Having been deprived of provisions from Charleston in an attempt by the South Carolina government to peaceably gain control of Sumter, Anderson had been forced into this position. His orders were to hold the fort. Yet, he was given no certainty as to when, or whether, relief would come. The *Star of the West* left New York Harbor in an attempt to relieve Fort Sumter on January 5, 1861. When it arrived outside Charleston on January 9, it was fired upon by batteries placed on Morris Island and the abandoned Fort Moultrie by the South Carolinians. On January 9, 1861, James Reilly, an ordnance sergeant at Fort Johnston in Smithville (Southport), N.C., transmitted a communication to his superior, Colonel S. Cooper, in Washington stating that a group of about 20 men from the town, led by a John J. Hedrick of Wilmington, had taken possession of the fort.[43] The party of men quickly were ordered by the governor to relinquish their preemptive conquest, but the incident proved that sentiment in the region extended beyond discourse at political meetings.

A communication dated January 10, 1861, from Governor Ellis to North Carolina congressman Warren Winslow (United States House of Representatives, 1855–1861) asked him to call upon General Winfield Scott demanding to know whether he intended to garrison the North Carolina forts. Ellis also corresponded with President James Buchanan on January 12, stating he had issued an order to those who had occupied Fort Johnston and Fort Caswell to restore the forts to the federal forces and asked the president if he intended to send troops to garrison them. He noted that the prevailing public opinion was that the federal government intended to reinforce the forts for the purpose of coercing the Southern states into submission; for the sake of maintaining civil order, he requested that the president provide assurances that troops would not be sent prior to March 4 (the inauguration of President Lincoln). The president referred the letter to Joseph Holt, secretary of war, who replied on January 15 that the president did not intend to garrison the forts, but he added that the United States was obliged to defend against seizure of its forts, arsenals, and prop-

This line drawing from *Frank Leslie's Illustrated Newspaper* shows Fort Caswell, another antebellum coastal fort. In the drawing, earthworks are built up around the walls of the fort. According to Jim McKee of the Brunswick Town–Fort Anderson Historic Site, earthworks proved to be effective in dissipating the force of exploding shells, whereas brick and stone walls could shatter into shrapnel (courtesy New Hanover Public Library, NCD Box 1 008).

erty.⁴⁴ In his *Chronicles of the Cape Fear River, 1660–1916*, James Sprunt includes a narrative of events concerning the fort seizures, written by Colonel John L. Cantwell, commander of the Thirtieth North Carolina Militia. Cantwell writes that at a meeting at the home of Robert G. Rankin, certain residents of Wilmington formed a Committee of Safety and initiated a call for volunteers to form the Cape Fear Minute Men, commanded by John J. Hedrick. Major Hedrick and his men embarked from Wilmington to Smithville on a small schooner with one week's provisions, and the pledge of continued support and supplies from the Committee of Safety. After arriving, they took possession of Fort Johnston. Reinforced by Captain S.D. Thurston and the Smithville Guards, they then proceeded to take Fort Caswell. Governor Ellis, learning of this action, sent orders to Colonel Cantwell on January 11 to restore the forts to the United States. Cantwell, along with Robert E. and William Calder, his temporary staff officers, sailed from Wilmington on January 12. The militia men relinquished the forts the next day. Hedrick's militiamen were organized into the Cape Fear Light Artillery after the event.⁴⁵

On January 19, 1861, the General Assembly of Virginia adopted resolutions to invite delegates for all the states, slave and non-slave holding, to meet in conference "in the spirit in which the Constitution was originally formed" in Washington on February 4 to mediate a solution to the mounting crisis. Delegates from 21 states were represented at the conference, but missing were California, Michigan, Minnesota, and Oregon. The states that had seceded before the conference were not represented, nor was Louisiana, whose senators had withdrawn from the U.S. Senate before the proposed constitutional amendments were reported to conference. North Carolina's delegates, Daniel M. Barringer, David S. Reid, John M. Morehead, Thomas Ruffin, and George Davis, were selected by the state legislature. Morehead and Reid were former governors, Ruffin was a retired state chief justice, Barringer a former congressman from North Carolina, and Davis a lawyer from Wilmington well known as a speaker, a supporter of the Union, and a former Whig (he had yet to hold public office).⁴⁶ The sessions were held in secret. In 1864, Lucius E. Chittenden, a delegate from Vermont, published the proceedings. (An editorial in *The New York Times*, published in June 1865, indicated that this "less interesting or more instructive" document was examined for its value in understanding the history of the war. The article continues by stating that had Senator John J. Crittenden's proposed amendments to the United States Constitution been ratified by conventions of three-fourths of the states, the resulting compromise would have placed slavery under constitutional protection, enabled the creation of "a vast and powerful aristocracy" in the agricultural core of the continent [including all territory south of 36°30'], and "totally changed the aim of American policy and the current of American ideal" by giving slavery the opportunity to grow, ensuring its perpetual existence.)[47] On Thursday, February 21, Mr. Davis delivered a speech, but unfortunately it was the only one that Chittenden did not hear, so he provides a second-hand summary of its content: Davis affirmed North Carolina's devotion to the Union, but agreed with the position that the Southern states required constitutional guarantees to protect their interests. Without those, North Carolina would have to align with South Carolina and the Gulf States that had seceded.[48] Earlier, on February 16, Davis commented on a resolution concerning the length to which delegates would be allowed to speak during discussions.

> I think thirty minutes quite too long. Our opinions are formed. Before this time probably every member has determined his course of action, and it will not be changed by debate. I move to strike out the word "thirty," and insert the word "ten."[49]

James Sprunt describes how Davis's views had changed from the conservative pro–Union position he had defended prior to the Peace Conference to advocating secession on returning to North Carolina. The citizenry of Wilmington was anxious to know the results of the conference, and Davis presented an address on that topic to a large audience at Thalian Hall, Wilmington's theater, on March 2. He had determined, Sprunt states, that the plan adopted by the convention was inconsistent with the interests of North Carolina, and nothing better could be expected. Wilmington had been divided on North Carolina's future in the Union. Local secessionist O.P. Meares, a gifted orator in his own right, swayed the town's youth element, but equally eloquent Union men, such as Dr. James H. Dickson, appealed to the older conservative establishment. When Mr. Davis reported on the failure of the Peace Conference, Sprunt was of the opinion that this was the turning point for Wilmington.[50] (Davis would be nominated as a delegate to the Provisional Confederate Congress in June, be elected to the Confederate Senate by September, and attain the cabinet position of attorney general in 1863. Impoverished after the war, he returned to Wilmington and resumed his law practice, never to seek office again. He would, however, maintain his place in the public eye as a critic of Reconstruction.[51] After his death, he would be honored with a bronze statue at Wilmington's most prominent location, the intersection of Third and Market streets.[52]) The forces for secession, however, seemed to have accelerated in pace before Davis gave his speech. The topic of holding a state convention to determine the position of North Carolina, secession or not, divided the political fac-

II. Events of 1860–1861 from the Wilmington Perspectiver 59

The City Hall–Thalian Hall, located on Third Street, was completed in 1858. Its theater, Thalian Hall, located in the rear of the building, was designed by John Montague Trimble. The theater was the site of political meetings during 1861, including a speech by George Davis concerning the failure of the Peace Conference held in Washington, D.C. (photograph by Dr. Cyn Johnson).

tions throughout the state, with even some firm pro-slavery opposition to the convention. Proceedings of the convention at Montgomery, Alabama, were published by the Wilmington press alongside articles concerning the North Carolina convention. A Mass Convention of States Rights was held on February 20 at the New Hanover County Courthouse,[53] and not long after, with positive reports of a solidifying Southern nation in the making, some citizens of Wilmington were of the opinion in the *Wilmington Herald* that the people of North Carolina had seen their neighbors to the south successfully organize a government to protect their own interests, while North Carolina remained "the tail-end of a Northern anti-slavery, consolidated despotism."[54] On February 28, the *Wilmington Herald* included items concerning the election that day for a state convention, and if approved, the selection of delegates. The Hon. W.S. Ashe, president of the Wilmington & Weldon Railroad, and Robert H. Cowan, Esq., a prominent merchant and shareholder in the railroad, appeared in an advertisement as "Immediate Secession Candidates" for delegates to the convention. On the same page is a report of a meeting held at the Oaks, the site of previously mentioned political activities located on the south side of Wilmington. Dispatches from George Davis, serving as a delegate to the Peace Conference in Washington, and dispatches concerning the Crittenden resolutions, were read, and a number of notables gave speeches. The Honorable Samuel Hall, the commissioner from the State of Georgia, was also at this meeting.[55] Hall had delivered an address to the North Carolina General Assembly on February 13 explaining the causes that led Georgia to separate from the Union and encouraging North Carolina to join the Confederate States of America. In his report to the delegates at the convention in Georgia a month later, he indicated he believed that the majority of people in North Carolina entertained the notion that the Peace Conference underway in Washington at the time of his address would yield constitutional protections that would be favorable to those states remaining in the United States, and that the Union would be reunited on those results. Henry Toole Clark, speaker of the Senate of North Carolina, permitted Hall to convey a message to the people of Georgia that North Carolina would not permit hostile forces to pass through the state to attack their state.[56] After learning of the disappointing results from Washington at the Oaks meeting, the writer for the *Wilmington Daily Herald* reported that Samuel Hall's speech elicited the warmest response: "Cheers were given for secession, Davis and Stephens and the Confederate States of America."[57] John Dawson and William A. Wright billed themselves as the "Conservative Ticket" to the state convention from New Hanover County, appealing to those "not disposed to be represented in the State Convention by men pledged to secession, without regard to circumstances or compromises," in an advertisement that appeared on the same page of the February 25 issue of the *Wilmington Herald* announcing the arrival of 1,819 shells and an advertisement directed to military companies that new "North Carolina Buttons" were available for their uniforms.[58]

Throughout February, the Wilmington newspapers speculated on the possible outcomes of the crisis in Charleston. On February 9, 1861, the *Wilmington Herald* commented on Major Anderson's plight: an attack on Fort Sumter would happen, and military code required that an attack must be resisted by all possible means unless it became apparent that the effort was futile and that continuing would result in a needless waste of life. Furthermore, without receiving reinforcements, Sumter's force was not sufficient to mount an effective resistance. The article continued by noting that Anderson was a southerner, members of his family supported the

Southern cause, and his property was located in a Southern state. For all these reasons, the writer thought it would be in the best interest of all that Anderson surrendered the fort.[59] On March 20, the *Wilmington Herald* reported that South Carolina, now a foreign country, had put in place a customs officer to inspect trains crossing the state line on the Wilmington & Manchester Railroad.

> In the course of a few days a custom house officer will be discharging his duty to the Confederate States on the line of the Wilmington and Manchester Rail Road where it enters the State of South Carolina. Then every passenger going or coming will be liable to have his trunks examined, and his baggage ransacked, and every freight train will be compelled to undergo the same scrutiny. What will be the effect of this on the business of the road, and of the town of Wilmington? This is a very interesting question to our people, the merchants and business men particularly, and we would like to hear what they have to say about it. Will anything be "going wrong" or will "anybody be hurt" by the new order of things?[60]

The fact that the boundary between North Carolina and South Carolina had become a national boundary could have been particularly problematic to the Wilmington & Manchester, since a substantial portion of its length was located in South Carolina, even if the two states remained on friendly terms. In the extreme unlikely scenario of Virginia and North Carolina not joining the Confederacy, the geography of the Lower Cape Fear, both physical and political, provided favorable conditions for offensive actions from the south: the Little Pee Dee, Little River, the Waccamaw, and the many low order streams and swamps of Brunswick and Columbus counties that intersected the line of the Wilmington & Manchester, made it difficult to defend. The North Carolina–South Carolina line in the Lower Cape Fear region plunges to approximately 33° 51' at it most southern point, placing it far below the more northern boundary of South Carolina, and the close proximity of Lumberton and Laurinburg to the South Carolina line allowed possible capture of the Wilmington, Charlotte and Rutherford Railroad. Also, the possible capture of Fayetteville offered the opportunity to launch an offensive on and along the Cape Fear, and to advance north to cut the Wilmington & Weldon. In addition, the Cape Fear River, not the North Carolina–South Carolina line, offered a more plausible opportunity for defense of the region. Adding to these problems, the Wilmington & Manchester was a five-foot gauge rail, as were the South Carolina railroads connecting to it. No bridge over the Cape Fear connected it to Wilmington. All of these are factors favorable to a southern invading force and a disadvantage to defending the state line. History provides two examples of how logistical disadvantages of the Lower Cape Fear have been exploited. In 1781, Cornwallis successfully captured Wilmington by invading through the Piedmont, then proceeding along the Cape Fear through Cross Creek and Campbell Town (Fayetteville) to Wilmington. Interestingly, his advance through North Carolina to Virginia follows closely the route of what would be the Wilmington & Weldon. More relevant to the times, in 1865, Union forces under General Sherman entered North Carolina through Robeson County, crossed the Lumber River, captured Fayetteville, and proceeded to Goldsboro, effecting a cut in the Wilmington & Weldon at its junction with the North Carolina Railroad. Confederate and Union wartime communications also exist that acknowledge the importance of controlling the Wilmington & Manchester. Confederate general William H.C. Whiting recognized in early 1863 how strategically important and vulnerable the Wilmington & Manchester was to the defense of Wilmington and the Lower Cape Fear. In a communication to Major John J. Hedrick at Fort Saint Phillip on January 15, 1863, Whiting instructed Hedrick to proceed to the Wilmington & Manchester's bridge on the Brunswick River to protect it if a number of enemy ships made it past his position. On the same day, he wrote to General Samuel Cooper, adjutant and inspector general in Richmond, that if an enemy force were able to advance to the Brunswick River, they could destroy the Wilmington & Manchester, cutting access to the south, gaining access to the upper Cape Fear, and commanding a position opposite Wilmington at Eagles Island. An example of a Union plan for the capture of Wilmington comes from a communication between Major-General J.G. Foster and Major-General H.W. Halleck on February 26, 1864, concerning a conversation with General Grant at Nashville, Tennessee. Foster reported that Grant was contemplating a force of 60,000 men advancing on Raleigh after capturing Weldon. Foster presented a revised plan, including an alternate objective that depended on the success or failure of specific engagements, which involved launching an attack from Norfolk on Weldon. The bridges at Weldon and Gaston would be destroyed, thus cutting off key rail connections to Petersburg and Richmond. Union forces occupying Plymouth, North Carolina, would attack Weldon from the rear. While a cavalry force would then move on to Raleigh, the main column would advance to Goldsboro, destroying the rails and bridges of the Wilmington & Weldon as they went. The thrust of the attack would be focused at Wilmington, and the force would be supplied by landing troops at Masonboro Inlet (New Hanover County, N.C.). To the south, a cavalry force would capture the Wilmington & Manchester. Wilmington would be cut off, and the defenses at the mouth of the Cape Fear would fall thereafter.[61] This particular plan

II. Events of 1860-1861 from the Wilmington Perspectiver

Fort Anderson was entirely an earthworks defense. From its position on the Cape Fear River, along with a battery located on Sugar Loaf on the opposite bank, enemy ships could be caught in a crossfire if they attempted to steam to Wilmington. There was also a minefield of remotely detonated and contact torpedoes (using Raines fuses) in the river (photograph by Dr. Cyn Johnson).

was not adopted, though it illustrates how both the coastal weaknesses of the Lower Cape Fear region and the geography of Brunswick and Columbus counties could be exploited to capture Wilmington. Considering the prospects of a conflict between the Union and Confederacy, one cannot imagine North Carolina being able to maintain a neutral position such as Kentucky had done at the beginning of hostilities. North Carolina would *be* the front line, and troops from either side would have to pass through it. Given the obsolescence of coastal defenses and the logistical advantages of any side gaining control over the eastern railroads, it is not surprising that the fear that the Union Army would garrison the coastal forts excited so much concern in early 1861, or that Wilmington's Committee of Safety prowled the depot at night looking for northern spies and agitators, or that South Carolina installed a customs agent on the Wilmington & Manchester, or that Fayetteville's mayor, Archibald McLean, was concerned about the safety of the United States arsenal in that town. In light of the purely military position of the Cape Fear, and despite the political debate in the state between the Secessionists and old guard Union Men (and the failed Peace Conference), the escalating tensions at Sumter, and ultimately, Lincoln's call for North Carolina troops overcame the "watch and wait" position. Setting aside politics, attachment to Southern heritage, and financial interests, North Carolina could not sidestep the collision from a military perspective.

Abraham Lincoln was inaugurated president of the United States on March 4, and the stalemate of the previous months immediately seemed threatened. North Carolina senator Thomas L. Clingman, in a letter dated March 19, 1861, to Governor Ellis, warned that it was believed that Lincoln would immediately garrison the North Carolina forts. In early April, as the newspapers circulated rumors that an expeditionary force was being prepared to sail from New York Harbor, the conservative resolve was appearing to end. Some speculated that the preparation of the expedition was a ploy to exert pressure on the Virginia Convention that had convened on February 13 (it would continue to May 1).[62] Indeed, one can find reference to the force during the proceedings of convention on April 8:

> These very ships that have just sailed from New York have gone, it is said, to Forts Sumter, Pickens and the Tortugas, with supplies and munitions of war, and they proceed, knowing that they will be attacked if they attempt to reinforce or land supplies; and yet it is said that Lincoln's policy is peace. Would it not bring disrepute upon any committee that would bring back such a report — that, forsooth, Lincoln's policy is peace, while he continued to hold the forts and reinforce them, knowing that he would thus provoke attack?[63]

The *Wilmington Herald* would report on April 9 that seven men-of-war were spotted off Charleston Harbor, and on April 10 it reprinted an article from the *Charleston Mercury* of the end of negotiations between Captain Talbot of the United States Army and R.S. Chew, confidential secretary to Secretary Chase, who were sent from Washington with dispatches to Major Anderson and Governor Pickens of South Carolina, and the Charleston authorities. General Beauregard did not allow him permission to communicate with Fort Sumter, but Talbot was able to deliver the official notification from the Lincoln administration that "Fort Sumter was to be provisioned — peaceably, if practicable, forcibly, if necessary." Chew and Talbot returned to Washington. By April 11, the *Herald* printed a report that the so-called armada of men-of-war was nothing more than a "fishing excursion," and none were present in Charleston Harbor. However, with all the exaggerated reports, the editor was certain that the administration intended to provoke war, and he said, "The most amiable and tenderhearted member of the "watch and wait" party could scarcely be expected to council an adherence to that motto, after war had actually been declared."[64]

An End to "Watch and Wait"

In Volume 1 of the 1863 edition of *My Diary North and South* by William Howard Russell, published by Bradbury and Evans, are a few passages concerning the British reporter's trip through North Carolina on the Wilmington & Weldon Railroad on April 15, 1861,[65] and the next morning in Wilmington, that provide a vivid picture of rail travel through North Carolina in the days following the bombardment and surrender of Fort Sumter. One is struck by Russell's observation about Confederate flags and cheers for Jefferson Davis, even though North Carolina had not yet seceded, and the militia at Goldsboro, called up by the governor of the

This illustration from *Pictorial History of the War of 1861* shows Fort Macon after it was captured by Union forces under the command of Major General Ambrose E. Burnside on April 26, 1862. Built of masonry, the fort was constructed in the early nineteenth century to protect Beaufort Harbor. Having captured New Bern more than a month earlier on March 14, the Union established a firm foothold in eastern North Carolina, leaving Wilmington the only viable port remaining in the state controlled by the Confederacy. From secure bases in New Bern, Union generals John G. Foster and Edward E. Potter launched raids against the Wilmington & Weldon Railroad (courtesy New Hanover Public Library, NCD Box 1 001).

state, readying to participate in the seizure of Fort Caswell and Fort Macon. The somewhat drunk members of Wilmington's Vigilance Committee contributed to several comic events associated with this frenzy after they grilled an artist friend sent out to post a letter. It appears they were looking for "Lincolnites and Abolitionists" that might be lurking about town. Other details, such as the descriptions of the railroad dining hall, the hotel and the lady running it, and the proximity of both to the trains contributes to an understanding of the depot site of that period, for which the sketchiest descriptions are known to exist. However, the one piece of information that Russell includes that begs further inquiry concerns the artillery shells stored on the railroad dock for the steamboat ferry. When he asked about them, he received the response that they had been there for about two months; but since Sumter had been taken, they might not be needed.[66]

The shells appear in a correspondence between Major W.H.C. Whiting, Confederate engineer, and Brigadier General Beauregard, who commanded the Confederate army at Charleston, dated April 22, 1861. Whiting mentioned that there were plenty of shells at the railroad depot in Wilmington, but he had a shortage of fuses and other equipment for the defenses at Fort Caswell. He was somewhat discouraged by the lack of military efficiency of his new post, but he commented on the enthusiasm of those under his command. He gave ladies the task of making cartridge bags and sand bags.[67] The ammunition arrived in Wilmington on February 23: Mentioned earlier, the notice of the arrival of "1819 bomb shells and balls and sundries" along with other items including cotton, flour, tobacco, ore, and bales domestic for a host of Wilmington merchants. The only individual that stands out is one J.L. Cantwell.[68] The comedy of community leaders in Wilmington playing the role of military commanders, the drunkenness of the vigilance committee, and the apparent public display of support for the Southern Confederacy aside,[69] while North Carolina had not yet withdrawn from the Union, suggestions are that the public support for the fading watch and wait position had collapsed after the fall of Sumter. The *Wilmington Journal* addresses the problems created by Lincoln's request for North Carolina troops on April 15 in an article entitled, "Where are we now? Assemble the Legislature!"

> The startling events of the last few days have effected changes in public sentiment and in relations of the people of the South to the Government at Washington that months of mere speculation and argument might have failed to compass. To use a common expression, "the thing is out," the issue is upon us and it must be met at once and firmly. Those who had heretofore been the strongest Union men were on Saturday last as fully prepared to go the utmost length to resist coercion, as

were those who had been original secessionists. It has been mainly a question of time, for in the last resort, when the worse comes to the worse we must all stand together and we *will*. No matter where any of our citizens was born, whether North or South, whether on this side of the Atlantic or the other side, we are all in the same boat, and every loyal North Carolina citizen will rally to the standard of resistance to sectional aggression. We have been anxious all along to make the issue in North Carolina peacefully, legally, and we are so now, so far as the issue between our own citizens is concerned, but the course of events — the progress of affairs, is too rapid to await the usual course of political actions.— The issue is no longer one confined to our citizens or under our own control. The Northern sword of Abe Lincoln has been thrown into the scale. He has issued his proclamation calling for the militia of the several States of the Union to make war upon the seceded States. Governor Ellis will be called upon for *his* quota, he will be required to call upon the different regiments for theirs, drafted to carry out the behests of Abraham Lincoln and William H. Seward — to initiate the irrepressible conflict — to fight against their friends and kinsmen of the Southern States. We ask any man to read the proclamation issued by Lincoln and Seward and answer whether it does not present an issue not only authorizing but demanding of Governor Ellis to call the Legislature together *immediately*. We say that it appears to be his duty to do so, a duty which he cannot evade and which he *will not* evade. Neither will he shrink from *any* responsibility that the circumstances may seem to demand. Will Governor Ellis respond to Lincoln's demand for troops? We do not pretend to answer for Governor Ellis, unless where we *know* his position, but in this case we have no hesitation in saying distinctly *No!* Governor Ellis will not do so. Will he agree that troops should pass freely from the North over the soil of North Carolina, to coerce our Southern sisters? Again we say —*No! Never*.[70]

The call for troops was not only the end of watch and wait, and the end of the old conservative Union Men holdout, but also the beginning of a rapid shift towards the Confederacy. Governor Ellis, responding to United States secretary of war Simon Cameron on April 15 concerning the call for troops from North Carolina, stated that he would not comply. The state was expected to supply two regiments, and Virginia was expected to provide three. The Virginia Convention went into secret session and on April 17 passed an ordinance of secession. Ellis soon ordered the taking of the forts and arsenals in North Carolina, and Wilmington's working men and a contingent of its free black work force were sent to the forts. The state took control of the mint at Charlotte.[71]

The neutrality of North Carolina during this period was questionable: on April 22, Governor Ellis received a request from Confederate secretary of war L.P. Walker to supply one regiment of state troops to Richmond, and he responded on April 24 by stating his willingness to send 1,000 to 10,000 volunteers as North Carolina troops within a few days. However, he added that funds would be required for their transportation, since he was not authorized to use state funds for that purpose.[72] Walker soon asked for muskets, and Ellis offered them from the arsenal at Fayetteville, in addition to sending arms and ammunition to Major Whiting at Wilmington. On May 1, Ellis offered the service of the mint at Charlotte to the Confederacy.[73] The *Wilmington Journal* defended his actions in an editorial.

> It is little over two weeks since Lincoln's proclamation was issued. Then, all was to be done. The Governor was in very feeble health — the treasury without means, the Executive without positive authority in the premises. Now, the forts are occupied, and the defenses of the coast fully organized and progressing under skillful officers.... The Legislature has been called — is in session and has already passed a convention bill and the convention will meet in less than twenty days.[74]

North Carolina seceded on May 20, 1861.

Organizational Deficiencies with Mobilization and Troop Transport

Hitherto, the railroads of North Carolina have only been mentioned in passing. It is at the annual meeting of stockholders at the end of the year that the impact of their changing functions became clear. The first wartime annual meeting of the stockholders of the Wilmington & Weldon Railroad was held on November 14, 1861, at the courthouse in Wilmington. William S. Ashe, president of the company, remarked on the increase in revenues over the past year in the opening paragraph of his report, and continued by stating that it had been predicted that the war would paralyze business on the railroad. Not omitting that "the prosecution of our business" was connected with rendering service to the Confederate cause, he assured the stockholders that they were justified in feeling some "patriotic pride." With confidence, he anticipated the war would not end before the Confederacy attained "complete social, commercial, and political independence," and the company should be prepared for the future. His vision for the future was a unified network of railroads for the South that focused on products to the Atlantic ports, connected by an "Atlantic line of Road." If the Cape Fear River were bridged, he anticipated an unbroken rail connection on the Atlantic from Norfolk to the Gulf.[75] It would be an exaggeration to credit William Shepperd Ashe with creating a long-term plan for a peacetime system of southern railroads. The idea of an Atlantic coast route had been discussed for decades, and Ashe, during his tenure in the Congress of the United States, was not disengaged from railroad issues, particularly those related to the Wilmington & Raleigh and the Wilmington & Manchester.[76] As president of the Wilmington & Weldon since 1855, he was proactive in refining the continuity of that railroad with the Wilmington & Manchester, and connecting both in North Carolina and neighboring states as well. As assistant quartermaster in charge of transport of troops and material for the Confederacy, he faced real-life logistical problems associated with organization and the nature of the Southern rail network. With such a background, he was not merely speaking from an abstract position of a visionary. Regardless, he was correct in some respects, even though the railroad network of the future would not be Confederate. R.R. Bridgers, a subscriber to the Tarboro Branch of the Wilmington & Weldon, would preside over the realization of some of this after the war. The Southern railroads of 1861, however, were not organized to function as a unified network.[77] An illustration can be found in a letter to Ashe from General Superintendent of the Virginia Central Railroad H.D. Whitcomb dated September 23, 1861. Whitcomb identifies three causes for delays of Confederate government freight on his railroad: that the railroad was not equipped with enough rolling stock to accommodate military needs, the supply of cities, and the needs of agriculture; that the shipments related to military needs did not follow an organized or predictable schedule, so there were periods when freight shipments were slow, followed by periods when the railroad was overwhelmed by both private and government freight; and because the volumes were greater than the available storage, freight often remained in the cars.[78] On the surface, the problems listed by Whitcomb appear to be the result of poor communications between the Confederate government and the Virginia Central only, but on a deeper level, it was a network problem: there were many different companies reacting with different degrees of efficiency to changing demands, rather than functioning as units within a hierarchical system, its organization equally suitable to respond to prioritized traffic flows in peacetime or war.[79] Aside from organizational difficulties, there existed physical barriers to continuous transportation that introduced logistical friction into the network. Ashe identified a significant problem in continuous rail transportation on the coastal corridor: the absence of a bridge across the Cape Fear River at Wilmington. He recommended to the stockholders as a joint investment such a bridge by his company and the Wilmington & Manchester.[80] The unloading of freight and passengers from railroad to steam ferry to railroad at Wilmington was a source of logistical friction, adding time, labor, and expense beyond the transfer from cars of one gauge to another. Transportation on the coastal corridor could never be exploited to its potential with the Cape Fear River remaining a stumbling block. When the river was bridged in 1869, the three railroads enjoyed the logistical advantages of a common hub.

The report of the chief engineer and superintendent, S.L. Fremont, provides a clear perspective of how the Wilmington & Weldon had fared during the months since North Carolina had seceded. As for improvements to the road, the filling in of trestlework had continued as it had since Fremont assumed his position in 1855, and the work, except for a half-mile, was complete. The board of directors, however, in January 1861, had suspended the use of the gravel train designated for this operation, so it cannot be considered a wartime improvement. He did not suggest any improvements to the road for the coming fiscal year, other than replacement of worn rail and the construction of masonry culverts. The renewal of the railroad in the early 1850s had gone forward without the installation of chairs or other fastenings between rail joints, a problem he raised in his report of 1855. Also, during the fiscal year 25,000 double-lipped rolled chairs had been installed, and an additional 20,000 were needed to complete the work. Under the existing conditions, however, he did not expect that Southern ironworks would be able to provide them with priorities placed on supplying the needs of the military. Other improvements to the road during the year included replacing 52,000 crossties and putting down 400 tons of new rail. During the year, the trains had logged 325,181 miles traveling the roads, an increase in transportation — operating trains at all times of day and night — due to troop transport, a change from the usual demands on the railroad that resulted in increased wear on the locomotives, rolling stock, and rails. The increased cost of lubrication was also attributed to the same.[81]

The number of through passengers carried over the road that year was 46,371, a significant increase from the previous year's total of 25,595. The number of way passengers increased from 81,051 in 1860 to 81,803 in 1861. Fremont notes that the 1861 figures group troops with passengers paying half or full ticket price; but in fact hundreds of North Carolina troops had been transported for free, because the state had not yet established a quartermaster department to allocate funds for the service. Fremont was skeptical of the net income figures for the year, considering that the ultimate cost resulting from repairs associated with increased traffic would be greater than an ordinary year's volume with full passenger and freight rates.[82] The consequence of adjusting the variable in the equation, prioritizing and altering the schedule to meet increase demand, could cancel out profits through a degradation of the rate structure, the system's operational components, or both. The Wilmington & Weldon, a reasonably well-equipped company, complete with foundry, machine shop, and all the necessities to build and repair their equipment, could operate under increased capacity[83] until its resources were exhausted, its facility to undertake self-maintenance had utterly failed, or outside forces rendered the entire railroad useless. The remarkable wartime history of the Wilmington & Weldon ended with the latter, segmented, isolated, its potential exhausted.

The report of S.L. Fremont indirectly exposes organizational deficiencies in both the Confederate and North Carolina governments. The scene at Goldsboro on April 15, 1861, described by William Howard Russell, reads much as the libretto of a comic opera, assumes a more disturbing aspect in the light of Fremont's words: the company of state militia, eccentrically costumed in their military regalia, but equipped with antique weapons, and commanded by an arrogant, inebriated "General," who assumed the authority for the railroad and would take "my cars" when and where he pleased, might have been stark reality.[84] Fremont, lumping passengers and paying troops together, could not provide any statistics on troops riding free in the early days of the war but believed they numbered in the hundreds. The poorly conceived mobilization had created a lingering irritation for railroads in the state. The North Carolina Railroad, seeking payment for transportation from the state for April 20, 1861, through August 20, 1861, found the North Carolina Legislature unwilling to pay the claim by insisting that the debt was incurred for the defense of the nation, thus the Confederate government was responsible for payment. The Confederate government, then paying half price for passengers and freight, also refused to pay, on the grounds that a certificate from an officer in the Confederate service was required to prove that the transportation was for the Confederate States. Thomas Webb, president of the company, showed open irritation by stating he had refused the government's payment on other debts using Confederate bonds rather than currency.[85]

"We work for the government at half price; it refuses to pay a portion of our claims although acknowledged just; it suspends others, and it should pay us in money or notes whatever is due. The State of North Carolina has paid us nothing."[86] By 1863, Confederate bonds would constitute a large portion on the company's sinking fund. In contrast, in 1861, the Wilmington & Weldon did not seem to have a problem with Confederate States bonds as evidenced by the $71,850.00 in this item that they had on hand. Claiming an increase in revenue that year of $71,026.67 from the previous year, the bonds rendered the profit to mere promise. Aside from this, the Confederate States and the State of North Carolina had a balance on transportation due the company of $57,667.95.[87]

The mobilization of North Carolina troops began before the state seceded on May 20, 1861. The legislature, after meeting in special session early in the month and again on May 8, authorized Governor Ellis to raise 10,000 troops that would be transferred to the Confederate command, an act that would siphon off the state's militia without establishing provisions for replenishing the state's home force. Then Ellis died of tuberculosis on July 7, leaving the task of state defense to his successor, Henry Toole Clark. As Clark would discover repeatedly during his tenure, the Confederate government did not consider defending the coastline of North Carolina a priority; that task fell to the state. Since August 31, 1861, S.L. Fremont had been working for the state as chief of the 1st Corps of North Carolina Volunteer Artillery and Engineers, and chief engineer of the coastal defenses for the southern coastal region (New River to the South Carolina line). This was at the time Fort Hatteras fell into Union hands. The greatest of the earthwork defenses that he worked on was Fort Fisher, named by Fremont for Charles F. Fisher, the president of the North Carolina Railroad, who had resigned his position to lead the 6th Regiment North Carolina

Fort Hatteras and Fort Clark fell under a combined assault by the United States naval and ground troops on August 28–29, 1861. The force was commanded by Commodore Stringham and Major General Butler. This illustration from *The Soldier in Our Civil War* shows Confederates raising the white flag of surrender (courtesy New Hanover Public Library, NCD Box 1 019).

State Troops, and was killed at the Battle of First Manassas. In late 1861, Fremont returned to his duties with the railroad.[88]

The fall of Fort Clark and Fort Hatteras on August 28–29, 1861, established a Union foothold in the Tidewater of North Carolina. As the war continued into 1862, Union forces achieved victories at Roanoke Island, New Bern, Fort Macon, and Tranter's Creek, and between December 14 and December 17 of that year, Brigadier General John G. Foster conducted his raid on Kinston, Whitehall, and Goldsboro with the intent of disrupting transportation on the Wilmington & Weldon. He managed to destroy the railroad bridge at Goldsboro before returning to base in New Bern. But before these events transpired, the railroad experienced its first sabotage attempts. Fremont, in his 1861 report to the stockholders, reported that in May someone had cut components of the trestle at Toisnot Creek (Wilson, North Carolina) with the intent of causing a train containing Confederate troops to tumble into the creek. An attempt at sawing through the stringers on the railroad bridge at Smith's Creek (Wilmington, North Carolina) had also failed; yet as of November, the saboteurs had yet to be apprehended, in spite of the reward that had been offered.[89] Every bridge along the line of the Wilmington & Weldon, and the Seaboard & Roanoke Railroad's bridge over the Roanoke, was a point of weakness that could exploited by the enemy to produce a catastrophic wreck or to interrupt transportation along the corridor. Fremont had, however, ample evidence of how the absence of a bridge on the road could foul its operations. Fortunately, it had not been destroyed; it simply had not been completed. Contractors working on the Tarboro Branch of the railroad had been originally scheduled to build a permanent bridge over the Tar River by September 1860, but were allowed additional time on the condition that they construct a temporary structure to allow trains to cross in the interim. They failed to complete either task and were employed elsewhere for the Confederate government. As a result, the bridge remained unfinished until June 1861. He continued that approximately 2,500 bales of cotton from the area that the company had anticipated would be transported by rail was instead sent to market on the river.[90] Delaying for nine months the replacement of a bridge on the main line that might be destroyed by the enemy was not an acceptable risk.

Freight

A comparison of freight statistics for fiscal years 1860 and 1861 shows a decrease in naval stores, with the exception of tar, from Wilmington on the Wilmington & Weldon: rosin dropped from 52,857 bbl. to 13,294

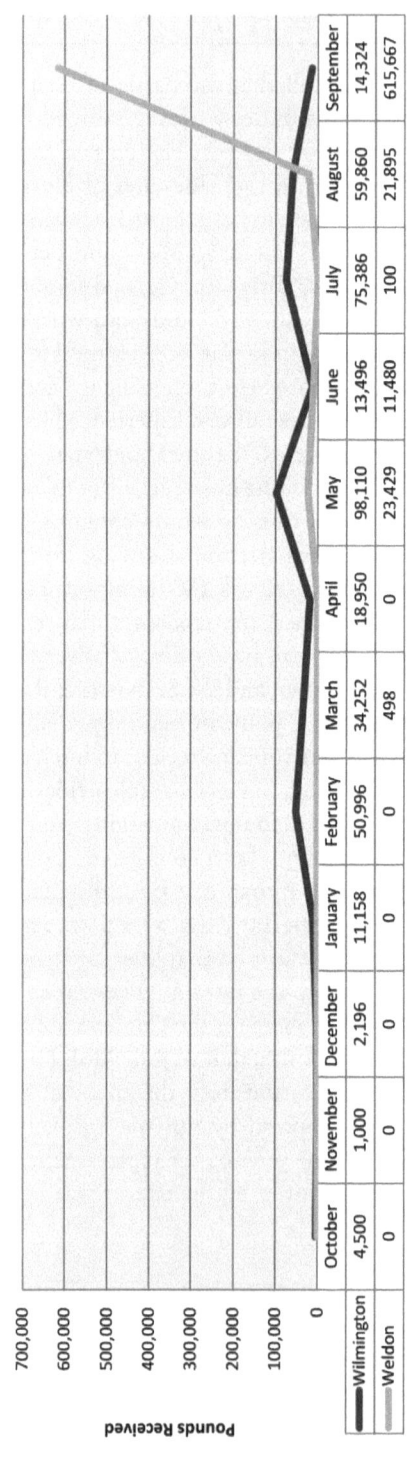

Monthly Freight Statistics, 1860–1861
(Bacon)

	October	November	December	January	February	March	April	May	June	July	August	September
Wilmington	4,500	1,000	2,196	11,158	50,996	34,252	18,950	98,110	13,496	75,386	59,860	14,324
Weldon	0	0	0	0	0	498	0	23,429	11,480	100	21,895	615,667

bbl.; spirits of turpentine dropped from 22,754 bbl. to 10,750 bbl.; crude turpentine dropped from 18,056 bbl. to 6,672 bbl.; while tar rose from 7,732 bbl. to 8,536 bbl. Cotton decreased from 15,893 bales in 1860 to 14,778 bales, and flour, from 10,893 bbl. to 8,491 bbl. The products reflecting a sharp increase at Wilmington in 1861 include bacon, corn, and wheat: bacon, from 377,082 lbs. to 384,228 lbs.; corn, dramatically from 8,448 bushels in 1860 to 101,464 bushels in 1861; and wheat, from 6,798 bushels to 10,303 bushels. At Weldon, the amount of bacon received climbed astronomically from 2,528 lbs. in 1860 to 673,669 lbs. in 1861. Corn, however, fell 4,256 bushels to 1,859 bushels; flour from 368 bbl. to 62 bbl.; and wheat from 618 bushels to 332 bushels. Decreasing, like that of Wilmington, were rosin, 10,716 bbl. to 3,556 bbl.; and spirits of turpentine, 569 bbl. to 226 bbl. No crude turpentine or tar was received at Weldon in 1860 or 1861, and bales of cotton received increased from 15,363 to 19,676. On closer examination, statistics covering the period from October 1860 to April 1861 follow the expected annual patterns. It is from May through September that the pattern changes.[91] Shipments of bacon received at Weldon, nearly nonexistent before March, climbed to 615,667 lbs. in September, while shipments of the same article declined at Wilmington. An examination of vouchers for the account of the State of North Carolina shows that on June 22, shipments of bacon, lard, and flour originating in Salisbury, Greensboro, and High Point were shipped on the Wilmington & Weldon; July 1 shows a shipment of bacon and lard. On July 16, 19, and 25, bacon originating in Salisbury, North Carolina, was shipped on the Wilmington & Weldon; butter was also shipped from Salisbury. A voucher from July 15 shows the same shipment of bacon was carried on the North Carolina Railroad and the Wilmington & Weldon.[92] These documents imply that the items were offloaded at Goldsboro and transported to Weldon. An earlier voucher from the State of North Carolina Commissary Department shows shipments from the Piedmont and transferred to the Wilmington & Weldon beginning in early May: 196 lbs. of bacon from Greensboro on May 4; on May 16, 1,759 lbs. of bacon and 56 bbl. and 11 sacks of flour from High Point; 312 lbs. of bacon and 14 bags of dried fruit; lard, bacon and sacks of peas were shipped from Salisbury and flour, bacon, and lard from both Greensboro and High Point on May 28.[93]

Opposite: The volume in pounds of bacon received at Wilmington and at Weldon during the fiscal year 1860–61 is shown on this chart. During the month of September, shipments of bacon received at Weldon climbed astoundingly, while at Wilmington they remained flat. The transportation of food was an essential role of the Wilmington & Weldon and its connecting lines.

The transportation pattern for freight that emerges during this period reflects the aid sent to Virginia prior to the secession of North Carolina, and the early mobilization of troops as well as the entry of North Carolina in the war. The vast quantities of foodstuffs, particularly from the North Carolina Piedmont, reflect the nature of the state's contribution to the war effort. The transportation patterns and the nature of shipments will be examined in detail.

Chapter III

The Freight of War

The freight transported by the Wilmington & Weldon Railroad in support of the war effort included provisions and arms. Freight entered the line at several locations: at Wilmington, loads arrived at the company wharf by boat from the depot of the Wilmington & Manchester Railroad; the depot of the Wilmington, Charlotte & Rutherford Railroad; or from other locations on the Cape Fear River. The Wilmington & Weldon transported the freight north to depots along the line, to the junction of the North Carolina Railroad and the Atlantic & North Carolina Railroad at Goldsboro, or to the hub at Weldon. Freight entered the line by the Tarboro Branch of the railroad and from the junction at Goldsboro. Southbound freight was transferred to the Wilmington & Weldon from the Petersburg Railroad (Petersburg & Weldon), the Seaboard & Roanoke Railroad, and from the branch line of the Raleigh & Gaston Railroad. Loads could then proceed to Wilmington and points south or be transferred at Goldsboro; southbound freight also entered the line at Goldsboro. The firm of Orrell & Hawes also provided transportation across the Cape Fear River between the depot of the Wilmington & Manchester Railroad and the depot of the Wilmington & Weldon Railroad.

Freight shipments on the account of the Confederate States can be divided into several broad categories: frequent shipments of food, including bacon, flour, corn, sugar, coffee; items such as tobacco and whiskey; military equipment excluding arms and powder consisting of items such as tents, shoes, soap, medicine, and tools; and cannons, projectiles, firearms, and articles associated with their production represent a distinct category. The vouchers also contained miscellaneous household items and those that were not identified but listed only as boxes, barrels, or packages; of this category, most were sent to individuals. For the purpose of analysis, food as a category of freight can be examined with respect to the attributes of destination (marks), origin, and weight within a time frame, and the same holds true for equipment and miscellaneous freight. Shipments of armaments require a more detailed examination since they can often be associated with specific deployments and needs. Heavy artillery shipped on the Wilmington & Weldon and the Wilmington & Manchester was more often than not intended for coastal defense. Field artillery and light arms traveled with the troops or as freight shipments to specific officers or consignees.

Artillery

Several instruction manuals printed in the Confederate States exist that provide a detailed description of the classes of artillery pieces, their ammunition, and all aspects of their maintenance and operation. *Instruction for Heavy Artillery; Prepared by a Board of Officers, for the use of the Army of the United States*, originally published in the early 1850s, was reprinted at Charleston in 1861, and at Richmond in 1862. Presented as a series of lessons, and including a number of illustrations, this work presents the extremely complex steps that constitute the chorography of loading, aiming and firing heavy artillery. It was a process that involves a team of men executing precise movements for a sequence of inflexible tasks using specific equipment; each man according to his task had his designated station around the piece. The handling and placement of equipment were also specific. Cannoneers were instructed in the "school of the piece" for field artillery before receiving training in heavy artillery. The classes of heavy artillery included siege and garrison guns, 12 pound, 18 pound, and 24 pound caliber; seacoast guns, 32 and 42 pound; siege and garrison howitzers, 8-inch and 24 pound; seacoast howitzers, 8-inch and 10-inch; columbiads, 8-inch and 10-inch; siege mortars, 8-inch and 10-inch, and seacoast mortars, 10-inch and 13-inch, all cast of iron; the stone mortars, 16-inch caliber, and the coehorn mortars, 24 pound caliber, were cast of bronze.[1] Howitzers and columbiads, and their carriages, appear in the transportation vouchers, along with the terms "cannons," "guns," and "gun carriages." More often, however, the vouchers refer to the transport of powder, shot, and shells.

A shipment of artillery sent via Weldon to Wilmington in August 1861 included four 10-inch columbiads, four 8-inch columbiads and wooden carriages; two 42 pounders; 200 10-inch shells, 200 8-inch shells, and six sets of carriage irons were ordered sent to Major J.H. Trapier, the engineer officer at Charleston, from the Quartermaster's Department at Richmond. Transportation for "one nine inch rifle gun" was also ordered on August 24 for Major Trapier.[2]

III. The Freight of War 79

A December 4, 1861, report concerning the bombardment of Fort Walker, written by Major Francis D. Lee, an engineer with the South Carolina Army, implies that the artillery was needed for the defense of Hilton Head.

Lee, having been engaged in the design of the battery there, had ordered seven 10-inch columbiads but had received them after completing his earthworks around September 1. They were an assortment of different pieces of varying calibers. A furnace for hot shot, ammunition heated to cause fire on impact, arrived just before the bombardment by Union forces on November 7.[3] A report by Acting Lieutenant John S. Barnes of the U.S. Navy provides an inventory of artillery pieces at Fort Beauregard and Fort Walker after their capture. At Fort Beauregard he found 13 guns guarding the approach to the Broad and Beaufort rivers that included five 32-pounders, navy pattern, 1845, one rifled 6-inch, new, marked "C.S.A., 1861" and "J.R.A. & Co., T.F." (Tredegar Iron Works in Richmond); five seacoast 42-pounders, one 10-inch columbiad with the "C.S.A., 1861" and Tredegar markings, the Palmetto coat of arms, and weighing 13,226 lbs., and one 8-inch columbiad with the same markings as the 10-inch. Mounted on the outer work of the fort were two 24-pounders marked "S.C." and three navy pattern 32-pounders. The interior of the fort contained two Spanish pattern 6-pounder field pieces, and two furnaces for hot shot. Fort Walker contained two new 6-inch rifled guns with Tredegar marks; seven navy pattern, 1845, 32-pounders; one new 10-inch columbiad, 13,220 lbs. and one new 8-inch columbiad, 9,018 lbs. with Tredegar marks; three old pattern seacoast howitzers marked "Charleston, with great haste"; and one 42-pounder seacoast howitzer that was not mounted. The outer work on the land side contained five 32-pounders marked "S.C." and dated 1851 and 1827; one 8-inch howitzer; two English siege guns marked "G.R." (Georgius Rex); and one 12-pounder. There were two furnaces for hot shot, and the shell room and magazine contained a quantity of ammunition, including 50 4-shell boxes of 6-inch shells, 250 10-inch shells, 100 8-inch shells, and other calibers of shell, shot, and canister.[4]

Invoices for freight ferried across the Cape Fear supplements the records of the railroads. The accounts of the firm of Orrell & Hawes, hired to provide ferriage, included information on the transfer of munitions and supplies between the depot of the Wilmington & Manchester Railroad and the depot of the Wilmington & Weldon Railroad. The invoices of the firm render some information on what weaponry was passing south over the Wilmington & Manchester. For example, a shipment of 200 kegs of powder from the WMRR depot to the WWRR depot was delivered on June 18, 1861, and the transportation of guns and ammunition is recorded on September 20, September 25, September 28, October 7, October 12, October 14, and October 22. The details of these shipments appear in reasonably legible script on partial sheets of lined paper: on September 25, the company delivered to the Wilmington & Manchester from the Wilmington & Weldon 375 units of shot and shell, five gun carriages, and two 8-inch guns with fixtures and carriages; the September 20 shipment included one rifled gun and iron carriage and three boxes; the September 25 shipment included one rifled cannon and carriage, three half-bbl. of powder, 15 boxes, one bundle of ramrods and sponges, and an additional unspecified box; on September 28, the delivery included two 32-pounders with fixtures and carriages, 39 shells and 200 balls; the October 7 shipment included six 18-inch howitzers and 600 shells, the October 12 shipment consisted of wheels, a carriage, and fixtures; three guns and 150 shells were delivered on October 14; and complete 8-inch columbiad was delivered on October 22. All deliveries were from the Wilmington & Weldon depot to the Wilmington & Manchester depot.[5]

From May 20 through June 1, 1861, the Wilmington & Weldon transported two carloads of gun carriages from Wilmington to Goldsboro for Fort Macon, seven cannons with 149 shot and 61 shells from Weldon to Wilmington, and two carloads of shells from Wilmington to Goldsboro.[6] In a letter dated August 29, 1861, written on behalf of the firm of Orrell & Hawes by Henry M. Drane, superintendent of the Wilmington & Manchester Railroad, the invoices for transportation of military freight across the Cape Fear River during the first months of the war were presented to the Confederate government for payment. Beginning with an invoice dated April 20, 1861, a D.K. McRae ordered a shipment to Fort Macon of 300 kegs of powder, four cannons, 200 balls and shells, seven barbette carriages, and five siege carriages. These items were transported from the depot of the Wilmington & Manchester to the depot of the Wilmington & Weldon. A shipment for Major Whiting of 8-inch carriages and platforms was delivered to the Wilmington & Weldon depot by Orrell & Hawes on May 7. On May 18, three 8-inch columbiad carriages and two platforms were delivered between the two depots for Fort Macon, and on May 20, thirteen 32-pounders were delivered from the Wilmington & Weldon depot to the Clarendon Iron Works for shipment to Fort Caswell. The weaponry was intended for coastal defenses, and the invoices were originally billed to the Ordinance Department of the State of North Carolina. There is also an invoice dated on August 7 for howitzers shipped via Weldon to Wilmington; an invoice for the shipment to Fort Fisher of an 8-inch columbiad carriage with platform and equipment, manufactured by the Richmond

This rifled and banded 6.4-inch, 32-pounder cannon at Fort Fisher on Shepard's Battery illustrates how coastal artillery was loaded and aimed. It is mounted in a barbette on a center pintle (photograph by Dr. Cyn Johnson).

firm of Ettenger & Edmond, dated September 19, 1861; and an invoice for the transportation of 61 shells on October 1 from Weldon to Wilmington.[7]

The Clarendon Iron Works at Wilmington was employed by the North Carolina State Ordnance Department in the summer of 1861 to fulfill requisitions by General Holmes, Colonel Tew, and Major Whiting. The orders, paid for by the Town of Wilmington and the State of North Carolina, were billed on June 8, June 29, July 16, and August 1 for an order of grapeshot, 12 complete 32-pounder barbette carriages and chasses, fourteen complete 24-pounder barbette carriages and chasses, three complete 8-inch columbiad carriages and chasses, and one complete 10-inch columbiad carriage and chassis.[8]

The previous example indicates that the transportation patterns of heavy artillery on the Wilmington & Weldon and the Wilmington & Manchester can be established early in the war, due to the necessity of coastal defense. Old pattern heavy artillery in the North Carolina and South Carolina state arsenals was moved east, and new ordnance, such as that manufactured by the Tredegar Iron Works, was transported on the railroads south. Gun carriages were manufactured separately, and those at the defenses at Wilmington and the area were made locally. Goldsboro is also a node where shipments were transferred. For example, on May 20 and June 1, 1861, several shipments of weapons for the state, to which Governor Ellis was the consignee, traveled over the Petersburg Railroad to the Wilmington & Weldon and were transferred at Goldsboro. These included a shipment of 2,119 shells and shot, gun equipment, two gun carriages; and another two cannons, 100 shot and 50 shells; on May 21, two howitzers; two gun carriages; and on May 30, 1,333 shell and shot were shipped.[9] Beginning in August, the consignee for these shipments was Col. J.D. Whitford, president of the Atlantic & North Carolina Railroad. On August 1, a shipment of gun accouterments from the Petersburg Railroad via the Wilmington & Weldon was transferred at Goldsboro; on August 12, two caissons and gun equipment, following the same route, were transferred; 1,040 shot were transferred on August 16 and 2,605 shot and shells on September 5; and on October 7, two cannons were transferred at Goldsboro for shipment via Weldon.[10]

By early 1862, the defenses on the Neuse River around New Bern consisted of Fort Dixie, which had one 6-inch rifled gun and three 32-pounders; Fort Ellis, which had eight guns including one 6-inch rifled gun and one 8-inch columbiad, a casemated work of two guns; Fort Thompson, which had ten 32-pounders and two 6-inch rifled guns; Fort Lane, with two 6-inch rifled guns and two 32-pounders; and two forts were in front of New Bern with two guns each.[11]

The movement of heavy artillery on the Wilmington & Weldon and the Wilmington & Manchester was to supply coastal defenses, and to this aim, the primary military purpose of the railroads being the through transportation of troops and provisions, was preserved, at least in theory. The Union objective was to overwhelm these defenses, establish a foothold there, and drive to the interior and cut the rail corridor to Virginia. At best, until the end of the war, the Union Army could accomplish only an occasional raid on the Wilmington & Weldon, then countermarch back to their coastal safe haven. The fortifications at the mouth of the Cape Fear remained unassailed until 1865.

Through Transportation Vouchers

The through transportation patterns for freight shipments on the Wilmington & Weldon for the Confederate States during the second half of 1861 are primarily connections from the Wilmington & Manchester—

indicating from sources south of the Cape Fear region to the junction of the South Carolina railroads at Florence, Manchester Junction, or Kingville — to Richmond by way of the Petersburg Railroad, or to Norfolk by way of the Seaboard & Roanoke Railroad. Transportation vouchers from the period beginning from August 1, 1861, through October 31, 1861, shows 82.4 percent of items shipped on the Wilmington & Weldon are destined for Richmond, and Manassas, at 5 percent of the list items, is the second most frequent destination. Excluding items shipped at a flat rate, 3,169,202 lbs. of food were shipped on the line, including 1,120,252 lbs. of rice; 812,368 lbs. of bacon; 643,750 lbs. of sugar; 343,402 lbs. of molasses; 134,050 lbs. of coffee; 100,430 lbs. of salt; 14,150 lbs. of flour; and two boxes of unspecified provisions weighing 200 lbs. Flat rate food items included 1,003 barrels of pork, 370 barrels of whiskey and other liquor, 17 barrels and two bags of salt, 13 bags of meal, 10 bags of rice flour, and two barrels of crackers (see Appendix C). The person to whom a great portion of the bulk food shipments sent to Richmond was Capt. J.H. Clairbourne, Capt. J.H. Claibone, or Capt. J.H. Claiborne. His name, misspelled again as J.H. Claibourne, Esq., appears on a correspondence dated September 18, 1861, presumably from the Virginia Central Railroad, complaining that all their cars were at Manassas and Millborough, and as a result of not getting them back, their depot was backed up. Therefore, if a shipment of flour was sent, the government would have to take the risk of having the shipment stored outside.[12] Major J.H. Claiborne served in the Commissary Department in Richmond, whose depot was located at the corner of Dock and Seventeenth streets.[13] The *Regulations for the Commissary's Department of the State of Virginia* describes a single ration as consisting of the following items:

> The ration is three-fourths of a pound of pork or bacon, or one and a fourth pounds of fresh or salt beef; eighteen ounces of bread or flour, or twelve ounces of hard bread, or one and a fourth pounds corn meal; and at the rate, to one hundred rations, of eight quarts of peas or beans, or, in lieu thereof, ten pounds of rice; six pounds coffee; twelve pounds sugar; four quarts of vinegar; one and a half pounds of tallow, or one and a fourth pounds adamantine, or one pound sperm candles; four pounds of soap, and two quarts of salt.[14]

Based upon these requirements, 1,083,157.33 rations of bacon, 112,025.20 rations of rice, and 53,645.83 rations of sugar were delivered to Richmond over the three month period; this amounts to 631,052.44 rations of bacon, 37,341.73 rations of rice, and 17,881.94 rations of sugar per month. Of these shipments of food, the vouchers contain the names of two individuals in Wilmington having shipped rice, R.G. Rankin and H.M. Drane. On

September 20, R.G. Rankin shipped a load of 14,045 lbs. of rice to Lynchburg and a load of rice to Richmond weighing 100,496 lbs. Then, he shipped a load of 81,455 lbs. of rice to Richmond on October 15, 1861. H.M. Drane shipped a load of 86,974 lbs. of rice on October 29 to Richmond. The remainder of the food arrived in Wilmington on the Wilmington & Manchester with the exception of two boxes of unlisted provisions, with a combined weight of 200 lbs. The latter entered the line at Goldsboro, bound for Yorktown.

The through transportation vouchers for the same period also contain details on 638,902 lbs. of supplies including axes, blankets, camp stools, candles, clothing, cots, kettles, soap, spades, and tents. Hospital stores were sent as well. Most shipments were marked for delivery to Richmond, but a few shipments went to Culpeper, Fairfax, Manassas, Norfolk, Portsmouth, and Staunton. Like the food, most shipments arrived in Wilmington on the Wilmington & Manchester. Only one shipment of clothing to Manassas entered the Wilmington & Weldon at Goldsboro. J. Dawson of Wilmington sent a shipment of axes to Richmond, and R.G. Rankin of Wilmington sent an unspecified box to the Richmond Armory. Some supplies were sent to the Alabama Soldiers, Georgia Hospital, the 16th Georgia Regiment, and Georgia Regiments. An entry also appeared for 152 kegs of gunpowder, a shipment of 1,800 lbs. of powder sent to Richmond, and 2,000 lbs. of powder sent to New Bern, all sent through Wilmington on the Wilmington & Manchester. A shipment of 9,615 lbs. of saltpeter was sent on October 3 and 4,220 lbs. of sulphur on October 15, both for Richmond. There is only one box of guns listed on the vouchers (see Appendix C).

Completing the examination of through freight vouchers for the three month period are the aggregate entries for items that are identified only as casks, bales, barrels, boxes, bundles, packages, trunks, and articles that do not fit under the categories of food or military supplies. The total weight of this type of freight transported by the Wilmington & Weldon amounted to 414,847 lbs. Many items addressed to individuals received a flat rate. While most were shipped to Richmond, boxes were sent to Aquila Creek, a grindstone to Asheville via Goldsboro, miscellaneous boxes, barrels, and bales to locations in Virginia including Bristow, Charlottesville, Culpeper, Fairfax, Fredericksburg, Lewisburg, Manassas, Norfolk, Petersburg, Portsmouth, Pratt's Point, Staunton, Suffolk, and Yorktown. A shipment of 3 boxes and 10 rolls of carpet was sent to Raleigh; and one undefined shipment weighing 270 lbs. was sent in the opposite direction from Weldon to Charleston. Notable shipments include a carriage and two horses sent to Jefferson Davis on October 11, and a 30 lb. box to General Lee at

Sewell's Mountain on October 29 on the Wilmington & Weldon. Also mentioned were the Alabama Soldiers, the Confederate Hospital, the Georgia Hospital, and the 7th Georgia Regiment marked for Richmond, and the 3rd Georgia Regiment marked for Portsmouth. The 11 boxes sent via Goldsboro to Weldon to the 2nd North Carolina Regiment at Pratt's Point on October 18. J. Dawson and E. Murray & Company were the only Wilmington interests in the entries under this category (see Appendix C).

The through freight vouchers for the period examined indicate that the flow of food and equipment for the military was predominately oriented south to north, originating south of Wilmington, directed towards Richmond and strategic positions in Virginia. The chief contribution to the commissary from the Wilmington area during these months appears to be rice dispatched by commission merchant R.G. Rankin. The Wilmington & Weldon Railroad at this point is functioning as a critical link in a network channeling food and military equipment from locations in the Deep South through its connection with the Wilmington & Manchester Railroad.

Gunpowder

In an address delivered before the Confederate Survivors' Association in 1882, George W. Rains, the officer and inventor responsible for the development of the Confederate Powder Works at Augusta, noted that at the beginning of the war, the South had no great reserve of powder to draw upon to supply its military.

Not anticipating secession led to a protracted conflict, Rains stated, because no provisions were made for accumulating stockpiles of the material of war. When the Confederates had captured the naval yard at Norfolk, they acquired a small quantity which was distributed quickly to critical locations. Jefferson Davis placed great importance upon establishing a powder factory in the South that could satisfy the need for a dependable supply, and it was to be one facility of large capacity situated in a secure place, rather than a number of small manufactories dispersed at different points. Rains was put in charge of gunpowder production. He selected land fronting the Augusta Canal as the site of one of the most impressive and extensive industrial operations of the era. Each phase of the operation, from the refining of saltpeter and sulphur, and the production of charcoal, to the storage of the finished product, was placed in its own dedicated facility, all adequately spaced along the canal to avert a potential accident from destroying the entire works. It had access to rail transportation. Many aspects of production relied on mechanization, the heavy machinery having been contracted from the Tredegar Iron Works. It was situated in a region where the water used in refining saltpeter was free of contaminating lime and salts. Augusta also had a suitable workforce to operate the factories. Construction commenced on the site on September 13, 1861; between April 10, 1862, and April 18, 1865, the factory complex produced 2,750,000 lbs. of gunpowder, including coarse grain powder for heavy guns.[15] Rains describes how the powder was packed for delivery in a box of his own design.

> The finished gunpowder was taken to the next building, one thousand five hundred feet beyond, up the canal, where it was weighed out and put into strong wood boxes about two and a half feet long, by one foot square, having the ends let into grooves; one of the ends had a strong wood screw, two inches diameter, with an octagonal head. Experience proved that these powder boxes, a devise [sic] of my own from necessity, were superior to barrels, being stronger, occupying less room, standing transportation better, and safer in use. No explosion ever occurred in their transportation, notwithstanding the occasional Railroad accidents, and the many thousands that were sent from the Powder Works during the war.[16]

Jefferson Davis would later write in *The Rise and Fall of the Confederate Government* that nitrates were collected from beds in Columbia, Charleston, Savannah, Augusta, Mobile, and Selma. In Greensboro, North Carolina, nitrate saturated soil was collected from under old houses and barns; and a chemical works was established at Charlotte, North Carolina, to counter the anticipated loss of access to foreign supplies. Josiah Gorgas, chief of Confederate ordinance, recommended the formation of a niter and mining bureau that not only developed domestic sources for potassium nitrate, but also supervised the production of iron, lead, copper, and other minerals. Sulphuric and nitric acid were produced for the manufacture of mercury fulminate for percussion caps for firearms. Fish oil was refined on the Cape Fear River for use as a lubricant. The principal armories were located at Richmond, Virginia, and Fayetteville, North Carolina (at the beginning of the war, the Fayetteville Arsenal held 2,000 rifles and 25,000 muskets); the machinery and materials from Harpers Ferry rescued by Armistead Ball were sent to these locations.[17]

The most direct route from Augusta to Wilmington was via Branchville and Kingville on the South Carolina to Manchester Junction, continuing on the Wilmington & Manchester Railroad to Florence, then to Wilmington. From there, the most direct route to Virginia through North Carolina was on the Wilmington & Weldon Railroad. An alternate, but longer route involved connections via the Charlotte & South Carolina Railroad and the North Carolina Railroad. That a substantial portion of the powder from Augusta destined for the Virginia theater would have passed on the Wilmington & Manchester and the Wilmington & Weldon seems obvious.

The stockholder reports, unfortunately, do not provide details on military shipments, and aggregate freight statistics. The vouchers for the firm of Orrell & Hawes, for 1862 through 1864, are helpful in that they show the transfer of powder and other materials used in explosives across the Cape Fear River. Some entries are marked from Col. Rains, and Col. Gorgas. Between the Wilmington & Manchester and the Wilmington & Weldon passed boxes of ammunition, boxes of rifles, boxes of percussion caps, artillery pieces, caissons, loads of sulphur and saltpeter, containers of mercury, and shipments of acid.[18] The record of these transfers of arms and ammunition, as well as the raw materials of explosives, confirms not only the route between the manufacturing centers for these materials, but also the names of officers receiving the shipments.

Blockade Runners

Major Caleb Huse, purchasing agent for the Confederate States in Europe, was commissioned prior to the firing upon Fort Sumter. Reporting for duty on April 12 to Col. Gorgas, Huse found that arrangements for his travel abroad, including the funding of his mission, had not advanced. The treasury of the Confederacy, only recently organized, lacked as yet any source of revenue. However, Huse was instructed to proceed to New York, and there, he received $500 in gold from the firm of Trenholm Brothers & Company for his expenses. Trenholm Brothers was connected to Fraser, Trenholm & Company of Liverpool, England, and John Fraser & Company of Charleston, South Carolina. Huse arrived in England via Canada. The Confederacy had no credit, but to pay for foreign goods, it acquired cotton through bonds or currency from the beginning of the war from producers. The shipped cotton was consigned to Fraser, Trenholm & Company of Liverpool. Cotton warrants were promises to pay in cotton and according to Huse, not worth the cost of printing, but they did have value when traded at a premium on the London market.[19] The warrant included in his book is worded as follows:

> The Government of the Confederate States of America hereby engage to deliver to the bearer within forty days after presentation of this Warrant at the Treasury of the said Confederate States Two Millions and Sixty

A Union warship gives chase to a vessel attempting to run the blockade below Wilmington in this drawing from *Le Monde Illustré* (courtesy New Hanover Public Library, NCD Box 1 018).

> Eight Thousands (2,068,000) pounds weight of cotton of the description and quality called and known in the usually Liverpool classification as Middling Orleans or the equivalent in value of any other description of cotton at the option of the Government. The cotton to be of the usual merchantable quality and delivered free of any duty or charges at the usual shipping places in the usual bales at any shipping port, if practicable to transport the cotton to the port selected (excepting such ports as may be then in possession of the enemy) in the Confederate States of America such shipping port to be declared by the holder of this warrant on presentation thereof.... This Warrant to be exchanged within Twenty one days for others representing the cotton in parcels of not less than Fifty Bales each Warrant.[20]

The theoretical value of the warrants was linked to the per pound market value of cotton, and offered the speculator the potential for profit if the item could be delivered. Otherwise, it was one of the more audacious gambling schemes in history, for success presupposed the cotton would eventually be shipped, and if the Confederate States ceased to exist, the warrants were worthless.

III. The Freight of War 89

The July 14, 1864, edition of *The Illustrated London News* included a drawing showing the steamer *Lillian* running the blockade into Wilmington (courtesy New Hanover Public Library, NCD Box 1 016).

From the safe ports of Bermuda, Nassau, and Havana, the blockade runners shuttled European cargo to the Southern ports and returned with cotton, tobacco, and other valuable cargo from the South. Running the blockade was a risk; not only the cargo, but vessel could be — and often was — lost. James Sprunt, in his book *Derelicts*, noted that the average blockade runner was constructed of iron and cost approximately $150,000 in gold. Several notable vessels were lost near the Cape Fear River. The *Modern Greece*, a British vessel, weight 1,000 tons, was lost near Fort Fisher on June 27, 1862. Its cargo included guns and 1,000 tons of powder. The *Elizabeth*, carrying a load of steel and saltpeter from Nassau to Wilmington, ran ashore at Lockwood's Folly on September 19, 1863. The *Georgiana McCaw*, a sidewheel steamer carrying 60 tons of provisions from Nassau to Wilmington, was fired upon and beached near Fort Caswell on June 2, 1864. On October 11, 1863, the blockade runner *Douro*, with a cargo belonging to the Confederate States consisting of 550 bales of cotton, 279 boxes of tobacco, 20 tierces of tobacco, and a quantity of naval stores, was run aground while trying to escape from the Union cruiser *Nansemond*. The *Dee*, loaded with a shipment from Bermuda of pig iron, bacon, and military supplies, was found by the U.S.S. *Cambridge* run aground and on fire on February 6, 1864. The steamer *Nutfield*, originating in Bermuda and bound for Wilmington, was loaded with drugs, munitions, Enfield rifles, eight Whitworth guns, and pig lead. After failing to enter New Inlet, it was engaged by the Union cruiser *Sassacus* at New River in early February 1864. Sprunt, however, provides some estimates as to the number of successful blockade running in *Chronicles of the Cape Fear River*. A year before the capture of Fort Fisher, it was estimated that British capitalists had invested $66,000,000 (gold) in ventures connected to the port of Wilmington alone, and $56,000,000 (gold) worth of cotton had been exported in return. A total of 397 steamers had run the blockade during that time. The Confederate steamer *R.E. Lee* alone ran 7,000 bales of cotton worth $2,000,000 (gold).[21] The Confederate cotton works was located near the depot of the Wilmington & Manchester Railroad opposite Wilmington. A fire on this site in April 1864 destroyed the government owned cotton, private cotton, the cotton press, and 18 cars on the railroad.[22]

The network thus included the imported food, military supplies, weapons, and explosive materials for distribution on the railroad, the cotton and other commodities for export delivered to Wilmington by the railroads, the goods of import and export traveling the Wilmington & Weldon and the Wilmington & Manchester from points of accumulation to the south (including Charleston, Savannah, etc.), and military related freight from domestic sources traveling north and south along the lines of both railroads. Though the statistics for the fiscal years embracing the war are not available, nor consistently represented in the stockholders reports of the Wilmington & Weldon Railroad, an examination of the comparative statement for fiscal year 1863 shows that bales of cotton delivered from and received at Wilmington between the beginning of fiscal year 1860 and the end of fiscal year 1863 had decreased: during fiscal year 1860, ending before the elections, 15,365 bales of cotton were delivered to the Wilmington depot for transportation; at the end of September 1861, the figure rose to 19,676 bales, but by September 1862, only 1,513 bales were received at Wilmington; during the year ending September 1863, 4,336 bales were delivered from and received for transportation at Wilmington. At Weldon, the statistics for cotton received for transportation are 15,483 bales in 1860, 19,667 bales in 1861, 10,444 bales in 1862, and 8,333 bales in 1863.[23] The pattern this implies is transition from rather balanced shipments of cotton from south to north and north to south on the line to most of the cotton being shipped south. Stephen Wallace, president of the Wilmington & Weldon, stated the difficulties in disposing of privately held stores of cotton in his report to the stockholders.

There are other needed articles which cannot be procured at home—a limited supply of which, in part, has been obtained by importation. To pay for these we have sent forward small lots of cotton as we could obtain ship room, and it is desirable to enlarge our operations in that line. The difficulty is in making shipments, as owners are less disposed to accommodate, in consequence of the Government claiming the use of a specified tonnage of each vessel, for transportation on its own account. An effort has been made to obtain, the consent of the department in charge, to allow us a small portion of its space for the purpose referred to, and it is believed continued representations will secure that object.[24]

The company had purchased a large quantity of cotton, but much of it was destroyed as the war drew to a close.[25] Cotton, as good as the coin, appears to have been less liquid for private interests due to priority placed upon the exchange abroad of government cotton. Neither was blockade running by privately sponsored steamers always beneficial for the government: valuable space would be devoted to merchandise for public sale rather than for military supplies. Critics of the Confederate bureaucracy charge that some speculators had bribed government officials to allow some private shipments of cotton. Considering that shipments of merchandise appear to make it through the blockade more often than vessels carrying supplies for the military, the belief also exists the speculators were, in addition, bribing the enemy to allow access.[26]

Freight Revenue

Data on monthly freight revenue exists for the fiscal years 1860–61, 1861–62, and 1862–63 in the annual reports. The annual report for the 1863–64 provides the aggregate amount of $1,484,378.68 for the whole fiscal year. The annual report for 1864–65 includes data for October, 1864 through February 1865 — the closing months of the war — as individual months; the data for months March and April 1865 and August and September 1865 are combined; and October 1865 through December 1865 are listed as individual months. There is, understandably, no data for the months April and May, June and July 1865 because the railroad was in the possession of the Union Army.[27]

Since no consistent presentation of data for all fiscal years during the war exists, they can be analyzed in groupings: 1860–61 through 1862–63, with 1863–64, and 1864–65 approached separately. Charting the data for 1860–61 through 1862–63 shows that pronounced spikes in freight revenue do not occur for the three fiscal years from the months of October through

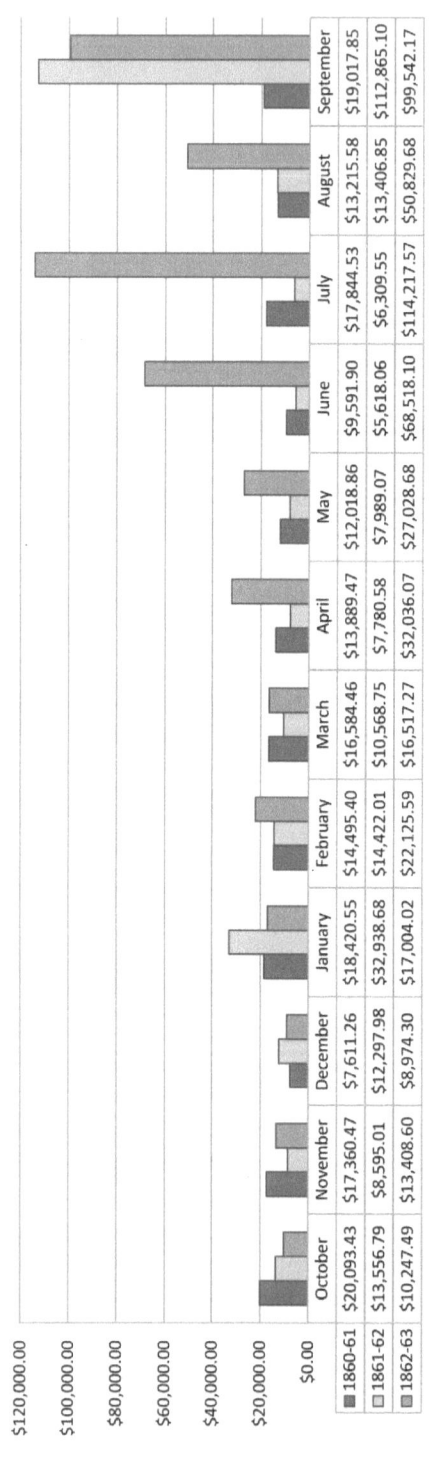

May. The monthly average for all these years, for these months, is $15,665.20, and when compared to the average of $15,493.58 for the pre-secession months of October 1860 through April 1861, the profit is not significant for these months, regardless of the volume of freight. If the average revenue of the months October 1860 through May 1861 is compared with the average revenue for October 1861 through May 1862, and October 1862 through May 1863 combined, the difference between two averages is merely $908.94. For the fiscal year 1860–61, the total freight revenue is $180,143.76, with a monthly average of $15,011.98. In the month of September 1862, freight revenue spikes by $93,847.25, compared with September 1861; but the total revenue for 1861–62 is only $66,204.67 more than the previous year, raising the monthly average for 1861–62 to $20,529.04. However, the median value for 1861–62 was $11,433.37, compared to $15.539.93 for 1860–61. That monthly freight revenue had dropped for most of the year is obvious. Freight revenue for the months of the yellow fever epidemic in Wilmington, August through November 1862, shows the largest revenue spike in September, at $112,865.10, with August, October, and November close to the totals for the same months the previous year. The epidemic does not appear to have had a noticeable impact on freight revenue in September; passenger travel, however, was diminished. Freight revenue for 1862–63 was $480,449.53, an average of $40,037.46 a month for the fiscal year. The spike in revenue began in the period of April to September, an average of $65,362.05 for those months, and the rest of the year is really below average at $14,712.88 for the remaining months.

The total of $1,484,378.68 for fiscal year 1863–64 appears extremely high in comparison with the figures examined thus far, averaging $123,698.22 a month. But upon examining the freight revenue for October 1864 ($127,607.47), November 1864 ($149,037.13), and December 1864 ($115,616.23), it appears that a monthly average of $123,698.22 was not out of the ordinary for the period beginning in September 1863. The problem, however, is that of currency, as S.L. Fremont explains in the 1864 report to the stockholders.

Opposite: Represented in this chart are three fiscal years of freight receipts compiled from the annual reports (1860–61, 1861–62, and 1862–63). The fiscal year ran from October to September. In September 1862, early during the yellow fever epidemic in Wilmington, freight receipts rose, though October and November receipts were modest at the height of the epidemic. From April to September 1863, freight receipts rose substantially, with spikes in both July and September. Union raids occurred in December 1862 and July 1863. The greatest volume of transportation for the Confederate government for 1863 occurred in July and September.

From the foregoing statement we have the net receipts for this year considerably larger than for any previous year of the Company's existence, but when we take into consideration the value of a dollar of currency as compared with the legal standard of value, (and this statement is given in currency,) we are reminded of the very poor exhibit we make? In fact, the net increase thus viewed is the smallest that has been made in several years. For the same reasons the cost of operating has been out of the usual proportion to the receipts — for while the company pays nearly specie value for all materials and supplies consumed — and for services rendered about half specie value — a much lower standard has ruled in the compensation received for transportation, and especially so in all cases of Government transportation. And when we consider that nine-tenths of all the transportation performed during the year, has been for the Government, we are at no loss to account for the unusual discrepancy between the receipts and expenditures. At the beginning of this conflict the Railroads represented in convention at Montgomery pledged themselves to work for the government at *half rates*. This was a generous offer, but one that they could well afford to make in view of the increased amount of business that it would give to all the principal lines. Could this principle have continued to rule in the payments for services rendered the Government, no one would have just cause to complain. But what do we see now, in comparing the present rates of compensation with those for 1861? Let us examine — In April, 1861, the compensation for transporting troops was two cents (2) per mile per man; in April, 1864, the rate was two and a half cents (2½) per man per mile, though in May following the rate was doubled and made five cents (5) per man per mile, which is the present rate. In April, 1861, our best machinists were in receipt of (2.50) two and a half dollars per day; the board of mechanics was about eighteen to twenty dollars per month; Flour six dollars per barrel, meat ten to twelve cents per pound, and a suit of clothes cost not over fifty dollars. In April, 1864, our best machinists are in receipt of twelve (and today it is twenty) dollars per day; their board is from ten to twelve dollars per day, or from $300 to $350 per month; Flour ($350) three hundred and fifty dollars per barrel; meat five to six dollars per pound, and a suit of clothes from one thousand to fifteen hundred dollars. In 1861, oil cost but one dollar per gallon, now it is worth fifty. — Iron but four cents per pound is now worth two to three dollars, nails four cents per pound, are now worth as many dollars. Yet with all this enormous increase in the cost of living the compensation by Government has at best only been doubled. How then, with all this increase in the cost of operating this line of Railroad, can the owners expect to maintain it in working order at the present rates for government service! I think it cannot be done, and it behooves the managers of the work to take immediate steps to apply a remedy.[28]

Fremont continues by suggesting two methods of remedying the problem: the government could be charged half of the private local rate, ten cents a mile, or the government could supply the railroad with materials and provisions.[29] The freight revenue increase should be compared in relation to gross income and gross expenses.

The total receipts for fiscal year 1861–62 was $965,750.35, the cost of operation was $295,693.54, and the interest and dividends amounting to $268,130.78; that left a balance of 398,323.44. The total freight revenue for that year was $246,348.43, (or 39.2 percent of the profits). When the freight revenue, total revenue, total expenses, and the difference between the total revenue and expenses are compared for the period from 1856 to 1864, it becomes apparent that by 1864, freight receipts had become nearly half of the total receipts, and the expenses had exceeded half of the total receipts. In the prewar years, other sources of revenue — passenger fares and mail contracts — were the greater part of the total revenue; expenses at times exceeded half of the total, but the company could be sure, within a play of tolerance, that the value of currency did not invalidate their statistics.

Using the price of a barrel of flour ($350) given by Superintendent Fremont in the 1864 as a measure of value, the total profit for that year ($1,232,302) would have purchased only 3,520.86 barrels of flour; whereas, at the 1861 price per barrel of flour ($6), the profits would purchase 205,383.66 barrels. The price per barrel would have doubled 58.33 times, so the same measure, the profits for 1864 would have been 58.33 times less, say a mere $21,126.38 for the year. This rather crude illustration should not be interpreted as indicative of the general rise in prices for all commodities, nor imply that the depreciation of the currency progressed on a smooth curve. The value of Confederate graybacks in relation to gold was a jagged curve that correlated to military and political events. Marc Weidenmier of Claremont McKenna College, plotted the value of Confederate money price in Richmond in weekly intervals for the years 1861 through 1865 and found depreciation of graybacks rose after the Battle of Antietam, again after the passage of the Finance–Conscription Bill by the United States, and with the battles of Gettysburg and Vicksburg; climbed steeply to plateau in late summer of 1863 before continuing depreciation to the Confederate Congress-instituted currency reform in February 1864. The grayback appreciated until the battle for and capture of Atlanta (July to September 1864), and then it began its sharp descent to values approaching 70 graybacks to one gold dollar.[30]

In light of the unstable nature of Confederate currency, the financial statements included in annual reports from 1863 onward require comparison in relation to the extremely transitory grayback to gold relationship. For the company, the high proportion of government to private trans-

Freight Receipts, Total Receipts, Total Expenses, 1856–1864

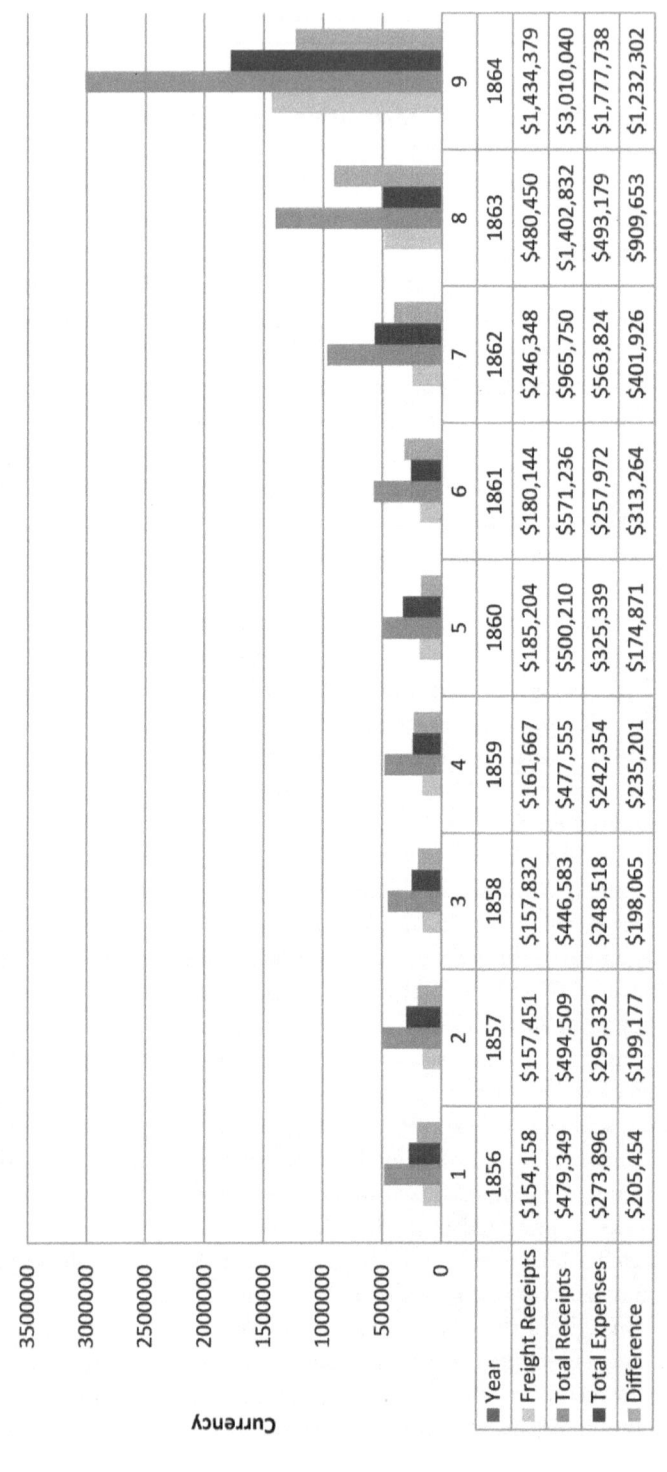

	1	2	3	4	5	6	7	8	9
Year	1856	1857	1858	1859	1860	1861	1862	1863	1864
Freight Receipts	$154,158	$157,451	$157,832	$161,667	$185,204	$180,144	$246,348	$480,450	$1,434,379
Total Receipts	$479,349	$494,509	$446,583	$477,555	$500,210	$571,236	$965,750	$1,402,832	$3,010,040
Total Expenses	$273,896	$295,332	$248,518	$242,354	$325,339	$257,972	$563,824	$493,179	$1,777,738
Difference	$205,454	$199,177	$198,065	$235,201	$174,871	$313,264	$401,926	$909,653	$1,232,302

portation actually represented a reduction of the revenue to expense ratio. The low rates of transporting government freight, and the high volumes of the same, coupled with a depreciating currency, suggests, even with the dangers of war aside, that the company eventually would not have the assets to maintain operations.

This is the essence of Fremont's warning in the 1864 report. In a letter in the Confederate Citizens Files dated March 22, 1862, Stephen Wallace, president of the Wilmington & Weldon Railroad, states that the rates for transporting passengers and freight for the Confederate States are too low in relation to the cost of maintaining the railroad, rolling stock, and other expenses. After conferring with presidents of other railroad companies, he found they held the same position. He proposed a convention to be held at Columbia, South Carolina, on April 13, 1864, to discuss the problem.

> It has also been suggested that statements be prepared, showing the earnings and expenditure for the twelve months preceding the 1st of March — the depreciation of Road and property — amount of Capital Stock that has changed owners since the 1st of January, 1861, with such other information as will enable a committee to prepare such an address to Congress, (if deemed expedient), as will exhibit to that body the true condition of our respective institutions, and place them right before the country.[31]

The convention also opposed the 25 percent surtax on profits exceeding one-quarter of capital investment in railroads, and memorialized Congress recommending a capital levy on the whole wealth of the South.[32]

The unstable currency of the Confederacy added to the difficulties of operating a railroad under conditions for which it had not been designed. Enemy attacks, germs, and twists of fate compounded the task exponentially.

Opposite: A compilation of the freight receipts, total receipts, and total expenditures for the years 1856 through 1864 shows a steady rise, the difference being $313,264 in 1861 to $1,232,302 in 1864. This suggests that the company had been making steady profits throughout the war. While indeed the railroad had seen an increase in business, the deflated value of the Confederate currency relative to gold, particularly when the war effort began to falter and access to foreign markets became constricted, the cost of everything the railroad needed to operate grew at a stupendous rate.

Chapter IV

The Enemy, Seen and Unseen

On Thursday, November 13, 1862, the annual meeting of the stockholders of the Wilmington & Weldon Railroad convened at the company offices, only to adjourn because there was an insufficient number of shares represented. The meeting was rescheduled for the first Thursday in December at a place designated by the president of the company. When the meeting reconvened at the New Hanover County Court House on December 4, 1862 at 11:00 A.M., a majority of shares were represented, but the meeting did not proceed with the usual smooth efficiency. As S.L. Fremont began reading his report, there was a call to have the reports printed into a pamphlet, and so the meeting was adjourned till 2:15 P.M. A committee comprising R.R. Bridgers, T.W. Walker, and E. Kidder was charged with the task of reviewing the reports in the interim. However, when the meeting resumed, the committee was able to render only a verbal report. Proceeding, the company elected S.D. Wallace president of the company, with R.R. Bridgers, B. Flanner, P.K. Dickinson, A.J. DeRosset, E.P. Hall, J.D. Bellamy, and E. Kidder directors representing the stockholders, and G.W. Collier, W.W. Brickle, and W.A. Wright directors representing the interests of the state. During the past year, two directors of the company, Gilbert Potter and William C. Bettencourt had died, and the president of the company, William S. Ashe, had been killed in an accident.[1]

On Friday, September 12, 1862, Ashe was heading in the direction of his home, 19 miles from Wilmington. He hoped to reach the turnout at North East before the southbound mail train passed. At 7:30 P.M., within a quarter of a mile of the turnout, his handcar made contact with the mail train. The others on the handcar escaped, but Mr. Ashe was mutilated and his right leg was crushed. The locomotive, recently purchased from the Seaboard & Roanoke Railroad, being brought to Wilmington behind the mail train, was put in the front after the mail train's locomotive experienced mechanical problems. It did not have a light; nor did Mr. Ashe's handcar have a light.[2]

It is indeed ironic that a double breach of the regulations would bring about the death of the person ultimately possessing the greatest responsibility for insuring safety on the line. The conductor should have placed a red light on the substitute locomotive before dark; and with all the resources available to Mr. Ashe, it seems strange that he would not bother to bring a lantern, knowing perhaps from the time he set out that the mail train was coming his way and that it would be dark before he made it safely to the turnout. It is equally puzzling, even to present-day urbanites accustomed to the perpetual din of automobile traffic, that something as loud as a steam locomotive, particularly in the quiet of a then rural landscape, did not arouse Mr. Ashe to action until it was too late.[3]

The secretary and treasurer of the company, James S. Green, also died that year.[4]

Green had been with the company in the position of secretary and treasurer since 1836, and to many, he was the public face of the company. Known for giving welcoming speeches to visitors to Wilmington at the depot, and presenting ladies with bouquets of flowers, Mr. Green represented the staff and directors of the company during the Wilmington & Raleigh Rail Road era. James Sprunt, who knew Green in his youth, described him as affable and kindly by nature. Sadly, he succumbed to yellow fever in September, his death following on the heels of the grisly demise of Mr. Ashe. William Bettencourt had also died of yellow fever. The directors of the company originally approached another of the old guard, in fact, the most enthusiastic of the early supporters of building the railroad, P.K. Dickinson, to replace Ashe as president. Mr. Dickinson declined the offer, so the position was offered to Stephen D. Wallace, who had originally been selected to replace Gilbert Potter.[5]

Yellow Fever

Nickolas Schenck provided in his diary a short, broken paragraph concerning the origin of the 1862 yellow fever epidemic in Wilmington.

> Yellow fever — was brought to Wilmington NC by Blockade Runner steamer Kate — who landed 2 sick seamen — below Kidders Mill — they died and the Negroes — who nursed those sailors died — this was in early July —1862 — There was no word of yellow fever — no knowledge or apprehension — though later it was known to exist and a week ( ) several mysterious cases of Death — yet no fear or thought of this dread disease — until Heyer — brother of Jonathan C. Heyer — died suddenly in late August or September — when Doctors Dickson and Thomas — medical record and the faculty — pronounced that Heyer had — black

vomit — the dread news — soon spread — quarantine put on — and soon — a panic to get away — citizens and family — going in all directions — Fayetteville — (Sumter) — the sound — Smithville — Clinton and every point — general sanitary measures commenced — a general cleanup — use of disinfectant — burning of tar barrels in the street — spreading lime — Everybody — who could get away — left town.[6]

The report of Dr. William T. Wragg, published in the *Confederate States Journal* in February 1864, mentions both the prevailing weather during that summer and a particular location in Wilmington: the months of July, August, and September had been a period of heavy rains. A particular pond on the Rouse Lot located near Roberts' Foundry (Clarendon Iron Works) was the object of his attention. Referencing the Schenck maps, the slime covered pond that Wragg describes is the Dudley Mill Pond, located downhill from Constable Rouse's house, occupying and overreaching the southern portion of the block bounded by Front, Second, Queen and Castle streets. The area on the hill appears to be the same location where William Alexander Graham addressed a crowd of Constitutional Union Party supporters in 1860. The Clarendon Iron Works, owned by Thomas E. Roberts, was located near the river at the intersection of Queen and Surry streets. Schenck noted that the disease did not cause any concern until the brother of Jonathan C. Heyer died. J.C. Heyer was a grocer whose store was located at 38 and 39 North Water Street. Dr. Thomas F. Wood of Wilmington would recount that a wood and coal dealer named Swartzman, who had his business on the wharf near the place where the blockade runner *Kate* was moored, was the first victim of the fever. Colonel Alfred M. Waddell, while traveling from Richmond to Augusta visited the sick Mr. Swartzman not long before his death and verified the he was the first death, "or at least it was the first recognized case."[7]

An article in the *New York Medical Journal* entitled "A Review of the 'Report on the Epidemic of Yellow Fever which prevailed at Wilmington, N.C., in the Fall of 1862. By William T. Wragg, M.D., of Charleston, S.C.,'" written by William George Thomas, M.D., of Wilmington, North Carolina, disputes the assertion that there were cases of yellow fever in the town before the arrival of the *Kate*. This report includes an exquisite map showing the location of specific cases and ponds around the town. While published in 1869, before the cause of yellow fever was connected to contact with mosquitos, Dr. Thomas identifies flaws in the diagnosis of yellow fever by Dr. Schonwald upon which Dr. Wragg bases some of his conclusions about cases appearing in June and July. (Schonwald was a homeopathic physician and druggist.) The statement that yellow fever first appeared in a "filthy alley" in June came from Schonwald's misdiagnosis of Private Fredrick Kling, who suffered chills and fever before his discharge on April 15 and return to service on September 10 in good health. Dr. Thomas continues his critique, eventually undermining the reports of early cases. After extensive investigation, Thomas found that the cases involved symptoms that had been of a longer term than those exhibited by yellow fever, or were inconsistent with them. Another problem with Dr. Wragg's report of was with the spelling of victims' names. Thomas provides the correct spellings and the locations of their dwellings.[8]

The problem with the early reports of yellow fever in Wilmington prior to the arrival of the *Kate* are twofold: while Dr. Schonwald might not have been a quack, his colleagues did not respect his methods or opinions (and he might have diagnosed the bilious symptoms associated with typhoid or malaria as yellow fever); since yellow fever had to be introduced into Wilmington from an outside source, it is unacceptable historical practice to claim a source other than the *Kate*, where the disease was known to exist with certainty, without identifying the possible source. Of the former, upon examining the reports of the railroad hospital for 1860 and 1861, one finds that Dr. James McRee treated 50 cases of bilious fever each year, and then Dr. William H. Hall treated 50 cases of bilious remittent fever the next year. These ailments top the list for both years.[9] The term archaic term bilious means bile in the vomit or stool, and can be associated with malaria and typhoid. It is also used in connection with a lung inflammation called "bilious" pneumonia in some typhoid cases. The death of Georgia Weeks, listed as hemorrhage of the lungs, supposedly having died on August 5 and been buried on August 23, is too poorly documented and incredible to base an alternative history of the epidemic upon. The location of her death could be merely circumstantial.[10]

The problem for the historian is much the same as that of Dr. Wragg: there is a difference between a documented idea and a documented fact. What Dr. Schonwald might have thought was yellow fever in retrospect — perhaps because yellow fever was the hot topic of the moment — ignores consideration of other diseases prevalent before the epidemic and that the existing sanitary condition in 1862 could only promote disease. Additionally, unlike Dr. Thomas, the historian does not always have the means to judge immediately the credibility of reported events, unlike opinions and ideas. Schenck, in his recollection of the epidemic, provides a general location, but having been away in the army when it started, he could base it only upon secondhand information at best. Thomas, unaware in his day that mosquitos were the vector for transmission of yellow fever, provides the necessary elements to reconstruct the scenario: a known infected person, a source of mosquitos, and someone else.

It has been shown that the several cases, which were supposed to have occurred before the arrival of the vessel, are not sustained by facts and circumstances; and more still, that all of them who did have yellow fever were attached subsequent to that date.[11]

On September 17, Lieutenant Commander George A. Stevens of the U.S.S. *Victoria* stationed off Wilmington, reported the escape of the *Kate* through New Inlet. He was aware of 15 deaths in Wilmington at that point, and he was also able to report that two ironclads were under construction there, one having an engine pulled from a tug called *Uncle Ben*. His information was obtained from five slaves that managed to escape from Smithville by boat. A report from the U.S. gunboat *Penobscot* on the 23rd confirmed the existence of the ironclads under construction, one in the shipyard of J.L. Cassidy & Sons, the other in Beery & Brothers shipyard. These were on the model of the *Merrimack*, and the iron for them was being manufactured in Richmond. Had not the yellow fever epidemic brought work to a stop, they would have been finished in mid–October. The only vessel reported to have run in or out of the port since the *Modern Greece* was the *Kate*. The tug *Mariner*, loaded with 100 bales of cotton and 100 barrels of rosin, was preparing to run the blockade to Nassau in late–September. Most of the soldiers in Wilmington had been moved to Fort Caswell and Fort Fisher because of yellow fever. They were being provisioned from the countryside.[12] (The steamer *Modern Greece* had run aground near Fort Fisher above New Inlet on June 27, 1862, while under fire by Union ships.[13]) On October 11, the U.S. consul at Nassau reported to acting Rear-Admiral Wilkes that the tug *Mariner* had arrived in port, transmitting the news that the *Kate* had escaped the blockade for the fortieth time. One steamer bound for the South, the *Anglia*, had to turn back due to the yellow fever spreading through her crew.[14] The long period between the wreck of the *Modern Greece* and subsequent non-arrival at Wilmington and the arrival of the *Kate* in port on August 6 does not strengthen the hypothesis that yellow fever arrived on another ship.

The testimony of George C. McDugal, chief engineer of the *Kate*, confirms that a crew member named Florence O'Donohoe had passed out drunk on the wharf at Nassau before the ship had left. He was chastised for doing so because of the yellow fever existing at that port. Two days after they setting sail, he complained of illness, and on docking in Wilmington, he ran away from the ship in a delirium. After being found in the woods near the Marine Hospital, located at Eighth and Nun streets, he eventually came under the care of a Dr. Custis, according to Dr. Thomas B. Carr, acting assistant surgeon of the hospital. After he jumped from an upper floor window, he was moved to the basement; and the next day began to vomit up what appeared to be coffee grounds. His body had turned yellow. He died the same day and was buried the following, with Dr. Custis recording his cause of death as delirium tremens. Two soldiers in the same ward as O'Donohoe named Gregory and Muse died suddenly two days later after their bodies turned yellow. After two more deaths, Dr. Custis recognized the cause as yellow fever, being the same as the cases observed downtown. By that time Dr. Thomas and Dr. James H. Dickson had reported the deaths of William Hyer (Wilhelm A. Heyer) and a Mrs. Orrel (Ester "Hester" E. Orrell) as being from yellow fever.[15]

Similar to the case of O'Donohoe, in late October, a sailor named Tobin, confined at the Seaman's Home Hospital at Front and Dock street, died in a delirium-induced jump from a third story window.[16] Another crew member from the *Kate* named Dennis Mitchell fell ill three days after

The white arrow denotes the general location of the Cassidy shipyard situated on South Water Street in Wilmington. The shipyard had a marine railway at the base of Church Street. This photograph was taken from Dram Tree Park at the base of Castle Street near the location of the establishment known as the Hole in the Wall (Mrs. McLin's house) where Georgia Weeks died. Her death, however, predates the arrival of the *Kate*, and Dr. Thomas disputed the diagnosis of yellow fever in this case (photograph by Dr. Cyn Johnson).

arriving in Wilmington. He was sent to lodge with Edward Laugherty, on Castle Street, two doors from Front Street. The *Kate* was moved to Cassidy's Shipyard on Water Street, between Nun and Church streets. Mitchell died on August 17, and Laugherty and his family contracted the disease, but survived. Their next door neighbor, Robert Campbell, contracted the disease, died, and was buried on September 8. Mrs. Thomas Clark, a neighbor of Laugherty who had nursed Dennis Mitchell, was buried on the same day. Mrs. Thomas J. Capps and J.W. Capps, residents of Castle Street, died the next month. Other deaths occurred in the surrounding blocks. Dr. Thomas corrected Dr. Wragg's report in identifying Laugherty's home, rather than Campbell's home, as the location of Mitchell's death and subsequent wake. With his body laid out for viewing, neighbors were invited in to visit. A town guard and butcher named Harry Smith (not Robert Smith, as reported by Dr. Schonwald) died on August 12, and was also given a wake. Sailors were seen at his home beginning on the night the *Kate* arrived, and thereafter, because he appeared to have been running a smuggling operation. His house, located on Third Street between

This postwar illustration identifies the location as the Rebel Navy Yard at Wilmington. There were two shipyards at Wilmington, J.L. Cassidy & Sons on South Water Street (where the CSS *Raleigh* was built) and Beery's Shipyard on Eagles Island (where the CSS *North Carolina* was built) (courtesy New Hanover Public Library, NCD Box 1 010).

IV. The Enemy, Seen and Unseen   105

Queen and Wooster, was one block removed from the Rouse Pond.[17] The death of Georgia Weeks appears to be a second-order variation of spatial autocorrelation. That is, the close proximity of the *Kate* and the prevalence of yellow fever deaths in the neighborhood might lead the researcher to include her death with the other victims, if not list her first. However, her death does not fall within the time frame of the contributing factors of the epidemic.

Of the citizens of Wilmington known to have contracted yellow fever, the first recognized case, as previously mentioned, was Louis Swartzman

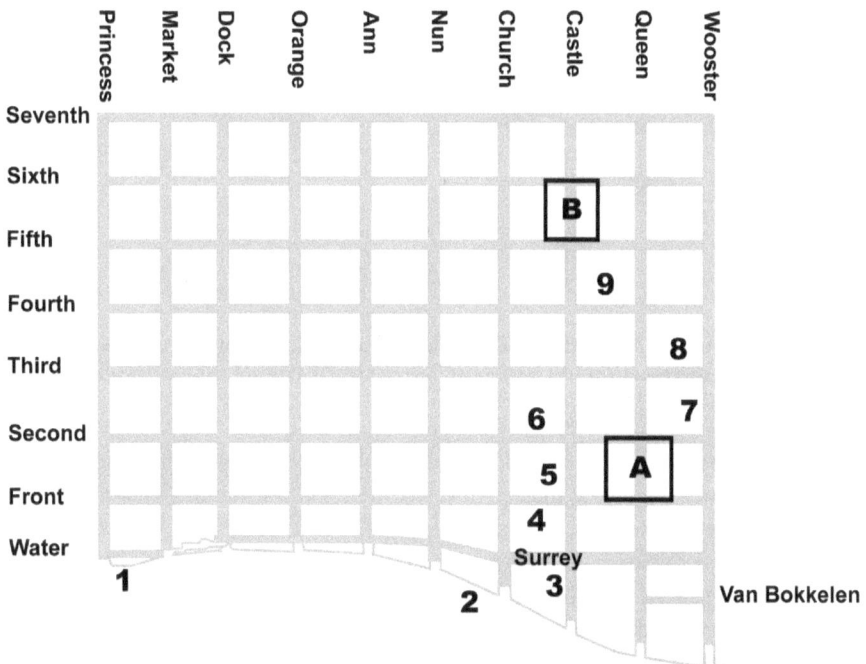

The author produced this map by overlaying information contained in Dr. Thomas's map concerning the south of Wilmington on the corresponding section of Turner's 1856 Plan of Wilmington, North Carolina: the numbers indicate (1) the wharf where the *Kate* was docked after arrival, (2) Cassidy's Shipyard, where the *Kate* was docked for repairs on the third day after her arrival, (3) the "Hole in the Wall" where Georgia Weeks died before the arrival of the *Kate* (not likely of yellow fever), (4) the Wilkins Morris house, (5) the Laugherty house where Dennis Mitchel died (6) Mrs. Peterson's house, (7) Lamon house, (8) where Harry Smith died, and (9) where Mrs. Johnson died. Letters denote the (A) Rouse Pond and (B) Dry Pond with the boxes for each approximating their extent (map by the author).

In Dr. Thomas' map, Mrs. McLin's house was located on the northeast side below the intersection of Castle and Surry streets (right) (photograph by Dr. Cyn Johnson).

(Lewis Swarzman), a coal and wood dealer and grocer whose business, Loeb & Swarzman, was located at the corner of Chestnut and Water streets. He boarded at Rockspring, run by Mrs. M.S. McCaleb on Chestnut, near his place of business. Dr. Thomas gave his place of death as being on the north side of Market Street between Second and Third streets. Though his partner, Jacob Loeb, claimed he did not board the *Kate*, Swarzman's friends and acquaintances reported he did so frequently. Mr. Heyer, according to his brothers, was on the ship constantly.[18] The report provide by Dr. Thomas, along with his map, identifies instances where yellow fever was transmitted to citizens of the town when they came in contact with the crew of the *Kate* on the vessel, and when crewmembers were in their homes. Dudley Mill Pond was a hotspot, and perhaps the presence of the mosquito breeding ground, and the wakes contributed to the spread of the disease.

The behavior of the citizens of Wilmington upon the entry into the port of a blockade runner was reported by a former Confederate officer in *Harper's New Monthly Magazine* after the war. His narrative describes the reception of a ship in the last year of the war, but the agents and officials would have been a constant, and the speculators would have made their appearance — the likes of Harry Smith not excluded.

> When a steamer came in, men, women, children rushed down to the wharves to see it, to buy, beg, or steal something. Everybody wanted to know if their "ventures"— the proceeds of the bales of cotton or boxes of tobacco sent out — had come in.... The first people aboard of course were agents — on such occasions very big men. Then swarmed officials and officers, "friends" and "bummers," hunting after drinks and dinners, and willing to accept any compliment, from a box of cigars or a bottle of brandy down to a bunch of bananas or a pocketful of oranges.[19]

Captain John Wilkinson of the Confederate States Navy confirmed the presence of speculators from all over the South in Wilmington bidding on the cargos from the blockade runners. However, he goes further by noting how the town had changed from its staid character before the war, to a place inhabited by all sorts of rogues and criminals, in addition to the soldiers posted in the town. The town officials were unable to prevent violence. The agents of the ships lived in high style and cornered the supplies going into the county market, while many Wilmingtonians retreated to the country, renting out their houses.[20]

It was no longer the town described by John MacLaurin or the 1860 Census. Dr. Thomas reported that the departure of permanent residents from the town did contribute to a decline in sanitary conditions, but it was not significantly different from the years before the epidemic or after the war up to 1868. At the time of the epidemic, however, garbage accumulated for want of a labor force to collect it.[21] While none of these factors can be associated with the cause of the yellow fever epidemic, the same can certainly not be said of typhoid fever or other diseases; nor do the social conditions present a favorable medium for official response: doctors, hospitals, civil authorities, or cemetery personnel.

Up to September 19, eight cases and six deaths attributed to yellow fever had been reported. On the week ending September 26, 26 cases had been reported with nine deaths. On September 29, S.L. Fremont announced that there would be only one train operating to and from Wilmington daily. The number of reported cases climbed to 267 with 82 deaths on October 3; then by October 10, the number of cases reached a new height of 395, with 40 deaths.[22] James Fulton, the editor of the *Wilmington Journal*, began printing a single page edition, having a sick printing staff and a shortage of paper.[23] The week ending October 17 was the peak for reported cases, being 431, with deaths reaching their peak of 111 the following week. Mr. Quigley of Oakdale Cemetery died during that week. Dr. Wragg arrived from Charleston, as well as a team of nurses under the command of a Captain Westerlund to help in the Seaman's Home Hospital. A public soup kitchen was set up on the southeast corner of Front and Dock near the hospital the next week. Food in the town had grown scarce since late September. On October 29, Mayor Dawson gave notice in the paper that he considered only one-twentieth of the people in town necessary, and recommended those who were not needed to leave town.[24] By November, many of the town's most prominent citizens, ministers, and Dr. James H. Dickson, the same gentleman who delivered the eloquent speeches on preserving the Union in early 1861, had died of yellow fever. Most of the population of Wilmington had fled, leaving about 3,000 individuals; more than half had contracted the disease.[25]

From a gentlemen who had left Richmond on passes provided by the Confederate authorities, the *Philadelphia Inquirer* published an article based on his statements on conditions in Wilmington and the South on November 18, 1862.

> Wilmington, N.C., is only a place in name. There is no trade, and when he was there not more than twenty soldiers were in the place. The town has the appearance of being perfectly dead to all activity or industry. Since his visit the yellow fever has made it still more desolate than before. Physicians were sent there from Richmond, and provisions were also forwarded. At Weldon the stores were all closed, and it was difficult to get a morsel of anything decent to eat or drink in the place. At Weldon, there was only a cavalry regiment stationed, under Gen. ROBERTSON, and two infantry regiments were posted near Franklin, at the Blackwater bridge. This comprised all the force assigned to protect the great Central Railroad running from Richmond via Petersburgh and Weldon to Wilmington, N.C., against the threatening forces of Gen. PECK, at Suffolk, and Gen. VIMLE, at Norfolk.[26]

S.L. Fremont, in a communication to the *Wilmington Journal* published on November 21, stated that the Wilmington & Weldon was ready to resume its regular schedule. The editor (Fulton) questioned why the telegraph office remained closed, now that the epidemic had subsided. He wondered if the operators would stay away until it was cold enough that "tophet" (Hell) froze over.[27] As mentioned earlier, the yellow fever epidemic had cause work to be curtailed on the ironclads in the Wilmington shipyard. All work on the defenses at Wilmington had stopped. Down river, it had also set back work on the torpedo defenses for the lack of proper labor.[28] The Union Army was fully aware of the conditions in Wilmington early in the epidemic. In a communication dated October 3, from his headquarters in the captured town of New Bern, Major General J.G. Foster wrote Major General H.W. Halleck in Washington that the yellow fever outbreak in Wilmington had a good chance of becoming an epidemic. The telegraph office was closed and all work on the ironclads was suspended. Foster received word in early December from William A. Parker, commander of U.S.S. *Cambridge*, that the epidemic had ended.[29]

The yellow fever outbreak in Wilmington occurred near the end of the fiscal year, so a detailed overview of its impact upon the operation of the Wilmington & Weldon requires examining the 1862 and 1863 annual reports. In the 1862 report (December 4), newly elected company president Stephen D. Wallace reported that due to the reduction of the schedule to one daily train, the transportation of mails did not follow the two train dispatch as was normal. He hoped that the schedule would be resumed as soon as the mechanics, which had been driven from town by the epidemic, returned. The receipts from the months of October and November were dismal, due to the general suspension of business in the town. The establishment of shops in Magnolia was underway, and Wallace anticipated they would be ready soon. S.L. Fremont's report calls attention to the increase cost of maintaining the line as compared to 1861: the cost of provisions, clothing, oil, grease, iron, labor, and other necessities had increased substantially. While the company had provided transportation beyond usual volume for the Confederate government and individuals, it had done so with its own equipment almost entirely. Exceptions were locomotives rented for three months from the Atlantic & North Carolina Railroad and one rented for one month from the Seaboard & Roanoke Road (surely the one involved in the accident that killed William Ashe). Fremont deemed it necessary that the company acquire two locomotives, 25 boxcars and 20 flatcars to fulfill the increased demand. The government had not supplied the company with any captured equipment. The locomotives of the company included ten passenger engines, seven freight engines, six old engines laid up, 15 first class passenger cars, six second class passenger cars, six mail and baggage cars, 100 boxcars and 25 flat cars. The repair shops were well equipped and were expected to be up to full capacity. While the bridges were in good order, he anticipated the possibility that they might be attacked, so he had ordered the lumber and other materials necessary to construct 400 feet of bridge, should the need arise. The report of Dr. William J. Love on the company hospital, covering the period from November 18, 1861, to October 1, 1862, does not contain any instances of yellow fever. Interesting are the diseases it does mention: of the cases treated, some patients had bilious fever, catarrhal fever, dysentery, diarrhea, cholera morbus, inflammation of the liver, painter's colic (from lead), pulmonary consumption, pneumonia, mumps, measles, gonorrhea, syphilis, and other diseases, not to mention a number of injuries. The company hospital treated 291 cases that fiscal year.[30] The report of the hospital physician was not included the 1862 annual report.

When the stockholders met next on November 18, 1863, the full impact of the yellow fever epidemic could be appreciated. The near standstill of operations at the beginning of the fiscal year meant "that the income, though stated, *was* for the whole fiscal year (terminating September 30, 1863), yet it was in reality but for little more than *ten* months." What little income there was during the epidemic was attributed for the most part to local business along the line. In October 1862, there were 94 northbound and 86 southbound through passengers and 1,812 way passengers. There were 235 northbound and 111 southbound through passengers and 7,239 way passengers the next month. Through passenger travel was at its lowest during the epidemic months, way travel was at its lowest in October, and November way travel was slightly more than December. By contrast, a comparison of agricultural products received at Wilmington and Weldon during the epidemic months show 25,100 lbs. of bacon, 4,536 bushels of corn, 295 bales of cotton, 306 barrels of flour, 1,422 bushels of wheat, and 619 bags of salt received at Wilmington in the month of October. At Weldon, 17,045 lbs. of bacon, 17,381 bushels of corn, 2,684 bales of cotton, and 66 bushels of wheat were received in the same month. In November, 10,497 lbs. of bacon, 8,158 bushels of corn, 41 bales of cotton, 850 barrels of flour, 2,254 bushels of wheat, and 2,587 bags of salt were delivered to Wilmington; and at Weldon, 4,454 lbs. of bacon, 6,083 bushels of corn, and 1,652 bales of cotton were delivered. These volumes are not the lowest or highest for the fiscal year.[31]

During the epidemic, Nicholas Schenck, while removing his family to Clinton, found that the hotels at Warsaw would not admit anyone coming from Wilmington. He was able to secure a carriage through friends to take them to Clinton. After ten days, he returned to Wilmington in a train that contained only S.D. Wallace and Sam Potter. Potter stopped short of entering the town when the train came to Smith Creek, and went to the home of G.J. Hill to get a canoe to proceed to his home on the Northwest Cape Fear. Schenck found a nearly deserted town when he arrived, not seeing a soul until he encountered a small group of men at the head of Market Street. The epidemic began to subside, according to Schenck, when there was a heavy frost on November 8, 1862. The total number of cases reported up to November 17, according to the *Wilmington Journal*, was 1,507, with 446 deaths.[32]

Foster's Raid

In a January 7, 1862, communication between Union generals McClellan and Burnside, a plan for destroying the Wilmington & Weldon Railroad at Goldsboro — and if situations proved favorable, advance to Raleigh — was outlined. It would begin with Burnside assuming command of the garrison at Hatteras Inlet, and then mounting an attack on Roanoke Island. Once the island was secured, defenses would be constructed so that it could be held with a small force. The next objective would be to seize New Bern and to gain control of the Atlantic & North Carolina Railroad up to Goldsboro. If an advance to Raleigh was advisable, then a large section of the Wilmington & Weldon, both north and south of Goldsboro, should be destroyed. Before moving into the interior to capture Raleigh, the force would march on Wilmington, the capture of which might require additional troops.[33]

New Bern fell to Union forces on March 14, not long after Burnside captured Roanoke Island in early February. The remainder of the plan was not carried through, however. Commencing on December 11, 1862, Union forces under the command of Major General John G. Foster launched a successful attack on Kinston, White Hall (Seven Springs), and the Wilmington & Weldon Railroad.

After leaving New Bern, Foster's troops advanced along the Kinston road for 14 miles, then encountered a half-mile length of the road blocked by downed trees. Making camp there, pioneers cleared the road during the night. At daylight the next morning, the troops resumed their march. The force was about 10,000 infantry, including General Wessells' brigade from General Peck's division, Colonel's Amory's brigade, Colonel Stevenson's brigade, and Colonel Lee's brigade. To this were added the 640 men of the Third New York Cavalry and 40 pieces of artillery. The cavalry had a brief skirmish four miles up the road from the place of the previous night's bivouac but routed the enemy. At a location called Vine Swamp (near the Lenoir-Jones county line, about eight miles south of Kinston), Foster ordered a detachment of three companies of cavalry up the road as a diversion, while the main column proceeded on Vine Swamp Road, thus avoiding defenses on the main road. The cavalry on the main road, under the command of Captain Hall, met the Confederates but defeated them after intense fighting. The main column was delayed by the destruction of the bridge over Beaver Creek, which had to be rebuilt. By stopping for the night, the main column advanced only four miles. By the afternoon of December 13, the main column had reached Southwest Creek, five miles south of Kinston. The Confederates had destroyed the bridge and dug in on the opposite bank, 400 men with three artillery pieces. Because the creek ran through a deep ravine, Foster ordered the Eighty-fifth Pennsylvania, part of Wessells' brigade, to make a crossing of the creek a half-mile below the bridge, and the Twenty-third Massachusetts, of Armory's division, to support the Ninth New Jersey crossing at the mill. The remainder from Wessells' brigade also crossed. The Confederates were overtaken. Continuing to advance on Kinston, Foster sent a company of cavalry on the second road into the town. There they encountered Confederate troops preparing to destroy the bridge. The cavalry charged, forcing the Confederates to withdraw, but not without destroying the bridge. The cavalry made a reconnaissance of the road leading to White Hall for about ten miles, and finding it undefended, they returned to the main column.[34]

On December 13, General Gustavus W. Smith, Department of North

The present-day Whitehall Bridge over the Neuse River at Seven Springs occupies the same site as its Civil War era predecessor. On December 15–16, 1862, Union troops under the command of Brigadier General John G. Foster, en route for a raid on the Wilmington & Weldon Railroad, bombarded Confederate positions on the other side of the Neuse. The Confederates set fire to the bridge in anticipation of the arrival of the Federals to protect the ironclad *Neuse*, then under construction (photograph by Dr. Cyn Johnson).

Carolina and Southern Virginia for the Confederate States Army, sent a dispatch to James A. Seddon, secretary of war for the Confederate States, apprising him of the situation at Kinston. General Nathan G. Evans, commanding the defenses there, had called for reinforcements. A regiment from Petersburg had left at 8:00 P.M. that day, and another was scheduled to depart at 6:00 A.M. as well as a regiment from Blackwater. Smith would leave on the afternoon of December 14, arriving at Goldsboro the next day at 3:00 P.M., and there meet Governor Zebulon B. Vance of North Carolina. Communications with General Evans had been lost, and the reports of scouts estimated that Union forces stood at 30,000, with more arriving from New Bern. Evans' last reported position was at Falling Creek, six miles west of Kinston (on the north side of the Neuse, nearly halfway to LaGrange following US 70 on modern maps). Before reaching Goldsboro, Smith had sent communications to Secretary Seddon: he had ordered three regiments from Daniel's brigade, three Mississippi regiments, and two batteries from Richmond in addition to the regiments from Petersburg and Blackwater. The batteries were to be installed at Goldsboro. General Beauregard was also sending 5,000 troops and three batteries. Smith requested that Quartermaster General Myers expedite their transportation. The Mississippi regiment was sent by rail the full distance that day and Daniel's brigade was on the march to Petersburg with the batteries to be sent by train south. A small guard was set up at Weldon, and at the battery at the obstructions at Hamilton on the Roanoke River. Evans requested cavalry support from Smith, but he had no troops to send. Around midnight on December 15, Smith received word that Union forces were passing on the south side of the Neuse River, heading towards Dudley Depot. Telegraph communication with Wilmington was lost.[35]

On Sunday, December 14, Foster had advanced within one mile of Kinston, where the Confederates had assumed a defensive position in the woods with the river on their left and swampland on their right. Foster ordered the Fifth Rhode Island, the Tenth Connecticut and the Forty-fourth Massachusetts to attack left and right with artillery support, with the intent that the latter would turn that flank. The Tenth Connecticut relieved the troops of Wessells' brigade, who had run low on ammunition. With the Ninety-sixth Regiment New York Volunteers, after 20 minutes under heavy fire, they charged, forcing the Confederate force across the bridge on the Neuse to retreat; and in their retreat, they fired the bridge. Foster's troops managed to put out the fire, and the Ninth New Jersey, the Seventeenth Massachusetts, and the troops of Wessells' brigade crossed and pushed into the town. Evans withdrew to a position two miles beyond the town. Foster sent a message to Evans under a flag of truce asking for his surrender, but he refused. Due to an inability to place his artillery before nightfall, Foster postponed pursuing an attack. He managed, however, to destroy an abandoned gun emplacement on the Neuse, capturing several field pieces in the process. At that point, he considered the objectives of his raid on Kinston accomplished. On December 15, Foster crossed back over the Neuse, and followed the river road to Goldsboro. He left a detachment of cavalry in the town to make a diversionary advance towards Goldsboro on that side of the river. Colonel Ledlie of the Third New York Artillery destroyed the commissary and quartermaster's stores in Kinston, and the bridge. Within nine miles of Goldsboro, three artillery rounds were fired in the direction of the nearby town; thereupon Union artillery returned fire. Sending a cavalry reconnaissance to White Hall, Foster found that it was defended by one regiment and four guns. They had retreated across the Neuse and fired the bridge.[36]

During December 16, General Smith continued to send communications to Secretary Seddon from Goldsboro reflecting anxiety over transportation delays and threatening communiques from the field of battle. The troops from Richmond had not arrived. Of Beauregard's troops, expected to have arrived in Wilmington earlier, he received no word. Smith needed cavalry reinforcements. He could hear an artillery bombardment from the direction of White Hall 15 miles away, and from General Whiting in Wilmington, he received intelligence about a possible landing of Union troops at Beaufort. Compounding Smith's concerns, his staff had yet to arrive. White Hall had been attacked in the morning. Later he learned that at 2:00 P.M. a cavalry force of about 500 men had attacked at Mount Olive, burning a turpentine still, destroying track, and cutting the telegraph.[37]

Foster had sent five companies of cavalry to Mount Olive on December 16 under the command of Major Garrard. In passing White Hall, they were fired upon, to which Garrard responded with artillery from the opposite side of the river until the main column arrived. Continuing to Mount Olive, he encountered no resistance. He was able to destroy about a mile of track and proceed to the trestle at Goshen Swamp, where he set fire to it in four places. At White Hall, the main column continued to bombard the Confederate entrenchments for an hour before their guns fell silent. The main column continued to Goldsboro, leaving sharpshooters in the rear to prolong the exchange. Eight miles short of Goldsboro, the main column bivouacked. On December 17, Foster sent two companies of cavalry as a diversion to Dudley Depot and Everettsville, where they burned two trestles, destroyed a train with four cars, the depot, and a water station before returning to the main column. On returning, Foster sent Garrard

General Foster sent a detachment of two regiments of cavalry as a diversion to Dudley Depot and Everettsville on December 17, 1862, where they burned two trestles, destroyed a train with four cars, the depot, and a water station before returning to the main column. The site of Dudley Depot, shown in this photograph, is located near the intersection of Old Mount Olive and Sleepy Creek roads. It is also the site where conductor Mr. William H. Laspeyre and a baggage master named Comann were killed in an 1860 rear end collision (photograph by Dr. Cyn Johnson).

on another diversion to Thompson's Bridge on the Neuse. At this point, the Confederates had a regiment and four artillery pieces in place, the bridge having already been set on fire. Foster sent the Forty-third Massachusetts and Angel's battery of the Third New York Artillery, further supporting the diversion, as he advanced to Goldsboro. At the railroad bridge over the Neuse at Goldsboro, Foster ordered his artillery to fire in the direction of the bridge. The Confederates returned fire from the opposite bank of the river and from an armored rail car situated on the bridge. Under heavy fire, Lieutenant Graham of the Twenty-third New York Battery succeeded in setting fire to the bridge, where others had failed. Foster's artillery continued firing to prevent any attempt at putting out the fire. Ordering a countermarch back to New Bern, he left a rear guard of infantry and artillery to counter an attack. This they did by firing spherical case

On December 17, 1862, Union forces under General Foster's command, including those of the 17th Massachusetts and the 9th New Jersey, supported by artillery batteries of Lee, Morrison, and Riggs, attacked the railroad bridge of the Wilmington & Weldon on the Neuse River near Goldsboro. The 51st and 52nd North Carolina on the south side of the bridge were supported by the artillery of Company B, 3rd North Carolina, Buntings' battery, Pool's battery, and Starr's battery on the north side of the bridge. These earthworks defended the approach to the bridge from the south (photograph by Dr. Cyn Johnson).

into the advance, inflicting heavy casualities and ultimately causing the Confederates to retreat. The rear guard withdrew and rejoined the main column. Foster reported 90 killed, 478 wounded, and 9 missing. On December 18, General Smith reported to Secretary Seddon that only a portion of the troops from Richmond had arrived, but none of the artillery and cavalry from Richmond and Petersburg were present. The Union forces, now estimated to be about 15,000, had withdrawn by night. The countryside was devastated, and the railroad was no longer fit for transporting ammunition.[38]

Foster's raid was not the full-scale invasion that might be imagined in reading the correspondence between McClellan and Burnside. If it had been, it is clear that the slow response in bringing reinforcements to the

IV. The Enemy, Seen and Unseen

The present-day railroad bridge over the Neuse River near Goldsboro stands on the site of the wooden bridge destroyed during Foster's raid. One man, Lieutenant Graham of the 23rd New York Battery, set fire to the bridge as the battle raged around him. Later, Col. S.L. Fremont, superintendent of the Wilmington & Weldon, would point to this fact when referencing the defense of the line (photograph by Dr. Cyn Johnson).

field on the Confederate side might have proven decisive, thus cutting transportation on the Wilmington & Weldon Railroad and the North Carolina Railroad at Goldsboro. As brilliant as it was, the raid disrupted transportation only temporarily without significantly damaging the Confederate war effort.

It should be recalled that the Battle of Fredericksburg, the most deadly battle of the war, occurred during the period December 11 to December 15, with Lee's army prevailing. As a result, Burnside was relieved of his command of the Army of the Potomac. The reduced traffic on the Wilmington & Weldon during the epidemic months shortly before the raid was a greater problem, whereas the railroad and bridges could be repaired quickly.

Shortly after the raid, Superintendent S.L. Fremont surveyed the damage to the track on a handcar up to the Neuse River. In his estimate, the track could be repaired in two days, with the bridge taking up to eight days to be ready for use again. He had scheduled the passenger train to run on December 22 up as far as the Neuse River, with one trip leaving Wilmington at 8:00 A.M. and returning at 8:00 P.M. A ferry served to make connections to the train going to Weldon.[39]

With regards to agricultural products delivered on the railroad during the month of December 1862, only 7,642 bushels of corn, 606 barrels of flour, 858 bushels of wheat, and 6,087 bags of salt were received at Wilmington, and at Weldon, 18,983 bushels of corn, 299 bbl. of rosin, and 7 bbl. of turpentine were received. January saw renewed volumes of bacon and cotton bales delivered over the line. Only in December had these commodities been absent from the statements; the epidemic months did not curtail their shipment. By February 1863, bacon, corn, cotton, flour wheat and salt were being delivered to Wilmington in large quantities.[40]

Prior to Foster's raid, S.L. Fremont had advertised contracts with a quarterly payment schedule for 300 slaves for tasks ranging from working in the shops to track hands. Slaves working on the track at Mount Olive and Goshen Swamp were ordered by Forster's cavalry to set the fires that destroyed sections of the trestlework.[41]

The labor force appears to have been sufficient to accomplish an opening of transportation to the Neuse in a matter of days. By January 18, 1863, the bridge over the Neuse River had been repaired. Way travel would rise to 10,206 passengers by the month's end, with no appreciable increase in through passenger volume; however, by February the passenger statistics rose to 50,308 way passengers, and 2,437 northbound through passengers, and 1,986 southbound through passengers. Freight revenues would also increase significantly. Overall, February passenger and freight volumes would not be surpassed until the summer months.[42]

The problems exposed by Foster's raid, however, are more significant than its immediate consequences for both sides. For the Confederates, bringing troops into the field to counter the attack was dismally inefficient, particularly regarding their transportation. As for the guarding of bridges on the railroad, General D.H. Hill had withdrawn the force assigned to bridge protection prior to the attack. S.L. Fremont considered that one man was able to set fire to the bridge on the Neuse River an embarrassment.[43] The Union foothold in eastern North Carolina presented the possibility that raids, even by small cavalry units, on lightly protected points on the line could take place without warning, and very little could be done to prevent it.

For the Union forces, nothing short of an occupation of Goldsboro could sever the railroad. General Gustavus W. Smith anticipated future raids and hoped that General Lee would send a portion of the forces he had at Fredericksburg. As long as Wilmington and Weldon could be held, a Union penetration into the interior could not be sustained. However, if they captured Wilmington, he doubted that the town could be retaken.[44] It would take the capture of both Wilmington and Goldsboro in 1865 to render the rail network of eastern North Carolina all but useless to the war effort, the Tarboro Branch and the hub at Weldon being the last connections.

The Skirmish at Warsaw

On July 3, 1863, General J.G. Foster sent 650 men of the Third New York Cavalry with artillery and pioneers of the First North Carolina Colored Regiment, under the command of Lieutenant Colonel George W.

On July 3, 1863, General J.G. Foster sent 650 men of the 3rd New York Cavalry with artillery and pioneers of the First North Carolina Colored Regiment, under the command of Lieutenant Colonel George W. Lewis, to disrupt transportation on the Wilmington & Weldon. At Warsaw Depot, two rail cars, a full warehouse, 4,000 barrels of naval stores, a store of gunpowder, and a safe containing a large amount of Confederate money were set alight. In addition, the troops pulled up and twisted rails, and destroyed telegraph lines. Warsaw is a small community approximately sixty miles from Wilmington but little more than seven miles from Magnolia, the site where that railroad had set up repair shops (photograph by Dr. Cyn Johnson).

Lewis from New Bern, to disrupt transportation on the Wilmington & Weldon. After successfully destroying a cache of weapons, commissary stores, and equipment for manufacturing knapsacks at Kenansville on the way, the raiders arrived at Warsaw on July 5, 1863. They occupied the undefended town and set to work pulling and twisting two miles of rails, and destroying telegraph lines. Culverts on the railroad were destroyed for a distance of five miles. At Warsaw Depot, two rail cars, a full warehouse, 4,000 barrels of naval stores, a store of gunpowder, and a safe containing a large amount of Confederate money were set alight. The raiders also took the mail. Anticipating the reinforcement of Confederate forces at nearby Magnolia and Rusk's Bridge, Colonel Lewis returned to the safety of New Bern. Along the way, in both directions, he encountered light resistance from squads of guerrillas and undermanned patrols. In the reports of the raid, however, Captain H.W. Wilson, the civil engineer commanding the 20 pioneers of the First North Carolina Colored Regiment, estimated that the length of track damaged was only about a quarter-mile, with 50 rails twisted and about another 50 turned over, with no crossties burned.[45]

The Raids on Tarboro and Rocky Mount

The report of S.L. Fremont, dated July 21, 1863, to General W.H.C. Whiting, commanding the Department of North Carolina in Wilmington, does not refrain from criticizing the decision not to have troops permanently assigned to Tarboro and continues by recommending that 1,000 cavalry troops should be stationed along the railroad. Fremont had learned early that morning that a Union cavalry force equipped with mountain howitzers had advanced towards Greenville, and he observed that their first objective was to destroy facilities and resources in the unprotected town. At 7:30 A.M., the conductor of the train from Tarboro sent a dispatch to Fremont from Rocky Mount stating that at daylight the Third New York Cavalry was in Tarboro. The telegraph went dead north of Wilson at 8:45 A.M. Then at 1 P.M., Fremont received a dispatch from Wilson reporting the burning of the Tar River Bridge and the Battle Cotton Mill at Rocky Mount.[46] The report of Union general J.G. Foster (July 25, 1863) on the expedition provides a detailed account of the damage.

> The bridge over the Tar River at Rocky Mount, a station on the Wilmington and Weldon Railroad, between Goldsborough and Weldon, was completely destroyed. The bridge was 350 feet long, and trestlework of 400 feet more. A cotton-mill, filled; a flour mill, containing

IV. The Enemy, Seen and Unseen

The cotton mill at Rocky Mount, six stories in height and built of stone, was destroyed during a raid by Major Ferris Jacobs, Jr., of the 3rd New York Cavalry under the command of Brigadier General Edward E. Potter on July 20, 1863. It was rebuilt after the war on the same site (photograph by Dr. Cyn Johnson).

>1,000 barrels of flour and large quantities of hard bread; machine-shop, containing shells, gunpowder, and every munition of war; a large depot, offices, &c.; an engine and a train of cars; a wagon train of 25 wagons, filled with stores and munitions; an armory and machine-shop, with the machinery and materials, and 800 bales of cotton, were all destroyed. At Tarborough two steamboats and one barge, and a fine iron-clad, in the process of construction, a saw-mill, a train of cars, 100 bales of cotton, and large quantities of subsistence and ordinance stores was also destroyed; likewise the bridges at Greenville and Sparta were destroyed. About 100 prisoners were taken, and some 300 animals — horses and mules. Some 300 contrabands followed the expedition into New Bern.[47]

Major Ferris Jacobs, Jr., of the Third New York Cavalry had volunteered to lead the raid on Rocky Mount. He described the cotton mill as being six stories in height, built of stone, and employing 150 white girls. The Confederate flour mill was a four-story structure, and appears to have been manufacturing hardtack in large quantity. He included an account of the heroics of Private George A. White, a cavalry soldier that chased down a passenger train eight miles from Rocky Mount, jumped from his horse into the cab of the locomotive, and with his revolver at the head of the engineer, forced the train to return to Rocky Mount in reverse. Union general Edward E. Potter, the expedition commander, reported charging into Tarboro between 7 and 8 A.M., meeting resistance from a few soldiers that fired shots and escaped across the Tar River. Potter destroyed the ironclad, described as modeled on the *Merrimack*, and two steamboats, and he burned rail cars at Tarboro.[48]

During the 1863 stockholders meeting, Superintendent Fremont would summarize the damage from the Union raids on December 12, 1862; the July 5, 1863 raid on Warsaw; and the expedition to Tarboro and Rocky Mount on July 20, 1863. The loss was estimated to have cost approximately $100,000 (or about one-sixth of the total expenditures for the year). One locomotive, two passenger cars, and seven freight cars had been burned in the Union raids, leaving the company with 24 locomotives, 19 passenger cars, 110 boxcars, and 25 flat cars. A warehouse burned at Dudley had been replaced, and the rebuilding of the warehouses at Warsaw and Rocky Mount were underway in November 1863. The company planned to rebuild the station and two warehouses at Tarboro in short order. Two wood and water stations and two covered bridges of two spans at Goldsboro and Rocky Mount destroyed during the raids had to be replaced. The bridges were rebuilt as temporary structures, to be rebuilt in proper fashion at the end of the war.[49]

Near the end of the 1863 stockholders report, Fremont addressed the rise in the cost of living for the employees of the company living in Wilmington. Where most had been able to "pay their way" during the summer months, the cost of heating their homes in winter had become a burden. Employees living along the line fared better, but the purchasing power of their salaries was half what it had been in 1860.[50]

The damage from the raids during the year had not crippled the transportation for any significant period of time nor visited upon the railroad such overwhelming destruction of property to permanently impair its operation, but it had diverted resources to repairs and was accompanied by the destruction of necessary stores of arms, munitions, commodities, and food that was needed at places up the line. The Confederate response to the raids was always too late to accomplish an interception, and the work of repairing the road was to shut down normal operations.

In early January 1863, Confederate general G.W. Smith correctly assumed that if Wilmington and Weldon could be held, a Union offensive penetrating the interior of North Carolina could not be maintained. At the time he had three regiments stationed at Rocky Mount, and 5,000 men stationed at Kinston. Yet, by May, it had become apparent to General D.H. Hill that General Foster had amassed sufficient forces to cut the railroad and make destructive raids in the lower regions of the Roanoke, Chowan, and Tar, and little could be done to prevent it. General Hill withdrew troops assigned to guard the railroad bridges, and it was particularly ironic that a handful of cavalry troops pulled off the burning of the bridges at the Neuse and Tar.[51]

It is more often than not the case for historians, particularly since the World Wars, to focus upon the clash of great forces and to place great weight in the numerical and technological superiority of one side over the other — a common and legitimate assessment of Civil War engagements — and to discount the effectiveness of commando attacks. The wars of the late-20th and early 21st century illustrate how well these attacks can introduce logistical friction into large scale military operations through disrupting supply lines, drawing off equipment and personnel to the site of the action, confounding and terrorizing the nearby population, and distracting military leaders from their primary objectives. There are proximate consequences of such attacks that fray the social and economic fabric of a region insofar as commerce and the routines of day-to-day life are impeded by preparing for a possible enemy attack that could come without warning.[52]

The Year to Come

At the time of the meeting of the stockholders in November 1863, the rails and equipment of the Wilmington & Weldon were in better condition than they had been the previous year, but at no point in the history of the railroad had more work been undertaken by its transportation department, a total of 475,000 miles of service. Half the line on the main branch needed to be renewed with 56 to 60 pounds per yard rail, and joint fastenings were needed to improve speed and safety. During the fiscal year, the speed of passenger trains was reduced to avoid deterioration of machinery. The company had put down 1,000 tons of mended rail and 500 tons of good as new rail during the year; however, Fremont urged the acquisition of 1,000 tons of rails from the Confederate government to continue maintaining the line until the end of the coming fiscal year. He also submitted recommendations contingent upon the ending of the war.[53]

> Should the war terminate during the present fiscal year, we should be in condition to procure, and probably be in need of ten Locomotive Engines of the best quality, and most approved description, one hundred

> Freight Cars, and from fifteen to twenty Passenger Cars. The entire reconstruction of the Warehouses, Track and Repair Shops at Wilmington, according to a plan heretofore submitted, should be made. To that end materials are now being accumulated and with ordinary energy during the year in collecting means, all these improvements may be made without affecting a reasonable and healthy dividend to the Stockholders.[54]

The coming year would present more challenges to the operation of the Wilmington & Weldon, and the war would continue months past the end of the calendar year.

"Our rails are gradually wearing out"

The 29th annual meeting of the stockholders of the Wilmington & Weldon Railroad Company convened on the morning of November 23, 1864, at the courthouse in Wilmington. In the president's report, Stephen D. Wallace commented on the consequences of the conditions of the rails, and the lack of suitable materials and labor.

> A constant cause of anxiety is acknowledged of the fact that our rails are gradually wearing out, and the means of renewal cannot at this time be relied on with any certainty. This consideration has counseled us to resort to every aid and appliance which would retard deterioration, and lengthen the period of durability. We, therefore, determined to run our trains at a low rate of speed, as a preservative both to the track and machinery, and most decided have been the results in favor of this policy.... The pressure of the war is felt in our mechanical departments with as much force as elsewhere. The want of proper materials prevents that rapid execution of work otherwise attainable, and the substitution of improper materials often renders the work, when performed, less satisfactory and durable. Labor of an inferior class is in many cases forced upon us, and these drawbacks are only fully realized by those in charge of the work, and who, with every disposition to remedy them, find themselves often unable, from the force of circumstance, to do so.[55]

Some of the rolling stock was left idle due to a want of replacement wheels and axles that were not being delivered to the company in a timely fashion. The Petersburg & Weldon Railroad (Petersburg Railroad), cut off by Union forces, had reduced receipts by about $300,000. Transportation to Petersburg and Richmond was rerouted via Goldsboro. The schedule was reduced to one train traveling daily to Weldon. Wallace concluded by lamenting the rising cost for all the necessary supplies to keep the railroad operating, but offered no alternative other than submit to the market.[56]

The Piedmont Railroad

The Battle of Weldon Railroad, fought August 18 through August 21, 1864, allowed Union forces under the command of General Ulysses S. Grant to extend their lines south of Petersburg near a location known as Globe Tavern. This cut transportation from Weldon and left the Southside Railroad, fronting the Appomattox River, as the remaining rail link; thus, the transportation between Wilmington and Petersburg had to be routed to Goldsboro, then Greensboro to Danville to Burkeville before continuing east to Petersburg. The trip was nearly twice the distance.[57] Adding to the logistical friction introduced by distance, the gauges of the Virginia railroads involved were incompatible with their North Carolina connections. The Greensboro to Danville line (Piedmont Railroad), built during the war, was particularly problematic due to a longstanding commercial conflict that predated the war. Its construction had long been resisted out of the fear that it would effectively divide the state into two parts, shifting the trade from western and central North Carolina away from ports and to the Virginia markets.[58] But it had become apparent by 1862–63 that the volume of food required to feed the army and the civilians in Virginia exceeded the capacity of the single connection at Weldon.[59]

In November 1862, when Union attacks threatened the railroads in eastern Virginia and North Carolina, Confederate secretary of war George W. Randolph offered to Governor Vance to supply "at cost rations, tools, horses, carts, &c.," and add "1,900 hands" to the work in anticipation of completing the railroad by March 1, 1863. Virginia would supply 650 hands, their owners paid $16 a month, and Randolph asked of North Carolina that the state supply 1,250 hands, suggesting that Vance appeal to the planters of the Roanoke. He also asked the governor to recommend a suitable person to raise a company of cavalry to patrol the work. Randolph's successor, James A. Seddon, presented the offer again to Governor Vance in early February 1863, assuring him the slaves assembled for the work would be safe, their comfort insured, and the full hire paid. He also stressed the importance of having the new line built in the same gauge to avoid the breaking of bulk at Danville, and he solicited the governor's support for a petition to the North Carolina Legislature for that purpose. Vance rebuffed Seddon's request to provide additional labor, citing the fact that the eastern part of the state had already provided slaves for a host of works from Wilmington to Petersburg, and about 20 counties already had their slaves engaged in similar work. The region through which the railroad was being built had few slaves, and it would present a hardship to the farmers in the region to deprive them of the labor they required for their subsistence. He was candid about the general aversion to the existence of this railroad for both commercial and military reasons: that the construction of the Danville connection had been viewed "with almost universal disfavor in the State," and had it not been for the war, its charter would not have been granted. At this point, there was concern that its construction would result in a relaxation of the defense of the eastern lines. Vance concluded by stating that the question of gauge had already been decided, and it would not be changed to conform to the gauge of the Virginia road (Richmond & Danville Railroad).[60]

The Piedmont Railroad was completed in May 1864. At the meeting of the stockholders of the North Carolina Railroad in July, Thomas Webb, president of the company, reported that a large quantity of government freight had been transported since as far as Greensboro. The railroad was now making two daily runs between Charlotte and Greensboro, while only one continued on to Raleigh. The potential of this connection was only then being realized by the company; it was proving indispensable to the war effort.

The April revenue from passenger travel of $152,908.99 increased to 176,142.43 in May; freight totals of $199,769.66 in April increased to $241,752.23 in May.[61] Thomas Webb did not mention it in his report, but he complained to Colonel Peter Mallett, the officer in charge of conscription in Raleigh, of the government's policy of drafting railroad workers into the army: "The Government can take its choice — either have the men and let the road and the Army suffer, or leave the men the men alone and let the road be worked as advantageously as possible."[62] In March 1865, as the war was drawing to a close, Governor Vance received a last-minute appeal to change the gauge of the North Carolina Railroad to that of the uncut Virginia railroads in order to speed along supplies to Lee's army, and to allow locomotives and rolling stock to be run, in the event that Virginia were to be lost.[63] Not only was the request unrealistic, it was entirely too late.

Union general Benjamin Butler had an opportunity to capture Petersburg, and he cut the railroads there on May 9, 1864; but on the same day, he was ordered to turn towards Richmond where General Grant and the Army of the Potomac appeared to be pushing back General Lee. However, Confederate troops under General Beauregard were able to slip past Butler and join the force south of Richmond. Butler had to withdraw to his defensive line, and the Union offensive lost momentum.[64] The time had come to evacuate Richmond.

Ironically, when the threat to Richmond had appeared a certainty in April, Jefferson Davis considered and rejected a plan to relocate the functions of the Confederate government farther south. Had the move been taken then, it would have also reduced demand on the food supply. Davis demurred from implementing the plan after the recapture of Plymouth, North Carolina, because he believed that ample provisions would be forthcoming from eastern North Carolina.[65] However, with the constriction of rail access to Petersburg in August 1864, the already serious food shortage had now become dire. General Lee, knowing that his army was too weak to drive the Union forces from their position on the Weldon Railroad, suggested using wagons to transport supplies around that access to Petersburg; and he also recommended accumulating stores of corn at Wilmington.[66]

Iron

At the 4 P.M. session of the November 23, 1864, meeting of the stockholders of the Wilmington & Weldon Railroad, General Walter Gwynn, the former superintendent and chief engineer of the Wilmington & Raleigh Rail Road, recommended that the company have its charter amended so it could acquire iron mines, coal fields, and woodlands for the purpose of manufacturing iron for the railroad. His proposal also included provisions for construction of a smelting facility.[67]

This suggestion was as old as the railroad itself and perhaps could have been envisioned in Joseph Caldwell's plan for the Central Rail Road and the aborted plan for the Cape Fear & Yadkin Rail Road in the early 1830s. The Chatham coal fields and iron deposits of the Deep River had long fueled interest in developing iron production in North Carolina. The Endor Furnace, located on the Deep River in Lee County, had produced pig iron since 1862. Yet, the railroad required iron in large quantities to renew their worn rails. The rails of the North Carolina Railroad, the principal artery supplying Richmond during the siege of Petersburg, were worn and laminated, even though the railbed had been as well maintained as possible.[68] In November 1864, the window of opportunity to utilize the iron resources of the state for the integrity of its rail network had closed.

That it was not undertaken prior to the war was the result of several flaws that shaped North Carolina's policy on internal improvements: the ability to obtain railroad iron and credit readily in Britain, sectional jealousies involving railroad development in regions that had industrial potential, the commercial rivalries with the neighboring states, and the failure to envision North Carolina as anything beyond an agricultural state.

The End of the War

When Fort Fisher fell on January 15, 1865, the lifeline of the Confederacy was broken. On February 25, the *New York Times* announced that the flag of the United States was flying over Wilmington. At the time, forces under General Sherman were advancing from the south.[69] With the fall of Wilmington, not only did the Confederacy lose its last connection to the outside world, but it also lost access to the Wilmington & Manchester Railroad. In the history of the railroad, the events following the fall of Wilmington would be reported after the end of the war.

On Tuesday, August 1, 1865, a special meeting of the stockholders of the Wilmington & Weldon Rail Road Company convened at the commercial house of John Dawson in Wilmington. Dr. B.F. Arrington, representing the shares in the company held by the State of North Carolina, conveyed the provisional governor's instruction that only shares held by

This drawing from the March 18, 1865, edition of *The Illustrated London News* depicts the interior of Fort Fisher during the second bombardment on January 13, 1865. After an infantry assault from the direction of the Wilmington Road on the afternoon of January 15, the fort was breached. By evening, the Confederate defense collapsed, and the fort was surrendered (courtesy New Hanover Public Library, NCD Box 1 023).

persons who had taken the amnesty oath be represented. Those who did not fall under the 14 classes excluded from the general amnesty unless they had received a pardon were not included in the total of shares represented at the meeting. He then excused himself from serving on the committee examining the shares. The resulting total consisted of 651 shares represented in person and 7,697 shares by proxy. There was insufficient evidence to establish the governor's qualifications in cases, so a large number of shares was excluded. The meeting took a recess.[70]

When the meeting resumed at 3 P.M. that day, then president of the company Stephen D. Wallace and the engineer and superintendent, Colonel S.L. Fremont, read their reports concerning the affairs of the company during the fiscal year to date. The receipts from October 1, 1864, to the suspension of service on March 30, 1865, were almost entirely from performing work for the Confederate government, a total of $1,275,000; the disbursements for the same period were $877,580.38; and the net profits were $397,419.62, all in Confederate currency. Other worthless assets of the company included bonds of the Confederate States, unsettled claims for transportation for the Confederate States, and treasury notes of the Confederate States, all amounting to $1,400,000. The debt of the company included bonds payable in London in sterling totaling $733,186.65 and secured by the property of the company, and another $47,059.03 due to parties in the North, unpaid dividends, and Negro bonds payable for the years 1844 through 1861. An additional $389,834.73 for liabilities contracted during the war was for the most part payable in Confederate currency, and subject to consideration by the directors at some later time. The value of property owned by company including the railroad, motive power and rolling stock, equipment, materials, real estate, and stock in other companies could not be valued. Only 159 bales of cotton valued at $25,000 and $22,803.86 in transportation cost due from the state were the only assets that had a known value.[71]

The report presented by Col. Fremont is a narrative describing the final days of the railroad's participation in the war. Earlier in the war, shops were erected at Magnolia (approximately 55 miles from Wilmington) to ensure the operation of the railroad should Wilmington be attacked.[72] Fremont left Wilmington for Magnolia on the night of February 20, 1865, two days before the fall of Wilmington. There, he oversaw the operation of the line until the railroad south of Goldsboro was surrendered to Union Forces under the command of General Alfred H. Terry, on March 19. Anticipating that the railroad would be cut at Goldsboro, Fremont dispatched his assistant, William Smith, with tools and rolling stock to set up a shop at Enfield on the division north of Goldsboro in early March.

While he could, Fremont continued operations at Magnolia with broken-down machinery, two worn out engines, and a few cars. The Union advance did not continue north of Goldsboro as expected, so the division of the railroad under Mr. Smith continued to operate. However, Confederate general Joseph E. Johnston ordered him to move all of his machinery west beyond Raleigh. Failing to accomplish this when cut off by Sherman's advance, he fell back to Weldon with all the stock and tools that could be saved from destruction at the hands of Confederate troops under the command of General Laurence S. Baker. With defenses falling back at Kinston, Fremont expected, as did some Confederate commanders, that Union forces would attempt to capture the northern division to prevent supplies from making their way from the vicinity of Tarboro. As a result, Confederate forces destroyed what they could. Seven miles of track between Goldsboro and Wilson were thoroughly ruined; the bridges over the Tar River near the end of the Tarboro branch of the railroad, as well as bridges on the main line over

This drawing of General Alfred H. Terry appeared in *Harper's Weekly Journal of Civilization* on February 4, 1865, after the fall of Fort Fisher. Fremont surrendered the railroad south of Goldsboro on March 19, 1865 (courtesy New Hanover Public Library, NCD Box 1 013).

Opposite, top: A longtime resident of Magnolia, Clarence Evans, is seen in this photograph marking the extent of the property the railroad once owned on Taylor Street (December 30, 2011) and ending before his shop at the near Main Street. The old brick depot, demolished years ago, was a small brick structure at the corner of South Railroad and East Carroll streets. The old concrete mile marker remains at that site. *Bottom*: The town of Enfield in Halifax County, North Carolina, was where William Smith ran the Wilmington & Weldon as the war was drawing to a close. Confederate general Joseph E. Johnston ordered him to move all of his machinery west beyond Raleigh, but he was cut off by General Sherman's advance. He had to return to Weldon. The station shown here dates from the 1920s (photographs by Dr. Cyn Johnson).

The old Seaboard & Roanoke Railroad Bridge over the Roanoke River marks the site of the Weldon Toll Bridge. In the early years of railroading in North Carolina it was an object around which there was considerable conflict, particularly between the Petersburg Rail Road and the Portsmouth & Roanoke Rail Road. Prior to the installation of iron, its spans were constructed of wood. As the Civil War was drawing to a close, Confederate troops ran locomotives and cars on to the bridge and set it on fire on April 13, 1865 (photograph by Dr. Cyn Johnson).

Fishing Creek and Quanky Creek near Enfield and Halifax, were destroyed. The bridge over the Roanoke River at Weldon was set on fire with locomotives and cars of the company on it. In total, the company lost four locomotives to fire at Enfield and Weldon, and 50 cars, including seven passenger cars.[73]

The Wilmington & Weldon was not the only railroad in North Carolina to experience damage to railroad property as the armies prepared for their final engagements on North Carolina soil. The bridges at Cedar Creek and Gaston were burned by Confederate soldiers, the first by Captain Webb, and the second by Captain White, both under the command of General Baker. The directors of the Raleigh & Gaston Railroad recommended that the bridge at Gaston not be rebuilt, but that the bridge at Weldon be used instead. The change would require that the charter of that company be amended. Huntsville Depot, south of the crossing of the Neuse River near Raleigh, was burned by Confederate cavalry under the command of Joseph "Fightin' Joe" Wheeler. Otherwise, the depots on the line remained intact. A portion of the rolling stock, along with the shops, was then being used by the U.S. military. The books of the company, like the Wilmington & Weldon, contained the uncertain assets and liabilities of the Confederacy.[74]

However, the North Carolina Railroad seemed to have fared much better. While the Confederate government had owed the company $1,379,941.80, the company was able to purchase 48 freight cars and a considerable amount of metal from its agents before the fall of Richmond, all valued at about $600,000. The Confederate Navy, being greatly indebted to the railroad and other companies, transferred its machine shop and tools at Charlotte to the North Carolina Railroad, the Charlotte and South Carolina Railroad, and the Wilmington, Charlotte & Rutherford Railroad. The North Carolina Railroad anticipated that the U.S. government would allow the company to keep the property. The railroad had lost five bridges, three to the Confederate Army and two to the Union Army. The warehouse, water stations, and train sheds at Salisbury and High Point were burned during Union raids by General George Stoneman's cavalry. The warehouse at Goldsboro had been burned as a result of carelessness on the part of Union soldiers after the town had fallen; and the section of the railroad from Goldsboro to Raleigh remained under its control at the time of the stockholders meeting. Yet, in spite of losses, the company had 16 locomotives at work on the line, and another five being repaired in the shops. The report recommended the acquisition of 20 miles of new rail to replace sections that had become unsafe. There were 860 bales of cotton stored by the company in Spartanburg and Union counties in South Carolina. The prospects for the future, however, were not as encouraging as the condition of its assets. The crops in the fields would be needed for home consumption, and few had the money to travel: the railroad could not expect receipts from freight or passengers to be sufficient until the population returned to their "wonted avocations" as the land settled into peacetime.[75]

Chapter V

Demanding the Impossible

That the railroads of the South were inadequate to the demands of service to the military needs of the Confederate States of America is accepted as a given. The reasons cited most often include the use of different gauges, gaps in the network, and the inability readily to acquire iron to replace worn rails. Aside from the obvious, the railroads were not designed to function under the sustained heavy conditions of wartime transport. It is, however, remarkable that the Wilmington & Weldon Railroad Company had the resourcefulness to maintain military transportation during an epidemic, resume operations quickly after the Union raids, and repair its worn equipment and rails in the company shops. Still, in spite of the best efforts of the company, the wartime activity of the railroad was a failed venture.

Working with the government of the Confederate States was a gamble at best, because, while struggling to become an independent nation, it had neither a standing army nor a navy, its treasury was meager, and its future depended on the paper promises of foreign commerce and an agricultural product both bulky and inedible. The government did not set prices, did not curtail inflation, and could not manage effectively the production and transportation of food to supply its troops or even its citizens. Whether through deliberate provocation or miscalculation, the secessionist cause had blundered into a war effort that it could not, over the long term, sustain.

For a business such as a railroad, an operation dependent upon the constant consumption of real things, the depreciating paper was a silent enemy inflicting continual damage on the ability of the enterprise to maintain either its equipment or its workforce. Yet, the question as to whether a business should expect to function in a normal economic environment during a national crisis — much less when an invading army is close at hand — is no worthy consideration. If it survived the end of the war, regardless of what that might bring, its functions would tend back towards the equilibrium of peacetime commerce, or the disequilibrium of an altered economic environment.

An analysis of the postwar economic condition of the Wilmington & Weldon Railroad suggests the latter. During the war, its significance was defined within the context of the lifeline, a set of transportation variables overlaying a geographic constant. Its existence outside this context, such as its ability to turn a profit, was irrelevant. If private interests would not run the railroad, the military certainly would take it over. The postwar context would not only force the company to work within the constraints of the free labor system, but also the rejuvenation could come only by mortgaging its railroad and property.

The Illusion of Doing Business

The business history of the Wilmington & Weldon Railroad during the years of the Civil War resembles the all too familiar paradigm for the failure of an industrial enterprise, the element of warfare excluded: the *real profits* of the operation over time were insufficient to maintain equipment and provide remunerative compensation for essential personnel, the *essential expenditures*, regardless of the demand for the product. Under normal conditions, the trajectory towards disorder is inherent, in that all physical processes and the frequency at which the process is repeated determine the regimen of maintenance. Assuming that any component can fail at any time in a mechanical system through intrinsic flaws, neglect, or improper usage, the level of maintenance will increase in relation to use in a trajectory approaching the replacement cost of the component or system. If we can consider capital as having a primary connection to objects and actions in the physical environment, then profit margins must be evaluated in light of the cost of maintaining the process at an optimal level of performance for the required task load. If the profit margin needed to be enhanced, the price of the product could be raised; if this could not be done, the company must reduce expenditures in aspects of its operations that do not compromise production.

The extraordinary conditions of wartime industrial demands transcend this model. In such a contest between nations, the role of citizens and corporations are that of participants, regardless of the nature of that participation, and each abnegates particular self-interest to serve the state. Conversely, it is the responsibility of the state, through imposing its prerogatives for waging war, to ensure for the benefit of all participants that the activity of military forces are supported by a social base that resembles normalcy — agriculture, a stable currency, an intact infrastructure, protection from profiteering, and an efficient bureaucracy — to administer civil and commercial intercourse while facilitating the war effort. The Confederate States government was ill-prepared to provide these — aside from the preexisting weaknesses in the Southern industrial capacity. Thus, for an industrial operation like a railroad — for which under peacetime commercial demands functioned within a play of tolerance between predictable revenues and expenses, and managing long-term debt obligations was a given — the inevitable moment would come when service to military necessity would overwhelm capacity, reduce more lucrative sources of revenue from private interests, and offer little in the way of offsetting maintenance expenditures.

Such was the situation in late 1864 when the superintendent of the Wilmington & Weldon Railroad, S.L. Fremont, declared to the stockholders that existing rates for government service were insufficient to maintain the railroad in working order. The proximity of the date of his report, November 23, 1864, to the fall of Fort Fisher, January 15, 1865, renders his proposed solutions irrelevant. The instinct to survive supplanted the desire to turn a profit, and all attention was directed to saving material assets: Fremont and Smith evacuated in February with Confederate troops, leaving behind consideration of the business of the road. Fremont would later write about the real company assets, aside from a store of cotton and transportation costs due from the State of North Carolina.

> The property of the Company consists of the Roadway, Machinery, Motive Power, Rolling Stock, Real Estate, &c., Old Iron, Wheels, Axles, &c., and Materials for Repairs, and the Stock owned in the W. & M.R.R. Co. and Telegraph Company, the value of all which I have not estimated.[1]

The debt of the company due in England, contracted for long prior to war, amounted to $587,555.56 with four years of interest; its domestic debt amounted to $63,994.43, in addition to $295,493.83 due in Confederate currency that had depreciated to a real value of approximately $15,000.[2] In essence, the company had labored under the illusion of doing business when all had merely been a gamble on the legitimacy of the financial institutions of the Confederate States.

However, the war cannot be viewed a commercial venture in the same way as the ordinary risks of business, though it might produce comparable ruinous results. War, in the modern sense, became an industrial process in the mid–19th century, and has henceforth remained inseparable from the financial mechanisms that underpin industrial manufacturing. The state, being the foundation for individual participation in social intercourse and corporate legitimacy, subsumes in law particular self-interest not only for the affirmation of its right to government by consensus, but also to defend its existence and prerogatives as defined in its constitution; thus, in theory, where the citizen enjoys the benefits of popular governance, also there comes responsibility for the common defense. While an individual or corporation might first seek to enhance particular security, no legitimate grounds exist for justifying it within the social contract. Regardless of the potential or actual profit or loss through war, the national objective is the complete overthrow of the enemy, not merely the enemy army, but also its government, institutions, and all complicitous parties to the acts of warfare. Business might be a practical concern, but it dims in significance when an enemy army is intent upon destroying company property. The profit margin is not a shield.

In the years before World War I, a British officer by the name of Major Stewart L. Murray reflecting in his companion text to the works of Karl von Clausewitz upon the great Prussian military theorist's concept of *Absolute War*:

> Yet, even now, so many years after Clausewitz wrote, in the hope, as he himself stated, "to iron out many creases in the heads of strategists and statesmen," the great transformation in the character of modern war, due to the participation of the people therein, has not yet been adequately realized by many men in this country who ought to know. It is earnestly to be hoped that they will endeavour to adjust their minds, as regards war, to the fact that we are living, not in the eighteenth century, but in the twentieth, and that they will consider that war has once for all become an affair of the people, that our opponents will be a people-in-arms, using the uttermost means of their whole manhood to crush us, and that disaster can only be prevented by a like utmost effort on our part, by an effort regardless of everything except self-preservation.[3]

The wartime activities of the Wilmington & Weldon Railroad and its companion lines are one expression of the "utmost force, the utmost effort, and the utmost energy"[4] that was required by the Confederacy. When S.L. Fremont left on the last train from Wilmington, the railroad was severed from its corporate constraints and was utmost an instrument of war, albeit approaching uselessness. Therefore, in the business history of the company, the period of the Civil War must be placed within the context of what happened before and what happened after. Unlike the Confederate States of America, the Wilmington & Weldon Railroad not only continued its corporate existence, but it would eventually, after years of struggle, thrive. Many of its officers and chief employees, as well as those of the other railroad companies, prospered and assumed places of prominence in Wilmington society.[5] With the political and military objectives of the United States achieved, it appears that the restoration of peacetime service and the retention of management was economically expedient, in addition to promoting social stability. The orderly transition back to commercial imperatives, regardless of its difficult choices, dissuaded a discouraged populace from reengaging in the struggle for Southern independence.

Strands of the Lifeline

At the close of the Civil War, Wilmington was the port in the Confederacy that had not been captured, and for this reason it continued to offer the opportunity to thwart the Union blockade. Supplies from foreign sources delivered by blockade runners were transported to the Virginia theater by rail. The reality of the lifeline, however, is more complex, and it existed long before the other major Southern ports had fallen. The Wilmington & Weldon Railroad and the Wilmington & Manchester Railroad formed a link, broken only by the Cape Fear River at Wilmington, between the railroads of Virginia and those of the Deep South. At Goldsboro, the Wilmington & Weldon connected to the North Carolina Railroad, and the Atlantic & North Carolina Railroad. Rates for transportation, in a patriotic gesture on the part of Southern railroad companies, had be set at one-half of private rates for the Confederate States at the convention of railroad companies held in Montgomery in April 1861, nearly a month prior to the secession of North Carolina.[6] Troops and munitions had to pass through North Carolina on the way to Virginia, and in North Carolina, the eastern railroad provided rapid movement of troops and equipment to fortify the coast.

Walter Gwynn, the West Point trained civil engineer that had surveyed and overseen the construction of the Wilmington & Weldon (formerly the Wilmington & Raleigh), had foreseen the military potential of the eastern line in coastal defense and suppressing insurrection, not hesitating to point out the virtue in the report of his survey to the company nearly 30 years earlier.[7] To his credit, the Union Army accomplished little more than brief interruptions of transportation until Sherman's forces captured Goldsboro in 1865. Thus, the defensive role of these railroads cannot be divorced from their corporate existence since in the planning phase such extraordinary functions were considered advantageous, if not essential. Coastal defenses, however, were vulnerable, or at best difficult to reinforce due to the physical geography of the coastline. Hatteras, Roanoke Island, and New Bern were captured, but Union forces were not able to make sustainable advances beyond the Outer Coastal Plains. Confederate troop response using the railroad, as exemplified by troops and artillery dispatched to counter Foster's raid, was less efficient than Gwynn's sell might imply, and incidents such as the burning of the railroad bridge at Goldsboro illustrate Confederate inconsistency in defending critical points along the line. The Union, severing of the Petersburg & Weldon Railroad during the Siege of Petersburg in the summer of 1864, accomplished much toward the ends of reducing the effectiveness of the Wilmington & Weldon that the raids could not. Passengers and freight en route to Petersburg and Richmond had to be transferred at Goldsboro to the North Carolina Railroad to make their way to those places from the rear. Only one train a day traveled the line north of Goldsboro to Weldon.[8]

The importance of the Wilmington & Manchester Railroad in the wartime transportation network cannot be overstressed. Troops and their munitions, originating in Georgia and Alabama, traveled north to Virginia on the Wilmington & Manchester and on the Wilmington & Weldon, as evidenced in transportation vouchers from 1861. By the same route, large shipments of food, clothing, equipment, and munitions were transported to Richmond. Bales of cotton for foreign shipment were stored in government warehouses near the depot of the Wilmington & Manchester opposite Wilmington. Transportation vouchers for the firm of Orrell & Hawes, a company engaged in providing ferriage across the Cape Fear River at Wilmington, show shipments of arms and supplies passing from the wharf of the Wilmington & Manchester to the wharf of the Wilmington & Weldon. Some of the explosive materials originated at the massive Confederate Powder Works at Augusta, Georgia. Southbound shipments from the Tredegar Iron Works also traveled the Wilmington & Weldon and the Wilmington & Manchester.

Through their agents in Europe, the Confederacy acquired weaponry, saltpeter, and provisions. The railroads of Wilmington were the means by which that freight was distributed. The Wilmington, Charlotte & Rutherford Railroad, yet to be completed, was to provide a vital link to the southwestern counties of North Carolina. Entries in the diary of author John Beauchamp Jones, kept while working in the Confederate War Department in Richmond, attest to the significance of the port to the survival of the Confederate States.

> Passengers from Bermuda say two monster guns were on the steamer, and were landed at Wilmington a few days ago, weighing each twenty-two tons; carriages, sixty tons; the balls, 15 inches in diameter, length

not stated, weighing 700 pounds; the shells, not filled, weigh 480 pounds; and 40 pounds of powder are used at each discharge. They say these guns can be fired with accuracy and with immense effect seven miles. I wonder if the President will send them to Charleston? They might save the city.[9]

But his diary is peppered with tales of the mismanagement of the transportation of food from Wilmington to Richmond, the ineptitude or corruption of Confederate officials in the issuing of passports, and the greed of speculators and profiteers.

Near the end of the war, Nickolas Schenck was making his way to Greensboro on the North Carolina Railroad, even as Union troops were advancing everywhere. At the site of the company shops, he was taken by the irony of finding large stores of food set outside to ruin — North Carolina hams, flour, sugar, candies, and coffee in great quantities — and thinking of the privation Lee's soldiers had suffered. As he beheld these "immense piles of stores" going to waste, it was apparent to him that transportation had been poorly managed.[10]

The logistical problems were serious, and perhaps revealed several fatal flaws. For example, in spite of the fact that agriculture in the Deep South was productive, it was waylaid in the eastern bottleneck on its way to Virginia. The Southern rail network had not been designed to handle heavy freight traffic, particularly the volume of food required for the troops.[11] From this single problem, come more: the inability to move cotton for foreign trade to locations where it could be exported; food shortages and high prices; deflated currency; speculation and profiteering; and the overused railroads' inability to maintain rails, locomotive, and rolling stock for want of materials, labor, and capital. But, can the obvious lack of foresight regarding transportation planning for the war effort lend support to the assertion that the supporters of secession did not anticipate that war would follow their actions?

The Blunder

In 1881, Jefferson Davis published his two volume set, *The Rise and Fall of the Confederate Government*. While it is difficult to approach this work as one would an impartial narrative, some of his statements imply that the movement toward secession lurched forward in the South. Set in motion in the halls of state legislatures, it acquired a momentum of its own. Countering claims that Southern members of Congress had orchestrated a plot for secession, he notes that plans for secession were coming together in some states during 1860, prior to the presidential election.[12]

The basis for assuming a peaceful course for secession rests upon the interpretation of early legislation concerning agreements between the United States government with the State of South Carolina and the Commonwealth of Virginia concerning forts, arsenals, and other facilities within those states. Davis presents the argument that a legal basis for terminating the agreement was provided for in the texts of the relevant acts. That the United States no longer represented the interests of these states after their secession appeared to satisfy the condition for the return of these properties. That the United States would not contest their claims was an assumption on the part of the delegation of commissioners from the State of South Carolina. Asserting the duty to protect the property of the United States, but unwilling to exercise that right in a way that might be construed as a provocation, he claimed that President Buchanan escalated tensions. However, by his own admission, Davis was aware that the recently formed Confederacy lacked the arms and munitions. The emphasis placed upon growing export crops had left the South lacking in the necessary food crops. Also, the feeling of attachment to the Union remained in the minds of most Southerners.[13]

If indeed all of these weaknesses were known, assuming the Lincoln administration would take a more aggressive stance to retain United States property, there existed no responsible course of military action other than standing down. Considering at that point that Virginia, North Carolina, Tennessee and Arkansas had yet to commit to the Confederacy, the advantages of taking possession of Fort Sumter paled in comparison to the overwhelming political, logistical, material, and financial risks; even with the then hypothetical support of the missing Southern states, the means for waging war hardly improved. However, there were known political risks for remaining quiescent.

South Carolina had attempted to secede in 1852, but was forced to abandon its ambitions for want of support from the other slave states. On this occasion, the benign mechanism of democratic discourse failed to entice revolutionary actions.

> The position of South Carolina at this time is a most difficult and embarrassing one. Suffering under injuries which render a continuance in the present Union incompatible with honor or safety; but deserted by other States, suffering under the same injuries, and whose solemn pledges of resistance gave South Carolina a right to expect very different action from them;— the citizens of the State became divided in opinion as to the course proper to be taken. One portion of them believed that

all hope being lost of any other States seceding from the Confederacy by a concerted movement, it was necessary for South Carolina to vindicate herself from intolerable wrongs by seceding alone. Another portion regarded this course as unwise, and thought it necessary to wait for the support of other States. The prospect of such support has grown fainter day by day, until it has receded to an indefinite distance; and that portion of our citizens who have placed their only hope in it, now find themselves powerless to effect their object. But by the popular majority which they have exhibited, opposed to exercising the right of secession at this time, they have also paralyzed the power of their fellow-citizens who desired to adopt that course.[14]

The few states of the Southern Confederacy of early 1861 faced the same prospect of having their revolution fizzle as the stalemate with the United States continued at Charleston. It was a matter of time before the moderates would grow weary of the bellicose posturing, and "paralyzed the power" of the ultras through concession — as had always happened in the past. Those who were pragmatic would have time to ponder the possible outcomes of provoking a war with the United States. Conservative "Union Men," the ever-vocal supporters of the *status quo*, might take the day, not only in the uncommitted slave states, but also in the fledgling Confederacy.

Pulling back from the brink is an act of political courage, and acquiring concessions in the process is the hallmark of political genius. The leaders of the Confederacy — as later with the monarchs of Europe on the eve of World War I — lacked both of these necessary qualities at that critical juncture when the value of standing down could have eminently served the common interest.

Rebuilding

By the fall of 1867, the Wilmington & Weldon Railroad Company had mortgaged the railroad and its equipment so that it could raise the capital for rebuilding. Dr. Thomas D. Hogg, one of the three directors on the board representing the interest of the state, was instrumental in securing the mortgage. The cost of reconstruction and improvement of the railroad was $935,306.15. The gross receipts of the company for the fiscal year 1866–67 were $583,836.98, with operating expenses amounting to $278,891.96. Of the remaining profit of $304,945.52, a portion was applied to paying interest on the debt, a sinking fund was established to address the future needs of the company, and some monies were set aside for future payment of a dividend of 8 percent (as if the railroad had been in normal working order and the floating debt did not exist). The sale of old iron yielded a sum of $105,063.99. The future of the company had been set to its debt clock, with the mortgage bonds — in English pounds — coming due in 1881 and 1886.[15]

The most remarkable statement appearing in the stockholders report for that year was that of chief engineer and superintendent S.L. Fremont.

> This result may be looked upon, under all the circumstances of the country — derangement of our labor system — the impoverished condition of our people — and a general distrust in commercial circles, as the most satisfactory and gratifying year's work that has ever been done by the corporation. If such results can be achieved by such a line under so many disadvantages, what may we reasonably look forward to when entire peace, happiness and prosperity shall again return to bless the industry and enterprise of our planters, our merchants and our artizans [*sic*]. Truly may we rejoice that we have a work so well located to command the business of the great agricultural portion of our country.[16]

The fact that the company could survive in the new normal of economic disequilibrium seems to place its Civil War corporate history within the same category of antebellum economic setbacks as the Panic of 1837, the Great Fire of 1843, the renewal of the road in 1849–50, and the Panic of 1857. These past events, however, had not radically altered the business paradigm or the socioeconomic environment under which it operated. The postwar Wilmington & Weldon would have to grow when economic conditions were stagnant; and it would have to adapt to the new business paradigm of free labor production.

Along with the eventual growth, or rebirth, of the railroad, Wilmington itself would be transformed by the railroad economy. The feedback loop of an expanded free labor base and the increased demand for transportation connection would leave its impression upon the human landscape of Wilmington, shaping it into the recognizable districts of the industrial urban model. The railroad could not exist as an appendage to the agricultural or maritime economy; to survive, it had to drive — if not force — new wealth producing models for exploiting these traditional resources.

The Men of the New South

The memoir of Dr. John H. Claiborne, a surgeon in the Twelfth Virginia Infantry, describes an event the occurred following the surrender of General Lee at Appomattox Court House that serves to place the arrogance and reckless irresponsibility of the social order that underpinned the regime. Claiborne and a small group of officers, including General William "Little Billy" Mahone, were traveling home on horseback. After riding all day, being "cold, hungry and tired," they stopped at an old country mansion a few miles from Charlotte Courthouse to spend the night. There they found an abundant corn crib and a host of livestock on the grounds of the estate, enough to make "a soldier's mouth water." The first officer sent to request the hospitality of the owner returned reporting that the owner had refused to help them, even though General Mahone had offered to pay for what they needed in gold. Claiborne was sent back to make another attempt. After carrying on negotiations at length with a household slave, he was escorted to the rear entrance of the mansion. There he met the eccentric mistress of the house, who without allowing him the courtesy of ascending the steps to make his request face to face, told him that she would have no soldiers on her property. To this he reminded her that they had fought four long years to keep the "Northern vandals" from seizing her property and killing her people. After acknowledging the fact, she nonetheless refused the request. On reporting back, General Mahone remarked that it would serve her right if they camped out on her lawn and paid for nothing, but thought riding the four miles farther to Charlotte Courthouse would be the honorable recourse.[17]

While Claiborne excused the insult as the peculiar behavior of an individual, it does not require too far a stretch of the imagination to extrapolate from this example the overall mindset that is representative of the social order created by the planter aristocracy and the crippling consequences of its built-in presumed entitlement. The aristocratic ideal rests upon the ancient foundation of agriculture, the ownership of land; it follows that if there is a state to defend the right of land ownership — a confederation governed by the properties class — then the landless must labor for the landed, directly or indirectly, to survive. The irony of such a social order is that the right to govern is not validated through the effective demonstration of industry and genius, qualities cultivated by addressing everyday necessity. At the end of the war, those who aspired to leadership in the New South required not only industry and genius to navigate the dangerous waters of Reconstruction, but also forbearance and guile.

General Mahone, in his response on hearing of the aristocratic woman's persistent rude rejection, momentarily wavered from his deference to the social order by suggesting defiance: "It would be serving her right to encamp on her lawn, take what we wanted, and pay for nothing," but he asserts his right to govern by realizing it would set a bad example.[18] Mahone, once the chief engineer of the Norfolk and Petersburg Railroad, represented the type of individuals that would overthrow the fraud of hierarchical privilege that had been perpetrated by the southern agriculturalists for 200 years: these were men of science, industry, and finance that defined themselves by their accomplishments, not by their birth. Their rise had begun in the era of antebellum railroad development; their time would come after the fall of the old order — even those who were born to and defended it. Mahone would participate in the politics of the New South and rise to the office of a United States senator from Virginia.

Chapter VI

The Aftermath

The history of the railroads of Wilmington during the Civil War era and its aftermath is a tale of three cities: first, the prewar town approached a population of 10,000 and consisted of a tightknit class of merchants, professionals, their families with their household dependence upon the business of the port, and the processing of agricultural and forest products. Second, the wartime port had a population reduced to about 3,000 at the height of the yellow fever epidemic in 1862. It was the abode of every category of unsavory element, speculators — domestic and foreign — the military, beleaguered civic authorities, and citizens of Wilmington that could not, or would not, vacate to safer environs. Finally, the City of Wilmington of Reconstruction and thereafter, being an urban milieu of the classic model, replete with identifiable neighborhoods self-organized according to socioeconomic and ethnic differences. This manifestation was primarily the result of the extinction of the slave labor economy, but the ascendency of the railroad economy also was a dominant force in the molding of its spatial functionality until the 1950s.

1865–66

From May 1, 1865, through May 1, 1866, Whitelaw Reid toured the defeated South, accompanying Chief Justice of the United States Salmon P. Chase. Early in his journey, the New York newspaperman had an opportunity to visit New Bern, Beaufort, Fort Fisher, and Wilmington. His description of old Wilmington appears familiar to those who have studied antebellum narratives, postwar photographs, and the remaining antebellum-built environment of the city that has survived.[1]

> One sees, at first, very little in the mere external appearance of Wilmington to indicate the sufferings of war. The city is finely built (for

VI. The Aftermath 147

This illustration, drawn by Joseph Becker, from *Frank Leslie's Illustrierte Zeitung* shows liberated Union prisoners of war walking to the transport ships. It is dated February 27, 1865. Several landmark buildings in Wilmington, some still in existence, are recognizable. These include the old Customs House (demolished), the old Presbyterian Church at Third and Orange streets (burned and was replaced), St. James Episcopal Church, City Hall-Thalian Hall, and a building east of St. James that appears to be the John A. Taylor house (courtesy New Hanover Public Library, NCD Box 1 022).

> the South); the streets are lined with noble avenues of trees; many of the residences are surrounded with elegant shrubbery; there is a bewildering wealth of flowers; the streets are full, and many of the stores are open.[2]

Reid, like so many other visitors and residents prior to the paving efforts, remarks on the "waste of sand which constitutes the streets," on observing a single horse drawing a cart (a dray) loaded with a poor white family with their household possessions.[3]

"Every Northern man in Wilmington lives in the very best style the place affords, no matter how slender his visible resources," writes Reid. But he also notes that the owners of these homes, having retreated from the town during the war, were anxious to return — their right to do so being in doubt due to the wartime policy on abandoned property. The old residents of the town, then returning, had not profited during the boom times of blockade running. The wharves were deserted. Speculators and profiteers, mostly foreigners and Confederate insiders, had had their day and vanished. Emancipated slaves of the town appeared more organized that those from the surrounding plantations. Poor whites, perhaps the greatest supporters of restoration of the Union and the end of slavery, were also the more vociferous opponents of racial equality. The former slaves of Wilmington had little faith that their freedom was permanent; they knew that in the country, slavery virtually still existed. None had faith that any contract for wages would be honored. Half of the town's families mourned the death of a soldier killed in the war. Reid did not believe that trade would readily return, as some Northern speculators imagined.[4]

Sir John Henry Kennaway, traveling the dilapidated railroads of the South in the autumn of 1866, was able to report that the Wilmington & Manchester was in service as far as the Brunswick River. The trestlework, destroyed during the war, had not been rebuilt. So, in spite of being able to see Wilmington across the Cape Fear, the passengers had to take a six mile journey that wound through a deserted rice plantation on a steamer to reach the town.[5]

In Wilmington, he found "a large park of artillery" surrendered by General Johnston at the end of the war, but nothing more of military

This drawing from an unidentified newspaper clipping in the collection of the New Hanover County Library shows sailors from Admiral Davis D. Porter's fleet removing obstructions placed in the Cape Fear River by the Confederates (courtesy New Hanover Public Library, NCD Box 1 014).

interest. He noted the existence of some fine houses, an abundance of churches, and as Reid mentioned, the "ankle-deep" sandy streets. Attending afternoon services at the Episcopal Church — no indication which one, St. James or St. John's — he found that a mournful atmosphere pervaded the service "so deep, I had never seen on any ordinary occasion, or should wish to see again." In the evening, he attended services in a church with a black congregation that proved more positive. Kennaway noted that the presence of smallpox in the population of freemen in the area had killed hundreds of their number; and the United States was providing rations for more than 1000.[6]

The railroad was running, albeit in a shabby fashion. Kennaway left Wilmington for Petersburg at 4:00 P.M., traveling as far as Weldon. The seats in the cars were broken; the rails were so worn and shaky that several times he thought that the train had run off the track. He considered this the worst leg of the journey. Traveling north on the same trains after leaving Savannah, he observed an old lady who appeared to have mastered the art of traveling without money. In Wilmington, she managed to have done well, entering the car with a store of coffee, sugar, and milk. The conductor, on finding that the lady had no ticket, considered letting her travel free of charge. However, after she had insulted him in a rage, he let her out at Weldon without her bag. Having traveled through the night, Kennaway and his party completed the whole 161 miles by morning. After a breakfast of "squirrel and scrambled eggs," the journey to Petersburg continued across the Roanoke River at Weldon, then west to Gaston. The passengers had to be ferried across the river because the bridge had not been rebuilt.[7]

The economic conditions in North Carolina of 1865–66 were chaotic, and the social fabric that had sustained it during the war years fell apart under the stress of the absence of cash, a lack of credit, and an undefined system of labor. The Stay Law, passed by the North Carolina Convention of 1865, repudiated state debt, thus placing the creditworthiness of North Carolina in doubt. The treasury notes of the state in which the middling and poor had invested their meager savings were of no value.

Repudiation had also destroyed the banks; the University of North Carolina, having all of its assets in the banks, was shut down, and the fund for commons schools ($1,000,000) vanished. The General Assembly passed a stronger version of the law, but that was eventually declared unconstitutional in the courts. The Northern creditors remained unencumbered by the law since the federal courts would not uphold their validity. The lack of cash and falling land values brought about the sale or break-up of large estates, some to Northern men.

The apprehensions of the emancipated slaves proved true: the contract labor system failed. Farmers found it more profitable to hire for short periods when the labor was most needed; but usually, for want of cash, the sharecropping systems prevailed. By the time General Sherman reached Fayetteville, 8,000 emancipated slaves were following behind his army. He sent them to Wilmington, where a large number had already gathered. At Wilmington, the fear of disease prompted General Hawley to disperse many into Brunswick County, where they were encouraged to grow their own crops. General Schofield advised the emancipated slaves at Wilmington to seek employment with their former masters.[8]

The epilogue to the wartime history of the Wilmington & Weldon Railroad begins with its dilapidated locomotives and rolling stock running on rough, worn rails — and with one locomotive still submerged in the Roanoke River. The bridges on the line destroyed during the war had been replaced with temporary structures, all in need of rebuilding. Its business was hampered by the absence of bridges north over the Roanoke. Assets of the company, outside a mass of worthless Confederate paper, included the railroad, stock in other companies, and a meager store of cotton. The economy of the state was at a standstill, and Wilmington, the once thriving port, was a place of occupation, not only by the Union Army, but also by a flood of refugees. The emancipated slaves and the destitute poor whites fashioned the perfect sinkhole for relief. The old residents of the town returned to an unrecognizable human landscape, uncertain that they would be ever able to occupy their homes again; some were in mourning, while others were scarred and broken.

Even today, the sandy streets of old are exposed for a brief time with street improvements and new construction. The ancient streams that once cut through the town, though now contained below the streets, still flow. It is not difficult to discern the build of the natural environment of antebellum Wilmington because so much has been preserved, at least south of Market Street. The robust economy of the late–19th century and early 20th century created nearly all of the downtown commercial district and pushed forward suburban development. The relics of this period have been acquired and restored through preservation and gentrification. Even the once bustling, dirty, and dangerous riverfront is now a place of recreation, contemplation, and romance. With the state ports removed downriver, the appearance of the occasional tug passing the picturesque decaying wharves and wild undergrowth of Eagle Island is a delightful scene. Preservation, however, can assemble from the relics of the built environment of the past a landscape that exists only in the present, if those who experience it cannot differentiate the edges of the periods of historical significance. For what remains of the Wilmington that existed immediately after the war, the surviving antebellum architecture, still "surrounded with elegant shrubbery," and the streets, still lined with "noble avenues of trees," merely suggests a backdrop that would serve equality well for other facets of the human drama.

The late 19th century would witness not only the restoration of the Wilmington & Weldon Railroad, but also the phenomenal ascendency of the company to the prime position in an evolving interstate rail network. Its existence, and the economic future — as well as the form — of Wilmington would become so enmeshed with it as to become indistinguishable. The regional base of traditional agriculture, supplemented by the introduction of new cash crops, would follow the lead of railroad consolidation. The tragedy accompanying this glorious rise from the ashes would culminate with the 1898 Wilmington Riots.

The Influence of the Civil War on the Transformation of Wilmington's Urban Form

Antebellum Wilmington, like Charleston, possessed some of the characteristics or the residential patterns described by the much disputed Sjoberg pre-industrial urban model: the urban core was occupied by the elite and their domestic servants, the lower class was situated in the zone surrounding the elite core, the outcast class resided in the extreme periphery and contained ethnic and occupational districts located inside the lower class and outcast zones. While Charleston conforms to some of the significant aspects of this model, it departs from the rigid three class divisions, the non-regulation of time, and lack of credit availability.[9]

Wilmington, in the decades before the war, appears to have been another variant somewhat resembling the Sjoberg preindustrial model but departing from the form's rigid structure. Some in the elite class held one or more plantations, but the most prominent and civically active were not merely planters. It also consisted of commission merchants and professionals, such as lawyers, physicians, bankers, and the owners of light manufactories (shipyards, turpentine distilleries, rice, and lumber mills). The lower class was thin and its gradient smooth: shopkeepers, clerks, foreigners, religious minorities, and Yankee transplants with the opportunity for social mobility. The marking of time was important: dealers extended credit to planters and farmers in the region on an annual arrangement. The time of day was marked by the ringing of bells; flags were raised to announce the arrival of the mail.[10] Mercantile capitalism was the foundation of the social structure.

However, boundaries, both administrative and physical, were virtual walls that contained the town core. The physical geography of Wilmington differs from Charleston. Located miles inland on a bluff near the confluence of the Northeast Cape Fear River and the Northwest Cape Fear River, the port was safe from violent storms on the ocean, and its wharves were situated on the river in a linear arrangement. Water Street, fronting the river, was the interface between maritime activities and the culture of commission merchants; and Front Street, located on the steep bluff, was the first street running south to north in the grid plan of the town. In antebellum times, this street contained a mix of commercial establishments, modest dwellings, and grand homes. Past and latter officers of the railroad, such as Governor Edward B. Dudley, James Owen, Robert Cowan, and P.K. Dickinson, owned impressive homes on Front Street.

Market Street, leading from the water's edge, and a portion of its intersecting streets, formed the commercial core of the town. The old boundaries of the town, from Castle Street on the south side to Red Cross on the north side, and from Front Street to Fifth Street, form the *genre de vie* that contained all the "time-geography routines," the symbolic, administrative, and technological places, and its natural context.[11] The noxious elements existed on the edge of these boundaries: antebellum Wilmington had its foundries, shipyards, wharves, saw mills, turpentine distilleries, gas works, and the railroads contained within their time-geography routines that were removed from the urban core and its institutions, but only at arm's length. The gentry were never too far from their commercial ventures. For example, Henry Nutt, the owner of a turpentine distillery near the wharves of the Wilmington & Weldon Railroad, had an office at the northeast corner of Red Cross and Nutt; but his grand home was located a block and a half up the bluff on Red Cross, between Front and Second streets. He was also an early director for the Wilmington & Weldon, and from his house, he had a view of the railroad facilities across the ravine. His home, though close to the noise and dirt of his business interests, was nonetheless at the edge of the elite enclave.

In the 1830s, the town boundaries abruptly terminated on the east, north, and south, beyond which rural land commenced. This land would later become developed and its use associated with the railroad. But even then, occasionally a locomotive would run over a farm animal just outside the town limits. Details about these plantations are sketchy, being derived from passing references in narratives on the town and from examining deeds. It wasn't a zone of the outcasts, it was not a part of the town, but rather simply rural county land. There were areas on the edge of town that were inhabited by the outcasts: Nickolas W. Schenck, in his diary, identifies a bad section of town located on the block bounded by Castle, Queen, Front and the waterfront. Ironically, it was only two blocks removed from Governor Dudley's mansion and three blocks from the early Baptist church. Other examples include a site known as the ruins of the brick home called "Williams Castle," at the corner of Ann and Third streets, "occupied by poor people." Schenck also mentions the site of a murder on Third Street, between Church and Nun streets.[12] These locations, like the close mix of commercial and residential spaces within the town, doesn't fit the clearly defined districts of familiar urban models.

The grid plan contributed to defining the *genre de vie* that appears to embody these contradictions. The blocks in most instances were 330 feet square and divided into five parcels 66 feet wide but usually subdivided into ten parcels that were 66 by 165 feet. This arrangement, however, did not allow even distribution of houses on all four sides, unless the parcels facing the street were 16 lots of 66 by 66 feet square. This presents the problem of having 39,204 square feet of the block (or 56.39 percent) enclosed by uniform parcels. The division of the block, therefore, followed a pattern of small parcels and alleys in the few blocks of the commercial core and large lots differing in arrangement from block to block in the residential core. These divisions of the block plan allowed for a certain spaciousness for gardens, outbuildings, and stands of trees within the old urban residential core that still remains evident in Wilmington's historic district, particularly in the area of South Third Street. The uneven residential densities and built-in green space imposed by the block plan ensured that the elite would dominate the cultural core and push the lower class to the periphery, while the outcasts were contained in pockets within zones of industrial activity.

The cultural core of old Wilmington would degenerate into near ruin for several decades after the Atlantic Coast Line Railroad moved its headquarters to Jacksonville, Florida. Even into the early 1980s, the old commercial district was not a place a respectable person would want to be after dark. Yet, even at the nadir of the economic decline following the end of the railroad era, Wilmington did not fall to the depths of an unkempt bawdyhouse as it did during the Civil War years. Wilmington of the war years was an anomaly, a rented out storefront in the guise of being a place, and at worst, a foreshadowing of the silver-strike boomtown of the territorial West of the coming decades. Compounding the coming and going of troops, soldiers and sailors were stationed in town. Add to this a transient aggregation of opportunists, prostitutes, and criminals of all degrees. Hometown ruffians indulged their propensities, and those citizens that were required to remain through necessity, obligation, or business had no choice but to negotiate chaotic conditions.¹³ To this mix was added a host of unsanitary conditions, some resulting from neglect of the city and its households, and others, pitfalls of nature that would have been a health hazard in any age.¹⁴

The degeneration of the town during the war years shares some aspects with the decline of the historic commercial and residential core after the departure of the ACL: the elite had relocated to safer environs, and the social walls that channeled the life paths of the town collapsed. While Wilmington might have been "one of the meanest places in the Confederacy,"¹⁵ the socioeconomic forces that created the condition were temporary and could not be sustained after Reconstruction. The restoration of a collective stewardship of property interests (or gentrification) restricted the avail-

The streets of old Wilmington, founded in 1739, are organized in the grid plan with most of it in blocks of uniform size. While this plan originally allowed residential parcels depth, it also limited the density of housing, which left green space. This is evident today in the residential neighborhoods of the historic district. With the breaking up of blocks for commercial usage, the size of the parcel would be more closely linked to the size of the building it contained. This photograph illustrates the current land usage density in the area including the northeast edge of Block 191, Block 204, and the southern edge of Block 217—all on the south side of the railroad cut. Prior to the late-nineteenth century, this was the residential neighborhood for North Front and North Second streets (photograph by Dr. Cyn Johnson).

ability of urban space for the low overhead and profit potential of unsavory activities, thus pushing outcasts back to marginal areas.

From the end of Reconstruction well into the early 20th century, the demands of the free labor industrial model transformed the urban space of Wilmington. Grand residences near the railroad were leveled to consolidate the downtown commercial district. The elite built their mansions east of Fifth and Market streets, and along Third, south of Market. Mill villages and streetcar suburbs replaced the rural farmlands and pastures that adjoined the town in former times; ethnic and blue collar neighborhoods formed on the former margins and around the key industries, where they were then incorporated into postwar city wards as Wilmington expanded. The reorganization of urban space was the direct result of the resurgence of social cohesiveness brought about by spatial revaluation according to functionality. The value of land is then based upon the value of the district rather than the value of the parcel.[16]

There are pitfalls to this economic model. The loss of a key industry can collapse an entire commercial district, and with it, the entire surrounding residential neighborhood can be lost. Land values fall, and urban decay follows as the opportunities to generate capital diminish. The social imperative of stewardship becomes unmanageable, and the demolition alternative appears increasingly attractive.

Conclusions

There are three significant periods in the history of the Wilmington & Weldon Railroad Company, with overlapping transitions. From 1833 through 1854, the Wilmington & Raleigh Rail Road period established the place of the railroad within the context of the early history of American railroads on the merits of its application of the prevailing technology and its management, as an early example of a multimodal system. The interval between 1855 and 1860 is a transition marked by the death of its first president, Governor Edward B. Dudley; the changing of the corporate name of the company; management changes that included the election of William S. Ashe as president, and the appointment of S.L. Fremont as chief engineer and superintendent; and a sustained period of financial stability, improvements, and the building of a branch line. The Wilmington & Weldon Railroad earned its place in American history during the second period — the Civil War — through its connection to the last open port in the Confederacy, Wilmington. The consequences of this involvement, in spite of all the heroic actions by Stephen Wallace and the directors, S.L.

Fremont, his mechanics and train crews, the Confederate soldiers that protected the railroad, and the associated railroad companies were a prolongation of the conflict and a more ruinous defeat. In certain respects, the Wilmington & Weldon was an essential element in getting the war started even before North Carolina seceded. Along with the Wilmington & Manchester Railroad, it was a conduit for the transport for troops, munitions, and food from the Deep South to Virginia during mobilization and thereafter, and with the port of Wilmington remaining the last hope for Lee's army, the railroad certainly extended the duration of the conflict. Its directors—notably, William S. Ashe—were active supporters of the secession movement. As significant a role as the railroad played in the war, the political forces at work impelled its participation. It was not a routine business program, nor could agile management mediate necessities with waretime demands, and the same can be said of Wilmington and its port.

The Civil War period in the history of the Wilmington & Weldon Railroad began during the election year of 1860 and ended with the securing of a mortgage of the railroad for its rebuilding in July 1867. The interval between the end of the war and 1876—the Reconstruction—is a transitional interval: the Cape Fear River is finally bridged, resulting in unbroken transportation through Wilmington; all the railroad terminating at Wilmington located facilities in the railroad district; the ever expanding force of railroad workers established neighborhoods within the city; and the Wilmington & Weldon entered into a lease agreement with the Wilmington, Columbia & Augusta Railroad. By 1875–76, work commenced on an ambitious program of improvements to the facilities at Wilmington.

Finally, the Post-Reconstruction period commenced with the expansion of the railroad facilities at Wilmington in 1876 and concluded with its merger into the Atlantic Coast Line Railroad in 1900. The period witnessed the transition from wood burning to coal burning locomotives, the replacement of iron rail with steel, the nationwide adoption of standard gauge on major rail networks, and the consolidation of railroad companies. The Wilmington & Weldon shops at Wilmington expanded for large-scale car production, and the railroads centered in the city became the major employers, driving the local economy. In the hinterland, the railroad provided new opportunities for agricultural and industrial development. This is the period that marks the beginning of the greatest impact of the railroad economy upon the physical and cultural landscape of Wilmington and the surrounding region. Directly and indirectly, much of the built environment of Wilmington would not exist if the Wilmington & Weldon had not entered this period of expansion.

The lasting legacy of the Civil War period upon the Wilmington &

Weldon Railroad Company was, as it was through the economy of the South, the immediate transition from the slave labor system to the wage-based labor system. While the Wilmington & Weldon offered few opportunities to black labor, the demise of slavery opened the market for railroad labor in general for all classes of workers, all of them participants in the general economy. The railroad was at the heart of an economic feedback loop.

For the student of military history, the wartime operation of the Wilmington & Weldon Railroad serves as a prime example of how railroad technology changed the nature of war in both a quantitative and qualitative sense.

> The railroad transformed the capabilities of armies along three dimensions: force, time and space. Railroads enabled armies to increase in size and accordingly in power. Transporting soldiers in rail cars, by carrying more men in a shorter period of time, increased the feasible size of armies. More troops could be brought to a potential battlefield in less time; battles could be fought with larger and larger armies. Larger armies of course meant that battles were more destructive and carried out over larger expanses of space.[17]

Field Marshal Count Helmuth von Moltke the Elder recognized the logistical advantages of planning warfare around rail transport and employed it effectively in the Austro-Prussian War (1866) and the Franco-Prussian War (1870). However, he was averse to large concentrations of troops, being difficult to provision and slow to move. By coordinating military use of the railroads, units could be mobilized efficiently.[18] The particular logistical advantages of coordinating rail transport were only occasionally exploited during the Civil War, but never with von Moltke's attention to detail. The propensity of the commanders on both sides to assemble large armies reduced the strategic potential of the railroads by burdening them with the task of transporting provisions.

Regardless of what could or could not have been achieved through detailed planning of military rail transport during the Civil War, the odds were against the Confederacy from the start: the South did not have the capital, the industrial base, or the manpower to prevail. The irresponsible and inflexible Southern ruling class accepted the odds and lost deadly, their ruination complete. Only the necessity to rebuild remained. Stephen D. Wallace closed the 1865 report to stockholders of the Wilmington & Weldon Railroad Company with the following statement.

> One thing is certain, the work is of too much importance to the public and the stockholders to be abandoned, and as there must be a commencement, the sooner that is entered upon the sooner will the desired benefits be realized. We have never appreciated the true value of Rail Roads to communities until now. Having enjoyed their advantage and then being deprived of their use, we forcibly realize their worth.[19]

Chapter VII

Rebuilding

The November 11, 1868, meeting of the stockholders of the Wilmington & Weldon Railroad Company illustrates the method of management employed to rebuild the railroad and at the same time to service debt: the company paid the interest on the debt and used the remaining funds to purchase new iron and rebuild bridges, particularly the ones over the Neuse River and the Northeast Cape Fear River. The gross receipts for the 1867–68 fiscal year amounted to $596,160.61; the ordinary operating expenses were $298,465.29, leaving a net income of $297,704.32. The total funded debt of the company was $1,474,644.80, of which $700,000 was from the sale of new bonds and $774,664.80 was from old sterling bonds. The rebuilding of the railroad and purchasing of new equipment was funded by the new issue of bonds.[1]

The receipts for the fiscal year appear to show a healthy increase in receipts when compared to the receipts of $500,209.57 found in the 1860 annual report. The ordinary operating expenses are $44,750.35 higher than in 1860, but the net profits for 1868 were $51,209.69 greater than in 1860. The increase in revenue offset the increased expenditures. When the receipts are broken down for these two years, it is apparent that the increase in revenue comes from a higher freight volume. Revenue from passenger travel, both through and way, as well as from the transportation of the mails, was less than in 1860. Robert Rufus "R.R." Bridgers, the president of the company, notes that in the early days of the railroad the main source of revenue had been through travel; as the region began to develop, way travel and freight increased. With the projected increase in population and the implementation of modern soil fertilization methods, he anticipated continued increases from these sources. As with the 1867 report, Bridgers stressed the importance of encouraging the cultivation of "trucks, fruits, and grapes." He did not think the cars for transporting the produce needed alteration other than providing more ventilation.[2]

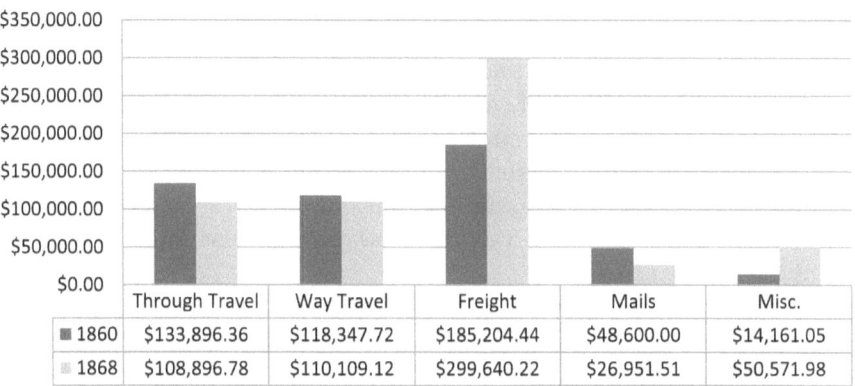

Receipts for 1860 and 1868

	Through Travel	Way Travel	Freight	Mails	Misc.
1860	$133,896.36	$118,347.72	$185,204.44	$48,600.00	$14,161.05
1868	$108,896.78	$110,109.12	$299,640.22	$26,951.51	$50,571.98

By comparing statistics on the total receipts from the annual reports for the fiscal years 1860 and 1868, one can see passenger receipts returning to their prewar level, and freight receipts are also on the increase from their prewar level. While the railroad was still recovering from its abuse during the war, the amount of receipts was not drastically different from its usual receipts from 1856 through 1860.

Agriculture After the War

There were good reasons for preparing the railroad for the transportation of fruits and vegetables. In the 1867 Wilmington City Directory, one can find an advertisement for the South Land, Emigration & Produce Company, a firm located at 71 Broadway, New York, near Wall Street, that was organized to introduce labor, capital, and modern farm machinery into the Southern states. Its secretary was W.H. Quincy, a South Carolinian. Aside from supplying machinery and the consignment of Southern products such as cotton and turpentine, it was an agent for labor: "White Labor (Germans, &c.,) [are] supplied" and they handled the "sale of State and Railroad bonds and all other Southern Securities." Its advertisement listed references from governors — North and South, presidents of banks, insurance companies, and railroads.[3] The *Daily Phoenix*, of Columbia, S.C., explained to its readers the purpose of this company and the American Land Company, also headquartered in New York City: they were to act as agents for Southern landowners who wanted to sell all or part of their holdings; to attract Northern investors who would want to invest in Southern land; and to "populate the South with white workers."[4]

The companies sold the land at cut rate prices: what was worth $25 to $50 an acre sold for $5 to $8 an acre. With Southern land such a bargain, former Northern soldiers, now familiar with the agriculture of the South, turned to trying their hands at being planters; even the journalist Whitelaw Reid made a failed attempt at farming in Louisiana.[5] In Wilmington, black land agent and State Senator George W. Price, Jr., offered "Land for the Poor!" in an advertisement printed in Haddock's 1871 city directory. The land was located near Town Creek in Brunswick County; farm lots of 40 acres, cut from a 3,000 acres parcel, were offered at $2.50 to $5 an acre, with 25 cents down payment the first year, and the balance for five years. A ten dollar cash down payment in hand could secure for the poor a 40 acre farm.

In New Hanover County, 8,000–10,000 acres of land, divided into 80-acre farms, were offered for sale on a six year arrangement. Ed R. Brink, postmaster of Wilmington and secretary of the local branch of the National Freedman's Savings and Trust Company, was the contact listed with this advertisement. Register of Deeds W.J. Bivens was another agent offering the sale of 40-acre farm lots in the Long Creek community in New Hanover County. This deal was 25 cents an acres for the first year (or $10 in cash), with five years to pay off the balance. The land also sold for $2.50 to $5.00 an acre, or a final cost of $100 to $200 over a period of six years.[6]

The breaking up of the old landholdings presented ideal conditions for encouraging truck farming. This was a trend that would continue into the era of the Atlantic Coastline Railroad; and land developers such as Hugh McRae would establish farming communities, populated by European emigrants, fronting the railroads, starting at the end of the century. R.R. Bridgers' vision, in recognizing the potential of small farms and a diverse agricultural economy, and the changing nature of agriculture, regardless of the dire economic conditions of the late 1860s, represented a long term trend. The new business model for the railroad placed an emphasis upon adapting to the transportation needs of diverse crops across harvest seasons. Looking ahead to the 1920s, the agricultural output of North Carolina, while still generating significant revenue from cotton and tobacco, had obviously expanded to include extensive cultivation of grains, vegetables, and fruits.[7] The railroads of North Carolina shipped out 13,405 carloads of vegetables and fruits in 1925. The truck farms and agricultural settlements in the eastern counties were proving to be particularly productive; Dutch farmers, settled near Wilmington, were growing ornamental plants and earning greater profits on their yield than could be made at any other location.[8]

The relationship between the Wilmington & Weldon and truck farming in the east appeared firmly established by end of the 19th century. Grapes, lettuce, and other truck farm crops were being grown near railroad station stops. Fertilizer manufacturing was in operation near rail lines feeding into Wilmington. New sources of lumber were being exploited in the surrounding counties.[9] The new agricultural economy and its transportation paradigm would render some traditional crops for the Cape Fear region unprofitable. For example, by the 1890s the rice lands on the Brunswick River near Wilmington would be used for grazing dairy cows. Diking, ditching, and irrigation of the river crops had become too costly when compared to rice grown on the lowlands in the Gulf States.[10]

Small farms fit well into Radical Republican Thaddeus Stevens' idea for Reconstruction. In September 1865, before a large meeting in Lancaster County, Pennsylvania, he advocated the confiscation of landholdings of "every rebel belligerent whose estate was worth $10,000, or whose land exceeded two hundred acres in quantity." Adult male freedmen would receive 40-acre farms from the 394,000,000 acres seized by the government, a total of 40,000,000 acres for a million former slaves. Southern estates below 200 acres would remain untouched, leaving 71,000,000 acres for white Southerners. That left 354,000,000 acres that the government could sell to the highest bidder with the resulting revenue applied to the federal debt. While most of Stevens' speech was well received, Northern newspapers were critical of his confiscation plan.[11] The Reconstruction Act of 1867 that Stevens helped draft reinforced the belief held by freemen that the government would fulfill their long-anticipated grant of forty acres and a mule. Instead, they would fall prey to opportunistic politicians willing to channel their hopes into votes, and swindlers representing themselves as agents of the government passing out wooden stakes to the freedmen for the plotting out of their homestead, with the requisite attorney fees. As late as 1903, prospects that the government would act on its promises of aid to former slaves left them vulnerable to confidence schemes.[12] Still, rural land ownership by blacks in the South would rise to a maximum of 200,000 farms by the World War I era. By 1969, large clusters of non-white farm operators — full and part time — in Virginia and North Carolina were located on the Inner Coastal Plain. The greatest concentration was around the North Carolina–Virginia line in the Roanoke Basin and in Brunswick, Bladen, and Scotland counties in the Cape Fear Region. Only a small fraction of the farms from South Carolina originated with land confiscated after the Civil War; nearly all the land was eventually restored to the original owners. Due to their limited capital, the freemen purchased small farms on less desirable tracts in coastal zones and the less populated pine barrens. Outmigration of whites from some rural areas of Virginia and other parts of the South provided more favorable conditions for black farm ownership.[13] With regards to the distribution of these farms, the clusters were centered on the coastal rail corridor in South Carolina, North Carolina, and Virginia.

While the new business model for the Wilmington & Weldon anticipated future freight increases from the produce of small farms, the demise of the slave labor system in agriculture required a more efficient approach to production: large farms would have to adopt modern techniques such as mechanization and fertilization with the aim of higher yields per acre, or more land would have to be put under cultivation on small farms using more traditional methods.

Connections

Stockholders of the Petersburg Rail Road met at the company's office in Petersburg on January 1, 1866. Federal authorities had turned over the operation of the railroad to the company on June 1, 1865. Ten miles of rail, including spikes, needed to be replaced, costing about $65,000, and a like amount was needed for the building of bridges and the repair and acquisition of rolling stock. Being without funds or credit, the company approved the issue of $150,000 in bonds. Judge W.T. Joynes, working in vain to find investors in Northern cities, secured only a few thousand dollars from this issue. Although unable to obtain a loan, the Petersburg Rail Road was, however, able to receive an advance from the Adams' Express Company and the Southern Express Company of $70,000 on an exclusive freight contract for four years. The company purchased from the United States government 800 tons of iron for $65,000, enough to replace ten miles of track.[14]

The Petersburg Railroad (Petersburg & Weldon) was a significant link in the coastal corridor, and without which an entire section of the Wilmington & Weldon — from Goldsboro to Weldon — was crippled. Unlike during the Siege of Petersburg, the bridges at Weldon and Gaston needed rebuilding. The three spans of the Weldon Bridge had been completely overhauled by the Seaboard & Roanoke Railroad by 1862, and in early 1866, the company was rebuilding and projecting that the work would be completed in April. The Petersburg Railroad had a three-year arrangement with the Seaboard & Roanoke to use the bridge for $7,000 annually. The rebuilding of the bridge at Gaston was dependent upon when the Raleigh & Gaston Railroad would have the funds to commit to the work; and the General Assembly of North Carolina had passed at its session "an Act to exempt the Raleigh and Gaston Railroad Company from rebuilding the bridge across the Roanoke at Gaston" in November 1865. Trains on the

Raleigh & Gaston could continue 12 miles east from Gaston to Weldon, thus avoiding the need to rebuild their own bridge. The Petersburg Rail Road saw little advantage in this detour.[15] In fact, the absence of a bridge at Gaston made the branch line of the Petersburg Rail Road, the Greensville & Roanoke Rail Road, a mere spur. However, for the interim, the route to Petersburg from the Wilmington & Weldon would continue from Weldon to Gaston. Their passengers and freight were ferried across the Roanoke to the Greensville & Roanoke.

The restoration of the Petersburg Rail Road was just as important to the future of the Wilmington & Weldon as were its connecting lines south. While the Petersburg Rail Road was able to improvise by reheating and straightening old rail and building temporary bridges, the rolling stock of the company was in poor order. As the war was drawing to a close, on acquiring knowledge that the bridge at Weldon might be destroyed, the company sent all the rolling stock in the area to the south side of the Roanoke. It became dispersed on the other railroads, and when collected again, it had suffered considerable damage at the hands of the military. The equipment had to be ferried across to Roanoke at Gaston. Once the company had a monopoly on travel north to Richmond; now the Piedmont Railroad offered an alternative via Danville for the commerce of the interior. The planned bridge over the Cape Fear at Wilmington would restore the traffic of the old corridor.[16]

Stephen D. Wallace

For much of this work, Colonel S.L. Fremont is featured prominently in the narrative; and rightly so, since he represented the arm of management closest to the physical reality of the railroad's wartime operations. However, the wartime history of the Wilmington & Weldon Railroad Company would be incomplete without due mention of Fremont's superior during the worst years of the war, company president Stephen D. Wallace. Because his postwar career as a civil leader and businessman contributes greatly to an understanding of his character, it seems fitting not to only place this discussion at the end of the work, but also to begin it with his obituary.

Stephen D. Wallace died on January 18, 1889, at the age of 75 after being ill for weeks. His tenure as president of the Wilmington & Weldon Railroad had been a brief episode in a long business and civic career. In addition to being the assistant secretary and general ticket agent of the railroad before the war, he had served as a town commissioner and on the Board of Superintendents of Common Schools, as well as an officer on the boards of the Wilmington Library Association and the Oakdale Cemetery Company. After the war, he was appointed chairman of the finance committee of the first Board of Aldermen for the City of Wilmington. After resigning as a director from the railroad, he was a partner in Wallace & Southerland, commission merchants, and an officer for both the Bank of New Hanover and the Wilmington, North Carolina Life Insurance Company.[17]

Wallace's obituary in the *Wilmington Messenger* states that he was a man of "high character" and "competent as a financier" who "attended strictly to his own business, and leaving that of others alone." He was amiable, sympathetic, and given to acts of charity.[18]

Stephen D. Wallace was the type of businessman one can easily recognize everywhere, past and present: competent in finance and administration, they prove their worth in their own line of business, and then, through the reputation of integrity they project, rise to a position of public trust. They are eminently useful in diverse enterprises, even where lacking specific expertise, because they delegate authority efficiently and possess a high degree of social reflexivity. As managers, they are constantly refining their craft, building upon the underlying principles of business and conscience of the constraining forces of the physical world. This breed of manager rises to a presidency from within, assuming the responsibility when necessity presents the opportunity.

When compared with previous presidents of the Wilmington & Weldon

Stephen D. Wallace, a Wilmington businessman, was elected president of the Wilmington & Weldon Railroad Company after the death of William S. Ashe in September 1862. Wallace continued to hold the office throughout the war, and appears to have managed the company conscientiously under the most difficult of circumstances. After the war, Robert Rufus "R.R." Bridgers replaced Wallace as president of the company. The town of Wallace, North Carolina, was named in honor of Wallace on March 4, 1899 (courtesy New Hanover Public Library, Robert M. Fales Collection).

(Wilmington & Raleigh), Wallace differed significantly. Edward B. Dudley, the first president, possessed both the vision and organizational genius, along with a sense of social responsibility, to transform a fading dream to reality; James Owen was figuratively the commander in the field during Dudley's governorship, overseeing the construction and operation of the railroad to completion. On Dudley's return to the presidency of the Wilmington & Raleigh, he guided it through a period of economic uncertainty and disastrous twists of fate — at one point, offering to place the whole of his personal fortune as collateral so the railroad could recover from the damage wrought by the Great Fire of 1843. His successor, Alexander McRae, had served as superintendent of the railroad. During his years as president (1847–1854), he was responsible for overseeing the rebuilding of the railroad with heavy iron rails and the improvement of its facilities. McRae was a military man. Having fought in the War of 1812, at age 70 he took up arms again during the Civil War; he served the duration to the Battle of Bentonville.[19]

The ill-fated William S. Ashe was not of the same mold as the original founders of the railroad. He was a charismatic politician and a masterful manager like Governor Dudley, but there the comparison ends. Where Dudley found the national political scene disturbing, Ashe was quick to embrace it. Even during the week of the 1860 meeting of stockholders, he became caught up in the activities surrounding the election and thereafter, was one of the "Immediate Secession Candidates" for the projected state convention. In enthusiastically exercising his authority as an officer in the Confederate Quartermasters Bureau, he provoked the ire of Governor Clark by seizing the firearms of private citizens without compensation to satisfy military needs.[20] Why he could not maintain the requisite detachment of a corporate officer — regardless of his political inclination and sense of duty — when the limits of what his railroad could possibly do would be put to the test is difficult to ascertain.

Whatever degree of reflexivity he possessed during the first five years as president of the Wilmington & Weldon dissipated as the events and potential opportunities of the times took hold. His demise was the result of his own impetuousness and inability to think expansively: he disregarded company rules in not displaying a light on his handcar; reaching the turnout before the expected train was his singular focus, and the ultimate benefits of arriving home earlier did not justify the endangerment of those in his service taking him there.

By contrast, as evidenced by his reports at the annual meeting of stockholders and other documentation previously presented, Wallace, upon accepting the role of president of the Wilmington & Weldon, directed his energies to the business of running a railroad. Assuming the position at a time of crisis (the death of Mr. Ashe, the capture of forts in the Tidewater, and the yellow fever epidemic), he met the challenges placed before him. While more a business technician than a managerial talent, his job description was unambiguous and his first report to the stockholders verifies that he was cognizant of its parameters. He knew that the railroad must be kept in good order to protect the stockholders' investment; the vital equipment of the shop must be removed to the interior in the event that Union forces invaded Wilmington; and the company needed a strategy for addressing its long-term debt. While the course of events would render it impossible for him to achieve any of these objectives, they are nevertheless in complete accord with the underlying principles that define the position. When Wallace interacted with the Confederate government it was for the purpose of securing adequate transportation rates and to acquire the necessities of the railroad regardless of his politics. It was for business, not politics.

In spite of his admirable performance in managing a corporation under the most difficult conditions, one cannot avoid contemplating that the end product of keeping the railroad going was a prolongation of hostilities in Virginia—the very thing that was impoverishing his employees, ruining his railroad, and bleeding the South. For a man of high character with an applied sense of social responsibility, if he had ever allowed himself to plumb the darkness beneath the sanctity of the administrative process, he might have realized how easily a great work intended for the purpose of economic and social development could be transformed into a weapon of war, placing management in a moral paradox between duty and regret for which refuge in the administrative process serves only self-denial. If Wallace did not ponder such questions, practitioners and scholars of business should, for it exposes the incompatibility between the governance of corporations and unstable political forces. Even the most well managed company performing at its highest degree of efficiency could be driven into the ground.

In 1899, the town of Wallace, a station stop along the route of the railroad named for the deceased railroad president, was established. The surrounding farms produced tobacco, fresh vegetables, strawberries, and livestock.[21]

War and Corporate Governance

From a business perspective, the wartime operation of the Wilmington & Weldon Railroad Company presents some unsettling paradoxes: politics, the demands of the wartime supply network, and unforeseen catastrophes propel the narrative, but not economic development; courage, perseverance, and decisive response exemplified the character of management, but exercising the positive qualities of leadership resulted only in the prolongation of the death struggle of the Confederacy. If the function of corporate governance is the preservation of company assets, protecting the interests of the stockholders, and striving to generate a profit, the prevailing external conditions of the war rendered these goals impossible: high volumes of military freight wore out rails and rolling stock; occasional Union raids destroyed equipment, bridges, and facilities, disrupting transportation; and the combination of low rates for military shipment and the unstable nature of Confederate currency rendered the profit margin of the company illusionary. Under the normal conditions of political and socioeconomic stability during peacetime, maintaining the sanctity of the administrative process ensures the protection of company assets — physical, financial, and intellectual — and provides accountability; it protects the interests of the stockholders, avoids conflicts of interests, and allows the company to function efficiently within the constraints of the law. It is the firewall between the operation and the outside world. From the election of 1860 to Assistant Superintendent William Smith's last futile attempt to protect the locomotives, rolling stock, and tools on the northern division of the railroad, the administrative process gradually lost its ability to protect the company. Politicians and generals became the true masters of the railroad.

War, by its nature, is capable of infecting all social and economic institutions and converting their functions to a singular purpose. Given the opportunity to commandeer all assets, all citizens are soldiers, everything grown or manufactured is a type of weapon, and every walk of life is a potential battlefield. No corporation, public or private, can rest assured of a certain future; all depends on the outcome. The American Civil War, like the World Wars, was a modern war: the fruits of the industrial revolution — mass manufacturing, steam power, and telegraphic communication — and the fruits of the Enlightenment — popular government — combined with the unconstrained lust for empire to form a deadly cocktail. In the unstable atmosphere of political conflict and popular agitation, the slightest misstep can set the war machine in motion.

That the company was to survive this greatest challenge is fortunate; but that it was able to recover during Reconstruction, then press forward to the apex of its corporate existence at the close of the century is remarkable. Wilmington would prosper from the railroad economy; its industries and merchants were dependent upon it, and much of its most stunning architectural treasures have a direct association with the railroad. After its merger into the Atlantic Coast Line Railroad, the monstrous steam locomotive of the 20th century would be pressed into service on the rails of the former Wilmington & Weldon during the World Wars.

Appendix A: Locomotives and Inventory of the Company Shops

Locomotives

1860

The following list of locomotives appears on pages 35 through 37 of the 1860 annual report. As of September 30, 1860, the Wilmington & Weldon Railroad Company owned 26 locomotives: 10 were passenger locomotives, and 10 were freight locomotives; two were being repaired, and one was being rebuilt; one pulled a gravel train, one was used as a yard engine, and one pulled a supply train. During the year, the total mileage runs by these locomotives was 318,701.

Passenger Locomotives

Number	Name	Builder	Engineer
22	*Orange*	Manchester Locomotive Works	G.W. Tarleton
23	*Wilmington*	Manchester Locomotive Works	Charles McQuestion
24	*Gov. Bragg*	Manchester Locomotive Works	C.H. Rice
17	*President*	R. Norris & Son	William A. Graham
18	*Express*	R. Norris & Son	D.F. Barnett
21	*Alex. McRae*	Company's Shops	William Paul
9	*Weldon*	Norris & Brothers	George Frailey
25	*P.K. Dickinson*	M.W. Baldwin & Company	J.W. Hollister
26	*Gov. Ellis*	M.W. Baldwin & Company	J.H. Stratton
19	*Goldsboro'*	M.W. Baldwin	William H. Graut

Freight Locomotives

Number	Name	Builder	Engineer
14	Director	Norris & Brothers	H. Hughes
15	Quickstep	Norris & Brothers	W.A. Gill
20	Guilford	M.W. Baldwin	James Knight
12	Merchant	M.W. Baldwin	G. Beasley
13	Industry	M.W. Baldwin	W.C. Corbett
4	W.H. Haywood	Burr, Pea & Sampson	G. Bea(s)ley
27	Gilbert Potter	M.W. Baldwin & Company	W.L. Trask
28	E.P. Hall	Rogers	A.W. Tolerman

Other Locomotives

Number	Name	Builder
6	J.K. Polk	M.W. Baldwin
7	Perseverance	M.W. Baldwin
10	North Carolina	M.W. Baldwin
1	Brunswick	William Norris
8	J.M. Morehead	Company's Shops
11	Farmer	Norris & Brothers
3	J.C. Calhoun	M.W. Baldwin
5	E.B. Dudley	Burr, Pea & Sampson

1866

The annual report for 1865 does not contain a consolidated report on the locomotives; however, it can be found on Pages 25 through 27 of the next annual report. The names of the engineers are no longer listed with their locomotives. The remarks on each locomotive in this particular report are interesting. The older locomotives *Farmer, J.M. Morehead, J.C. Calhoun, Brunswick,* and *J.K. Polk* were sold during 1866. In all, the locomotives logged 221,993 miles of service during the year, less than the year 1860.

Passenger Locomotives

Number	Name	Builder	Remarks
23	Wilmington	Manchester Locomotive Works	Thoroughly repaired, (by U.S. mostly), and sold to W.C. & R. R.R.
25	P.K. Dickinson	M.W. Baldwin	Thoroughly repaired
26	Gov. Ellis	M.W. Baldwin	Has been thoroughly Repaired
30	Gov. Vance	J.R. Anderson	Undergoing repairs
31	Wm. A. Wright	Rogers	In good order

Locomotives and Inventory of the Company Shops

32	A.J. DeRosset	Rogers	In good order
33	Edward Kidder	William Mason	In good order
34	S.L. Fremont	William Mason	In good order
35	Gov. Worth	Rogers	In good order
36	S.D. Wallace	Rogers	In good order

Freight Locomotives

Number	Name	Builder	Remarks
(none)	Commodore	Smith & Jackson	Thoroughly repaired, and sold to Orange and Alexandria Rail Road
(none)	Chief	Taunton Locomotive Works	Thoroughly repaired, and sold to Orange and Alexandria Rail Road
(none)	Spark	Norris & Son	Undergoing repairs
4	W.H. Haywood	Burr, Pea & Samson	Repaired and in fair Order, (on Tarboro' Branch Rail Road
7	Perseverance	M.W. Baldwin	Needs rebuilding
15	Quickstep	Norris & Son	Needs a general overhauling
18	Jeff. Davis	Norris & Son	Needs a general overhauling
27	Gilbert Potter	M.W. Baldwin & Company	Thoroughly repaired
28	E.P. Hall	Rogers	Thoroughly repaired
37	James Knight	Rogers	In good order

Other Locomotives

Number	Name	Builder	Remarks
22	Orange	Manchester Locomotive Works	Undergoing repairs
19	Goldsboro'	M.W. Baldwin	Undergoing repairs
10	North Carolina	M.W. Baldwin	Undergoing repairs
24	Gov. Bragg	Manchester Locomotive Works	Needs rebuilding–burnt
21	Alexander McRae	Wilmington & Weldon Rail Road	Needs rebuilding–burnt
5	E.B. Dudley	Burr, Pea & Samson	Needs rebuilding
13	Industry	M.W. Baldwin	Needs general overhauling
29	Tarboro'	J.R. Anderson	Needs general overhauling
17	President	Norris & Son	Needs general overhauling
20	Guilford	M.W. Baldwin	In Roanoke River
12	Merchant	M.W. Baldwin	Totally unfit for service

| 14 | *Director* | Norris & Son | Totally unfit for service |
| (none) | *Job Terry* | (none) | Totally unfit for service |

Shops

The annual report for 1859 contains the most detailed inventory of the equipment and supplies in the shops of the Wilmington & Weldon Railroad Company. This inventory can be found on pages 15 through 20 under the heading "Return of Machinery, Tools and Stock on hand in the Machine Shops of the W. & W. R. R. Co., Sept. 30th, 1859."

Machinery and Tools

Finishing Shop

1	new stationary Engine
1	boiler built in Company Shops
1	old stationary engine and boiler
1	14 feet lathe, geared
1	12 feet lathe, geared
1	8 feet lathe, geared
1	5 feet lathe, geared
1	large engine lathe, geared
1	14 feet engine lathe, geared
1	10 feet engine lathe, geared
5	planers
2	bolt cutters
9	pair dies to bolt cutters
16	taps to bolt cutters
3	holders to bolt cutters
10	nut blocks
1	old drill press
6	drills for old drill press
1	new drill press
39	drills for new drill press
2	drill sockets
1	wheel press
2	grind stones
11	vices
9	screw wrenches
14	oil cans
76	flat chisels
12	cape chisels
12	scribers
6	center punches
3	ratchet braces
23	drills for ratchet braces
1	clamp ratchet
12	drills for clamp ratchet
5	die stocks
9	pairs of dies for die stocks
30	taps for shops
7	tap wrenches
1	screw plate
4	hand-hole taps
41	reamers
10	numbers
38	letters
2	sledges
4	large bed screws
2	large jack screws
10	hammers
170	files assorted, in use
2	spirit levels
1	set corking tools for flues
1	hacksaw
76	cold chisels
1	new test gauge and pump
2	Ashcroft's steam gauges

Foundry

1	large cupola
1	small cupola
1	brass furnace
5	shovels
6	riddles

8	rammers
6	ladles
3	skimmers
4	hammers
1	core bench
1	core oven
1	core mill
1	wheel barrow
3	pair of tongs
12	crucibles
1	pair of balances
1	small ladder
1	cupboard
100	good flasks
150	inferior flasks
2	slings
50	iron clamps

Blacksmith Shop

1	fan
4	cast iron forges
2	No. 1 anvils
6	common anvils
12	sledge hammers
10	hand hammers
120	pairs of tongs
180	swages, ½ inch to 6 inches
30	fullers and flatters
28	cast steel chisels
18	mandrills
60	heading tools, ¼ inch to 2 inches
2	vises
1	bolt hammer
4	wrenches
10	squares
1	pair of straight edges
1	bellows
1	crane
10	buckets
1	trip hammer

Rail Mending Shop

2	cast iron furnaces
2	swage blocks
6	cast steel chisels
20	swages
6	sledge hammers

Coppersmith Shop

1	large bellows
1	forge
4	ladles
1	pair of soldering irons
1	solder mold
4	pair of roofing tongs
5	pair of gas tongs
19	stakes
3	pair of shears
2	screw wrenches
1	hammer
1	saw
3	mallets
4	cold chisels
6	files
2	rasps
1	scraper
6	punches
1	former
1	vise
1	hand bellows
2	double seamers for roofing
1	swaging machine
2	grooving machines
2	beading machines
2	folding machines
1	rolling machine
2	setting down machines
2	small burr machines
2	thick edge machines
1	thin edge machine
1	wiring machine
1	gutting machine
8	oil cans

Boiler Shop

1	pair of boiler makers' shears
2	punching [shears]
1	screw punch
3	pairs of bellows
2	anvils
1	pair of clamps
1	pair of rollers
2	sets of corking tools
3	sledge hammers
3	riveting hammers
4	hand hammers
1	riveting machine
20	pair of tongs

5	swages	5	gauges
3	punches	6	gimblets [gimlet]
4	cold chisels	11	pairs of compasses
4	flatters	2	bead planes
4	heading tools	2	boring machines
3	reamers	1	bolt machine
1	brace	16	augers
12	riveting tools		
3	cast iron blocks		
1	pair of calipers		
1	pair of dividers		
1	vise		

Paint Shop

15	paint brushes
4	varnish brushes
4	dusters
42	pencil brushes
1	hammer

Car Shop

1	stationary engine	6	putty knives
1	molding machine	1	pallet
1	McDaniel's planning machine	1	iron pot
1	tenon machine	4	funnels
1	circular saw	1	pair of scales
1	scroll saw	1	sprinkling pot
1	gig saw	6	water buckets
34	chisels	1	stove
21	hand planes	6	30 gallon tin cans
10	hand saws	5	5 gallon tin cans
2	cross cut saws	12	assorted tin cans
7	hatchets	25	paint pots
3	try squares [tri-squares]	3	paint mills
2	framing squares	2	paint stones
3	hammers		

Stock Materials

Finishing Shop

11,000 lbs.	new driving wheel tires	8 lbs.	sheet copper
3,600 lbs.	old driving wheel tires	6 quires	emery paper
15,000 lbs.	assorted iron	50 lbs.	spun yarn
1,500 lbs.	steel	48 lbs.	Spelter solder
14,000 lbs.	new castings	10 sides	belt lacing
560 lbs.	new log chains		
90	sheets of Russia iron		
100 feet	wrought iron pipe		
4	new driving axles		
	3 barrels fire clay		
336 lbs.	sheet lead		
2 sheets	No. 10 copper		
½ pig	antimony		
46 feet	rubber hose		
200 lbs.	rivets		

Blacksmith Shop

50 tons	bituminous coal
50 tons	white ash coal

Foundry

500 lbs.	pig iron
2 pigs	block tin
1 pig	antimony
12 tons	molding sand

Boiler Shop

1 plate	No. 3 copper
4,000 lbs.	plate iron
800 lbs.	sheet iron
200 lbs.	rivets

Copper Shop

25 lbs.	solder
25 lbs.	copper
1 sheet	No. 1 copper
120 sheets	galvanized iron
50 sheets	common iron
1 box	tin

Car Shop

9,000 feet	white oak
2,000 feet	white oak, refuse
1,500 feet	walnut
3,000 feet	poplar, refuse
6,000 feet	ash
11,000 feet	white pine
20,000 feet	yellow pine

Paint Shop

60 gallons	linseed oil
45 lbs.	dry white lead
100 lbs.	ground white lead
100 lbs.	white zinc
50 lbs.	brown zinc
10 lbs.	burnt sienna
3 lbs.	sugar of lead
100 lbs.	Brandon yellow
20 lbs.	rotten stone
18 lbs.	Vandyke brown
34 lbs.	chrome green
21 lbs.	Chinese blue
24 lbs.	chrome yellow
50 lbs.	black lead
28 lbs.	India red
15 lbs.	red lead
60 lbs.	Venetian red
2 lbs.	gum shellac
100 lbs.	Brandon red
10 lbs.	rose pink
4 lbs.	flower of emery
50 lbs.	block pumice stone
35 gallons	coach varnish
8 gallons	furniture varnish
1 gallons	Japan varnish
30 gallons	asphaltum

Cross ties, new rails laid, and bridge and trestle timber used—fiscal year 1858–59

52,200	cross ties
194,920 feet	bridge and trestle timber
200 tons	new rails
2,085	new iron rail chairs

Appendix B: Railroad Employees Living in Wilmington, 1865–1871

Abbreviations

1865 Dir   Frank D. Smaw, Jr., *Wilmington Directory, including a General and City Business Directory for 1865–66* (Wilmington, NC: Heinsberger, 1865).

1867 Dir   Frank D. Smaw, Jr., *Smaw's Wilmington Directory comprising a General and City Business Directory, and a Directory of Colored Persons, to Which Is Added a Complete Historical and Commercial Sketch of the City* (Wilmington, NC: Smaw, 1867).

1871 Dir   T.M. Haddock, *Haddock's Wilmington, N.C., Directory, and General Advertiser, Containing a General and Business Directory of the City, Historical Sketch, State, County, City Government, &c., &c.* (Wilmington, NC: Engelhard, 1871).

WCARR   Wilmington, Columbia & Augusta Railroad Company
WCRRR   Wilmington, Charlotte & Rutherford Railroad Company
WMRR   Wilmington & Manchester Railroad Company
WWRR   Wilmington & Weldon Railroad Company

Example: The data entered in the list found on page 65 in the 1871 Wilmington city directory is abbreviated as 1871 Dir-65.

Railroad Employees Living in Wilmington, 1865–1871 177

Name	Title	Company	Address	Directory
Adams, M.L.	Engineer	WWRR	City Hotel	1865 Dir-17
Adams, Geo. H.	Route Agent	WCARR	9th. and Swann, cor.	1871 Dir-49
Adkins, William	Machinist	WMRR	Henry Penny	1867 Dir-53
Alderman, I.T.	Freight Inspector	WCRRR	Edwin T Love	1865 Dir-17
Alderman, I.T.	Freight Agent	WCRRR	Front and Mulberry, cor.	1867 Dir-55
Alexander, J.	Laborer	WWRR	unlisted	1871 Dir-50
Allen, Wm. H.	Treasurer, Master of Transportation	WCRRR	unlisted	1865 Dir-17
Allen, William	Treasurer	WCRRR	unlisted	1867 Dir-55
Allen, Miles	Section Master	WCRRR	3rd., near Harnett	1871 Dir-50
Allen, William H.	Master Transportation, Eastern Division	WCRRR	7th., between Mulberry and Chestnut	1871 Dir-50
Atkinson, Roger P.	Superintendent	WCRRR	unlisted	1865 Dir-19
Bailey, Burt	Baggage Master	WWRR	unlisted	1865 Dir-21
Banks, David	Baggage Master	WWRR	unlisted	1865 Dir-21
Barratt, T.S.	Carpenter	WWRR	unlisted	1871 Dir-56
Barry, John	Road Master	WWRR	4th., Between Brunswick and Bladen	1871 Dir-56
Bates, Capt. B.G.	unlisted	WMRR	4th. and Walnut cor.	1865 Dir-19
Beck, Thomas	unlisted	WWRR	6th. and Red Cross	1865 Dir-23
Beck, Thomas W.	unlisted	WMRR	6th. and Red Cross, cor.	1867 Dir-59
Bectol, R.	Machinist	WWRR	unlisted	1865 Dir-23
Beery, Stephen W.	Clerk	WWRR	Red Cross, between 2nd. and 3rd.	1865 Dir-23
Bell, Wm.	Machinist	WWRR	unlisted	1865 Dir-23
Bell, William K.	Machinist	WWRR	5th., between Castle and Queen	1867 Dir-61
Bell, James	Blacksmith	WMRR	Walnut and Anderson, cor.	1867 Dir-61
Bell, Daniel	unlisted	WWRR	Near Anderson, near Grimes	1871 Dir-58
Bell, W.K.	Machinist	WWRR	unlisted	1871 Dir-58
Bell, Wm. T.	Machinist	WWRR	5th., between Castle and Queen	1871 Dir-58
Berry, Robert	Mechanic	WWRR	6th., between Red Cross and Campbell	1867 Dir-207 (Black)
Best, James	Engineer	WMRR	3rd., Harnett and Cowan	1867 Dir-61

178   Appendix B

Name	Title	Company	Address	Directory
Bisset, John F.	Foreman, Machine Shop	WWRR	Hanover and 3rd., cor.	1871 Dir-60
Blackman, E.	Engineer	WWRR	2nd., between Hanover and Brunswick	1871 Dir-62
Boatwright, J. Hal	Clerk	WCARR	2nd., between Chestnut and Mulberry	1871 Dir-62
Boland, J.	Laborer	WWRR	unlisted	1871 Dir-62
Boney, C.	Machinist	WWRR	P. Dahmer	1865 Dir-25
Boon, Alexander	Machinist	WWRR	Hanover, between 2nd. and 3rd.	1867 Dir-63
Borden J.C.	Conductor	WWRR	Railroad Hotel	1865 Dir-25
Borden J.C.	Conductor	WWRR	Purcell House	1871 Dir-64
Bowden, Jos. N.	Baggage Master	WMRR	Princess and 4th.	1865 Dir-25
Bowden, Joseph N.	Baggage Master	WMRR	John C. Bowden	1867 Dir-63
Bowden, Joseph	Conductor	WCARR	4th. and Princess, cor.	1871 Dir-64
Bowden, William N.	Book Keeper	WCARR	2nd. and Chestnut, cor.	1871 Dir-64
Bowen, Samuel	Machinist	WCARR	Front, below Dock	1871 Dir-64
Boyd, Adam	Carpenter	WMRR	R. Walker	1867 Dir-63
Bradley, John	Machinist	WWRR	Hanover, between 2nd. and 3rd.	1871 Dir-66
Brewer, A.	Carpenter	WWRR	unlisted	1871 Dir-66
Bridgers, R.R.	President	WWRR and WCARR		
Britt, William	Moulder	WCARR	Front and Chestnut (res.)	1871 Dir-66
Brooks, E.H.	Post Office Route Agent	WCARR	4th., between Queen and Wooster	1871 Dir-66
Browning, E.D.	Conductor	WWRR	Front, between Market and Princess	1871 Dir-68
Browning, E.D.	Conductor	WWRR	Jas Lumsden	1865 Dir-25
Browning, E.D.	Conductor	WWRR	James C. Lumsden	1867 Dir-65
Browning, S.M.	Laborer	WWRR	Purcell House	1871 Dir-70
Brunson, Isaac N.	Carpenter	WCARR	unlisted	1871 Dir-70
Brunson, Frances M.	Watchman	WCARR	Castle, between 7th. and 8th.	1871 Dir-70
Bryan, Henry	Engineer	WMRR	unlisted	1871 Dir-70
Bryan, Alfred D.	Carpenter	WWRR	Railroad Hotel	1865 Dir-25
Bryant, B.F.	Conductor	WCARR	unlisted	1871 Dir-70
			Mulberry and 4th., cor.	1871 Dir-70

Railroad Employees Living in Wilmington, 1865–1871 179

Name	Occupation	Railroad	Address	Year	Source
Burgess, J.W.	Carpenter	WWRR	unlisted	1871	Dir-70
Burnett, J.	Laborer	WWRR	unlisted	1871	Dir-72
Burr, Charles	Painter	WCARR	49 Market	1871	Dir-72
Calais, Wm. J.	Master Carpenter	WCARR	4th., between Mulberry and Walnut	1871	Dir-72
Calder, W.	Clerk	WMRR	Market and 6th., cor.	1865	Dir-27
Cantwell, Jno. L.	Freight Agent	WMRR	Mrs. C.K. Price	1865	Dir-27
Cantwell, John L.	Freight Agent	WMRR	122 Market	1867	Dir-69
Capley, J.L.	Engineer	WWRR	unlisted	1871	Dir-76
Carey, Joseph W.	Carpenter	WMRR	William Kinyon	1867	Dir-69
Carpenter, J.H.	Engineer	WWRR	unlisted	1871	Dir-76
Carroll, John	Post Office Route Agent	WWRR	Front, between Market and Princess	1871	Dir-76
Carroll, Michael	Laborer	WWRR	3rd. and Brunswick, cor.	1871	Dir-76
Carter, Robert	Engineer	WCARR	Swann, between 5th. and 6th.	1871	Dir-76
Casey, Richard	Engineer	WWRR	4th., between Brunswick and Hanover	1871	Dir-78
Cason, Edward F.	Clerk	WWRR	Mrs. M.S. McCaleb	1867	Dir-69
Cates, James J.	Carpenter	WMRR	Bladen and 6th., cor.	1867	Dir-69
Ceggin, C.	Engineer	WMRR	5th. and Bladen, cor.	1867	Dir-69
Chilson, Henry E.	Post Office Route Agent	WCRRR	unlisted	1871	Dir-78
Clark, William	Carpenter	WWRR	unlisted	1871	Dir-80
Clowe, C.R.	Master Carpenter	WWRR	unlisted	1871	Dir-80
Cogden, Caisen	Machinist	WCARR	5th. and Bladen, cor.	1871	Dir-80
Condon, D.	Laborer	WWRR	unlisted	1871	Dir-82
Conner, David	Carpenter	WWRR	S.G. Northrop	1865	Dir-29
Corbett, Wm.	Mechanic	WCARR	Market and 7th., cor.	1871	Dir-82
Corbett, William F.	Machinist	WCARR	4th., between Nun and Church	1871	Dir-82
Corbett, William J.	Engineer	WCRRR	Mulberry, between 7th. and 8th.	1871	Dir-82
Corden, W.W.	Carpenter	WCARR	8th., between Mulberry and Walnut	1871	Dir-82
Cormon, Samuel W.	Watchman	WCARR	unlisted	1871	Dir-82
Cowan, R.H.	President	WCRRR	unlisted	1865	Dir-29
Cowan, John	Conductor	WCRRR	Mrs. S. Cowan, Chestnut and 4th., cor.	1865	Dir-29

Appendix B

Name	Title	Company	Address	Directory
Cowan, Platt D.	Clerk	WCRRR	Mrs. Sarah Cowan	1867 Dir-73
Cowan, John	Ticket Agent	WCRRR	Mrs. Sarah Cowan	1867 Dir-73
Cowan, Robert H.	President	WCRRR	Front between Chestnut & Mulberry (res.)	1867 Dir-73
Cowan, Platt D.	Freight Agent	WCRRR	Chestnut and 4th., cor.	1871 Dir-82
Craig, W.G.	Carpenter	WWRR	unlisted	1871 Dir-84
Crone, John	Engineer	WWRR	unlisted	1871 Dir-84
Cumber, J.A.	Blacksmith	WWRR	unlisted	1871 Dir-86
Cumber, J.T.	Blacksmith	WWRR	unlisted	1871 Dir-86
Cummings, James M.	Painter	WWRR	4th., between Hanover and Brunswick	1871 Dir-86
Custice, M.A.	Conductor	WCARR	3rd. and Market, cor.	1871 Dir-86
Cutts, A.H.	Conductor	WWRR	City Hotel	1865 Dir-31
Cutts, A.H.	Conductor	WWRR	Red Cross, between 4th. and 5th.	1867 Dir-75
Cutts, A.H.	Conductor	WWRR	5th. and Red Cross, cor.	1871 Dir-88
Darden, J.S.	Laborer	WWRR	unlisted	1871 Dir-88
Davis, Thomas J.	Carpenter	WCARR	4th. and Hanover, cor.	1871 Dir-90
Davis, W.A.H.	Baggage Agent	WCARR	3rd., between Red Cross and Campbell	1871 Dir-90
Dawson, Geo.	Machinist	WWRR	unlisted	1865 Dir-31
Dawson, George	Machinist	WWRR	unlisted	1867 Dir-77
Delane, Piper	Post Office Route Agent	WCARR	Grist Station	1871 Dir-92
Dent, William	Pattern Maker	WWRR	Mrs. Hiram Sholar	1867 Dir-77
Dent, William	Pattern Maker	WWRR	Hanover, between 2nd. and 3rd.	1871 Dir-94
Dickerson, John	Blacksmith	WWRR	Mrs. Hiram Sholar	1867 Dir-77
Dicksey, P.T.	Baggage Master	WWRR	6th. and Castle, cor.	1871 Dir-94
Divine, John F.	Master Machinist	WWRR	4th., north of railroad	1865 Dir-33
Divine, John F.	Master Machinist	WWRR	4th. and Walnut, cor.	1867 Dir-79
Doughty, Henry S.	Carpenter	WWRR	Campbell, between 3rd. and 4th.	1871 Dir-96
Dove, James	Carpenter	WWRR	unlisted	1871 Dir-96
Drane, Henry M.	Superintendent	WMRR	5th. and Chestnut, cor.	1865 Dir-33
Drane, Henry M.	President	WMRR	5th. and Chestnut, cor.	1867 Dir-79

Railroad Employees Living in Wilmington, 1865–1871

Name	Position	Railroad	Address	Year	Dir
Dudley, Guilford L.	Freight Agent	WWRR	A. Martin	1865	Dir-33
Dudley, Guildford L.	Freight Agent	WWRR	Alfred Martin	1867	Dir-79
Dudley, G.L.	Auditor	WWRR	Market, between 4th. and 5th.	1871	Dir-96
Dugid, W.H.	Carpenter	WWRR	8th., between Mulberry and Walnut	1865	Dir-33
Dugid, W.H.	Carpenter	WWRR	Eight, between Mulberry and Walnut	1867	Dir-79
Edwards, Amos	Machinist	WWRR	4th. and Queen, cor.	1867	Dir-81
Ellis, James H.	Carpenter	WWRR	3rd. and Walnut, cor.	1865	Dir-35
Ellis, James H.	Carpenter	WWRR	Walnut, between Secord and 3rd.	1867	Dir-81
Ellis, J.H.	Carpenter	WWRR	unlisted	1871	Dir-98
Ellis, Joseph J.	unlisted	WCARR	Farmers' Hotel	1871	Dir-98
Etheridge, S.R.	Carpenter	WWRR	unlisted	1871	Dir-100
Evans, J.J.	Conductor	WMRR	unlisted	1865	Dir-35
Evans, John J.	Conductor	WMRR	Red Cross, between 4th. and 5th.	1867	Dir-83
Evans, J.J.	Conductor	WCARR	4th. and Red Cross, cor.	1871	Dir-100
Everett, Edward	Conductor	WWRR	Front and Nun, cor.	1871	Dir-100
Fillyaw, De Leon	Transfer Agent	WWRR and WCARR	4th., between Bladen and Harnett	1871	Dir-102
Fillyaw, D.L.	Conductor	WWRR	4th., between Bladen and Harnett	1871	Dir-102
Finlay, Robert	Mechanic	WWRR	Front and Harnet, cor.	1867	Dir-83
Finley, Robert	Machinist	WWRR	2nd., between Bladen and Harnett	1871	Dir-104
Flanner, Charles	Master of Transportation	WWRR	Front, between Red Cross and Walnut	1871	Dir-104
Folstead, John A.	Blacksmith	WCARR	Church, between 4th. and 5th.	1871	Dir-106
Folstead, John P.	Blacksmith	WCARR	Church, between 4th. and 5th.	1871	Dir-106
Foster, David P.	Machinist	WMRR	Hanover, between 2nd. and 3rd.	1867	Dir-85
Fox, George A.	Carpenter	WMRR	9th., between Princess and Chestnut	1867	Dir-85
Fox, George A.	Engineer	WWRR	9th., between Princess and Chestnut	1871	Dir-106
Fremont, Col. S.L.	Superintendent	WWRR	Front and Walnut, cor.	1865	Dir-37
Fremont, S.L.	Superintendent	WWRR	Front and Walnut, cor.	1867	Dir-85
Fremont, S.L.	Engineer and Superintendent	WWRR and WCARR	Front, between Princess and Chestnut	1871	Dir-106

Appendix B

Name	Title	Company	Address	Directory
French, William R.	Clerk	WCRRR	unlisted	1867 Dir-85
Freshwater, S.	Carpenter	WWRR	unlisted	1871 Dir-108
Galvin, C.M.	Chief of Watch	WWRR	unlisted	1871 Dir-112
Galvin, Edward	Watchman	WWRR	Farmers' Hotel	1871 Dir-112
Galvin, Patrick	Boiler Maker	WWRR	Walnut, between 3rd. and 4th.	1871 Dir-112
Gardner, Geo G.	Engineer	WCRRR	unlisted	1865 Dir-39
Gardner, George	Engineer	WCRRR	James D. Gardner	1867 Dir-87
Gardner, J.D., Jr.	Conductor	WCARR	Chestnut, between 8th. and 9th.	1871 Dir-110
Gardner, A.	Laborer	WWRR	unlisted	1871 Dir-108
Garrity, Jas H.	Moulder	WWRR	North of railroad	1865 Dir-39
Gates, Geo W.	Machinist	WWRR	unlisted	1865 Dir-39
Gay, H.B.	Carpenter	WWRR	unlisted	1871 Dir-110
Gilbert, James	Tinner	WWRR	unlisted	1871 Dir-112
Giles, Norwood	Clerk	WMRR	3rd. and Chestnut, cor.	1867 Dir-87
Gill, R.J.	Foreman, Blacksmith Shop	WWRR	Hanover, between 2nd. and 3rd.	1867 Dir-87
Gill, R.J.	Blacksmith	WWRR	Farmers' Hotel	1871 Dir-112
Goodman, William	Watchman	WWRR	8th. and Dawson, cor.	1871 Dir-112
Gordon, William	Watchman	WWRR	3rd. and Wooster, cor.	1867 Dir-89
Gordon, William	Watchman	WCARR	Dawson, between 6th. and 7th.	1871 Dir-114
Grant, William	Machinist	WWRR	Hanover, between 2nd. and 3rd.	1871 Dir-114
Green, James	unlisted	WMRR	Nun and 2nd., cor.	1865 Dir-39
Green, James G.	Yard Master	WMRR	2nd. and Nun, cor.	1867 Dir-89
Green, James G.	Master of Transportation	WCARR	Nun and 2nd., cor.	1871 Dir-116
Green, M.M.	Post Office Route Agent	WWRR	Front, between Market and Princess	1871 Dir-116
Gregory, Wm. H.	Carpenter	WWRR	unlisted	1871 Dir-116
Griffith, W.H.	Baggage Master	WWRR	6th. and Castle, cor.	1871 Dir-116
Gutenberg, (not given)	Laborer	WCARR	unlisted	1871 Dir-116
Hale, David L.	Blacksmith	WWRR	Front, between Church and Castle	1871 Dir-118
Hall, David	Machinist	WMRR	Henry Penny	1867 Dir-91

Railroad Employees Living in Wilmington, 1865-1871   183

Name	Occupation	Address	Railroad	Year	Source
Hall, George	Master Machinist	Mr. W.G. Milligan	WMRR	1867	Dir-91
Hall, George	Master Machinist	4th., near Orange	WCARR	1871	Dir-118
Hanby, Joseph H.	Carpenter	unlisted	WWRR	1871	Dir-118
Hankins, M.M.	Mechanic	4th., between Brunswick and Bladen	WWRR	1867	Dir-91
Hankins, M.M.	Machinist	4th., between Bladen and Brunswick	WWRR	1871	Dir-118
Hardy, J.W.	Machinist	unlisted	WWRR	1871	Dir-120
Harker, Wm.	unlisted	5th. and Queen, cor.	WWRR	1871	Dir-120
Harris, Charles M.	Carpenter	7th. and Hanover, cor.	WCARR	1871	Dir-120
Harsfield, W.B.	Coppersmith	3rd. and Campbell, cor.	WWRR	1865	Dir-41
Harsfield, Wm.	Coppersmith	Hanover, between 2nd. and 3rd.	WWRR	1871	Dir-122
Hayden, P.	Blacksmith	Chestnut, between 4th. and 5th.	WMRR	1867	Dir-93
Haynie, Wm.	Conductor	City Hotel	WMRR	1865	Dir-41
Haynie, William	Conductor	unlisted	WMRR	1867	Dir-93
Heath, Daniel W.	Moulder	2nd., between Hanover and Brunswick	WCRRR	1871	Dir-124
Hessinger, J.G.	Engineer	5th. and Walnut, cor.	WWRR	1871	Dir-124
Hicks, Hardy	Machinist	3rd. and Campbell, cor.	WWRR	1871	Dir-126
High, W.H.	Conductor	Purcell House	WCARR	1871	Dir-128
Hill, James H.	Freight Agent	Market, between Front and 2nd.	WWRR	1871	Dir-128
Hill, Charles E.	Watchman	2nd., between Hanover and Brunswick	WCRRR	1871	Dir-128
Hines, Enoch J.	Machinist	3rd. and Campbell, cor.	WWRR	1871	Dir-128
Hines, Eli W.	Carpenter	Swann, between 5th. and 6th.	WWRR	1871	Dir-128
Hines, Clarence	Carpenter	Swann, between 5th. and 6th.	WCARR	1871	Dir-128
Hines, E.J.	Carpenter	unlisted	WWRR	1871	Dir-128
Hodges, Charles	Painter	5th. and Chestnut, cor.	WCARR	1871	Dir-128
Hogan, J.	Car and Pump Repairer	8th. and McRae, cor.	WWRR	1871	Dir-132
Hodges, Fred	Cabinet Maker	Front, below Dock	WCARR	1871	Dir-132
Horn, Guildford	Engineer	Campbell, between 3rd. and 4th.	WWRR	1871	Dir-132
Hoster, J.O.	Post Office Route Agent	5th. and Brunswick, cor.	WWRR	1871	Dir-134
Howell, J.M.	Conductor	Weldon	WWRR	1871	Dir-134
Howland, Samuel	Conductor	7th., between Mulberry and Chestnut	WCRRR	1871	Dir-134

Appendix B

Name	Title	Company	Address	Directory
Hunter, S.J.	Carpenter	WWRR	Campbell, between 3rd. and 4th.	1871 Dir-136
Ives, Frank	Carpenter	WWRR	Unlisted	1871 Dir-136
Ives, Jesse	Carpenter	WWRR	4th. and Harnett, cor.	1871 Dir-136
Ivey, John R.	Conductor	WWRR	City Hotel	1865 Dir-45
Ivey, John R.	Conductor	WWRR	Jno. C. Bowden	1867 Dir-97
Jacobs, William L.	Baggage Master	WMRR	4th. and Princess, cor.	1867 Dir-97
James, Theo C.	Special Traveling Agent	WWRR and WCARR		
Jarvis, Wm. J.	Conductor	WCARR	3rd. and Dock, cor.	1871 Dir-138
Jobson, William	Carpenter	WMRR	Front and Red Cross, cor.	1871 Dir-138
Jobson, William A.	Car Builder	WCARR	Princess, between 8th. and 9th.	1867 Dir-99
Jones, S.	Machinist	WMRR	Nun, between 5th. and 6th.	1871 Dir-140
Joyce, Richard	Laborer	WWRR	Chestnut, between 9th. and 10th.	1867 Dir-101
Keith, J.	Carpenter	WWRR	Mulberry, between Front and Water	1871 Dir-142
Kelly, Augustus H.	Clerk	WWRR	unlisted	1871 Dir-142
Kelly, Bartholomew	Carpenter	WCARR	2nd. and Walnut	1871 Dir-142
Kelly, Oliver	Clerk	WCRRR	Church, between 4th. and 5th.	1871 Dir-143
Kenyon, Thomas	Carpenter	WCARR	Walnut and 7th., cor.	1871 Dir-143
Kinder, Thos D.	Painter	WWRR	5th. and Chestnut, cor.	1865 Dir-47
King, C.C.	Carpenter	WWRR	P. Dahmer	1871 Dir-144
King, J.A.	Car Inspector	WWRR	unlisted	1871 Dir-144
King, James	Greaser	WWRR	unlisted	1871 Dir-144
Knight, James	Conductor	WWRR	Campbell, between 3rd. and 4th.	1871 Dir-146
Knight, J.S.	Engineer	WWRR	Goldsboro	1871 Dir-146
Knowles, T.M.	Conductor, Sleeping Car	WWRR	Farmers' Hotel	1871 Dir-146
Lamon, W.W.	Machinist	WWRR	Purcell House	1865 Dir-49
Lan[?]ton, B.J.	Engineer	WWRR	6th. and Walnut, cor.	1871 Dir-148
Langdon, Richard F.	Clerk	WWRR	Market, between 4th. and 5th.	1865 Dir-49
Langdon, Richard F.	Clerk	WWRR	Market, between 7th. and Eight	1867 Dir-105

Railroad Employees Living in Wilmington, 1865–1871 185

Name	Position	Railroad	Address	Year/Dir
Langdon, R.F.	Trace Clerk	WWRR	Market and 8th., cor.	1871 Dir-148
Laspeyre, M.	Engineer	WCRRR	Asa J. Murray	1865 Dir-49
Laspeyre, Mathew	Engineer	WMRR	Asa J. Murray	1867 Dir-105
Latta, John R.	Clerk	WMRR	7th., between Mulberry and Walnut	1867 Dir-105
Latta, John R.	General Freight and Ticket Agent	WCARR	7th., between Walnut and Mulberry	1871 Dir-148
Lawther, T.H.	Engineer	WWRR	unlisted	1871 Dir-148
Ledbetter, Robert	Carpenter	WWRR	J.F. Legwin	1867 Dir-107
Leggett, John E.	Conductor	WWRR	6th. and Walnut, cor.	1865 Dir-49
Leggett, John E.	Conductor	WWRR	6th. and Walnut, cor.	1867 Dir-107
Leggett, J.E.	Conductor	WWRR	Mulberry, near Front	1871 Dir-148
Lippitt, Thos. B.	Clerk	WWRR	Mrs. J.J. Lippitt	1865 Dir-51
Lippitt, Thomas B.	Clerk	WMRR	Dock, between Front and 2nd.	1867 Dir-107
Lord, John B.	Prov. Agent	WCARR	Market, between 2nd. and 3rd.	1871 Dir-152
Lotzin, H.L.	Watchman	WWRR	P. Dahmer	1865 Dir-51
Love, A.D.	Clerk	WCRRR	Mulberry, between 4th. and 5th.	1871 Dir-152
Love, Armand D.	Freight Clerk	WCRRR	Mulberry, between 4th. and 5th.	1871 Dir-152
Love, E.T.	Engineer	WCRRR	2nd., between Mulberry and Chestnut	1871 Dir-154
Love, Richard S.	Conductor	WCRRR	Mulberry and Front, cor.	1871 Dir-154
Love, Thomas L.	Clerk	WCARR	6th. and Bladen, cor.	1871 Dir-154
Lyons, L.B.	Conductor	WMRR	6th., between Princess and Chestnut	1865 Dir-51
Lyons, James W.	Machinist	WCARR	3rd., between Red Cross and Campbell	1871 Dir-156
Lyons, Lawrence B.	Engineer	WCARR	3rd., between Red Cross and Campbell	1871 Dir-156
Mahoney, Wm. B.	Carpenter	WWRR	Campbell, between 3rd. and 4th.	1871 Dir-164
Manning, Edward W.	Captain, steamer *Gen. Howard*	WCRRR	3rd. and Mulberry	1865 Dir-53
Manning, Edward W.	Commander, Steamer *General Howard*	WCRRR	3rd. and Mulberry, cor.	1867 Dir-111
Marble, L.W.	Engineer	WWRR	E. Hansley	1865 Dir-53
Marshall, A.	Laborer	WWRR	unlisted	1871 Dir-164
Martin, Silas N.	President	WCRRR	Market, between 2nd. and 3rd.	1871 Dir-164
Mayo, William E.	Machinist	WMRR	4th., between Brunswick and Bladen	1867 Dir-111
McClenny, Absalom	Engineer	not listed	Front and Ann, cor.	1871 Dir-158

Appendix B

Name	Title	Company	Address	Directory
McCumber, James	Blacksmith	WWRR	Church, between 6th. and 7th.	1871 Dir-158
McCumber, Thomas	Blacksmith	WWRR	4th. and Queen, cor.	1871 Dir-158
McEnessey, Dennis	Laborer	WWRR	Hanover, below 3rd.	1871 Dir-158
McEntee, John	Carpenter	WWRR	4th., between Hanover and Brunswick	1871 Dir-158
McEvoy, J.	Carpenter	WWRR	unlisted	1871 Dir-158
McFarland, Wm. H.	Baggage Agent	WWRR	Campbell, between 2nd. and 3rd.	1871 Dir-158
McGarity, James H.	Moulder	WCARR	4th., between Nun and Church	1871 Dir-158
McIntee, J.	Carpenter	WWRR	unlisted	1871 Dir-160
McKay, J.S.	Mechanic	WWRR	L. Lyons	1865 Dir-55
McMillian, F.A.	Engineer	WCARR	Hanover, between 2nd. and 3rd.	1871 Dir-160
McMillian, F.A., Jr.	Machinist	WWRR	Hanover, between 2nd. and 3rd.	1871 Dir-160
McRae, Walter G.	Store-keeper	WWRR	Mrs. C.K. Price	1865 Dir-55
McRae, Roderick	Clerk	WMRR	Gen. Alex. McRae	1867 Dir-113
McRae, Walter G.	Clerk	WWRR	Market, between 7th. and 8th.	1867 Dir-133
Meredith, S.L.	Engineer	WWRR	Red Cross, between 2nd. and 3rd.	1871 Dir-168
Meredith, James T.	Passenger Train Hand	WWRR	Mulberry, cor Walnut	1871 Dir-168
Merritt, R.	Laborer	WWRR	unlisted	1871 Dir-168
Miller, Edgar	Post Office Route Agent	WWRR	Harnett, between 6th. and 7th.	1871 Dir-168
Moore, John	Watchman	WCARR	2nd., between Nun and Church	1871 Dir-172
Morris, Richard	Clerk	WCARR	2nd., between Ann and Nun	1871 Dir-172
Morrison, R.	Engineer	unlisted	W.G. Fowler's	1865 Dir-57
Morrison, George	Conductor	WWRR	Front, between Mulberry and Walnut	1865 Dir-57
Morrison, T	Engineer	unlisted	5th. and Princess, cor.	1865 Dir-57
Morrison, George	Conductor	WWRR	Front, between Mulberry and Walnut	1867 Dir-117
Morrison, Robert	Engineer	no listed	Wm. G. Fowler	1867 Dir-117
Morrison, George	Conductor	WWRR	Front, between Dock and Orange	1871 Dir-172
Murphy, B.F.	Carpenter	WWRR	unlisted	1871 Dir-174
Murphy, [?]	Blacksmith	WWRR	Hanover, between 2nd. and 3rd.	1871 Dir-176
Murray, Asa J.	unlisted	WWRR	Market, between 6th. and 7th.	1865 Dir-59

Name	Occupation	Railroad	Address	Year	Source
Murrin, E.	Cupola Tender	WWRR	Railroad	1871	Dir-176
Neilen, M.	Laborer	WWRR	unlisted	1871	Dir-178
Nettles, Joseph	Carpenter	WMRR	Richard Walker	1867	Dir-119
Newton, James	Blacksmith	WWRR	Mrs. Em. Elwell	1867	Dir-119
Niemeyer, J.E.	Engineer	WWRR	unlisted	1871	Dir-178
Nutt, H.	Baggage Master	WWRR	Jno. Nutt	1865	Dir-59
Nutt, Henry	Mechanic	WWRR	John Nutt	1867	Dir-121
Pae, Archie	Machinist	WWRR	2nd. and Harnett	1871	Dir-182
Palmer, [?]	Conductor	WWRR	4th., between Hanover and Brunswick	1871	Dir-182
Penny, Henry W.	Post Office Route Agent	WCARR	Chestnut, between 5th. and 6th.	1871	Dir-184
Peterson, C.W.	Tel Operator	WWRR	3rd., between Red Cross and Campbell	1871	Dir-186
Petteway, Wm. H.	Engineer	WWRR	Market, between 6th. and 7th	1865	Dir-63
Petteway, William H.	Engineer	WWRR	Market, between 6th. and 7th.	1867	Dir-125
Petteway, Wm. H.	Engineer	WCARR	Market, between 6th. and 7th.	1871	Dir-186
Plumbe, Charles	Conductor, Sleeping Car	WWRR	Front and Red Cross, cor.	1871	Dir-188
Poisson, W.M.	Ticket Agent	WWRR	Chestnut, between 3rd. and 4th.	1865	Dir-63
Poisson, William M.	General Ticket Agent	WWRR	Chestnut, between 3rd. and 4th.	1867	Dir-125
Poisson, J.D.	Passenger Dept. Agent	WWRR	5th. and Mulberry, cor.	1871	Dir-188
Poisson, Wm. M.	General Ticket Agent and Clerk	WWRR	Mulberry, between 2nd. and 3rd.	1871	Dir-188
Pool, John	Clerk	WCARR	Farmers' Hotel	1871	Dir-188
Potter, L.D.	Watchman	WCRRR	2nd. and Harnet, cor.	1867	Dir-125
Price, Joseph	Conductor	WCARR	Market, between 5th. and 6th.	1871	Dir-190
Price, R.W.	Clerk	WCARR	5th. and Orange, cor.	1871	Dir-190
Price, B.T.	Boiler Maker	WWRR	unlisted	1871	Dir-190
Pundt, John M.	Boiler Maker	WCARR	Church, between Front and 2nd.	1871	Dir-192
Quinlan, D.	Blacksmith	WWRR	unlisted	1871	Dir-194
Quinn, A.	Carpenter	WMRR	4th. and Harnet, cor.	1867	Dir-127
Rankin, Robert	Clerk	WCARR	Front and Princess	1871	Dir-194
Rankin, Robert G.	Clerk	WCARR	2nd., between Ann and Nun	1871	Dir-194
Reddick, John	Engineer	WCARR	4th., between Nun and Church	1871	Dir-196

Appendix B

Name	Title	Company	Address	Directory
Register, Gibson	Foundryman	WWRR	5th., between Ann and Nun	1871 Dir-196
Rockford, P.	Laborer	WWRR	unlisted	1871 Dir-198
Rosafy, E.M.	Post Office Route Agent	WWRR	Princess, between 8th. and 9th.	1871 Dir-198
Rotchford, Peter	Laborer	WWRR	2nd. and Princess, cor.	1871 Dir-198
Rowell, Joseph W.	Carpenter	WMRR	5th., between Dock and Orange	1867 Dir-131
Rowell, J.W.	Carpenter	WCARR	5th., between Dock and Orange	1871 Dir-198
Ruark, John H.	Blacksmith	WCARR	Castle, ab. Front	1871 Dir-198
Savage, D.F.	Engineer	WWRR	unlisted	1871 Dir-202
Sheno, H.W.	Clerk	WWRR	Purcell House	1871 Dir-206
Sheppard, J.	Laborer	WWRR	unlisted	1871 Dir-206
Sholar, A.M.	Pattern Maker	WCARR	5th., between Church and Nun	1871 Dir-206
Simpson, Thomas	Watchman	WWRR	6th. and Hanover, cor.	1871 Dir-208
Skipper, Ira	Greaser	WWRR	unlisted	1871 Dir-208
Sledge, [?]	Engineer	WWRR	4th., between Brunswick and Hanover	1871 Dir-210
Smith, Wm.	Sup't. Transportation	WWRR	Mulberry, between Front and 2nd.	1865 Dir-69
Smith, William	Superintendent of Transportation	WWRR	Mulberry, between Front and Secord	1867 Dir-137
Smith, Jefferson	Engineer	WCARR	Dock and 7th., cor.	1871 Dir-210
Smith, W.	Machinist	WWRR	unlisted	1871 Dir-210
Smith, Wm.	Master of Transportation	WWRR	5th. and Chestnut, NW cor.	1871 Dir-212
Spicer, Isaac	Blacksmith	WMRR	Front and Meares, cor.	1867 Dir-211 (Black)
Stewart, J.S.	Carpenter	WWRR	unlisted	1871 Dir-216
Strickland, Wm. H.	Boiler Maker	WWRR	unlisted	1871 Dir-218
Sullivan, Frederick	Blacksmith	WWRR	5th. and Bladen, cor.	1871 Dir-218
Swann, B.	Carpenter	WWRR	unlisted	1871 Dir-218
Swann, F. Alex	Ticket Agent	WCARR	5th., near Ann	1871 Dir-218
Swann, B.F.	Carpenter	WWRR	Mulberry and McRae, cor.	1871 Dir-222
Sweeney, Thomas U.	Machinist	WWRR	Edward C. Sweeney	1867 Dir-139
Sykes, Wm H.	Conductor	WMRR	Dock, between 6th. and 7th	1865 Dir-73

Railroad Employees Living in Wilmington, 1865–1871 189

Name	Occupation	Railroad	Address	Year	Source
Sykes, Wm. H.	Conductor	WMRR	unlisted	1867	Dir-139
Sykes, Augustus V.	not listed	WCARR	5th. and Bladen, cor.	1871	Dir-222
Sykes, W.H.	Road Master	WCARR	unlisted	1871	Dir-222
Sylva, Antone P.	Watchman	WWRR	McRae, between Walnut and Red Cross	1867	Dir-139
Taft, W.L.	Laborer	WWRR	unlisted	1871	Dir-222
Taylor, H.	Machinist	WWRR	unlisted	1871	Dir-223
Terry, Martin V.	Post Office Route Agent	WCRRR	unlisted	1871	Dir-223
Thomason, W.H.	Boiler Maker	WWRR	unlisted	1865	Dir-73
Thompson, J.W.	Secretary and Treasurer	WWRR	2nd., between Walnut and Red Cross	1867	Dir-141
Thompson, John W.	Secretary and Treasurer	WWRR	2nd., between Walnut and Red Cross	1871	Dir-223
Thompson, J.S.	Secretary and Treasurer	WWRR	Walnut, between 2nd. and 3rd.	1867	Dir-141
Thornton, Thomas	Engineer	WWRR	3rd. and Harnet, cor.	1871	Dir-224
Timelick, [?]	Moulder	WWRR	Hanover, between 2nd. and 3rd.	1871	Dir-224
Toft, William	Blacksmith	WWRR	unlisted	1871	Dir-226
Townsend, R.S.	Blacksmith	WWRR	unlisted	1871	Dir-226
Trachsler, J.	Painter	WWRR	Thompson Alley	1871	Dir-228
Vegers, M.	Watchman	WCARR	Front, between Princess and Chestnut	1871	Dir-230
Wade, William	Post Office Route Agent	WMRR	6th. and Market, cor.	1865	Dir-75
Walker, Wm A.	Secretary and Treasurer	WMRR	6th. and Market, cor.	1867	Dir-145
Walker, William A.	Secretary and Treasurer	WWRR	Orange, between 4th. and 5th.	1871	Dir-230
Walker, Jas. A.	Conductor, Sleeping Car	WCARR	Market and 6th., cor.	1871	Dir-230
Walker, William A.	Treasurer	WWRR	unlisted	1871	Dir-230
Wallace, S.D., Jr.	Conductor	WCARR	6th., between Bladen and Harnett	1871	Dir-232
Watkins, Bunyon	Carpenter	WWRR	unlisted	1871	Dir-234
Wheeler, C.F.	Carpenter	WCRRR	unlisted	1871	Dir-234
White, B.F.	Engineer	WCARR	unlisted	1865	Dir-77
Wilkins, B.W.	Road Master	WWRR	4th., between Hanover and Brunswick	1871	Dir-236
Wilkinson, John E.	Tinner	WWRR	unlisted	1871	Dir-236
Williams, A.	Painter	WWRR	unlisted	1871	Dir-236
Williams, B.W.	Engineer	WWRR	unlisted	1871	Dir-236

Appendix B

Name	Title	Company	Address	Directory
Williams, C.C.	Blacksmith	WWRR	unlisted	1871 Dir-236
Williams, J.M.	Laborer	WWRR	unlisted	1871 Dir-238
Williamson, George	Watchman	WCARR	unlisted	1871 Dir-238
Wilson, James	Moulder	WWRR	2nd., between Orange and Ann	1865 Dir-77
Wilson, Walter A.	Machinist	WWRR	Red Cross, between 3rd. and 4th	1865 Dir-77
Wilson, Walter A.	Engineer	WMRR	3rd. and Harnet, cor.	1867 Dir-149
Wilson, J.	Moulder	WWRR	4th., between Hanover and Brunswick	1871 Dir-240
Winder, John C.	Superintendent	WCARR	2nd., between Chestnut and Mulberry	1871 Dir-240
Woodliff, Wm. T.	Carpenter	WWRR	Harnett, between 3rd. and 4th.	1871 Dir-242
Woodward, J.H.	Coppersmith	WWRR	unlisted	1871 Dir-242
Woodward, J.F.	Carpenter	WWRR	unlisted	1871 Dir-242
Wright, Thos. H.	Conductor	WWRR	J.W. Wright	1867 Dir-151
Wright, J.G.	Assistant Freight Agent	WWRR	Market and Eight, cor.	1871 Dir-244
Yopp, Samuel	Carpenter	WWRR	8th., between Mulberry and Walnut	1865 Dir-81
Yopp, William J.	Clerk	WWRR	5th., between Princess and Chestnut	1867 Dir-151
Yopp, W.J.	Assistant Freight Agent	WWRR	5th., between Princess and Chestnutt	1871 Dir-246
Yopp, Alfred P.	Machinist	WWRR	5th., between Chestnut and Mulberry	1871 Dir-246
Yopp, C.M.	Blacksmith	WWRR	5th., between Princess and Chestnut	1871 Dir-246
Yopp, G.W.	Painter	WWRR	unlisted	1871 Dir-246
Young, Armand D., Jr.	Conductor, Sleeping Cars	WWRR	A.D. Young	1867 Dir-151

Railroad Employees in Wilmington, 1865–66

Living in Hotels

Name	Position	Railroad	Address
Adams, M.L.	Engineer	WWRR	City Hotel
Borden, J.C.	Conductor	WWRR	Railroad Hotel
Bryan, Henry	Engineer	WMRR	Railroad Hotel
Cutts, A.H.	Conductor	WWRR	City Hotel
Haynie, Wm.	Conductor	WMRR	City Hotel
Ivey, John R.	Conductor	WWRR	City Hotel

Boarding House, Living with a Fellow Employee or Relative

Name	Position	Railroad	Address
CLERICAL			
Alderman, I.T.	Freight Inspector	WCRRR	Edwin T. Love
Cantwell, Jno L.	Freight Agent	WMRR	Mrs. C.K. Price
Dudley, Guilford L.	Freight Agent	WWRR	A. Martin
Lippitt, Thos B.	Clerk	WWRR	Mrs. J.J. Lippitt
McRae, Walter G.	Store-keeper	WWRR	Mrs. C.K. Price
Nutt, H.	Baggage Master	WWRR	Jno. Nutt
SHOPS			
Boney, C.	Machinist	WWRR	P. Dahmer (store)
Conner, David	Carpenter	WWRR	S.G. Northrop (engineer)
Kinder, Thos. D.	Painter	WWRR	P. Dahmer (store)
Lotzin, H.L.	Watchman	WWRR	P. Dahmer (store)
McKay, J.S.	Mechanic	WWRR	L. Lyons
Wilson, Walter A.	Machinist	WWRR	W. Wilson
TRAIN CREW			
Browning, E.D.	Conductor	WWRR	Jas. Lumsden (saloon)
Cowan, John	Conductor	WCRRR	Mrs. S. Cowan
Laspeyre, M.	Engineer	WCRRR	Asa J. Murray
Marble, L.W.	Engineer	WWRR	E. Hansley
Morrison, R.	Engineer	unlisted	W.G. Fowler

North Front Sector (Market to Red Cross, and North Front to North Fifth)

Name	Position	Railroad	Address
OFFICERS			
Drane, Henry M.	Superintendent	WMRR	5th and Chestnut, cor.
Fremont, Col. S.L.	Superintendent	WWRR	Front and Walnut, cor.
Smith, Wm.	Sup't. Transportation	WWRR	Mulberry, between Front and 2nd
Thompson, J.W.	Secretary and Treasurer	WWRR	2nd between Walnut and Red Cross

CLERICAL

Beery, Stephen W.	Clerk	WWRR	Red Cross, between 2nd and 3rd
Bowden, Jos. N.	Baggage Master	WMRR	Princess and 4th
Poisson, W.M.	Ticket Agent	WWRR	Chestnut, between 3rd and 4th

SHOPS

Ellis, James H.	Carpenter	WWRR	3rd and Walnut, cor.

TRAIN CREW

Morrison, George	Conductor	WWRR	Front, between Mulberry and Walnut
Morrison, T.	Engineer	unlisted	5th and Princess, cor.

OTHER

Manning, E.W.	passenger boat	WCRRR	3rd and Mulberry
Bates, B.G.	unlisted	WMRR	4th and Walnut, cor.

Market Street Sector

Name	Position	Railroad	Address

OFFICERS

Walker, Wm. A.	Secretary and Treasurer	WMRR	6th and Market, cor.

CLERICAL

Calder, W.	Clerk	WMRR	Market and 6th, cor.
Langdon, Richard F.	Clerk	WWRR	Market, between 4th and 5th

TRAIN CREW

Petteway, Wh. H.	Engineer	WWRR	Market, between 6th and 7th

OTHER

Murray, Asa J.	unlisted	WWRR	Market, between 6th and 7th

Northeast Sector (east of Fifth Street and south of the railroad cut)

Name	Position	Railroad	Address

SHOPS

Dugid, W.H.	Carpenter	WWRR	8th, between Mulberry and Walnut
Lamon, W.W.	Machinist	WWRR	6th and Walnut, cor.
Yopp, Samuel	Carpenter	WWRR	8th, between Mulberry and Walnut

TRAIN CREW

Leggett, John E.	Conductor	WWRR	6th and Walnut, cor.
Lyons, L.B.	Conductor	WMRR	6th, between Princess and Chestnut

OTHER
Beck, Thomas	unlisted	WWRR	6th and Red Cross

Railroad Cut Sector (Campbell Street and north of the cut)

Name	Position	Railroad	Address
SHOPS			
Divine, John F.	Master Machinist	WWRR	4th, north of railroad
Garrity, Jas. H.	moulder	WWRR	North of railroad
Hartsfield, W.B.	Coppersmith	WWRR	3rd and Campbell, cor.

South Wilmington Sector (south of Market to Castle Street)

Name	Position	Railroad	Address
TRAIN CREW			
Sykes, Wm. H.	Conductor	WMRR	Dock, between 6th and 7th
SHOPS			
Wilson, James	Moulder	WWRR	2nd, between Orange and Ann
OTHER			
Green, James	unlisted	WMRR	Nun and 2nd, cor.

Railroad Employees in Wilmington, 1866–67

Boarding House, Living with a Fellow Employee or Relative

Name	Position	Railroad	Address
CLERICAL			
Bowden, Joseph N.	Baggage Master	WMRR	John C. Bowden
Cason, Edward F.	Clerk	WWRR	Mrs. M.S. McCaleb
Cowan, Platt D.	Clerk	WCRRR	Mrs. Sarah Cowan
Cowan, John	Ticket Agent	WCRRR	Mrs. Sarah Cowan
Dudley, Guildford L.	Freight Agent	WWRR	Alfred Martin
Latta, John R.	Clerk	WMRR	John C. Latta
McRae, Roderick	Clerk	WMRR	Gen. Alex. McRae
SHOPS			
Adkins, William	Machinist	WMRR	Henry Penny
Boyd, Adam	Carpenter	WMRR	R. Walker
Carey, Joseph W.	Carpenter	WMRR	William Kinyon
Dent, William	Pattern Maker	WWRR	Mrs. Hiram Sholar
Dickerson, John	Blacksmith	WWRR	Mrs. Hiram Sholar
Hall, David	Machinist	WMRR	Henry Penny
Hall, George	Master Machinist	WMRR	Mr. W.G. Milligan
Ledbetter, Robert	Carpenter	WWRR	J.F. Legwin
Nettles, Joseph	Carpenter	WMRR	Richard Walker
Newton, James	Blacksmith	WWRR	Mrs. Elwell

194   Appendix B

Nutt, Henry	Mechanic	WWRR	John Nutt
Sweeney, T. U.	Machinist	WWRR	Edward C. Sweeney

TRAIN CREW

Browning, E.D.	Conductor	WWRR	James C. Lumsden
Gardner, George	Engineer	WCRRR	James D. Gardner
Ivey, John R.	Conductor	WWRR	Jno. C. Bowden
Laspeyre, Mathew	Engineer	WMRR	Asa J. Murray
Morrison, Robert	Engineer	unlisted	Wm. G. Fowler
Wilson, Walter A.	Engineer	WMRR	W. Wilson, Third and Harnet, cor.
Wright, Thos. H.	Conductor	WWRR	J.W. Wright
Young, A. D. Jr.	Conductor	WWRR	A.D. Young

North Front Sector (Market to Red Cross, and North Front to North Fifth)

Name	*Position*	*Railroad*	*Address*

OFFICERS

Cowan, Robert H.	President	WCRRR	Front between Chestnut and Mulberry
Drane, Henry M.	President	WMRR	Fifth and Chestnut, cor.
Fremont, S.L.	Superintendent	WWRR	Front and Walnut, cor.
Smith, William	Sup't. Transportation	WWRR	Mulberry, between Front and 2nd
Thompson, John W.	Secretary and Treasurer	WWRR	2nd, between Walnut and Red Cross

CLERICAL

Alderman, I.T.	Freight Agent	WCRRR	Front and Mulberry, cor.
Giles, Norwood	Clerk	WMRR	3rd and Chestnut, cor.
Jacobs, William L.	Baggage Master	WMRR	4th and Princess, cor.
Poisson, William M.	General Ticket Agent	WWRR	Chestnut, between 3rd and 4th
Yopp, William J.	Clerk	WWRR	5th, between Princess and Chestnut

SHOPS

Divine, John F.	Master Machinist	WWRR	4th and Walnut, cor.
Ellis, James H.	Carpenter	WWRR	Walnut, between 2nd and 3rd
Hayden, P.	Blacksmith	WMRR	Chestnut, between 4th and 5th

TRAIN CREW

Cutts, A.H.	Conductor	WWRR	Red Cross, between 4th and 5th
Evans, John J.	Conductor	WMRR	Red Cross, between 4th and 5th
Morrison, George	Conductor	WWRR	Front, between Mulberry and Walnut

Railroad Employees Living in Wilmington, 1865–1871   195

OTHER
  Manning, E. W.   Steamer *Gen. Howard*   WCRRR   3rd and Mulberry, cor.

Market Street Sector

Name	Position	Railroad	Address
OFFICERS			
Walker, William A.	Secretary and Treasurer	WMRR	6th and Market, cor.
CLERICAL			
Cantwell, John L.	Freight Agent	WMRR	122 Market
Langdon, Richard F.	Clerk	WWRR	Market, between 7th and 8th
McRae, Walter G.	Clerk	WWRR	Market, between 7th and 8th
TRAIN CREW			
Petteway, Wm H.	Engineer	WWRR	Market, between 6th and 7th

Northeast Sector (east of Fifth Street and south of the railroad cut)

Name	Position	Railroad	Address
SHOPS			
Bell, James	Blacksmith	WMRR	Walnut and Anderson, cor.
Berry, Robert	Mechanic	WWRR	6th, between Red Cross and Campbell
Dugid, W.H.	Carpenter	WWRR	8th, between Mulberry and Walnut
Fox, George A.	Carpenter	WMRR	9th, between Princess and Chestnut
Jobson, William	Carpenter	WMRR	Princess, between 8th and 9th
Jones, S.	Machinist	WMRR	Chestnut, between 9th and 10th
TRAIN CREW			
Leggett, John E.	Conductor	WWRR	6th and Walnut, cor.
OTHER			
Beck, Thomas W.	unlisted	WMRR	6th and Red Cross, cor.
Sylva, Antone P.	Watchman	WWRR	McRae, between Walnut and Red Cross

Railroad Cut Sector (Campbell Street and north of the cut)

Name	Position	Railroad	Address
SHOPS			
Boon, Alexander	Machinist	WWRR	Hanover, between 2nd and 3rd

Name	Position	Railroad	Address
Cates, James J.	Carpenter	WMRR	Bladen and Sixth, cor.
Finlay, Robert	Mechanic	WWRR	Front and Harnet, cor.
Foster, David P.	Machinist	WMRR	Hanover, between 2nd and 3rd
Gill, R.J.	Foreman, Machine Shop	WWRR	Hanover, between 2nd and 3rd
Hankins, M.M.	Mechanic	WWRR	4th, between Brunswick and Bladen
Mayo, William E.	Machinist	WMRR	4th, between Brunswick and Bladen
Quinn, A.	Carpenter	WMRR	4th and Harnet, cor.
TRAIN CREW			
Best, James	Engineer	WMRR	3rd, between Harnett and Cowan
Ceggin, C.	Engineer	WMRR	5th and Bladen, cor.
Thornton, Thomas	Engineer	WWRR	3rd and Harnet, cor.
OTHER			
Potter, L.D.	Watchman	WCRRR	2nd and Harnet, cor.

South Wilmington Sector
(south of Market to Castle Street)

Name	Position	Railroad	Address
CLERICAL			
Lippitt, Thomas B.	Clerk	WMRR	Dock, between Front and 2nd
SHOPS			
Bell, William K.	Machinist	WWRR	5th, between Castle and Queen
Edwards, Amos	Machinist	WWRR	Fourth and Queen, cor.
Rowell, Joseph W.	Carpenter	WMRR	5th, between Dock and Orange
TRAIN CREW			
Green, James G.	Yard Master	WMRR	2nd and Nun, cor.

South of Castle Street Sector

Name	Position	Railroad	Address
SHOPS			
Spicer, Isaac	Blacksmith	WMRR	Front and Meares, cor.
OTHER			
Gordon, William	Watchman	WWRR	3rd and Wooster, cor.

Railroad Employees in Wilmington, 1870-71

Living in Hotels

Name	Position	Railroad	Address
Borden, J.C.	Conductor	WWRR	Purcell House
Browning, E.D.	Conductor	WWRR	Purcell House
Ellis, Joseph J.	unlisted	WCARR	Farmers' Hotel
Galvin, Edward	Watchman	WWRR	Farmers' Hotel
Gill, R.J.	Blacksmith	WWRR	Farmers' Hotel
High, W.H.	Conductor	WCARR	Purcell House
Knight, J.S.	Engineer	WWRR	Farmers' Hotel
Knowles, T.M.	Conductor	WWRR	Purcell House
Pool, John	Clerk	WCARR	Farmers' Hotel
Sheno, H.W.	Clerk	WWRR	Purcell House

North Front Sector (Market to Red Cross, and North Front to North Fifth)

Name	Position	Railroad	Address
Officers			
Bridgers, R.R.	President	WWRR*	Front and Chestnut
Flanner, Charles	Master of Transportation	WWRR	Front, between Red Cross and Walnut
Fremont, S.L.	Superintendent	WWRR*	Front, between Princess and Chestnut
Thompson, J.S.	Secretary and Treasurer	WWRR	Walnut, between 2nd and 3rd
Winder, John C.	Superintendent	WCARR	2nd, between Chestnut and Mulberry
*Also for the WCARR			
Clerical			
Boatwright, J. Hal	Clerk	WCARR	2nd, between Chestnut and Mulberry
Bowden, William N.	Book Keeper	WCARR	2nd and Chestnut, cor.
Brooks, E.H.	Post Office Route Agent	WCARR	Front, between Market and Princess
Carroll, John	Post Office Route Agent	WWRR	Front, between Market and Princess
Cowan, Platt D.	Freight Agent	WCRRR	Chestnut and 4th, cor.
Davis, W.A.H.	Baggage Agent	WCARR	3rd, between Red Cross and Campbell
Green, M.M.	Post Office Route Agent	WWRR	Front, between Market and Princess
Kelly, Augustus H.	Clerk	WWRR	2nd and Walnut
Love, A.D.	Clerk	WCRRR	Mulberry, between 4th and 5th
Love, Armand D.	Freight Clerk	WCRRR	Mulberry, between 4th and 5th

198   Appendix B

Penny, Henry W.	Post Office Route Agent	WCARR	Chestnut, between 5th and 6th
Poisson, J.D.	Passenger Dept. Agent	WWRR	5th and Mulberry, cor.
Poisson, Wm. M.	General Ticket Agent	WWRR	Mulberry, between 2nd and 3rd
Rankin, Robert	Clerk	WCARR	Front and Princess
Smith, Wm.	Master of Transportation	WWRR	5th and Chestnut, NW cor.
Wade, William	Post Office Route Agent	WCARR	Front, between Princess and Chestnut
Yopp, W.J.	Assistant Freight Agent	WWRR	5th, between Princess and Chestnut

SHOPS

Calais, Wm. J.	Master Carpenter	WCARR	4th, between Mulberry and Walnut
Galvin, Patrick	Boiler Maker	WWRR	Walnut, between 3rd and 4th
Hodges, Charles	Painter	WCARR	5th and Chestnut, cor.
Kenyon, Thomas	Carpenter	WCARR	5th and Chestnut, cor.
Joyce, Richard	Laborer	WWRR	Mulberry, between Front and Water
Lyons, James W.	Machinist	WCARR	3rd, between Red Cross and Campbell
Rotchford, Peter	Laborer	WWRR	2nd and Princess, cor.
Yopp, Alfred P.	Machinist	WWRR	5th, between Chestnut and Mulberry
Yopp, C.M.	Blacksmith	WWRR	5th, between Chestnut and Mulberry

TRAIN CREW

Bowden, Joseph	Conductor	WCARR	4th and Princess, cor.
Bryant, B.F.	Conductor	WCARR	Mulberry and 4th, cor.
Cutts, A.H.	Conductor	WWRR	5th and Red Cross, cor.
Evans, J.J.	Conductor	WCARR	4th and Red Cross, cor.
Hessinger, J.G.	Engineer	WWRR	5th and Walnut, cor.
Jarvis, Wm. J.	Conductor	WCARR	Front and Red Cross, cor.
Leggett, J.E.	Conductor	WWRR	Mulberry, near Front
Love, E.T.	Engineer	WCRRR	2nd, between Mulberry and Chestnut
Love, Richard S.	Conductor	WCRRR	Mulberry and Front, cor.
Lyons, Lawrence B.	Engineer	WCARR	3rd, between Red Cross and Campbell
Meredith, James T.	Passenger Train Hand	WWRR	Mulberry, cor Walnut [?]
Meredith, S.L.	Engineer	WWRR	Red Cross, between 2nd and 3rd
Plumbe, Charles	Conductor, Sleeping Car	WWRR	Front and Red Cross, cor.

OTHER

Name	Position	Railroad	Address
Peterson, C.W.	Tel. Operator	WWRR	3rd, between Red Cross and Campbell

Market Street Sector

Name	Position	Railroad	Address
OFFICERS			
Dudley, G.L.	Auditor	WWRR	Market, between 4th and 5th
Martin, Silas N.	President	WCRRR	Market, between 2nd and 3rd
Walker, William A.	Treasurer	WCARR	Market and 6th, cor.
CLERICAL			
Hill, James H.	Freight Agent	WCARR	Market, between Front and 2nd
Langdon, R.F.	Trace Clerk	WWRR	Market and 8th, cor.
Lord, John B.	Prov. Agent	WCARR	Market, between 2nd and 3rd
Wright, J.G.	Assistant Freight Agent	WWRR	Market and 8th, cor.
SHOPS			
Burr, Charles	Painter	WCARR	49 Market
Corbett, Wm.	Mechanic	WCARR	Market and 7th, cor.
TRAIN CREW			
Custice, M.A.	Conductor	WCARR	3rd and Market, cor.
Petteway, Wm. H.	Engineer	WCARR	Market, between 6th and 7th
Price, Joseph	Conductor	WCARR	Market, between 5th and 6th

Northeast Sector (east of Fifth Street and south of the railroad cut)

Name	Position	Railroad	Address
CLERICAL			
Allen, William H.	Master Transportation	WCRRR	7th, between Mulberry and Chestnut
Kelly, Oliver	Clerk	WCRRR	Walnut and 7th, cor.
Latta, John R.	Freight and Ticket Agent	WCARR	7th, between Walnut and Mulberry
Rosafy, E.M.	Post Office Route Agent	WWRR	Princess, between 8th and 9th
SHOPS			
Corden, W.W.	Carpenter	WCARR	8th, between Mulberry and Walnut
Hogan, J.	Car and Pump Repairer	WWRR	8th and McRae, cor.

Swann, B.F.	Carpenter	WWRR	Mulberry and McRae, cor.
TRAIN CREW			
Corbett, William J.	Engineer	WCRRR	Mulberry, between 7th and 8th
Gardner, J.D., Jr.	Conductor	WCARR	Chestnut, between 8th and 9th
Fox, George A.	Engineer	WWRR	9th, between Princess and Chestnut
Howland, Samuel	Conductor	WCRRR	7th, between Mulberry and Chestnut
OTHER			
Bell, Daniel	not listed	WWRR	near Anderson, near Gwynn
Vegers, M.	Watchman	WWRR	Thompson Alley

Railroad Cut Sector (Campbell Street and north of the cut)

Name	Position	Railroad	Address
CLERICAL			
Adams, Geo. H.	Route Agent	WCARR	9th and Swann, cor.
Allen, Miles	Section Master	WCRRR	3rd, near Harnett
Barry, John	Road Master	WWRR	4th, between Brunswick and Bladen
Fillyaw, De Leon	Transfer Agent	WWRR*	4th, between Bladen and Harnett
Hoster, J.O.	Post Office Route Agent	WWRR	5th and Brunswick, cor.
Love, Thomas L.	Clerk	WCARR	6th and Bladen, cor.
McFarland, Wm. H.	Baggage Agent	WWRR	Campbell, between 2nd and 3rd
Miller, Edgar	Post Office Route Agent	WWRR	Harnett, between 6th and 7th
*Also for the WCARR			
SHOPS			
Bisset, John F.	Foreman, Machine Shop	WWRR	Hanover and Third, cor.
Bradley, John	Machinist	WWRR	Hanover, between 2nd and 3rd
Carroll, Michael	Laborer	WWRR	3rd and Brunswick, cor.
Cogden, Caisen	Machinist	WCARR	5th and Bladen, cor.
Cummings, James M.	Painter	WWRR	4th, between Hanover and Brunswick
Davis, Thomas J.	Carpenter	WCARR	4th and Hanover, cor.
Dent, William	Pattern Maker	WWRR	Hanover, between 2nd and 3rd
Doughty, Henry S.	Carpenter	WWRR	Campbell, between 3rd and 4th
Finley, Robert	Machinist	WWRR	2nd, between Bladen and Harnett

Railroad Employees Living in Wilmington, 1865-1871

Grant, William	Machinist	WWRR	Hanover, between 2nd and 3rd
Hankins, M.M.	Machinist	WWRR	4th, between Bladen and Brunswick
Harris, Charles M.	Carpenter	WCARR	7th and Hanover, cor.
Hartsfield, Wm.	Coppersmith	WWRR	Hanover, between 2nd and 3rd
Heath, Daniel W.	Moulder	WCRRR	2nd, between Hanover and Brunswick
Hicks, Hardy	Machinist	WWRR	3rd and Campbell, cor.
Hines, Clarence	Carpenter	WCARR	Swann, between 5th and 6th
Hines, Enoch J.	Machinist	WWRR	3rd and Campbell, cor.
Hines, Eli W.	Carpenter	WWRR	Swann, between 5th and 6th
Hunter, S.J.	Carpenter	WWRR	Campbell, between 3rd and 4th
Ives, Jesse	Carpenter	WWRR	4th and Harnett, cor.
King, James	Greaser	WWRR	Campbell, between 3rd and 4th
Mahoney, Wm. B.	Carpenter	WWRR	Campbell, between 3rd and 4th
McEnessey, Dennis	Laborer	WWRR	Hanover, below 3rd
McEntee, John	Carpenter	WWRR	4th, between Hanover and Brunswick
McMillian, F.A. Jr.	Machinist	WWRR	Hanover, between 2nd and 3rd
Murphy, (not given)	Blacksmith	WWRR	Hanover, between 2nd and 3rd
Murrin, E.	Cupola Tender	WWRR	Railroad
Pae, Archie	Machinist	WWRR	2nd and Harnett
Sullivan, Frederick	Blacksmith	WWRR	5th and Bladen, cor.
Timelick, (not given)	Moulder	WWRR	Hanover, between 2nd and 3rd
Watkins, Bunyon	Carpenter	WCARR	6th, between Bladen and Harnett
Wilkinson, John E.	Tinner	WWRR	4th, between Hanover and Brunswick
Wilson, J.	Moulder	WWRR	4th, between Hanover and Brunswick
Woodliff, Wm. T.	Carpenter	WWRR	Harnett, between 3rd and 4th

TRAIN CREW

Blackman, E.	Engineer	WWRR	2nd, between Hanover and Brunswick
Carter, Robert	Engineer	WCARR	Swann, between 5th and 6th
Casey, Richard	Engineer	WWRR	4th, between Brunswick and Hanover
Fillyaw, D.L.	Conductor	WWRR	4th, between Bladen and Harnett

Name	Position	Railroad	Address
Horn, Guildford	Engineer	WWRR	Campbell, between 3rd and 4th
McMillian, F.A.	Engineer	WCARR	Hanover, between 2nd and 3rd
Palmer, (not given)	Conductor	WWRR	4th, between Hanover and Brunswick
Sledge, (not given)	Engineer	WWRR	4th, between Brunswick and Hanover

OTHER

Name	Position	Railroad	Address
Hill, Charles E.	Watchman	WCRRR	2nd, between Hanover and Brunswick
Moore, John	Watchman	WCARR	2nd, between Nun and Church
Simpson, Thomas	Watchman	WWRR	6th and Hanover, cor.
Sykes, Augustus V.	unlisted	WCARR	5th and Bladen, cor.

South Wilmington Sector (south of Market to Castle Street)

Name	Position	Railroad	Address

CLERICAL

Name	Position	Railroad	Address
Dicksey, P.T.	Baggage Master	WWRR	6th and Castle, cor.
Green, James G.	Master Transportation	WCARR	Nun and 2nd, cor.
Griffith, W.H.	Baggage Master	WWRR	6th and Castle, cor.
James, Theo. C.	Special Traveling Agent	WWRR*	3rd and Dock, cor.
Morris, Richard	Clerk	WCARR	2nd, between Ann and Nun
Price, R.W.	Clerk	WCARR	5th and Orange, cor.
Rankin, Robert G.	Clerk	WCARR	2nd, between Ann and Nun
Swann, F. Alex	Ticket Agent	WCARR	5th, near Ann

*Also for the WCARR

SHOPS

Name	Position	Railroad	Address
Bowen, Samuel	Machinist	WCARR	Front, below Dock
Brunson, Isaac N.	Carpenter	WCARR	Castle, between 7th and 8th
Corbett, William F.	Machinist	WCARR	4th, between Nun and Church
Folstead, John A.	Blacksmith	WCARR	Church, between 4th and 5th
Folstead, John P.	Blacksmith	WCARR	Church, between 4th and 5th
Hale, David L.	Blacksmith	WCARR	Front, between Church and Castle
Hall, George	Master Machinist	WCARR	4th, near Orange
Hodges, Fred	Cabinet Maker	WCARR	Front, below Dock
Jobson, William A.	Car Builder	WCARR	Nun, between 5th and 6th

Kelly, Bartholomew	Carpenter	WCARR	Church, between 4th and 5th
McCumber, James	Blacksmith	WWRR	Church, between 6th and 7th
McGarity, James H.	Moulder	WCARR	4th, between Nun and Church
Pundt, John M.	Boiler Maker	WCARR	Church, between Front and 2nd
Register, Gibson	Foundryman	WWRR	5th, between Ann and Nun
Rowell, J.W.	Carpenter	WCARR	5th, between Dock and Orange
Ruark, John H.	Blacksmith	WCARR	Castle, ab. Front
Sholar, A.M.	Pattern Maker	WCARR	5th, between Church and Nun

TRAIN CREW

Everett, Edward	Conductor	WWRR	Front and Nun, cor.
McClenny, Absalom	Engineer	not listed	Front and Ann, cor.
Morrison, George	Conductor	WWRR	Front, between Dock and Orange
Reddick, John	Engineer	WCARR	4th, between Nun and Church
Smith, Jefferson	Engineer	WCARR	Dock and 7th, cor.
Walker, Jas. A.	Conductor, Sleeping Car	WCARR	Orange, between 4th and 5th

South of Castle Street Sector

Name	Position	Railroad	Address

SHOPS

Bell, Wm. T.	Machinist	WWRR	5th, between Castle and Queen
Britt, William	Moulder	WCARR	4th, between Queen and Wooster
McCumber, Thomas	Blacksmith	WWRR	4th and Queen, cor.

OTHER

Goodman, William	Watchman	WWRR	8th and Dawson, cor.
Gordon, William	Watchman	WCARR	Dawson, between 6th and 7th
Harker, Wm.	unlisted	WWRR	5th and Queen, cor.

Appendix C: Freight Shipments for the Confederate Government, 1861

Source

United States, National Archive, *Confederate Papers Relating to Citizens or Business Firms, compiled 1874–1899, documenting the period 1861–1865* (Washington, DC: National Archives, 1874–1899), Records Group 109, ARC Identifier 2133274 / MLR Number PI101 180, Roll 1122, Document 261.

Abbreviations

WMRR	Wilmington & Manchester Railroad Company
*	No weight value given

Freight Shipments for the Confederate Government, 1861 205

Date	Source	Destination	Item	Weight
FOOD				
8/01/1861	WMRR	PRR	Rice	32,000
8/02/1861	WMRR	PRR	Rice	10,559
8/03/1861	WMRR	PRR	Rice	14,707
8/05/1861	WMRR	Richmond	Rice	700
8/05/1861	WMRR	Richmond	Rice	14,161
8/08/1861	WMRR	Richmond	Rice	143,552
8/20/1861	WMRR	Richmond	Rice	6,857
8/21/1861	WMRR	Richmond	Rice	23,325
8/26/1861	WMRR	Richmond	Rice	8,255
8/30/1861	WMRR	Richmond	Salt	20,760
8/31/1861	WMRR	Richmond	Bacon	12,864
8/31/1861	WMRR	Richmond	Salt	12,580
8/31/1861	WMRR	Richmond	Bacon	54,216
8/31/1861	WMRR	Richmond	Rice	12,357
8/31/1861	WMRR	Richmond	Salt	13,600
8/31/1861	WMRR	Richmond	Rice	682
8/31/1861	WMRR	Richmond	Rice	1,551
9/03/1861	WWRR	Richmond	Rice	27,796
9/04/1861	WWRR	Manassas	Bacon	48,982
9/04/1861	WWRR	Richmond	Bacon	17,393
9/04/1861	WWRR	Richmond	Salt	13,320
9/05/1861	WMRR	Richmond	Bacon	23,718
9/08/1861	WMRR	Richmond	Salt	9,900
9/08/1861	WMRR	Manassas	Bacon	34,700
9/08/1861	WMRR	Richmond	Pork	*
9/08/1861	WMRR	Manassas	Pork	*
9/08/1861	WMRR	Richmond	Bacon	47,945
9/08/1861	WMRR	Richmond	Salt	14,520

Appendix C

Date	Source	Destination	Item	Weight
9/08/1861	WMRR	Richmond	Coffee	48,900
9/09/1861	WMRR	Staunton, VA	Bacon	13,474
9/09/1861	WMRR	Manassas	Bacon	2,100
9/10/1861	WMRR	Manassas	Bacon	15,480
9/10/1861	WMRR	Lynchburg	Bacon	14,669
9/10/1861	*	Lynchburg	Rice	14,745
9/10/1861	WMRR	Richmond	Bacon	14,261
9/10/1861	WMRR	Richmond	Molasses	16,400
9/10/1861	WMRR	Manassas	Bacon	13,824
9/10/1861	WMRR	Richmond	Bacon	858
9/10/1861	WMRR	Manassas	50 bbl. Pork	*
9/10/1861	WMRR	Manassas	50 bbl. Pork	*
9/10/1861	WMRR	Richmond	Molasses	15,660
9/10/1861	WMRR	Richmond	Molasses	540
9/10/1861	WMRR	Manassas	Bacon	15,115
9/10/1861	WMRR	Manassas	Bacon	5,683
9/10/1861	WMRR	Richmond	Bacon	9,145
9/10/1861	WMRR	Manassas	37 bbl. Pork	*
9/10/1861	WMRR	Richmond	Bacon	13,165
9/10/1861	WMRR	Manassas	35 bbl. Pork	*
9/10/1861	WMRR	Manassas	Bacon	1,095
9/10/1861	WMRR	Richmond	6 bbl. Pork	*
9/10/1861	WMRR	Richmond	10 bags Rice Flour	*
9/10/1861	WMRR	Manassas	20 bbl. Pork	*
9/11/1861	WMRR	Manassas	200 bbl. Pork	*
9/11/1861	WMRR	Richmond	Molasses	77,761
9/11/1861	WMRR	Richmond	Bacon	16,097
9/11/1861	WMRR	Richmond	Bacon	15,015
9/11/1861	WMRR	Richmond	Bacon	4,594

Freight Shipments for the Confederate Government, 1861   207

Date	Carrier		Destination	Commodity	Amount
9/11/1861	WMRR		Richmond	Molasses	3,240
9/11/1861	WMRR		Manassas	Bacon	7,550
9/12/1861	WMRR		Richmond	Bacon	22,846
9/12/1861	WMRR		Richmond	Bacon	2,252
9/14/1861	WMRR		Richmond	Bacon	6,522
9/14/1861	WMRR		Manassas	Bacon	8,517
9/14/1861	WMRR		Manassas	Bacon	8,718
9/14/1861	WMRR		Richmond	Bacon	4,312
9/14/1861	WMRR		Richmond	Sugar	2,510
9/14/1861	WMRR		Richmond	Sugar	13,693
9/17/1861	WMRR		Richmond	Molasses	1,080
9/17/1861	WMRR		Richmond	Rice	29,595
9/17/1861	WMRR		Richmond	37 bbl. Whiskey	*
9/17/1861	WMRR		Richmond	Molasses	30,421
9/17/1861	WMRR		Manassas	34 bbl. Pork	*
9/17/1861	WMRR		Lynchburg	Salt	15,750
9/17/1861	WMRR		Richmond	Sugar	17,345
9/17/1861	WMRR		Richmond	Rice	2,800
9/18/1861	WMRR		Richmond	Sugar	12,335
9/18/1861	WMRR		Richmond	Bacon	11,730
9/20/1861	R.G. Rankin (Wilmington)		Lynchburg	Rice	14,045
9/20/1861	R.G. Rankin (Wilmington)		Richmond	Rice	100,496
9/20/1861	WMRR		Richmond	40 bbl. Whiskey	*
9/20/1861	WMRR		Richmond	50 bbl. Pork	*
9/20/1861	WMRR		Richmond	Bacon	16,878
9/20/1861	WMRR		Manassas	Bacon	14,522
9/20/1861	WMRR		Manassas	50 bbl. Pork	*
9/27/1861	WMRR		Richmond	Molasses	14,040
9/27/1861	WMRR		Richmond	5 bbl. Whiskey	*
9/21/1861	WMRR		Richmond	50 bbl. Pork	*

Appendix C

Date	Source	Destination	Item	Weight
9/21/1861	WMRR	Richmond	Molasses	27,540
9/21/1861	WMRR	Richmond	2 sacks Salt, 13 bags Meal	*
9/21/1861	WMRR	Richmond	Bacon	28,784
9/21/1861	WMRR	Richmond	Bacon	3,650
9/21/1861	WMRR	Richmond	36 bbl. Pork	*
9/21/1861	WMRR	Richmond	Sugar	14,445
9/23/1861	WMRR	Richmond	130 bbl. Whiskey	*
9/23/1861	WMRR	Richmond	Sugar	17,080
9/23/1861	WMRR	Richmond	Bacon	15,015
9/23/1861	WMRR	Richmond	Molasses	55,620
9/23/1861	WMRR	Richmond	Rice	11,145
9/23/1861	WMRR	Richmond	37 bbl. Pork	*
9/23/1861	WMRR	Richmond	Molasses	16,200
9/25/1861	WMRR	Manassas	50 bbl. Pork	*
9/25/1861	WMRR	Richmond	Molasses	24,840
9/25/1861	WMRR	Richmond	Sugar	14,805
9/25/1861	WMRR	Richmond	Bacon	21,058
9/25/1861	WMRR	Richmond	45 bbl. Whiskey	*
9/25/1861	WMRR	Richmond	Rice	5,557
9/25/1861	WMRR	Richmond	Molasses	6,100
9/25/1861	WMRR	Richmond	Molasses	13,500
9/25/1861	WMRR	Richmond	Molasses	6,440
9/25/1861	WMRR	Richmond	Coffee	16,200
9/26/1861	WMRR	Richmond	Rice	39,328
9/26/1861	WMRR	Richmond	Sugar	32,955
9/26/1861	WMRR	Richmond	Molasses	21,600
9/26/1861	WMRR	Richmond	Bacon	7,302
9/26/1861	WMRR	Richmond	4 bbl. Pork	*
9/27/1861	WMRR	Richmond	59 bbl. Pork	*

Freight Shipments for the Confederate Government, 1861 209

Date	RR	Destination	Commodity	Amount
9/27/1861	WMRR	Manassas	16 bbl. Pork	*
9/27/1861	WMRR	Richmond	Rice	4,255
9/27/1861	WMRR	Richmond	5 bbl. Whiskey	*
9/27/1861	WMRR	Richmond	Bacon	3,633
9/27/1861	WMRR	Richmond	Sugar	2,700
9/27/1861	WMRR	Manassas	Bacon	4,332
10/01/1861	WMRR	Richmond	Sugar	23,560
10/01/1861	WMRR	Richmond	Rice	34,230
10/01/1861	WMRR	Richmond	Coffee	3,200
10/01/1861	WMRR	Richmond	Coffee	8,400
10/03/1861	WMRR	Richmond	Sugar	47,845
10/03/1861	WMRR	Richmond	Sugar	9,225
10/03/1861	WMRR	Richmond	Bacon	1,865
10/03/1861	WMRR	Richmond	5 bbl. Whiskey	*
10/03/1861	WMRR	Richmond	Rice	16,100
10/04/1861	WMRR	Richmond	Sugar	29,485
10/05/1861	WMRR	Richmond	45 bbl. Whiskey	*
10/05/1861	WMRR	Richmond	Rice	12,745
10/05/1861	WMRR	Richmond	Bacon	7,824
10/08/1861	WMRR	Richmond	Sugar	57,515
10/09/1861	WMRR	Richmond	Bacon	5,087
10/09/1861	WMRR	Richmond	Bacon	974
10/09/1861	WMRR	Richmond	Rice	117,721
10/10/1861	WMRR	Richmond	40 bbl. Whiskey	*
10/10/1861	WMRR	Richmond	Bacon	786
10/10/1861	WMRR	Richmond	Sugar	9,590
10/10/1861	WMRR	Richmond	Rice	6,965
10/11/1861	WMRR	Richmond	Sugar	2,785
10/14/1861	WMRR	Richmond	Rice	2,435
10/14/1861	WMRR	Richmond	Bacon	3,431

210 Appendix C

Date	Source	Destination	Item	Weight
10/14/1861	WMRR	Richmond	7 bbl. Pork	*
10/14/1861	WMRR	Richmond	Coffee	350
10/14/1861	WMRR	Richmond	Rice	12,585
10/14/1861	WMRR	Richmond	Rice	30,064
10/14/1861	WMRR	Richmond	Coffee	22,400
10/15/1861	WMRR	Richmond	Coffee	20,800
10/15/1861	WMRR	Richmond	Rice	82,863
10/15/1861	WMRR	Richmond	50 bbl. Pork	*
10/15/1861	R.G. Rankin (Wilmington)	Richmond	Rice	81,455
10/15/1861	WMRR	Richmond	Sugar	14,420
10/16/1861	WMRR	Manassas	69 bbl. Pork	*
10/16/1861	WMRR	Richmond	Rice	13,251
10/16/1861	WMRR	Richmond	Sugar	14,440
10/16/1861	WMRR	Richmond	Bacon	4,205
10/16/1861	WMRR	Richmond	Bacon	7,628
10/16/1861	WMRR	Richmond	Flour, Rice, misc.	14,150
10/16/1861	WMRR	Richmond	Bacon	6,688
10/16/1861	WMRR	Richmond	Bacon	20,762
10/16/1861	WMRR	Richmond	Bacon	1,009
10/17/1861	WMRR	Richmond	Rice	14,015
10/17/1861	WMRR	Richmond	47 bbl. Pork	*
10/17/1861	WMRR	Richmond	Sugar	13,815
10/17/1861	WMRR	Richmond	Rice	740
10/17/1861	WMRR	Richmond	Sugar	7,360
10/17/1861	WMRR	Richmond	Sugar	7,800
10/18/1861	WMRR	Richmond	Sugar	16,135
10/18/1861	WMRR	Richmond	Sugar	1,420
10/18/1861	WMRR	Richmond	2 bbl. Crackers	*
10/18/1861	WMRR	Richmond	11 bbl. Liquor	*

Freight Shipments for the Confederate Government, 1861   211

Date	RR	Destination	Commodity	Amount
10/19/1861	WMRR	Richmond	Sugar	6,150
10/19/1861	WMRR	Richmond	Sugar	5,460
10/19/1861	WMRR	Richmond	7 bbl. Liquor	*
10/19/1861	WMRR	Richmond	Sugar	15,195
10/19/1861	WMRR	Richmond	1 bbl. Pork	*
10/19/1861	WMRR	Richmond	Molasses	5,400
10/19/1861	WMRR	Manassas	Bacon	11,648
10/19/1861	WMRR	Richmond	Bacon	3,963
10/19/1861	WMRR	Richmond	45 bbl. Pork	*
10/21/1861	WMRR	Richmond	Rice	41,811
10/22/1861	WMRR	Richmond	Molasses	7,020
10/22/1861	WMRR	Richmond	Sugar	6,855
10/23/1861	WMRR	Richmond	Sugar	16,820
10/23/1861	WMRR	Richmond	Bacon	12,468
10/23/1861	WMRR	Richmond	Sugar	9,765
10/23/1861	WMRR	Richmond	Sugar	14,390
10/23/1861	WMRR	Richmond	Sugar	14,560
10/23/1861	WMRR	Richmond	Sugar	10,538
10/23/1861	WMRR	Richmond	Bacon	5,756
10/23/1861	WMRR	Richmond	Bacon	13,665
10/23/1861	WMRR	Richmond	Bacon	6,931
10/24/1861	WMRR	Richmond	Sugar	8,827
10/24/1861	WMRR	Richmond	Bacon	4,976
10/25/1861	WMRR	Richmond	Bacon	6,578
10/25/1861	WMRR	Richmond	Sugar	4,500
10/25/1861	WMRR	Charlottesville	Sugar	9,805
10/25/1861	WMRR	Richmond	Bacon	9,131
10/25/1861	WMRR	Richmond	Bacon	6,436
10/25/1861	WMRR	Charlottesville	Sugar	5,715
10/25/1861	WMRR	Richmond	Bacon	11,278

212   Appendix C

Date	Source	Destination	Item	Weight
10/25/1861	WMRR	Richmond	Bacon	300
10/25/1861	WMRR	Richmond	Bacon	4,983
10/25/1861	WMRR	Charlottesville	Sugar	8,230
10/25/1861	WMRR	Richmond	Sugar	4,410
10/25/1861	WMRR	Richmond	Sugar	4,495
10/25/1861	WMRR	Richmond	Bacon	1,902
10/29/1861	H.M. Drane (Wilmington)	Richmond	Rice	86,974
10/29/1861	WMRR	Richmond	Rice	30,800
10/29/1861	WMRR	Richmond	Sugar	9,010
10/29/1861	WMRR	Richmond	Bacon	33,056
10/29/1861	WMRR	Richmond	Sugar	74,325
10/29/1861	WMRR	Richmond	Bacon	25,242
10/31/1861	WMRR	Richmond	Sugar	31,437
10/31/1861	WMRR	Richmond	Bacon	11,782
10/31/1861	WMRR	Richmond	Rice	17,030
10/31/1861	WMRR	Richmond	17 bbl. Salt	*
10/31/1861	WMRR	Richmond	Coffee	14,400
10/21/1861	Goldsboro to Weldon	Yorktown	2 boxes Provisions	200

ARMS AND EQUIPMENT

Date	Source	Destination	Item	Weight
8/03/1861	WMRR	Weldon	Tents	3,400
8/07/1861	WMRR	Richmond	Powder	*
8/12/1861	WMRR	Richmond	Tents	725
8/12/1861	WMRR	Richmond	Tents	22,712
8/15/1861	WMRR	Richmond	Tents	12,860
8/15/1861	WMRR	Richmond	Tents and Blankets	13,769
8/15/1861	WMRR	Richmond	Tents	700

Freight Shipments for the Confederate Government, 1861 — 213

Date	Carrier	Destination	Contents	Weight
8/21/1861	WMRR	Richmond	25 bales domestic, 3 boxes	8,590
8/21/1861	WMRR	Richmond	Tents	1,750
8/22/1861	WMRR	Richmond	Tents	7,756
8/26/1861	WMRR	Richmond	Tents	11,350
8/26/1861	WMRR	Culpeper C.H.	Cots, 4 boxes, camp stoves	2,757
8/29/1861	WMRR	Richmond	20 bales Drills	7,500
8/29/1861	WMRR	Richmond	Tents	5,358
8/29/1861	WMRR	Richmond	Hospital stores	600
8/29/1861	WMRR	Richmond	Hospital stores	3,465
8/27/1861	WMRR	Richmond	Tents, Shoes, Blankets	8,482
8/27/1861	WMRR	Richmond	Tent	4,845
8/27/1861	WMRR	Richmond	Tents, Axes, Tin Ware	1,200
8/30/1861	WMRR	Richmond	1 bale, 12 boxes, Tents	7,080
8/30/1861	WMRR	Richmond	Tents	6,258
8/30/1861	WMRR	Richmond	Camp Stools, Cots. boxes, bales	1,018
8/31/1861	WMRR	New Bern	Gun Powder	2,000
9/05/1861	WMRR	Richmond	Knap Sacks	3,040
9/08/1861	WMRR	Richmond	Haversacks	1,920
9/08/1861	WMRR	Richmond	Tents, Shoes, Blankets	6,441
9/08/1861	WMRR	Richmond	152 Kegs Powder	*
9/08/1861	WMRR	Richmond	Cots, Stools	646
9/09/1861	WMRR	Richmond	Tents	7,566
9/09/1861	WMRR	Staunton, VA	Cots, Camp stools, Tents, bales, boxes	3,056
9/08/1861	WMRR	Richmond	Cannon	3,200
9/10/1861	WMRR	Richmond	Tents	9,900
9/10/1861	WMRR	Fairfax, VA	Tents	190
9/11/1861	WMRR	Richmond	Candles, Soap	16,000
9/11/1861	WMRR	Richmond	Tents	10,208
9/11/1861	WMRR	Richmond	Cots, Stools	685
9/11/1861	WMRR	Richmond	Hospital stores	1,200

Appendix C

Date	Source	Destination	Item	Weight
9/11/1861	WMRR	Richmond	Blankets	1,180
9/14/1861	Goldsboro	Manassas	Clothing	1,329
9/17/1861	WMRR	Richmond	Cots, Camp stools	650
9/17/1861	WMRR	Richmond	Hospital stores	311
9/17/1861	WMRR	Richmond	Hospital stores	575
9/17/1861	WMRR	Fairfax, VA	Clothing	1,270
9/17/1861	WMRR	Richmond	Blankets	2,590
9/19/1861	WMRR	Richmond	Hospital stores	960
9/20/1861	WMRR	Richmond	Hospital stores	100
9/20/1861	WMRR	Richmond	Tents	4,200
9/20/1861	WMRR	Richmond	Cots, Stools	680
9/20/1861	WMRR	Richmond	Bunks, Stools	6,028
9/27/1861	WMRR	Richmond	Soap	28,400
9/27/1861	WMRR	Richmond	Boxes etc. and Tents	9,720
9/21/1861	WMRR	Richmond	Hospital stores	600
9/21/1861	WMRR	Richmond	Hospital stores	3,400
9/21/1861	WMRR	Richmond	Soap	4,200
9/21/1861	WMRR	Richmond	Tents	6,600
9/21/1861	WMRR	Richmond	Hospital stores	2,000
9/21/1861	WMRR	Richmond	Hospital stores	3,000
9/23/1861	WMRR	Richmond	Hospital stores	2,000
9/25/1861	WMRR	Richmond	Soap	16,940
9/25/1861	WMRR	Richmond	Tents	4,200
9/26/1861	WMRR	Richmond	Soap	16,490
9/27/1861	WMRR	Richmond	Soap	2,070
9/27/1861	WMRR	Richmond	Clothing	1,200
9/27/1861	WMRR	Richmond	Clothing	4,400
9/27/1861	WMRR	Richmond	Clothing	600
10/01/1861	WMRR	Richmond	Tents	4,500

Freight Shipments for the Confederate Government, 1861 — 215

Date	RR	Destination	Item	Quantity
10/01/1861	WMRR	Richmond	Soap	9,000
10/03/1861	WMRR	Richmond	Candles	32,000
10/03/1861	WMRR	Richmond	Saltpeter	9,615
10/11/1861	WMRR	Richmond	Clothing (Georgia Regiments)	11,400
10/11/1861	WMRR	Richmond	Boxes, bales, blankets, etc.	47,720
10/14/1861	WMRR	Richmond	Candles	7,800
10/14/1861	WMRR	Richmond	Soap	2,000
10/14/1861	WMRR	Richmond	Soap	800
10/14/1861	WMRR	Richmond	Shoes	12,700
10/14/1861	WMRR	Richmond	Haversacks	3,500
10/15/1861	WMRR	Richmond	Boxes of Guns	800
10/15/1861	WMRR	Richmond	Sulphur	4,220
10/15/1861	WMRR	Richmond	Horseshoes and nails	550
10/15/1861	WMRR	Richmond	Clothing	300
10/15/1861	WMRR	Richmond	Overcoats	7,200
10/15/1861	WMRR	Richmond	Shoes	3,500
10/16/1861	WMRR	Richmond	Tents	4,130
10/16/1861	WMRR	Richmond	Shoes	400
10/16/1861	WMRR	Richmond	Soap	9,600
10/16/1861	WMRR	Richmond	18 bales, 35 boxes of Shoes, Clothing (Alabama Soldiers)	14,150
10/16/1861	WMRR	Richmond		16,224
10/16/1861	WMRR	Norfolk	Clothing	1,200
10/16/1861	WMRR	Richmond	Clothing	1,500
10/16/1861	WMRR	Richmond	Clothing	2,400
10/16/1861	WMRR	Richmond	1 Horse	*
10/16/1861	WMRR	Richmond	4 boxes for 16th. Georgia Regiment	*
10/17/1861	WMRR	Richmond	Clothing	1 car
10/18/1861	WMRR	Richmond	Shoes	6,460
10/18/1861	WMRR	Richmond	Hospital stores	*
10/18/1861	WMRR	Richmond	Clothing	1,170

Appendix C

Date	Source	Destination	Item	Weight
10/18/1861	WMRR	Richmond	2 bundles, 1 Saddle	120
10/19/1861	WMRR	Portsmouth	Blankets	*
10/19/1861	WMRR	Richmond	55 boxes Soap, 3 boxes, wheat	3,815
10/22/1861	WMRR	Richmond	Axes, Spades, boxes	3,965
10/23/1861	WMRR	Richmond	Horseshoes	1,100
10/23/1861	J. Dawson (Wilmington)	Richmond	6 boxes 16 pieces Axes	*
10/23/1861	R.G. Rankin (Wilmington)	Richmond	1 box (Richmond Armory)	800
10/24/1861	WMRR	Richmond	1 box Shoes, 1 package Axes	175
10/24/1861	WMRR	Richmond	Mattresses (Georgia Hospital)	1,200
10/24/1861	WMRR	Richmond	1 box (Soldiers Clothing)	*
10/24/1861	WMRR	Richmond	1 box (Soldiers Clothing)	*
10/24/1861	WMRR	Richmond	1 box (Soldiers Clothing)	*
10/24/1861	WMRR	Richmond	1 box (Soldiers Clothing)	*
10/24/1861	WMRR	Richmond	1 box (Soldiers Clothing)	*
10/24/1861	WMRR	Richmond	1 box (Soldiers Clothing)	100
10/24/1861	WMRR	Richmond	2 boxes (Soldiers Clothing)	600
10/24/1861	WMRR	Richmond	1 trunk (Soldiers Clothing)	100
10/24/1861	WMRR	Norfolk	1 box (Soldiers Clothing)	*
10/25/1861	WMRR	Richmond	Shoes	4,986
10/25/1861	WMRR	Richmond	3 casks, Camp Kettles	1,500
10/25/1861	WMRR	Richmond	Soap	1,350
10/25/1861	WMRR	Richmond	Tents	3,310
10/25/1861	WMRR	Richmond	Overcoats	8,335
10/25/1861	WMRR	Richmond	31 packages Axes, 1 box	3,950
10/25/1861	WMRR	Richmond	Soap	2,500
10/25/1861	WMRR	Richmond	3 boxes Camp Kettles	750
10/25/1861	WMRR	Richmond	1 horse	*
10/29/1861	WMRR	Richmond	Soap	15,750
10/29/1861	WMRR	Richmond	4 boxes (Soldiers Clothing)	970

Freight Shipments for the Confederate Government, 1861   217

Date	Source	Destination	Item	Weight
10/29/1861	WMRR	Richmond	5 boxes (Soldiers Clothing)	1,400
10/30/1861	WMRR	Richmond	Shovels, 25 boxes, 4 casks	12,955
10/31/1861	WMRR	Richmond	Soap	6,257
10/31/1861	WMRR	Richmond	Gun Powder	1,800
10/31/1861	WMRR	Richmond	Soap	16,000
10/31/1861	WMRR	Richmond	Horseshoes	900
10/31/1861	WMRR	Richmond	30 bales Oakum	1,440

OTHER FREIGHT

Date	Source	Destination	Item	Weight
8/02/1861	WMRR	Mile Post 65	10 bales	2,600
8/02/1861	WMRR	Weldon	163 boxes, 8 bales	26,520
8/05/1861	WMRR	Richmond	6 boxes, 1 bag	900
8/05/1861	WMRR	Richmond	paper	10,000
8/05/1861	WMRR	Richmond	2 boxes	410
8/05/1861	Weldon	Charleston	misc.	270
8/07/1861	WMRR	Richmond	149 boxes	9,710
8/08/1861	WMRR	Norfolk	3 boxes	850
8/12/1861	WMRR	Richmond	5 bales Domestic, 3 boxes, 3 bales mds.	14,230
8/22/1861	WMRR	Richmond	16 boxes	2,650
8/22/1861	WMRR	Richmond	2 boxes	*
8/22/1861	WMRR	Richmond	10 boxes	2,685
8/22/1861	WMRR	Richmond	33 boxes	10,950
8/26/1861	WMRR	Richmond	5 bales domestic	1,250
8/26/1861	WMRR	Richmond	2 boxes	500
8/26/1861	WMRR	Richmond	2 boxes	360
8/27/1861	WMRR	Richmond	3 boxes	670
8/26/1861	WMRR	Asheville via Goldsboro	1 Grindstone	500
9/05/1861	WMRR	Richmond	2 bales	360

Appendix C

Date	Source	Destination	Item	Weight
9/05/1861	WMRR	Richmond	1 box, Confederate Hospital	176
9/05/1861	WMRR	Culpeper	1 box, Confederate Hospital	170
9/05/1861	WMRR	Richmond	18 boxes, 3 bales	5,493
9/08/1861	WMRR	Richmond	Potash	1,771
9/08/1861	WMRR	Richmond	25 bales domestic	6,770
9/08/1861	WMRR	Richmond	1 box	180
9/08/1861	WMRR	Richmond	2 boxes	480
9/08/1861	WMRR	Richmond	6 boxes	1,000
9/10/1861	WMRR	Richmond	1 box	200
9/10/1861	WMRR	Richmond	18 boxes	3,680
9/10/1861	WMRR	Richmond	20 boxes	3,000
9/10/1861	WMRR	Richmond	2 bags, 3 bales	400
9/10/1861	WMRR	Richmond	1 box	80
9/10/1861	WMRR	Norfolk	2 boxes	300
9/11/1861	WMRR	Staunton, VA	3 boxes	227
9/11/1861	WMRR	Richmond	24 boxes	4,800
9/11/1861	WMRR	Richmond	10 boxes, 1 bbl.	980
9/12/1861	WMRR	Richmond	1 tierce, 1 keg	200
9/12/1861	WMRR	Richmond	2 boxes	530
9/12/1861	WMRR	Richmond	2 boxes	460
9/12/1861	WMRR	Richmond	Soda	15,941
9/14/1861	Goldsboro	Manassas	4 boxes, 1 package	260
9/17/1861	WMRR	Richmond	10 boxes	4,574
9/17/1861	WMRR	Charlottesville, VA	11 boxes, 2 bales	800
9/19/1861	Goldsboro	Bristoe	16 boxes, 1 barrel	800
9/20/1861	WMRR	Richmond	29 boxes	11,300
9/20/1861	WMRR	Richmond	2 boxes	540
9/20/1861	WMRR	Richmond	20 boxes	10,805
9/27/1861	WMRR	Richmond	1 bundle	*

Freight Shipments for the Confederate Government, 1861

Date	RR	Destination	Description	Weight
9/27/1861	WMRR	Richmond	23 boxes, 4 trunks	2,000
9/27/1861	WMRR	Richmond	24 boxes	4,000
9/21/1861	WMRR	Richmond	18 boxes	6,009
9/21/1861	WMRR	Richmond	27 bales, 2 boxes	5,919
9/21/1861	WMRR	Petersburg	1 box	200
9/23/1861	WMRR	Richmond	3 boxes	600
9/25/1861	WMRR	Richmond	5 boxes, 1 bale	500
9/25/1861	WMRR	Richmond	43 boxes	13,769
9/25/1861	WMRR	Richmond	19 boxes	10,260
9/25/1861	WMRR	Richmond	1 box	325
9/25/1861	WMRR	Richmond	1 box	242
9/25/1861	WMRR	Richmond	18 boxes	1,907
9/25/1861	WMRR	Richmond	1 box	330
9/25/1861	WMRR	Richmond	2 boxes	495
9/25/1861	WMRR	Richmond	bales, boxes, bundles, etc.	3,910
9/27/1861	WMRR	Richmond	bales, boxes	15,716
9/27/1861	WMRR	Richmond	boxes, casks	22,068
9/27/1861	WMRR	Richmond	boxes	1,590
10/01/1861	WMRR	Richmond	15 boxes	5,800
10/01/1861	WMRR	Richmond	75 boxes	3,000
10/03/1861	WMRR	Richmond	3 boxes	1,200
10/03/1861	WMRR	Richmond	7 boxes	1,400
10/04/1861	WMRR	Richmond	2 boxes. 1 cask	1,200
10/04/1861	WMRR	Richmond	12 boxes	1,200
10/04/1861	WMRR	Richmond	10 boxes, 1 bale	1,890
10/08/1861	WMRR	Yorktown	4 bags of cement, carriages, 3 boxes	3 cars
10/08/1861	WMRR	Richmond	1 case, trunks	300
10/08/1861	WMRR	Richmond	4 boxes	200
10/08/1861	WMRR	Norfolk	1 box	100
10/08/1861	WMRR	Norfolk	1 box	*

Appendix C

Date	Source	Destination	Item	Weight
10/08/1861	WMRR	Richmond	1 box	*
10/10/1861	WMRR	Richmond	10 boxes	3,080
10/10/1861	WMRR	Richmond	boxes, bales, demijohns	4,150
10/10/1861	WMRR	Richmond	2 boxes	365
10/11/1861	WMRR	Richmond	boxes, bales, bags, bbl., cask	2,765
10/11/1861	WMRR	Richmond	1 carriage, 2 horses for Jefferson Davis	*
10/11/1861	WMRR	Richmond	32 bags (Certificate)	*
10/14/1861	WMRR	Richmond	4 boxes	800
10/14/1861	WMRR	Richmond	10 boxes	1,500
10/14/1861	WMRR	Richmond	2 boxes	600
10/14/1861	WMRR	Richmond	Potash	1,409
10/14/1861	WMRR	Richmond	1 bale	200
10/14/1861	WMRR	Richmond	5 boxes	1,500
10/14/1861	WMRR	Richmond	12 boxes, 2 bales	4,000
10/14/1861	WMRR	Richmond	4 boxes	1,000
10/14/1861	WMRR	Richmond	paper	7,216
10/15/1861	WMRR	Richmond	6 boxes	3,000
10/15/1861	WMRR	Richmond	1 box	115
10/18/1861	WMRR	Richmond	2 boxes, 2 bales (Hospital)	1,800
10/18/1861	WMRR	Richmond	2 boxes	600
10/18/1861	WMRR	Richmond	1 box	*
10/18/1861	WMRR	Richmond	16 boxes, 2 bbl., 3 kegs	3,108
10/18/1861	WMRR	Richmond	13 boxes	1,670
10/18/1861	WMRR	Richmond	1 box	50
10/18/1861	WMRR	Richmond	1 box	50
10/18/1861	WMRR	Richmond	1 box	75
10/18/1861	WMRR	Richmond	1 box	45
10/18/1861	WMRR	Richmond	1 box	50
10/18/1861	WMRR	Richmond	1 box	90

Freight Shipments for the Confederate Government, 1861 — 221

Date	RR	Destination	Contents	Amount
10/18/1861	WMRR	Richmond	1 box	110
10/18/1861	WMRR	Richmond	2 boxes	100
10/18/1861	WMRR	Richmond	4 boxes	200
10/18/1861	WMRR	Richmond	5 boxes	300
10/18/1861	WMRR	Richmond	5 boxes, 3 packages	500
10/19/1861	WMRR	Richmond	1 package	*
10/19/1861	WMRR	Richmond	1 box	*
10/19/1861	WMRR	Richmond	21 boxes, 37 polls, carpet, 5 bales	12,000
10/19/1861	WMRR	Richmond	13 bales, 2 boxes, 1 roll carpet	4,000
10/19/1861	WMRR	Richmond	2 bundles, 5 boxes	500
10/19/1861	WMRR	Richmond	6 boxes	1,500
10/19/1861	WMRR	Richmond	4 boxes	600
10/19/1861	WMRR	Richmond	5 boxes	1,065
10/19/1861	WMRR	Richmond	1 box	100
10/19/1861	WMRR	Richmond	2 boxes	200
10/19/1861	WMRR	Richmond	1 box	*
10/19/1861	WMRR	Richmond	1 box	*
10/19/1861	WMRR	Richmond	1 box	*
10/19/1861	WMRR	Richmond	1 box	*
10/19/1861	WMRR	Richmond	1 box	*
10/19/1861	WMRR	Richmond	2 boxes	220
10/19/1861	WMRR	Richmond	1 box	*
10/19/1861	WMRR	Richmond	1 box	*
10/19/1861	WMRR	Richmond	1 box	*
10/19/1861	WMRR	Richmond	12 bales	3,216
10/19/1861	WMRR	Norfolk	1 box	*
10/19/1861	WMRR	Norfolk	1 box	*
10/19/1861	WMRR	Norfolk	1 box	*
10/19/1861	WMRR	Norfolk	1 box	*
10/19/1861	WMRR	Norfolk	1 box	*

Appendix C

Date	Source	Destination	Item	Weight
10/19/1861	WMRR	Norfolk	2 boxes	*
10/21/1861	Baggage	Richmond	1 box	*
10/21/1861	Baggage	Richmond	1 box	*
10/21/1861	Baggage	Richmond	1 box	*
10/21/1861	Baggage	Richmond	1 box	*
10/21/1861	Baggage	Richmond	2 boxes	120
10/21/1861	Baggage	Richmond	4 boxes	150
10/21/1861	Baggage	Richmond	7 boxes, 1 trunk	700
10/23/1861	Wilmington to Goldsboro	Raleigh	3 boxes, 10 rolls Carpet	1,800
10/23/1861	WMRR	Richmond	7 boxes	1,400
10/23/1861	WMRR	Richmond	2 boxes	530
10/23/1861	WMRR	Richmond	7 boxes	300
10/23/1861	WMRR	Richmond	3 boxes	450
10/23/1861	WMRR	Richmond	1 box	75
10/23/1861	WMRR	Richmond	1 box	170
10/23/1861	WMRR	Richmond	1 box	75
10/23/1861	WMRR	Richmond	2 boxes	*
10/24/1861	WMRR	Richmond	17 boxes	8,800
10/24/1861	WMRR	Richmond	1 box	520
10/24/1861	WMRR	Richmond	6 boxes	2,500
10/24/1861	WMRR	Richmond	1 box	50
10/24/1861	WMRR	Richmond	2 boxes (Georgia Hospital)	530
10/19/1861	WMRR	Richmond	3 boxes (Georgia Hospital)	*
10/19/1861	WMRR	Richmond	2 boxes (Georgia Hospital)	150
9/19/1861	WMRR	Portsmouth	Boxes, etc. (Georgia Hospital)	10,686
10/24/1861	WMRR	Richmond	boxes, trunks, keg (3rd. Georgia Regiment)	Certificate
10/24/1861	WMRR	Richmond	boxes, bags, trunks, bbl., cotton etc.	Certificate
10/24/1861	WMRR	Richmond	25 boxes	Requisition

Freight Shipments for the Confederate Government, 1861

Date	Via	Destination	Contents	Amount
10/25/1861	WMRR	Richmond	10 boxes	3,620
10/25/1861	WMRR	Richmond	1 box	150
10/25/1861	WMRR	Portsmouth	1 box	40
10/25/1861	WMRR	Portsmouth	10 boxes, 2 bags (3rd. Georgia Regiment)	1,836
10/25/1861	WMRR	Portsmouth	13 boxes (3rd. Georgia Regiment)	Requisition
10/25/1861	WMRR	Portsmouth	1 box	100
10/25/1861	WMRR	Portsmouth	1 box	90
10/25/1861	WMRR	Portsmouth	1 box	275
10/25/1861	WMRR	Portsmouth	1 trunk	40
10/25/1861	WMRR	Richmond	1 box	*
10/25/1861	WMRR	Richmond	1 box	*
10/25/1861	WMRR	Richmond	1 box	*
10/25/1861	WMRR	Richmond	3 boxes	1,000
10/28/1861	E. Murray & Co. (Wilmington)	Richmond	25 bales	5,781
10/28/1861	J. Dawson (Wilmington)	Richmond	4 cases mds.	950
10/28/1861	WMRR	Richmond	6 boxes, 1 bag	1,000
10/28/1861	WMRR	Richmond	1 car load (Alabama soldiers)	*
10/28/1861	WMRR	Richmond	14 boxes, 2 bbl. (7th. Georgia Regiment)	3,500
10/28/1861	WMRR	Richmond	3 boxes	807
10/28/1861	WMRR	Richmond	1 box	50
10/28/1861	WMRR	Portsmouth	20 packages (3rd. Georgia Regiment)	2,360
10/28/1861	WMRR	Richmond	25 boxes, 1 keg	4,800
10/28/1861	WMRR	Richmond	10 boxes, 1 trunk	640
10/29/1861	Baggage	Richmond	7 boxes, 1 basket	Requisition
10/29/1861	Baggage	Richmond	1 bundle	Certificate
10/29/1861	Baggage	Richmond	1 bales	*
10/29/1861	Baggage	Suffolk	15 packages	Requisition
10/29/1861	Goldsboro to Weldon	Lewisburg, VA	1 box	100
10/29/1861	Goldsboro to Weldon	Sewell's Mountain, (WV)	1 box (Major General Lee)	30

Appendix C

Date	Source	Destination	Item	Weight
10/29/1861	Goldsboro to Weldon	Fredericksburg	1 box	150
10/29/1861	WMRR	Richmond	boxes, bales, etc.	4,735
10/29/1861	WMRR	Richmond	1 box	130
10/29/1861	WMRR	Suffolk	1 box	245
10/29/1861	WMRR	Richmond	1 box	200
10/30/1861	WMRR	Richmond	10 bales	3,160
10/30/1861	WMRR	Richmond	boxes, trunks, etc.	4,547
10/31/1861	WMRR	Richmond	25 bales	6,875
10/31/1861	WMRR	Richmond	boxes, bales	4,000
10/03/1861	Goldsboro to Weldon	Yorktown	1 box	100
10/03/1861	Goldsboro to Weldon	Yorktown	1 box	100
10/03/1861	Goldsboro to Weldon	Yorktown	1 box	100
10/03/1861	Goldsboro to Weldon	Yorktown	1 box	50
10/15/1861	Goldsboro to Weldon	Aquila Creek	1 box	110
10/15/1861	Goldsboro to Weldon	Aquila Creek	2 boxes, 1 trunk	200
10/15/1861	Goldsboro to Weldon	Aquila Creek	5 boxes	350
10/15/1861	Goldsboro to Weldon	Aquila Creek	2 boxes	75
10/17/1861	Goldsboro to Weldon	Fredericksburg	1 box	20
10/17/1861	Goldsboro to Weldon	Fairfax Station	1 box	64
10/18/1861	Goldsboro to Weldon	Pratt's Point	10 Boxes (2nd Regiment NC Troops)	1,500
10/18/1861	Goldsboro to Weldon	Pratt's Point	1 Box (2nd Regiment NC Troops)	100
10/21/1861	Goldsboro to Weldon	Fredericksburg	1 box	50
10/21/1861	Goldsboro to Weldon	Fredericksburg	1 box	50
10/21/1861	Goldsboro to Weldon	Fredericksburg	1 box	100
10/21/1861	Goldsboro to Weldon	Fredericksburg	1 box	40
10/21/1861	Goldsboro to Weldon	Fredericksburg	1 box	10
10/21/1861	Goldsboro to Weldon	Yorktown	1 box	100
10/21/1861	Goldsboro to Weldon	Yorktown	1 box	100
10/21/1861	Goldsboro to Weldon	Yorktown	2 boxes	100

Chapter Notes

Abbreviations

CL   Cornell University Library
CL MOA   Cornell University Library, "The War of Rebellion, A Compilation of the Official Records of the Union and Confederate Armies," *Making of America* (2011), http://ebooks.library.cornell.edu/m/moawar//waro.html
NHCL   The collection housed in the North Carolina Room located in the New Hanover County Library at 201 Chestnut Street, Wilmington, North Carolina, 28401
NHCL-R   The Bill Reaves Collection housed in the North Carolina Room located in the New Hanover County Library
NCSA   North Carolina State Archives
UNCCH   The North Carolina Collection housed in Louis Round Wilson Library on the campus of the University of North Carolina at Chapel Hill
UNCW   Collections housed in William Madison Randall Library on the campus of the University of North Carolina at Wilmington

Chapter I

1. The early years of the railroad are chronicled in the author's previous volume, *The Wilmington & Raleigh Rail Road Company, 1833–1854*. The year 1854 was a significant turning point in the history of the railroads of Wilmington, North Carolina. The Wilmington & Manchester Railroad would be completed, thus allowing for a southbound rail connection to the South Carolina railroads. The steamboat fleet of the Wilmington & Raleigh Rail Road Company, an element of its transportation plan that allowed for continuous service to Charleston even as the railroad was under construction during the 1830s, would no longer be needed. The Wilmington & Raleigh would change its corporate name to the more accurate Wilmington & Weldon Railroad Company; near year's end, the stockholders would select Samuel Ashe as president of the company. As a notable figure in Democratic Party politics, his election was met with some resistance by the Whig establishment that viewed his attainment of this office as being rigged, utilizing the vote representing the state's shares. He would, however, retain the presidency of the company until his unusual death in 1862.

2. Wilmington & Weldon Rail Road Company, *Annual Reports of the President and Directors, and the Chief Engineer and Superintendent of the Wilmington & Weldon R.R. Co., with the Proceedings of the General Meeting of the Stockholders, November 23D. 1864* (Wilmington, NC: Fulton & Price, 1864), 3–5, UNCCH, Cp 385.1 W78. This is one of the few annual reports that list the name of each shareholder, his place of residence, and the amount of shares. The last would appear after the war in 1866.

3. Wilmington & Weldon Rail Road Company, *Annual Reports of the President and*

Directors, and the Chief Engineer and Superintendent of the Wilmington & Weldon R.R. Co., with the Proceedings of the General Meeting of the Stockholders, November 8th, 1860 (Wilmington, NC: Fulton & Price, 1860), 29–30, NHCL, NC 385 W.

4. *Ibid.*, 33.

5. *Ibid.*, 24.

6. *Ibid.*, 32.

7. Wilmington & Weldon Rail Road Company, *Annual Reports of the President and Directors, and the Chief Engineer and Superintendent of the Wilmington & Weldon R.R. Co., with the Proceedings of the General Meeting of the Stockholders, December 14th, 1862* (Wilmington, NC: Fulton & Price, 1862), 16, UNCCH, Cp 385.1 W78r.

8. Edward L. Ayers, *The Promise of the New South: Life After Reconstruction* (Oxford and New York: Oxford University Press, 2007), 9–11.

9. Wilmington, Columbia & Augusta Rail Road Company and the Wilmington & Weldon Rail Road Company, *Annual Reports of the President and Directors and the General Superintendents of the Wilmington, Columbia & Augusta and the Wilmington & Weldon Rail Road Companies, with the Proceedings if the General Meeting of Stockholders, November 20th, 1877* (Wilmington, NC: Morning Star, 1877), 16, UNCCH, Cp 385.1 W78.

The Rail Roads of the country which have been the great lever of American development, do not pay three per cent. on the cost of construction. The Wilmington & Weldon Rail Road has worked about one-half the time, since it was built, on construction account, and to-day does not pay three and one-half per cent. on its actual cost. The capital stock and bond debt represents but little over one-half the cost. But for the wise policy of improving the Road with its earnings, instead of making dividends, the present rate of dividends could not be maintained. The Stockholders of the Wilmington & Weldon Rail Road, who reside in the State, are invited to examine the condition of the Road and its equipment, and to compare rates, both of freights and passengers, with former years, when the Road was controlled entirely by persons living in the State.

10. Wilmington, Columbia & Augusta Rail Road Company and the Wilmington & Weldon Rail Road Company, *Annual Reports of the President and Directors and the General Superintendents of the Wilmington, Columbia & Augusta and the Wilmington & Weldon Rail R.R. Co's., with the Proceedings if the General Meeting of Stockholders, November 19th, 1873* (Wilmington, NC: Englehard & Saunders, 1873), 5–13, UNCCH, Cp 385.1 W78; Wilmington & Weldon Rail Road Company, *Annual Reports of the President and Directors, and the General Superintendent of the Wilmington & Weldon Rail Road Company, with the Proceedings of the General Meeting of the Stockholders, November 19th, 1878* (Wilmington, NC: Morning Star, 1878), 10, UNCCH, Cp 385.1 W78.

11. *Wilmington Morning Star*, August 13, 1935, New Hanover County Library, Reaves Collection (abbreviated hereafter as NCHL-R).

12. Wilmington & Weldon Rail Road Company, *Proceedings of the Stockholders of the Wilmington & Weldon R.R. Co., at their Special Meeting, August 1st, 1865; together with the Proceedings of the 30th Annual Meeting, held at Wilmington, North Carolina, November 22, 1865, with the Reports of the President and Directors, and the Chief Engineer and Superintendent* (Wilmington, NC: Englehard & Price, 1866), 26, UNCCH, Cp 385.1 W78r.

The labor question is one that seems likely to give the future management of the railways in the South the most trouble and anxiety. I am unable to see a satisfactory solution of the difficulty. How many negroes in one hundred will prove reliable and steady laborers, it is hardly possible to determine; but if we could believe there would be one, it would be a hopeful condition of things compared to the present uncertainty. I am confident it cannot reach two in the hundred that now inhabit this section of country. The remedy is, I think, white labor, if it can be had; as a consequence I have authorized the employment of all the industrious and sober white laborers on the track, and while we do not get more than three-fourths the amount of work for each hand we formerly obtained, we pay about the same price for it. In constant trials, with patience and time, we may find a solution of this difficulty.

13. Wilmington & Weldon Rail Road Company, 1860, 27.
In closing this report, allow me to call your attention to the great difficulty we have experienced during the past year in procuring a sufficient number of good, reliable freight train hands, to work those trains efficiently and economically. This difficulty commenced with the calendar year, and still exists. Finding it impracticable to obtain slaves or free blacks, a resort was had to white men, but with few exceptions, they were found far inferior to slaves, or even the free blacks we had heretofore employed. They come into our service generally from necessity, and finding the labor much harder than they anticipated, leave us as soon as their most pressing wants are satisfied; and most frequently at the very moment their services are most needed.

14. Reggie L. Pearson, "'There Are Many Sick, Feeble, and Suffering Freedmen': The Freedmen's Bureau's Health Care Activities during Reconstruction in North Carolina, 1865–1868," *North Carolina Historical Review* 79, no. 2 (April, 2002), 141–181.

15. Frank D. Smaw, Jr., *Smaw's Wilmington Directory comprising a General and City Business Directory, and a Directory of Colored Persons, to which is added A Complete Historical and Commercial Sketch of the City* (Wilmington, NC: Smaw, 1867), 207, 211, NHCL, NC 917.56 K.

16. Wilmington & Weldon Rail Road Company, 1866, *ibid.*

17. *Wilmington Journal,* January 12, 1849; January 30, 1854.

18. *Wilmington Journal,* January 30, September 22, October 9, 1854.

19. *Wilmington Journal,* October 13, 1854.

20. *Wilmington Journal,* January 30, 1854.

21. *Wilmington Journal,* February 17, 1854.

22. L.C. Turner, C.E., *Plan of Wilmington, North Carolina* (Philadelphia: Duval & Son's, 1856), NHCL, A 16.

23. *Wilmington Journal,* February 3, February 10, March 3, March 10, 1854.

24. *Wilmington Journal,* February 10, 1854.

25. *Wilmington Journal,* January 12, 1855.

26. *Wilmington Journal,* February 1, 1856.

27. *Ibid.*
By the route surveyed, the distance from Kingsville to Hamburg is 89 miles, which cannot be materially reduced. The distance by the South Carolina Railroad between the same points is 117 miles, or 28 miles greater, and the saving in time would, if both Roads were operated at the same speed, be a little over one hour. If the present schedule on that Road was adhered to the difference of time would be upwards of four hours; but competition in Railways always produces increase of speed. It is proper, therefore, to compare the characteristics of two roads with reference to the same perfection of construction and management in each and the result in this case will be a saving of only two hours of time.... All the estimates of the income of Railways are based on uncertain data, and generally fall below the actual results. This Road would, in some degree, be in direct competition with the South Carolina Road, both for the through travel and the local business, and the country through which it passes has so sparse a population, and but few elements capable of being developed, to add materially to its receipts, that it must rely in a great measure upon the former for its support. If the income be estimated at the same rate as the receipts of your Road the past year ($2,400 per mile,) and the working expenses at the minimum of 50 per cent of the receipts, it would yield 4¾ per cent on the investment, which leaves too little margin to recommend its construction. An examination of the map of South Carolina will show that if a Road be constructed from Orangeburg on the Columbia branch to Blackville on the Hamburg Road, it would reduce the distance between Kingsville and Hamburg to about 96 miles, or about seven miles greater than the direct line. This connection would require the construction of about 25 miles of Road, through a country presenting but few obstacles to easy grades and curves, with no heavy bridging or other structures. The investment required would be comparatively small, and the distance and time saved nearly equal to the direct line.

28. United States War Department, *The War of Rebellion: A Compilation of the Official Records of the Union and Confederate Armies* (Washington, DC: Government Printing Office, 1895), Ser. 1, Vol. 47, Pt. 2, 594–595, Ser. 1, Vol. 47, Pt. 2, 1292, Cornell University Library, "The War of Rebellion: A Compilation of the Official Records of the Union and Confederate Armies," *Making of America* (2011) http://ebooks.library.cornell.edu/m/moawar//waro.html (Accessed on October 5, 2011) (abbreviated hereafter as CL MOA).

29. *New York Times*, December 11, 1865.

30. United States War Department, 1895, Ser. 1, Vol. 47, Pt. 3, 549–551, CL MOA; Harvey S. Teal, "Experiencing History: A Visit to a Railroad 'Stonehenge,'" *USCS Newsletter* (Columbia: University of South Carolina, University South Caroliniana Society, 1997), 3.

31. *New York Times*, February 7, 1866, May 9, 1867.

32. *Daily Review* (Wilmington, NC), November 3, 1866, NHCL-R.

33. James Sprunt, *Chronicles of the Cape Fear River, 1660–1916* (Raleigh, NC: Edwards & Broughton, 1916),671; *Wilmington Journal*, March 19, 1855.

At a meeting of the Commissioners appointed under the act of incorporation for the purpose of creating the capital stock of the Wilmington, Charlotte and Rutherford Rail Road Company, held this 14th day of March, 1855 at the town of Wadesborough, General Alexander McRae of Wilmington, was elected Chairman, and Robert S. French, of Lumberton, was requested to act as Secretary. The Chairman explained the object of the meeting. Present-General Alexander McRae, of Wilmington; Alfred Smith, of Whitesville; Thomas A. Norment of Lumberton; James P. Leake, of Rockingham; Walter P. Leake, of Wadesborough; D.A. Covington, of Monroe. It was resolved, That books be opened for subscription to the capital stock in the Wilmington, Charlotte and Rutherford Rail Road, at the places and by the persons designated in the act of incorporation of said road, on the second Monday in April next, and that the Chairman cause publication of the same to be made in the Shelbyville, Charlotte, Wadesborough, Fayetteville and Wilmington papers. It was ordered that the name of Peter A. McEachin be added to the Commissioners for the County of Robeson, at Floral College; That Haynes Lennon, Thomas L. Vail, Lovett Peacock and Marmaduke Powell be added to the Commissioners of Columbus County, at Lennon's Store; That W.W. Hart of Monroe; William Hamilton, William L. Stigall, C. Tolson, at Hamilton's; William Houston, Capt. James Houston and William Hudson, at the Davis Gold Mine; George McCain, John Stewart, Col. William Walkup and Hugh Wilson, at Wilson's Store; Robert Howard, Robert Howie, Col. James A. Dunn, at Howard's Store, be added to the Commissioners for the County of Union; That William Maxwell, William H. Mathews and _____ Williamson be added to the Commissioners for the County of Mecklenburg. It was resolved, That the Directors of the Company hereafter to be appointed, be requested, in all contracts for work on the road, or for materials for said road, to prefer stockholders over all others, to the amount of their stock, all other things being equal. It was resolved, That it be recommended to hold mass-meetings in the different counties on the line of the road. On the motion of Mr. Norment, it was resolved, That it be recommended to the Commissioners that a subscription be taken up as early as practicable to pay the expenses of a survey from the town of Wilmington, and from Whitesville to Lumberton, and that John C. McRae, of Wilmington, be appointed to make the surveys. The following form was adopted as a caption to the lists of subscription: "Subscription list for the Wilmington, Charlotte and Rutherford Railroad Company. State of North Carolina,} County.} "We, the subscribers, agree to take the number of shares opposite our several names in the capital stock of the Wilmington, Charlotte and Rutherford Railroad Company, in accordance with the provisions of the charter of said Company," The following form was adopted for the receipts to be given by the Commissioners: County of _____) _____, A.D.,_____.) Received of _____ _____, _____ dollars, it being five per cent, on _____ shares subscribed by him to the stock of the Wilmington, Charlotte and Rutherford Railroad Company. _____ Ch'n of Comm'rs. The meeting adjourned subject to the call of the Chairman. R.S. French, Sec'y.

34. *Wilmington Journal*, March 26, 1855; James C. Burke, *The Wilmington & Raleigh Rail Road Company, 1833–1854* (Jefferson, NC: McFarland), 162.
  35. Wilmington, Charlotte & Rutherford Railroad Company, *Proceedings of the Stockholders of the Wilmington, Charlotte & Rutherford Rail Road Company, Wilmington, N.C., October 20th, 1870* (Wilmington, NC: Carolina Farmer & Morning Star, 1870), 20–21, NHCL NC 385 W.
  36. *New York Times*, July 21, 1865; Wilmington, Charlotte & Rutherford Railroad Company, 21.
  37. *Wilmington Journal*, November 8, 13, December 4, 1868; *New York Times*, August 29, 1869.
  38. *New York Times*, July 12, 1866; Wilmington, Charlotte & Rutherford Railroad Company, 4–5, 7–9. John F. Pickrell is mentioned as a defendant in *BALTZER and another v. RALEIGH & AUGUSTA AIR-LINE R. CO. and others* (United States Supreme Court, 115 U.S. 634 (6 S.Ct. 216, 29 L.Ed. 505), Decided on December 7, 1885.
  On September 1, 1868, the company had received the $1,200,000 authorized by the convention, and on October 19, 1868, the company having complied with the conditions prescribed by the act of the general assembly, the $2,000,000 in bonds of the state authorized by the general assembly were delivered to it. On September 1, 1868, the defendant John F. Pickrell, who was a resident of the city of New York, doing business in Wall street as a banker and broker, and being in good credit, made an offer in writing, in which he represented himself and John D. Whitford, of North Carolina, to W. J. Hawkins, the president of the Chatham Railroad Company, to do the entire work on the Chatham Railroad, such as grading, superstructure, and masonry, and furnish all material for the same, including the iron rails, and to take the state bonds in payment. This proposition was accepted by resolution adopted by the board of directors of the railroad company on September 4, 1868. The firm of Greenleaf, Norris & Co. and Charles Gould, of New York, were interested with Pickrell and Whitford in the performance and profits of the contract.... The validity of the bonds of the state of North Carolina issued by authority of the ordinance of the convention of March 11, 1868, and the act of the general assembly of August 15, 1868, having been questioned in the latter part of the year 1868, they became discredited, and both the railroad company and Pickrell were embarrassed thereby. The contract between Pickrell and the railroad company was changed, and the length of the road to be built by Pickrell was, by contract dated March 6, 1869, reduced. Under the contract as amended he built the railroad from Raleigh to Haw River, a distance of 30 miles, furnishing therefor the iron rails. The company paid him in full for the rails and for constructing the road. In consequence of the embarrassment resulting to Pickrell from the discrediting of the North Carolina bonds, no iron was received by him after November 2, 1868, from Baltzer & Taaks on the contract of September 11, 1868; and on August 11, 1869, Baltzer & Taaks, by a letter of that date addressed to Pickrell, released him, as far as they were concerned, "from obligations of receiving any more iron under contract dated eleventh September, 1868, and," they added, "we consider the same as closed." The balance sued for was, therefore, for iron delivered on November 2, 1868.
  39. *New York Times*, March 31, May 24, August 4, November 14, 1873; United States, *The Federal Reporter, Volume 97, Cases Argued and Determined in Circuit Courts of Appeal and Circuit and District Courts of the United States, Permanent Edition, November, 1899–January, 1900* (St. Paul: West, 1900), 401–404, Harvard University Library, KF105.F42 v.97–98; Jerry L. Cross, *Biographical Sketches of Seven State Treasurers* (Raleigh: North Carolina Department of Cultural Resources, 1994), 1; J.D. de Roulhac Hamilton, *History of North Carolina* (Chicago: Lewis, 1919), Vol. 3, 119–128, UNCW, F 254 .H67; Hugh Talmage Lefler, Albert Ray Newsome, *The History of a Southern State, North Carolina* (Chapel Hill: University of North Carolina Press, 1954), 464–465, UNCW, F 254.139 1954; Sprunt, 671–672.
  40. Charles Post, "Plantation Slavery and Economic Development in the Southern

United States," *Journal of Agrarian Change* 3, no. 3 (July 2003), 311–314, 323, 327; Otto H. Olsen, "Historians and the Extent of Slave Ownership in the Southern United States," *Civil War History* 50, no. 4 (2004), 414, 417.

41. Wilmington & Weldon Rail Road Company, 1860, 27.

42. *Wilmington Journal*, February 26, 1856.

43. Burke, *The Wilmington & Raleigh Rail Road Company*, 9, 20, 65, 74, 122, 125, 128–130, 159; *Wilmington Journal*, January 12, February 2, March 23, April 13, April 20, June 1, August 10, August 31, October 5, 1849, April 28, 1854.

44. *The Wilmington Journal*, October 9, 1854, July 6, 1855, April 25, 1856. James Dyson, a white man living in Columbus County, was killed by the mail train on the Wilmington & Manchester near Porter Swamp after becoming intoxicated at Cerro Gordo. He was walking home at night. In the same week an overseer on the Wilmington & Raleigh (Weldon) named Marshburn was run over by a freight train near Teachey's Depot and died the next day. William Mitchell was passed out on the tracks near mile post 72 on the Wilmington & Weldon on the morning of April 17, 1856, when he was run over and killed instantly by a southbound train. A man named Spencer, living near Wilmington, was found in the woods near the tracks of the Wilmington & Weldon about eight miles from town, but buzzards and other animals had been consuming his body for several days.

45. *Wilmington Journal*, August 14, 1854.

46. *Wilmington Journal*, November 24, December 23, 1854, January 5, 1855; Wilmington & Weldon Rail Road Company, 1860, 13–14, 29; *Wilmington Journal*, February 26, March 2, 1855. A locomotive and tender on an express train belonging to the Wilmington & Raleigh ran off the company wharf at Wilmington and ended up beneath ten feet of water in the Cape Fear River. *The Wilmington Journal* reported that the train came into the inclined plane leading to the wharf at a high rate of speed, and that the locomotive could not be reversed to slow it because of a mechanical problem that was known to exist the entire day. The mail agent on the train jumped and injured his arm. Mr. William H. Laspeyre, the conductor, applied a third brake in addition to the usual two, but it was sufficient to stop the train. Mr. William Piedmont (presumably the engineer) went into the river with the locomotive and tender but was uninjured. The fault, the newspaper conjectures, was with the engineer disregarding the mechanical problem. Mr. Laspeyre would be killed, along with a young baggage master named Mr. Comann, in a rear end collision in late 1860. The company set aside twenty shares of stock to be held in trust for the benefit of his widow and their children.

47. *Wilmington Journal*, October 15, 1854, February 26, March 2, 1855. On February 24, 1855, an express train was stopped at the depot when a freight train came in behind it at a high speed. "The freight train was running when it ought not to have been running." The engineer of the express train put his train into motion to avoid the collision, but the freight train impacted the rear of his train. A Dr. Cowper, a resident of Murfreesboro, had the flesh on his heel torn off in the crash, but his injury was not considered debilitating. The engineer of the freight train, a Mr. Marsh, escaped into the woods to avoid "summary punishment." Later, *The Wilmington Journal* published his side of the story. Mr. Marsh, being a new engineer on the line, encountered dense smoke in the woods two miles north of the depot, and became confused as to his location. When he and Mr. Thompson, the conductor of the freight train, realized he was coming up on the depot, they made every effort to stop.

48. *Wilmington Journal*, June 12, November 13, 1854. At the 1854 meeting of the stockholders of the Wilmington & Raleigh Rail Road Company, the outgoing president, Alexander McRae, noted that the requirement that the railroad meet its obligation to transport the mails in a timely manner necessitated the running of trains at 25 to 30 mph, and at that speed, would take 1,500 to 1,800 feet to come to a stop of level terrain. Free roaming cows and hogs wandered onto the track and were not seen until it was too late to stop. Mr. McRae noted that the expense of compensating the farmer for his killed livestock was a minor consideration compared to the damage and loss of life that might occur if the train

was derailed. He did not feel that the law as it existed provided adequately for the new traveling conditions and that farmers should be required to keep their livestock penned.

49. *Wilmington Journal*, August 25, 1855.

50. *Wilmington Journal*, January 14, 1856.

51. *Wilmington Journal*, March 14, March 21, 1856; *New York Times*, March 15, 1856. Octavius Cook, a passenger, later died of his burns. The injured included George C. Bourdett, the conductor; William Weymouth, the engineer; passengers Woodis Niemeyer of Portsmouth, Leon Clary of Windsor, North Carolina, J.P. Allison of Brooklyn, New York, and Dr. Williamson, a dentist from Northampton County, North Carolina, received injuries ranging from broken bones to bruises and gashes. There were twelve passengers total including two women, but their names are not included in the newspaper reports of the accident. The Adams Express Company's losses amounted to about $50,000. Some of their packages, of a total of six to seven tons of material, included notes for the Bank of Wilmington in denominations of fives and tens. The mail was reduced to ashes; only the brass pouch locks remained. A reporter from the *Richmond Dispatch* from Weldon noted the Seaboard & Roanoke Railroad didn't have any trains at the Weldon terminus after the accident, so Mr. C. Sanford of the Petersburg Railroad loaned a locomotive and cars to the Seaboard & Roanoke so that service would continue from Weldon to the site of the accident until the trestle had been repaired. The reporter acknowledged that Capt. Corbett of the Seaboard & Roanoke provided him with details about the accident. The trestlework near Margarettsville had been regarded by some to be unsafe; however, later investigation proved that a freight train pulling forty cars had passed over it two day before with no problem, and the true cause of the accident was the breaking of an axle on the tender of the train. The editor of the *Wilmington Journal* remarked, "We suppose the inference is legitimately drawable that any train, on any trestle work is at the mercy of every axle and truck in the train." In this statement, the editor sums up the uncertainty associated with rail travel, and to a degree, the weakness of mechanical contrivances upon which agrarian America was being propelled into modernity. Yet, could not the stay-at-home die just as surely from yellow fever, small pox, cholera, or malaria? Mr. Daughtry found himself being congratulated on having escaped the yellow fever epidemic, only to be "roasted" in the accident at Margarettsville.

52. *Wilmington Journal*, April 21, 1854.

One act of a negro belonging to a gentleman near this village, I will mention. It seems that the negro was going home, when he discovered a tree blown down and lying across the track. Having nothing with which to remove the obstruction, he went several miles to a neighbor's house, borrowed an axe, returned and cut the tree away. This was certainly a praise worthy deed. Had this faithful negro went on without clearing out the obstruction, in all human probability the lives of many persons, with perhaps the entire train, would have been destroyed. But, as it was, we are firmly of the opinion that he should be well rewarded. We hope that he will be as it will incite others to remove trees or other obstructions from the Road.

53. *New York Times*, December 11, 1865.

54. *Wilmington Star*, June 25, 1868, NHCL-R.

55. *Wilmington Star*, August 27, 1868, NHCL-R.

56. *Daily Journal*, January 20, 1874, NHCL-R.

57. *Daily Journal*, January 1, February 4, 1874, NHCL-R; Beverly Tetterton, *Wilmington: Lost But Not Forgotten* (Wilmington, NC: Dram Tree Books, 2005), 75, 109–110.

58. Wilmington & Weldon Rail Road Company, *Annual Reports of the President and Directors, and the Chief Engineer and Superintendent of the Wilmington & Weldon Rail Road Company, with the Proceedings of the General Meeting of Stockholders, November 21st, 1866* (Wilmington, NC: Engelhard & Price, 1866), 2; Wilmington & Weldon Rail Road Company, 1860, 17. The president of the company received $2,000 for his annual services, and the chief engineer and superintendent received an annual salary of $3,000. Station agents earned from $60 to $500 per year, with most earning below $200; and engineers earned $80 monthly in 1860.

Chapter II

1. United States, *Population of the United States in 1860; Compiled from the Original Returns of the Eighth Census, Under the Direction of the Secretary of the Interior*, by Joseph C.G. Kennedy, Superintendent of Census (Washington: Government Printing Office, 1864), 349, 353–355, 357–359, 361.

2. United States, *Manufactures of the United States in 1860; Compiled from the Original Returns of The Eighth Census, Under the Direction of the Secretary of the Interior* (Washington, DC: Government Printing Office, 1865), 429; United States, *Statistics of the United States (Including Mortality, Property, &c.,) in 1860; Compiled from the Original Returns and Being the Final Exhibit of the Eighth Census, Under the Direction of the Secretary of the Interior* (Washington, DC: Government Printing Office, 1866), 309.

3. *Wilmington Journal*, November 8, 1860.

4. T. Tuther, Jr., *Kelley's Wilmington Directory, to which is added a Business Directory for 1860* (Wilmington, NC: Fulton & Price, 1860), 12–13, NHCL NC917.56K.

5. James Sprunt, *Chronicles of the Cape Fear River, 1660–1916* (Raleigh, NC: Edwards & Broughton, 1916), 160; Tuther, 21, 23, 51, 87. John MacLaurin, writing under the pen name Senex, Jr., composed a series of articles about life in Wilmington during the 1840s. The town boundaries of that day extended from the river to Fifth Street and from Campbell Street to what would be known as Wooster Street. The population of Wilmington was 4,268 with 1,004 white males, 916 white females, 356 free persons of color, and 1,992 slaves. It appears that households acquired the services of a slave on a year contract with the owner, and MacLaurin notes the day of one such event as January 1, 1840.

6. Nickolas W. Schenck, transcribed by LuAnne Mims, *The Diary of Nicholas W. Schenck* (Wilmington: University of North Carolina, William Madison Randall Library, Special Collections (1905), 2000), http://library.uncw.edu/web/collections/Schenck/schenck intro.html (accessed on October 7, 2011).

7. Tuther, 37, 54–55, 79, 95, 106.

8. *Wilmington Herald*, November 6, 1860.

9. *Ibid.*, November 8, 1860.

10. There were two newspaper publishers in Wilmington, North Carolina, during the Civil War era. The firm of Fulton & Price published *The Wilmington Journal*, established in 1844, and *The Daily Journal*, established in 1851. The office of *The Wilmington Journal* was located on Princess Street between Front Street and 2nd Street. The firm of C. E. & R. Burr (later A. M. Waddell) published *The Wilmington Daily Herald*. The office of *The Wilmington Herald* was located at 40 1/2 Market Street. Because of Wilmington's location at the terminus of three railroads (The Wilmington & Weldon Railroad, The Wilmington & Manchester Railroad, and The Wilmington, Charlotte and Rutherford Railroad), *The Wilmington Journal* and *The Wilmington Herald* became the most widely circulated newspapers in the state. *The Wilmington Journal* boasts of this fact in an 1860 advertisement in the 1860 *Wilmington Directory*. These newspapers had access to telegraphic transmissions and had correspondents to cover stories first hand. The corresponding editor for the *Wilmington Herald* was Duncan McNeill.

11. *Wilmington Journal*, November 1, 1860. The Democrats held a mass meeting at Peacock's Store in Columbus County. William S. Ashe, former congressman and president of the Wilmington & Weldon Railroad, along with Warren Winslow, former governor of North Carolina from 1845 to 1855 and then congressman serving from 1855 to March 1861, were the featured speakers. The meeting included a public dinner and flag-raising ceremony.

12. *Wilmington Journal*, October 27, 1860.

13. William W. Freehling, *The Road to Disunion*, Vol. 1 (New York: Oxford University Press, 1990), 367–368.

14. The Hunkers represented the conservative wing of the party that supported business friendly policies and avoided as much as possible discourse on slavery; the Barnburners were concerned with reform, rooting out corruption, and arresting the expansion of slavery.

The Free Soil Party attracted the Barnburners and some Whigs during the 1848 election, upsetting Democratic unity and allowing Whig candidate Zachary Taylor to win the presidency.

15. *Wilmington Journal*, October 27, 1860.
16. *Ibid*.
17. *Wilmington Herald*, October 3, 1860.
18. *Ibid*.
19. *Ibid*.
20. Sprunt, 186; Schenck, 114.
21. *Wilmington Journal*, November 3, 1860.
22. *Ibid*.; *Wilmington Herald*, October 3, 1860.
23. Wilmington & Weldon Rail Road Company, *Annual Reports of the President and Directors, and the Chief Engineer and Superintendent of the Wilmington & Weldon R.R. Co., with the Proceedings of the General Meeting of the Stockholders, November 8TH, 1860* (Wilmington, NC: Fulton & Price, 1860), 11, NHCL, NC 385 W; Tuther, 65.
24. Wilmington & Weldon Rail Road Company, *Annual Reports of the President and Directors, and the Chief Engineer and Superintendent of the Wilmington & Weldon R.R. Co., with the Proceedings of the General Meeting of the Stockholders, November 8TH, 1860* (Wilmington, NC: Fulton & Price, 1860), 11, NHCL, NC 385 W, 9–10, 12–14.
25. *Wilmington Journal*, November 8, 1860.

It will be a matter of grave consideration for our Legislature how this position of affairs should be met. It is not ours now to make any suggestions upon this subject, save this, that if only half-way measures are to be adopted, it would be better to adopt none at all. If *only* talking is to be resorted to, we go decidedly against talking at all. We have had too much of that already. For *anything* in the way of true and earnest action we must have due respect; with anything short of this we have no concern.

New Hanover County

District	Ellis	Pool	Breckinridge	Bell	Douglas
Wilmington	578	539	593	567	5
Federal Point	15	10	..	..	..
Masonboro	28	40	33	28	..
Middle Sound	71	65	63	19	..
Sandy Run	121	..	121	..	..
Holly Shelter	80	..	70	..	..
Rocky Point	101	8	95	6	..
Long Creek	154	5	167	5	..
Caintuck	65	1	51	..	..
Upper Black River	96	1	96	1	..
Moore's Creek	53	3	106	..	..
Piney Woods	108	11	67	9	..
South Washington	129	22	144	9	..

26. Wilmington & Weldon Railroad Company, 1860, 15–16, 21–22, 27, 32.
27. *Wilmington Journal*, November 8, 1860.
28. *Ibid*.; *Wilmington Journal*, November 10, 1860. The federal officers that resigned in Charleston were Judge A. G. Magrath of the U.S. District Court, and James Conner, the U.S. District Attorney. The widespread coverage of these and other resignations encouraged other federal officers in South Carolina to resign their positions. In a real sense, the resignation of these officers was what jump-started the revolution in South Carolina. Governor William H. Gist called the legislature of South Carolina into session for the appointment of electors of president and vice president of the United States. However, the mission of this assembly was guided toward a formal action on secession.
29. *Wilmington Herald*, November 10, 1860.

What we have already said will apply to the subject of secession generally even in those States that have declared their intention, and their right to secede (and which it is proper to observe, notwithstanding their clamor, have suffered less from the aggressions of the abolitionists than any other southern States;) but, when applied to North Carolina and the border States, it is all-important. The greatest injustice, connected with this movement, which is done to us, first became known in Mr. Yancey's celebrated programme, by which it was proposed to deny us admission into the contemplated Southern Confederacy, and to compel us to "remain in the Union," and serve as a barrier between the Cotton States and the North — a sort of frontier territory to be used for the benefit of the Cotton States! Gov. Gist avowed, in his message to the South Carolina Legislature the other day, that the action of that State was expected to forestall the action of her sister States.

30. *Wilmington Journal*, November 10, 1860.
31. *Wilmington Herald*, November 15, 1860.
32. *Wilmington Herald*, November 16, 1860; *Wilmington Journal*, November 22, 1860
33. South Carolina, *Journal of the Convention of the People of South Carolina, Held in 1860–61, together with the Reports, Resolutions, &c.* (Charleston, SC: Evans & Cogswell, Printer to the Convention, 1861), 3–5, Duke University Library, http://babel.hathitrust.org/cgi/pt?id=mdp.35112105061941 (accessed on January 10, 2012).
34. Alexander H. Stephens, *Extract from a Speech by Alexander H. Stephens, Vice-President of the Confederate States, Delivered in the Secession Convention of Georgia, January, 1861* (no publisher), 2, Library of Congress, E440.5 .S83.
35. Louis Pendleton, *Alexander H. Stephens* (Philadelphia: Jacobs, 1908), 103–116, UNCCH, E 467.1.S85 P2.
36. South Carolina, 6, 17, 19.
37. *Ibid.*, 41–45.
38. *Ibid.*, 33.
39. *Ibid.*, 34–35, 98.
40. *Ibid.*, 121.
41. Yale University, Lillian Goldman Library, "Amendments Proposed in Congress by Senator John J. Crittenden: December 18, 1860," *The Avalon Project, Documents in Law, History and Diplomacy* (2008), http://avalon.law.yale.edu/19th_century/critten.asp (accessed on September 14, 2011).
42. *Wilmington Herald*, January 10, 1861; United States War Department, *The War of Rebellion: A Compilation of the Official Records of the Union and Confederate Armies* (Washington, DC: Government Printing Office, 1880), Ser. 1, Vol. 1, 9–10, CU-MOA.
43. United States War Department, *O.R.*, 1880, Ser. 1, Vol. 1, 474–475; Chris E. Fonvielle, Jr., *Fort Fisher 1865: The Photographs of T.H. O'Sullivan* (Carolina Beach, NC: Slap-Dash, 2011), 9–10.
44. United States War Department, *O.R.*, 1880, Ser. 1, Vol. 1, 484–485.
45. James Sprunt, 276–279; Tuther, 22, 27, 107, 108; *The Wilmington Daily Herald*, April 18, 1861. Mr. Hedrick is given as Captain J.H. Hedrick of the Cape Fear Light Artillery Company in a newspaper announcement. Mail for his troops was to be forward to his business, Hedrick & Ryan. The 1860–61 Wilmington directory lists John L. Cantwell as a produce broker, clerk of the U.S. District Court, and treasurer of St. John's Masonic Lodge, and J.J. Hedrick as a dry goods merchant.
46. Lucius E. Chittenden, *A Report on the Debates and Proceedings in the Secret Sessions on the Conference Convention, for Proposing Amendments to the Constitution of the United States, held at Washington, DC in February, A.D. 1861* (New York: Appleton, 1864), 9, 453, Internet Archive, http://www.archive.org/details/reportofdebatesp00inchit (accessed on September 14, 2011); North Carolina, "Governor's Letter Book," *Governor's Papers, John Willis Ellis* (Raleigh: North Carolina State Archives, 1861), 384–385, GLB 49; William S. Powell, *Dictionary of North Carolina Biography* (Chapel Hill: University of North Carolina Press, 1986), Vol. 2, 32. George Davis served as general counsel for the Wilmington & Raleigh–Wilmington & Weldon Railroad from 1848 until his death in 1896.
47. *The New York Times*, June 18, 1865.

48. Chittenden, 259–260.
49. *Ibid.*, 57.
50. Sprunt, 269–271.
51. Powell, *Dictionary of North Carolina Biography*, Vol. 2, 32.
52. The legacy of George Davis is a curiosity. While Sprunt admiringly assigns Davis the honor of "beloved leader of the Lower Cape Fear," and the object of "increased veneration," around the turn of the twentieth century, a generation later would jest that the dramatically outstretched right hand of the statue was said to be pointing to a liquor store, now long gone. In more recent times, student pranksters would place a beer can in the same hand transforming the great orator into historic jolly reveler — a ritual indignity that inevitably befalls lifelike statues on every college campus. Had Davis remained tenacious in his position on preserving the Union, it is unlikely it would have changed anything; however, that he not only endorsed secession after the failed peace conference, but also rendered his services to the Confederate government, remains a testament to the fallibility of genius, the cost of which is to become an artifact of one's times rather than an object of veneration for the ages.
53. *Wilmington Herald*, February 14, February 21.
That the natural destiny as well as the truest interests of North Carolina, impel her to cast her fate with her sisters of the South, and not with her enemies of the North, and that therefore, we urge upon the Convention to be assembled the promptest practicable action, by which the State of North Carolina can be enabled to take her place with the Southern Confederate States.
54. *Wilmington Herald*, February 28, 1861.
55. *Ibid.*; Tuther, 29: Wilmington & Weldon Rail Road Company, 1860, 14, 47.
56. Georgia, *Journal of the Public and Secret Proceeding of the Convention of the People of Georgia, Held in Milledgeville and Savannah in 1861. Together with the Ordinances Adopted. Published by Order of the Convention* (Milledgeville, GA: Broughton, Nisbet & Barnes, State Printers, 1861), 343–345, Georgia State University, University Library, JK 9784 .A15 1861.
57. *Wilmington Herald*, February 28, 1861.
58. *Wilmington Herald*, February 25, 1861.
59. *Wilmington Herald*, February 9, 1861.
The public mind seems now satisfied that an attack on Fort Sumter is inevitable within a very short time — perhaps a few days. That it will be taken no one doubts, and that, — if its capture is resisted — a great sacrifice of life will be required, is equally certain. The contemplation of such an event is painful in the extreme, and in view of it, the question naturally suggests itself, what is Maj. Anderson's duty under all the circumstances? The military code adjudges a surrender, except where resistance would be futile, and accompanied with unnecessary loss of life, as disgraceful — and it requires these consequences of resistance to be apparent, and certain beyond a doubt. Major Anderson, according to the generally received opinion, not only has the benefit of this exception, but the circumstances which surround him are novel, and of such a character as, in our opinion, to justify him in an immediate surrender upon demand of the authorities of South Carolina. The government, to whose protection he has a right to look as long as he is in its service, has not reinforced him, although it is well aware that his present force is inadequate to the defense of his post. The policy of sending such reinforcements cannot affect the question at all. If resistance is intended by the government, it must make that resistance effectual at every hazard, possible. To leave its officer in a position of such imminent danger and to throw the whole responsibility of defending his post upon him, and a handful of men while the possibility of strengthening his force exists, is not only inhuman, and barbarous, but such instructions cannot, in any point of view, be regarded as binding. Besides Major Anderson's sympathies are, we are told, all with the South — he believes, they say, that a State has a right to secede — his family are among those who occupy the position of enemies to his government — his property lies in a Southern State, and consists to a great extent in slaves. It

may be said that this — if not an additional reason for self-abnegation — is still only at most sufficient to justify his resignation. But the same military code would, under the circumstances which surround him, make it more disgraceful to resign than surrender, inasmuch as the former would only shift the responsibility to another's shoulders. It seems to us that Major Anderson has done his whole duty in this matter and that he is not bound by any consideration of faith to the government, or personal honor to resist an attack upon Fort Sumter. On the contrary we think that it is his duty to his country, to the South, to himself, and to humanity to surrender that post to the State of South Carolina.

60. *Wilmington Herald*, March 26, 1861.

61. United States War Department, *The War of Rebellion, A Compilation of the Official Records of the Union and Confederate Armies* (Washington, DC: Government Printing Office, 1887), Ser. 1, Vol. 18, 848–849, CU-MOA; *The War of Rebellion, A Compilation of the Official Records of the Union and Confederate Armies* (Washington, DC: Government Printing Office, 1891), Series 1, Volume 33, 602–604, CU-MOA

62. United States War Department, *O.R.*, 1880, Ser. 1, Vol. 1, 486; *Wilmington Herald*, April 6, 1861.

63. Virginia, *Proceedings of the Virginia State Convention of 1861, February 13–May 1*, George H. Reese, ed., Richmond Enquirer (Richmond, VA: Virginia State Library, 1965), 362, University of Richmond, Boatwright Memorial Library, "Monday, April 8, 1861," Virginia Secession Convention, http://collections.richmond.edu/secession/documents/index.html?id=pb.3.372 (accessed on September 25, 2011).

64. *Wilmington Herald*, April 9, 10, 11, 1861.

65. Major Robert Anderson and his garrison had been evacuated by Union ships.

66. William Howard Russell, *My Diary North and South* (London: Bradbury and Evans, 1863), Vol. 1, 134–138, Library of Congress, E 167 .R963; *Wilmington Herald*, April 16, 1861. The Committee of Safety, for the Town of Wilmington was chaired by John Dawson, Esq., dry goods merchant, president of the branch of the Bank of North Carolina, and mayor of Wilmington. The secretary of the committee was S.D. Wallace, chairman of the Board of Superintendents of Common School, a town commissioner, assistant secretary and general ticket agent for the Wilmington & Weldon Railroad, and from 1862 to 1865, president of the railroad.

67. United States War Department, *O.R.*, 1880, Ser. 1, Vol. 1, 477, 487–488.

68. *Wilmington Herald*, February 25, 1861. The presence of such a large quantity of ordinance on the railroad docks as early as February 23, however, suggests that the individuals to whom it was delivered were acting as agents for South Carolina or were stockpiling it for use in connection with the seizure of the North Carolina coastal defenses. The presence of Major W.H.C. Whiting in April, an officer serving in the then foreign army, assisting state militia refitting federal forts less than a month before the state seceded implies that state had informally sided with the Confederacy.

69. *Wilmington Journal*, April 15, 1861.

The news of the capture of Fort Sumter was received here on Saturday afternoon and created the wildest excitement. We need hardly attempt a description. It may be enough to say that the tone of feeling was unmistakeable (sic.) and the effect was evidently to convince the most skeptical that the time for resistance had come. Men who before had clung to the hope however feeble of being able to preserve or reconstruct the Union, were at last forced to confess that they could cling to that hope no longer. No doubt they will now be as strong Southern Rights men as the strongest. Speeches were made from the steps of the Cape Fear Bank and from other points by George Davis, T.D. Meares, R.H. Cowan and Eli W, Hall, Esqrs., and the Hon. S.J. Person and John L. Holmes, Esq. They all breathed the same spirit of resistance to aggression. Guns were fired on the wharf, a lone star flag was hoisted on Princess street, and a flag of the Confederate States near the corner of Front and Market streets.

70. *Wilmington Journal*, April 15, 1861.

71. United States War Department, *O.R.*, 1880, Ser. 1, Vol. 1, 486; *Wilmington Herald*, April 16, 17, 18, 1861; *Wilmington Journal*, April 20, 25, 1861.
72. United States, War Department, *O.R.*, 1880, Ser. 1, Vol. 1, 486.
73. *Ibid*, 487–488.
74. *Wilmington Journal*, May 4, 1861.
75. Wilmington & Weldon Railroad Company, *Annual Reports of the President and Directors, and the Chief Engineer and Superintendent of the Wilmington & Weldon R. R. Co., with the Proceeding of the General Meeting of the Stockholders, November 14, 1861* (Wilmington, NC: Fulton & Price, 1861), 5–6, UNCCH, Cp 385.1 W78a1; United States, Congress, *Railroads — Atlantic to the Mississippi* (Washington, DC: 23rd Congress, 2nd Session, 1835), Document 177, 34–58. The peacetime vision that Ashe suggests in his report, "the Atlantic line of Road," might have been something like the Atlantic Coastline Railroad as it existed around 1900; or it might have been the Southern Route (Memphis, Tennessee, to Savannah, Georgia) of Lt. Col. S.H. Long's *Atlantic to the Mississippi* survey with the post-Texas acquisition addition of continuing the full length of the coast to Brownsville. Pondering at length on a counterfactual coastal corridor that he may, or may have not, imagined invites wasteful consideration of alternate outcomes. The value of his statements stands only where relevant to the aggregation of different lines that constituted the extent of his responsibility to the Confederate government.
76. United States, Congress, *Journal of the House of Representatives of the United States, 1849–1850* (Washington, DC: 31st Congress, First Session, 1849–50), February 21, 1850, 588; *Journal of the House of Representatives of the United States, 1850–51* (Washington, DC: 32nd Congress, First Session, 1851–52), December 22, 1851, 121.
77. Robert C. Black III, *Railroads of the Confederacy* (Chapel Hill: University of North Carolina Press, 1952), xxi-xxiii. A glance at the maps in Black illustrates two critical shortcomings of the southern rail network: inconsistent gauges and gaps. The Atlantic coast corridor extended from the neighborhood of Fredericksburg, Virginia, to Thomasville, Georgia, with standard gauge commencing north of Wilmington, North Carolina, and five-foot gauge south. Ideally, a continuation from Thomasville to Baton Rouge would have allowed the coastal corridor access to the Gulf of Mexico and the Mississippi corridor (New Orleans to the Memphis hub). The eastern interior corridor in the Piedmont lacked a direct (and initially discontinuous) connection between Charlotte, North Carolina, and Atlanta, Georgia; thus, to travel from Montgomery, Alabama, to the hub at Richmond, Virginia, a shipment would travel on standard gauge as far as West Point, Georgia, be transferred to five-foot cars there to continue to Atlanta, be diverted east to Branchville, South Carolina, then west to Charlotte, North Carolina, and be transferred back to standard gauge cars to continue to the hub at Goldsboro, North Carolina. The competition of the connection between Greensboro, North Carolina, and Danville, Virginia, during the war offered another occasion to transfer the shipment from standard gauge cars to five-foot gauge cars. The western corridor from the hub at Richmond to the hub at Memphis maintained five-foot gauge along its length, as did the Mississippi corridor from Memphis to New Orleans.
78. United States, War Department, *The War of Rebellion, A Compilation of the Official Records of the Union and Confederate Armies* (Washington, DC: Government Printing Office, 1881), Ser. 1, Vol. 5, 867, CU-MOA; United States, *Journal of the Confederate States of America, 1861–1865* (Washington, DC: Government Printing Office, 1904), Vol. 1, January 24, 1862, 701, Library of Congress, KFZ8618.2 1861.
79. The fluid nature of war requires agile allocation of resources, but a seamless network of railroads branching off one or more trunk lines allows for the distribution of troops and material to be distributed over a large geographic area as reserve, ready to be deployed along the line to reinforce static defenses, or to attack the flanks of the opposing force, if the distribution of the reserve is consistently apportioned to the capacity of the branch line. Additionally, the wartime use of a railroad network is not necessarily incompatible with serving the needs of the civilian population if judicious prioritization and schedule modifications are exploited. The peacetime functions of a unified network represent a pattern of asset dis-

tribution and flow that is not radically different from that in war: the time a shipment (freight or passengers) is at rest between dispatch and final destination should be minimal; accumulation of excessive numbers of loaded or empty cars, aside from the marshaling yards at hub depots, must be avoided; the network must be organized hierarchically from a trunk line connecting hubs descending through lesser order branch lines down to the lowest order of lines akin to the classification of stream order in a drainage basin or the distribution of the mails; and the flexible coordination of scheduled dispatches, a prioritization, in a hierarchical network is a variable that can be adjusted within limits to accommodate to address unforeseen demands. In contemporary terms, the network is a hard wired, but it can run a multitude of programs.

80. Wilmington & Weldon Railroad Company, 6.

81. Wilmington & Weldon Railroad Company, 1861, 11–13; Wilmington & Weldon Railroad Company, *Proceedings of the Wilmington & Weldon Rail Road Co. at their Twentieth Annual Meeting, held at Wilmington, North Carolina, November 9th 1855* (Wilmington, NC: Loring, 1855), 13, UNCCH, NC 385 W, 1855.

82. Wilmington & Weldon Railroad Company, 1861, 13.

83. *Ibid.*

84. William Howard Russell, 1863, Vol. 1, 134–135; Wilmington & Weldon Rail Road Company, 1861, 16. Fremont, in the closing remarks of his report, warns military officers not to interfere with the train schedules.

85. Wilmington & Weldon Rail Road Company, 1861, 13; North Carolina Rail Road Company, *Proceedings of the Thirteenth Annual Meeting of the Stockholder of the North Carolina Rail Road Company, held at Hillsboro, Thursday and Friday, July 10th and 11th, 1862* (Raleigh: North Carolina Institute for the Deaf & Dumb and the Blind, 1862), 10–11, UNCCH, C 385.1 N87p.

86. North Carolina Rail Road Company, 1862, 11.

87. North Carolina Rail Road Company, *Proceedings of the Fourteenth Annual Meeting of the Stockholder of the North Carolina Rail Road Company, held at Greensboro, on Thursday, the 9th day of July, 1863* (Raleigh: North Carolina Institute for the Deaf & Dumb and the Blind, 1863), 18–21, UNCCH, C 385.1 N87p; Wilmington & Weldon Railroad Company, 1861, 9, 24.

88. R. Matthew Poteat, "Part 1: 'A Modest Estimate of His Own Abilities': Governor Henry Toole Clark and the Early Civil War Leadership of North Carolina," *North Carolina Historical Review* 84:1 (January 2007), 1, 12, 14–15, 22; William S. Powell, *Dictionary of North Carolina Biography* (Chapel Hill: University of North Carolina Press, 1986), Volume 2, 151–152. Wilmington & Weldon Railroad Company, 1861, 16; Fonvielle, *Fort Fisher 1865*, 8–9; North Carolina Railroad Company, *Proceedings of the Twelfth Annual Meeting of the Stockholder of the North Carolina Rail Road Company, held a Salisbury, on Thursday and Friday, July 11th & 12th, 1861* (Raleigh: North Carolina Institute for the Deaf & Dumb and the Blind, 1861), 5, UNCCH, C 385.1 N87p.

89. Wilmington & Weldon Railroad Company, 1861, 12; *Wilmington Journal*, April 25, 1861. Stringers were sawed through on the railroad bridge of Toisnot Creek, near Wilson, in an attempt to derail a train carrying Georgia volunteers to Virginia.

90. Wilmington & Weldon Railroad Company, *Ibid.*, 14.

91. Wilmington & Weldon Railroad Company, 1861, 23

92. United States National Archives, *Confederate Papers Relating to Citizens or Business Firms, compiled 1874–1899, documenting the period 1861–1865* (Washington, DC: National Archives, 1874–1899), Records Group 109, ARC Identifier 2133274 / MLR Number PI101 180, Roll 1122, Document 261.

93. *Ibid.*

Chapter III

1. United States, *Instruction for Heavy Artillery; Prepared by a Board of Officers, for the use of the Army of the United States* (Charleston, NC: Evan & Cogswell, 1861; reprinted, Richmond, VA: West & Johnston, 1862), 1–84, Duke University Library, http://babel.hathitrust.org/cgi/pt?id=dul1.ark:/13960/t5db8sn88. Accessed on October 20, 2012.

2. United States National Archive, *Confederate Papers Relating to Citizens or Business Firms, compiled 1874–1899, documenting the period 1861–1865* (Washington, DC: National Archives, 1874–1899), Records Group 109, ARC Identifier 2133274 / MLR Number PI101 180, Roll 1122, Document 261, no. 223, 230; E. Milby Burton, *The Siege of Charleston, 1861–1865* (Columbia: University of South Carolina, 1982), 64.

3. United States, Naval War Records Office, *Official Records of the Union and Confederate Navies in the War of Rebellion* (Washington, DC: Government Printing Office, 1901), Series I, Volume 12, 312, CU-MOA.

The armament of the water front, as ordered by General Beauregard, consisted of seven X-inch columbiads, and my plans were arranged for such a battery. The interior slopes of the water battery were consequently intended for seven circular traverses against enfilading fire. The labor having arrived, the work was rapidly pressed forward, and by September 1, 1861, was ready to receive its armament. In place of receiving seven X-inch guns but one could be procured, together with one X-inch columbiad, model to be a 32-pounder and rifled; one VIII-inch columbiad, model bored to a 24-pounder and rifled; one VIII-inch columbiad; nine navy 32-pounders; three navy 42-pounders; three navy VIII-inch howitzers; two 24-pounders; two 42-pounder carronnades [carronades], and two long English 12-pounders. Thirteen of these, viz, one X-inch columbiad; one X-inch columbiad, pattern bored to a 32-pounder and rifled; one VIII-inch columbiad, pattern bored to a 24-pounder and rifled; one VIII-inch columbiad; six navy 32-pounders, and three navy 42-pounders, being in all thirteen guns, were ordered to be placed on the water front.

4. United States, 1901, 270–271, 313.
5. United States National Archive, *op. cit.*, Roll 0761, Document 4, v1-v3.
6. *Ibid.*, Roll 1122, Document 261, no. 249.
7. *Ibid.*, Roll 0761, Document 4, no. v1-v3, Roll 1122, Document 261, no. 172, 159.
8. *Ibid.*, Roll 0872, Document 93, no. 3.
9. *Ibid.*, Roll 1122, Document 261, no. 162.
10. J.M. Hollowell, *War-Time Reminiscences and Other Selections* (Goldsboro, NC: Goldsboro Herald, 1939), 16, Wayne County Public Library, LH NC WAY .86 HOL; United States National Archive, *op. cit.*, Roll 1122, Document 261, no. 159, 161, 161A-161M.
11. United States Naval War Records Office, *Official Records of the Union and Confederate Navies in the War of Rebellion* (Washington, DC: Government Printing Office, 1898), Ser. 1, Vol. 7, 109, CU-MOA.
12. United States War Department, *The War of Rebellion: A Compilation of the Official Records of the Union and Confederate Armies* (Washington, DC: Government Printing Office, 1881), Ser. 1, Vol. 5, 858, CU-MOA.
13. Anonymous, *The Stranger's Guide and Official Directory for the City of Richmond. Showing the Location of the Public Buildings and Offices of the Confederate, State and City Governments, Residences of the Principal Officers, etc.* (Richmond, VA: Evans, 1863), 10; UNCCH, *Documenting the American South*, http://docsouth.unc.edu/imls/stranger/stranger.html. Accessed on October 5, 2011.
14. Virginia, *Regulations for the Commissary's Department of the State of Virginia* (Richmond, VA: Wynne, 1861), 5, Duke University Libraries, http://babel.hathitrust.org/cgi/pt?id=dul1.ark:/13960/t8z900n28/ Accessed on November 20, 2011.
15. George W. Rains, *History of the Confederate Powder Works* (Newburg, NY: Newburg Daily News Print, n.d.), 3–4, 8, 9–10, 20, 24, Duke University Libraries, http://babel.hathitrust.org/cgi/pt?id=ucl.b61807. Copper boilers for the powder works in Augusta were

reworked turpentine stills from Wilmington. Powder manufacturing on a less ambitious scale occurred at sites in Petersburg, then Charlotte, and then Columbia, under the auspices of the Confederate Navy Department, and an unknown quantity was produced at powder mills in Richmond and Raleigh.

16. Rains, 21–22.

17. Jefferson Davis, *The Rise and Fall of the Confederate Government*, Vol. 1 (New York: Appleton, 1881), 317–318, 471, 476–483, UNCW, E487 .D263 v.1. Fayetteville would produce about 400 stands per month during the war.

18. United States National Archive, *op. cit.*, Roll 1122, Document 261. For example, on July 10, 1862, 619 kegs of powder were shipped on the Wilmington & Manchester; on July 23, 1862, there was a shipment of 32 kegs of powder marked from Col. Rains, Augusta, Georgia; on August 10, 1862, the firm transported 300 boxes of powder marked from Col. Gorgas; and on April 30, 1863, a shipment of 76 boxes of cartridges and two boxes of percussion caps were marked as coming from Col. Rains.

19. Caleb Huse, *The Supplies for the Confederate Army, How they were obtained in Europe and how they paid for* (Boston: Marvin, 1904), 9–10, 15–16, 22–23, 36, UNCCH, Cp970 .72H96; United States War Department, *The War of Rebellion: A Compilation of the Official Records of the Union and Confederate Armies* (Washington, DC: Government Printing Office, 1897), Ser. 2, Vol. 2, 191, CU-MOA. Trenholm Brothers & Company was located at 42 Pine Street, near Wall Street. By early 1862, William Seward was soliciting information from the superintendent of police for New York City concerning the relationship between the company with Fraser, Trenholm & Company of Liverpool, England and John Fraser & Company of Charleston, South Carolina. The Liverpool and Charleston companies had owned vessels running the blockade from the onset of the war. William Trenholm became the secretary of the treasury for the Confederate States.

20. Huse, plate on unnumbered page.

21. James Sprunt, *Derelicts: An Account of Ships Lost at Sea in General Commercial Traffic and a Brief History of Blockade Runners Stranded Along the North Carolina Coast, 1861–1865* (Wilmington, NC: Sprunt, 1920), 52, 59–62, 66, 79–82, NHCL, NC 973.758 S; James Sprunt, *Chronicles of the Cape Fear River, 1660–1916* (Raleigh, NC: Edwards & Broughton, 1916), 387–388.

22. United States, *The War of Rebellion: A Compilation of the Official Records of the Union and Confederate Armies* (Washington, DC: Government Printing Office, 1891), Ser. 1, Vol. 33, 1328, CU-MOA.

23. Wilmington & Weldon Railroad Company, *Annual Reports of the President and Directors, and the Chief Engineer and Superintendent, of the Wilmington & Weldon R.R. Co., with the Proceeding of the General Meeting of Stockholder, November 18th, 1863* (Wilmington, NC: Fulton & Price, 1863), 38, UNCCH, Cp385.1 W78a1 1861.

24. *Ibid.*, 17.

25. Wilmington & Weldon Rail Road Company, *Proceedings of the Stockholders of the Wilmington & Weldon R.R. Co., at their Special Meeting, August 1st, 1865; together with the Proceedings of the 30th Annual Meeting, held at Wilmington, North Carolina, November 22, 1865, with the Reports of the President and Directors, and the Chief Engineer and Superintendent* (Wilmington, NC: Engelhard & Price, 1866), 8, 19, UNCCH, Cp385.1 W78r. Only 159 bales, valued at $25,000, remained after the war.

26. J.B. Jones, *A Rebel War Clerk's Diary at the Confederate States Capital* (Philadelphia: Lippincott, 1866), Vol., 2, 13–14, 94, 244, 317–319, State Library of North Carolina, 973.782 Jr 1866 v.2.

27. Wilmington & Weldon Railroad Company, *Annual Reports of the President and Directors, and the Chief Engineer and Superintendent of the Wilmington & Weldon R. R. Co., with the Proceeding of the General Meeting of the Stockholders, November 14, 1861* (Wilmington, NC: Fulton & Price, 1861), 31, UNCCH, Cp385.1 W78a1 1861; Wilmington & Weldon Rail Road Company, *Annual Reports of the President and Directors, and the Chief Engineer and Superintendent of the Wilmington & Weldon R.R. Co., with the Proceedings of the General*

Meeting of the Stockholders, December 14th, 1862 (Wilmington, NC: Fulton & Price, 1862), 27, UNCCH, UNCCH, Cp385.1 W78; Wilmington & Weldon Railroad, 1863, 31; Wilmington & Weldon Rail Road Company, *Annual Reports of the President and Directors, and the Chief Engineer and Superintendent of the Wilmington & Weldon R.R. Co., with the Proceedings of the General Meeting of the Stockholders, November 23D. 1864* (Wilmington, NC: Fulton & Price, 1864), 7, UNCCH, Cp385.1 W78 1864; Wilmington & Weldon Railroad Company, 1866, 22, 27, 32.
    28. Wilmington & Weldon Railroad, 1864, 8–9.
    29. *Ibid.*, 9.
    30. Marc Weidenmier, "Money and Finance in the Confederate States of America," *EH.Net* (Economic History Association, February 1, 2010), http://eh.net/encyclopedia/article/weidenmier.finance.confederacy.us. Accessed on December 2, 2011.
    31. United States National Archive, *op. cit.*, Records Group 109, Document 151.
    32. Robert C. Black, *Railroads of the Confederacy* (Chapel Hill: University of North Carolina Press, 1998), 220.

Chapter IV

    1. Wilmington & Weldon Railroad Company, *Annual Reports of the President and Directors, and the Chief Engineer and Superintendent of the Wilmington & Weldon R.R. Co., with the Proceedings of the General Meeting of Stockholders, December 14, 1862* (Wilmington, NC: Fulton & Price, 1862), 11–15, UNCCH, Cp385.1 W78r 1862.
    2. *Raleigh Register*, September 17, 1862.
    3. Wilmington & Weldon Railroad Company, *Regulations for the Government of Officers and Employees of the Company, and for the Running of Trains of the Wilmington & Weldon Rail Road, Adopted March 2d, 1855; and Revised, March, 1867, to which is attached the By Laws of the Company, Now in Forces—March, 1867* (Wilmington, NC: Bernard, 1867), 8–9, 12, 14–15, 18, 20, WRRM.
    4. Wilmington & Weldon Railroad Company, 1862, 15; The Oakdale Cemetery Company Inc., Burial Database (Wilmington, NC: Oakdale Cemetery, 2007), Section D, Lot 14, http://www.oakdalecemetery.org/burial_database.asp?id=6728&page=&txtFirstName=James&txtLastName=Green&txtDOD=. Accessed on October 18, 2011; First Presbyterian Church, *Memorial of the First Presbyterian Church, Wilmington, N.C., Seventy-Fifth Anniversary, 1817–1892* (Richmond, VA: Whittet & Shepperson, 1892), 18, East Carolina University, Joyner Library, BX9211.W7 F57X 1893.
    5. James Sprunt, *Chronicles of the Cape Fear River, 1660–1916* (Raleigh, NC: Edwards & Broughton, 1916), 149–150, 155, 266, 286; The Oakdale Cemetery Company Inc., Burial Database; *Wilmington Journal*, September 20, 1862; Harold Havelock Kynett, Samuel Worcester Butler, D G Brinton, "News and Miscellany," *The Medical and Surgical Reporter* 9, no. 2 (October 11, 1862), 54.
    6. Nickolas W. Schenck, transcribed by LuAnne Mims, *The Diary of Nicholas W. Schenck* (Wilmington, NC: University of North Carolina, William Madison Randall Library, Special Collections (1905), 2000), http://library.uncw.edu/web/collections/Schenck/schenckintro.html (accessed on October 7, 2011), 28–29.
    7. Joseph Janvier Woodward, *Report on Epidemic Cholera and Yellow Fever in the Army of the United States, during the Year 1867* (Washington, DC: Government Printing Office, 1868), xxxiv-xxv; United States Sanitary Commission, *Sanitary Memoirs of the War of Rebellion*, Vol. 1 (New York: Hurd and Houghton, 1867), 238–240, http://books.google.com/books?id=HAUvDHr0gM4C&pg=PA238&lpg=PA238&dq=Yellow+Fever+Victims,+Wilmington,+NC&source=bl&ots=jTOLTwdmZe&sig=U5SlM00qTFPlXQKhq7Z8pPrQvlk&hl=en&ei=qS2bTqPRFsuBtge6orRE&sa=X&oi=book_result&ct=result&resnum=8&ved=0CFUQ6AEwBzgK#v=onepage&q&f=false. Accessed on October 19, 2011; Schenck, 128–130; Frank D. Smaw, Jr., *Wilmington Directory, including a General and City Business Di-*

rectory for 1865–66 (Wilmington, NC: Heinsberger, 1865), 65, 104, UNCCH, CC971.65 W74wl; T. Tuther, Jr., *Kelley's Wilmington Directory, to which is added a Business Directory for 1860* (Wilmington, NC: Fulton & Price, 1860), 98, NHCL, NC385W; Sprunt, 286, 290–291.

8. William George Thomas, "A Review of the 'Report on the Epidemic of Yellow Fever which prevailed at Wilmington, N.C., in the Fall of 1862. By William T. Wragg, M.D., of Charleston, S.C.,'" *New York Medical Journal* 10, no. 3 (December 1869), 225–253.

9. Wilmington & Weldon Rail Road Company, *Annual Reports of the President and Directors, and the Chief Engineer and Superintendent of the Wilmington & Weldon R.R. Co., with the Proceedings of the General Meeting of the Stockholders, November 8th, 1860* (Wilmington, NC: Fulton & Price, 1860), 31, NHCL, NC 385 W; Wilmington & Weldon Railroad Company, *Annual Reports of the President and Directors, and the Chief Engineer and Superintendent of the Wilmington & Weldon R. R. Co., with the Proceeding of the General Meeting of the Stockholders, November 14, 1861* (Wilmington, NC: Fulton & Price, 1861), 17, UNCCH, Cp385.1 W 78al 1861.

10. Thomas, 239.

11. *Ibid.*, 250.

12. United States Naval War Records Office, *Official Records of the Union and Confederate Navies in the War of the Rebellion* (Washington, DC: Government Printing Office, 1899), Ser. 1, Vol. 8, 82, 89–90, CU-MOA.

13. Mark Wilde-Ramsing, and Wilson Angley, *National Register of Historic Places Nomination, Cape Fear Civil War Shipwreck District* (Raleigh: North Carolina Department of Cultural Resources, Archaeology, 1985), 14–15, 38.

14. United States Naval War Records Office, *Official Records of the Union and Confederate Navies in the War of the Rebellion* (Washington, DC: Government Printing Office, 1894), Ser. 1, Vol. 1, 501, CU-MOA.

15. Thomas, 244–245; The Oakdale Cemetery Company, Inc., Burial Database (Wilmington, NC: Oakdale Cemetery, 2007), Section K, Lot 63, Section J, 38, http://www.oakdalecemetery.org/burial_database.asp?id=6728&page=&txtFirstName=James&txtLastName=Green&txtDOD=. Accessed on October 25, 2011.

16. *Wilmington Journal*, October 27, 1862, NHCL, LCPF No. 508.

17. Thomas, 240–241, 247–248, 250–251. Incidentally, the Hole in the Wall, where Georgia Weeks was listed as having died on August 22, was in the next block south from Cassidy's Shipyard. Unfortunately, the date of her death is questionable, and Dr. Thomas was unable to question the clerk at Oakdale Cemetery because he had died of yellow fever.

18. Tuther, 55, 81, 95, 98–99, 101–102; Thomas, 251–252.

19. John Johns, "Wilmington During the Blockade," *Harper's New Monthly Magazine* 33, no. 196 (September 1866), 498.

20. Sprunt, 413–414.

21. Thomas, 227.

22. *Wilmington Journal*, September 29, November 17, 1862.

23. Sprunt, 284.

24. *Wilmington Journal*, October 20, October 21, October 27, October 29, 1862, September 20, November 17, 1862, NHCL, LCPF No. 508.

25. Sprunt, 269–271, 286–287.

26. *New York Times*, November 19, 1862.

27. *Wilmington Journal*, November 21, 1862.

28. United States War Department, *The War of Rebellion: A Compilation of the Official Records of the Union and Confederate Armies* (Washington, DC: Government Printing Office, 1887), Ser. 1, Vol. 18, 848, CU-MOA; *ibid.*, Ser. 1, Vol. 42 (1895), 1220, CU-MOA

29. *Ibid.*, Ser. 1, Vol. 18, 1887, 416, 475.

30. Wilmington & Weldon Railroad Company, 1862, 6–7, 21–24.

31. Wilmington & Weldon Railroad Company, *Annual Reports of the President and*

Directors, and the Chief Engineer and Superintendent, of the Wilmington & Weldon R.R. Co., with the Proceeding of the General Meeting of Stockholder, November 18th, 1863 (Wilmington, NC: Fulton & Price, 1863), 15, 24–25, 31, 38, UNCCH, Cp385.1 W78a1 1863. Volumes of naval stores for the whole fiscal year (1862–63) were not significant, and in some months nothing was transported. Wilmington received 172 bbl. of turpentine; and 2,735 bbl. of rosin, 438 bbl. of turpentine, and 396 bbl. of tar was received at Weldon.

32. Schenck, 29–30; *Wilmington Journal*, November 17, 1862.
33. United States Naval War Records Office, *O. R.*, Ser. 1, Vol. 6, 507–508, CU-MOA.
34. *O.R.*, Ser. 1, Vol. 18, 53–55, CU-MOA.
35. *Ibid.*, 106–108.
36. *Ibid.*, 56–57.
37. *Ibid*, 108.
38. *Ibid*, 58–59, 108–109.
39. *Wilmington Journal*, December 20, December 22, 1862.
40. Wilmington & Weldon Railroad Company, 1863, 38.
41. *Wilmington Journal*, December 2, December 18, 1862.
42. *Wilmington Journal*, January 17, 1863; Wilmington & Weldon Railroad, 1863, 31.
43. Wilmington & Weldon Railroad, 1863, 26–27.
44. *O.R.*, Ser. 1, Vol. 18, 837.
45. O.R., Ser. 1, Vol. 27, Pt. 2, 859–867, CU-MOA.
46. *Ibid.*, 975–976.
47. *Ibid.*, 963–964.
48. *Ibid.*, 965, 968–969.
49. Wilmington & Weldon Railroad Company, 1863, 23, 25–26.
50. *Ibid.*, 29.
51. O.R., Ser. 1, Vol. 18, 837, 1051; Wilmington & Weldon Railroad Company, 1863, 26–27.
52. O.R., Ser. 1, Vol. 18, 769. For example, the Union presence in the extreme east of North Carolina, prior to the December 1862 raid, was cause for Colonel L.B. Northrop of the Confederate Commissary Department to request that Governor Vance remove stores of food, including hogs, west of areas that might be accessible to the enemy.
53. Wilmington & Weldon Railroad Company, 1863, 24–28.
54. *Ibid.*, 29.
55. Wilmington & Weldon Rail Road Company, *Annual Reports of the President and Directors, and the Chief Engineer and Superintendent of the Wilmington & Weldon R.R. Co., with the Proceedings of the General Meeting of the Stockholders, November 23D. 1864* (Wilmington, NC: Fulton & Price, 1864), 2–3, UNCCH, Cp385.1 W78 1864.
56. *Ibid.*, 3–4.
57. For a modern motorist, the journey from Wilmington to Petersburg via Goldsboro, Greensboro, Danville and Burkeville would be 406 miles compared to the 237 miles following the direct route.
58. *Wilmington Journal*, November 16, 1849.
We hope that we will not be assailed with the hackneyed outcry of being illiberal, or "behind the age," when we aver, that had not the North Carolina Railroad project been presented to us as a State work — as eminently North Carolinian in its inception, character and tendencies — we would have opposed it "tooth and toe-nail" from the start — nay more, we feel perfectly confident, that had it not appealed to the State pride of the Legislature, it would never have become a law. When it was introduced, the partizans [sic] of the Charlotte and Danville Road, backed by the Virginia interest, were knocking at the door of the Legislature for a charter to connect those two points. It was as a substitute for this project, which would have cut the State in two, and carried all its central and western trade to the Virginia markets, that the Central Railroad bill was passed. Nothing but a desire to build up a market within our own borders — to foster

our own trade — to avert the impending ruin of our own public works already constructed, and to prevent the draining of our own resources to swell the commerce and prosperity of our neighbors at the price of our own increased impoverishment, could have overcome the scruples which existed against the State's becoming farther involved in any projects of internal improvement which, as they must in some measure, be confined in their effects to special localities, should, if possible, be constructed by those who expect to be the peculiar recipients of the benefits to be derived from them. Such being the facts of the case, we cannot regard without jealousy and apprehension, the strenuous efforts which are being made in advance to divert the work from the legitimate object, and make it subservient to the interests and wishes of our Virginia rivals.

59. O.R., Ser. 4, Vol. 2, 175–176, 971, CU-MOA. Confederate commissary general L.B. Northrop stated in a report on subsistence in November 1863 that there was a sufficient quantity of corn to make up for a lack of wheat to provide bread to the army and the civilians, but it was widely distributed in other states and had to be transported by rail. He emphasized the fact that the connection at Weldon could not carry the amount of corn needed, even if it remained undisturbed by the enemy. He recommended that the government offer additional labor for the construction of the railroad from Greensboro to Danville, on the advice of the president of the company, so that it could be completed in three months.

60. *Ibid.*, 175–176, 385–386, 393–394.

61. North Carolina Railroad Company, *Fifteenth Annual Meeting of the Stockholders of the North Carolina Rail Road Company, Held at Raleigh, Thursday, July 14, 1864* (Raleigh: North Carolina Institute for the Deaf and Dumb and the Blind, 1864), 16, 25, UNCCH, C385.1 N78p 1850.7a.

62. United States Naval War Records Office, *Official Records of the Union and Confederate Navies in the War of the Rebellion* (Washington, DC: Government Printing Office, 1900), Ser. 4, Vol. 3, 599–600, CU-MOA.

63. J.B. Jones, vol. 2, 463.

64. Howard C. Westwood, "Ulysses S. Grant and Benjamin Butler in the Appomattox Campaign," *Illinois Historical Journal* 84, no. 1 (Spring 1991), 41–46.

65. Jones, 190–191.

66. *Ibid.*, 270–271. Throughout the war, Confederate clerk J.B. Jones recorded the daily travails of life in Richmond. His entries include the prices of food and household items in the market, the weather, and the progress of his vegetable garden. At times, he railed against the speculators, profiteers, and extortionists that exploded the price for the common necessities of life to a stupendous level; for the government officials that accepted their bribes, he spared no contempt. Clinging tenaciously to the ideal of Southern independence, Jones deplored the inequities of the social system of his South as they became more obviously manifest: wealthy slave owners could buy their way out of military service or obtain positions safe behind the lines; the speculators could hog space on railroad freight shipments needed for food and military supplies; and the government turned a blind eye on the sufferings of the poor, civilian and soldier alike. With Grant's army on the attack at Richmond and Petersburg, Jones's diary entries state the urgency of prioritizing rail transport, with disregard for the speculators, for the sake of preventing the poor from abandoning the fight.

AUGUST 24TH. Clear and pleasant. Operations now must be initiated by the enemy. Gen. Lee writes that he is too weak to attempt to dislodge the Yankees from the Weldon Railroad. He cannot afford the loss of men necessary to accomplish it. He says the enemy, however, was "worsted" in the two conflicts, that of Friday and Sunday. And if he were to drive him away, the road would still be subject to interruption. He thinks we can still get supplies, by wagons, round the enemy's position, as well as by the Danville Road. He also suggests that corn be imported at Wilmington, and that every effort be made to accumulate supplies here; and he thinks we can hold out until corn matures some six weeks hence, so that the moral effect will be good, when it is apparent the efforts of the enemy to cut off our supplies are thwarted. He thinks the enemy has relinquished the idea of forcing our fortifications. But he says that Grant intended to force his way into Richmond last week. I wrote a letter to the President to-day, urging the necessity of preventing the transportation of any supplies on the railroads except for distribution at cost, and thus exterminating the speculators. The poor must be fed and protected, if they be relied upon to defend the country. The rich bribe the conscription officers, and keep out of the ranks, invest their Confederate money and bonds in real estate, and would be the first to submit to the United States Government; and the poor, whom they oppress, are in danger of demoralization from suffering and disgust, and might also embrace reunion rather than a prolongation of such miseries as they have so long experienced.

67. Wilmington & Weldon Railroad Company, 14.
68. North Carolina Railroad Company, 1864, 14, 21.
69. *New York Times,* February 25, 1865.
70. Wilmington & Weldon Rail Road Company, *Proceedings of the Stockholders of the Wilmington & Weldon R.R. Co., at their Special Meeting, August 1st, 1865; together with the Proceedings of the 30th Annual Meeting, held at Wilmington, North Carolina, November 22, 1865, with the Reports of the President and Directors, and the Chief Engineer and Superintendent* (Wilmington, NC: Engelhard & Price, 1866), 3–4, UNCCH, Cp385.1 W78r 1865.
71. *Ibid.,* 4, 7–8, 22.
72. Wilmington & Weldon Rail Road Company, *Annual Reports of the President and Directors, and the Chief Engineer and Superintendent of the Wilmington & Weldon R.R. Co., with the Proceedings of the General Meeting of the Stockholders, December 14th, 1862* (Wilmington, NC: Fulton & Price, 1862), 16, 20, UNCCH, Cp385.1 W78r 1862.
73. Wilmington & Weldon Rail Road Company, 1866, 10–12.
74. Raleigh & Gaston Rail Road Company, *Proceedings of the Fifteenth Annual Meeting of the Stockholders of the Raleigh & Gaston Railroad Company, with the Reports of the President, Treasurer, &c.* (Raleigh: North Carolina Institute for the Deaf and Dumb and the Blind, 1865), 6–8, NHCL.
75. North Carolina Railroad Company, *Proceeding of the Sixteenth Annual Meeting of the Stockholders of the North Carolina Railroad Company, held at Salisbury, July 13, 1865* (Raleigh: North Carolina Institute for the Deaf and Dumb and the Blind, 1865), 7–15, UNCCH, C385.1 M87e 1865.

Chapter V

1. Wilmington & Weldon Rail Road Company, *Proceedings of the Stockholders of the Wilmington & Weldon R.R. Co., at their Special Meeting, August 1st, 1865; together with the Proceedings of the 30th Annual Meeting, held at Wilmington, North Carolina, November 22, 1865, with the Reports of the President and Directors, and the Chief Engineer and Superintendent* (Wilmington, NC: Engelhard & Price, 1866), 8, UNCCH, Cp385.1 W78r 1866.
2. *Ibid.,* 21.
3. Stewart L. Murray, *The Reality of War, A Companion to Clausewitz* (London: Hodder and Stoughton, 1914), 60–61.
4. *Ibid.,* 48.
5. Leslie N. Boney, Jr., and James L. Allegood, *The Cape Fear Club* (Wilmington, NC: Wilmington, 1984), 1–4, 11–17, 46, 51–52.
6. Wilmington & Weldon Rail Road Company, *Annual Reports of the President and Directors, and the Chief Engineer and Superintendent of the Wilmington & Weldon R.R. Co., with the Proceedings of the General Meeting of the Stockholders, November 23D. 1864* (Wilmington, NC: Fulton & Price, 1864), 9, UNCCH, Cp385.1 W78 1864.
7. *Farmers' Register,* "Extracts from the Report of Walter Gwynn, Esq., Engineer, to the President and Directors of the Wilmington and Raleigh Rail Road Company," October 1836, 348–351.

8. Wilmington & Weldon Railroad Company, 1864, 4.
9. J.B. Jones, *A Rebel War Clerk's Diary at the Confederate States Capital*, vol. 2 (Philadelphia: Lippincott, 1866), 21, State Library of North Carolina, 973.782 Jr 1866 v.2.
10. William W. Freehling, *The South vs. The South, How Anti-Confederate Southerners Shaped the Course of the Civil War* (New York: Oxford University Press, 2001), 142.
11. Nickolas W. Schenck, transcribed by LuAnne Mims, *The Diary of Nicholas W. Schenck* (Wilmington: University of North Carolina, William Madison Randall Library, Special Collections (1905), 2000), http://library.uncw.edu/web/collections/Schenck/schenck intro.html. Accessed on December 25, 2011, 39.
12. Jefferson Davis, *The Rise and Fall of the Confederate Government*, vol. 1 (New York: Appleton, 1881), Volume I, 208, UNCW, E487.D283 v.1.
The "plan of secession," if any, and the purpose of secession, unquestionably, originated, not in Washington City, or with the Senators or Representatives of the South, but among the people of the several States, many months before it was attempted. They followed no leaders at Washington or elsewhere, but acted for themselves, with an independence and unanimity unprecedented in any movement of such magnitude. Before the meeting of the caucus of January 5, 1861, South Carolina had seceded, and Alabama, Mississippi, Florida, Louisiana, and Texas had taken the initial step of secession, by calling conventions for its accomplishment. Before the election of Lincoln, all the Southern States, excepting one or two, had pledged themselves to separate from the Union upon the triumph of a sectional party in the Presidential election, by acts or resolutions of their Legislatures, resolves of both Democratic and Whig State Conventions, and of primary assemblies of the people in every way in which they could commit themselves to any future act.
13. *Ibid.*, 209–217, 301–302, 304. Only on February 28, 1861, did the Confederate Congress enact legislation for national defense.
14. South Carolina, *Journal of the State Convention of South Carolina; Together with the Resolution and Ordinance* (Columbia, SC: Johnston & Cavis, 1852), 25, University of South Carolina, USC School of Law, Coleman Karesh Library, F273 .S68 1852.
15. Wilmington & Weldon Rail Road Company, *Annual Reports of the President and Directors, and the Chief Engineer and Superintendent, of the Wilmington & Weldon Rail Road Co., with the Proceeding of the Stockholders, November 13th, 1867* (Wilmington, NC: Englehard & Price, 1867), 5–6, UNCCH, C385.1 W78r 1867.
16. *Ibid.*, 11.
17. John H. Claiborne, *Seventy-five Years in Old Virginia* (New York: Neale, 1904), 298–301, State Library of North Carolina, 975.503 C585s.
18. *Ibid.*, 301.

Chapter VI

1. Of the surviving structures, a present-day resident of Wilmington can recite instantly a list of the architectural gems: the Bellamy Mansion, the Burgwin-Wright House, City Hall, the DeRosset House, the Latimer House, and St. James Episcopal Church define the historic downtown. Yet, one finds a rather nice collection of antebellum buildings scattered through the old town. On Market Street, the Dawson Building (1855) and the Thomas Henry Wright Building (1846), and the Quince Building (1835) on Water Street are representatives of the commercial buildings of the period. St. Thomas the Apostle Catholic Church (1847) on Dock Street contains the grave of Father Thomas Murphy, the parish priest who died while attending the sick during the yellow fever epidemic of 1862. Other representative homes from the 1840s and 1850s include the Ballard-Potter-Bellamy House (1844), the Dudley-Chadbourne House (1843), the Edward Savage House (1851), the Fanning House (1852), and the Parker-Saunders House (1844), to name a few. The John A. Taylor House (1847), faced with slabs of marble, is one of the more unusual homes of this period.

The Hart Carriage House (1852) on Cottage Lane is one of the few surviving service structures of the period. Some of the earlier homes include the Cameron-Hollman House (1790), the Governor Dudley Mansion (1825), the Hogg-Anderson House (1810), and the oldest. The Mitchell-Anderson House (1738). St. John's Lodge (1804) was the earlier meeting place for the masons. The Masonic Building (1841), another hall, remains in a somewhat altered state on Market Street. There are other antebellum structures, altered and unaltered, distributed throughout the old town mixed with later examples of Italianate Style homes, and late-nineteenth century Queen Anne Style homes.

2. Whitelaw Reid, *After the War: A Southern Tour* (Cincinnati: Moore, Wilstach & Baldwin, 1866), 48, UNCCH, http://www.worldcat.org/wcpa/oclc/12009895?page=frame&url=http%3A%2F%2Fsearch.lib.unc.edu%2Fsearch%3FN%3D0%26Nty%3D1%26Ntk%3DOCLCNumber%26Ntt%3D51310326%26checksum%3De392424c1bfb6b7e1032c1e05cf936f9&title=University+of+North+Carolina+at+Chapel+Hill&linktype=opac&detail=NOC%3AUniversity+of+North+Carolina+at+Chapel+Hill%3AARL+Library.

3. *Ibid.*, 49.

4. *Ibid.*, 46, 48–55.

5. John H. Kennaway, *On Sherman's Track; or the South after the War* (London: Seeley, Jackson, and Halliday, 1867), 188, State Library of North Carolina, 975.04 K34o.

6. *Ibid.*, 189–191.

7. *Ibid.*, 186–187, 193–198.

8. J.D. de Roulhac Hamilton, *Reconstruction in North Carolina* (Chicago: Lewis, 1906), 180–183, UNCW, F254.H23; J.T. Trowbridge. *The South: A Tour of its Battlefields and Ruined Cities, A Journey Through the Desolate States and Talks with the People* (Hartford, CT: Stebbins, 1866), 578–580, Hathi Trust Digital Library, F216 .T85 1969, http://catalog.hathitrust.org/Record/006235675. Accessed December 28, 2011.); *New York Times*, January 11, 1866.

9. John P. Radford, "Testing the Model of the Pre-Industrial City: The Case of Ante-Bellum Charleston, South Carolina," *Transactions of the Institute of British Geographers*, New Series 4, no. 3 (1979), 397–400, 406–407.

10. James Sprunt, *Chronicles of the Cape Fear River, 1660–1916* (Raleigh, NC: Edwards & Broughton, 1916), 159–200.

11. Allen Pred, "The Choreography of Existence: Comments on Hagerstrand's Time-Geography and Its Usefulness," *Economic Geography* 53, no. 4 (April 1977), 214.

12. Nickolas W. Schenck, transcribed by LuAnne Mims, *The Diary of Nicholas W. Schenck* (Wilmington, NC: University of North Carolina, William Madison Randall Library, Special Collections (1905), 2000), http://library.uncw.edu/web/collections/Schenck/schenckintro.html, , *128, 133, 136*. Accessed on December 12, 2011.

13. Robert J. Cooke, *Wild, Wicked, Wartime Wilmington: Being an Account of Murder, Mayhem and Other Assorted Malice in North Carolina's Largest City during the Civil War* (Wilmington, NC: Dram Tree Books, 2009), 9–19, 33, 39–42, 79–80.

14. William George Thomas, "A Review of the 'Report on the Epidemic of Yellow Fever which prevailed at Wilmington, N.C., in the Fall of 1862' by William T. Wragg, M.D., of Charleston, S.C.," *New York Medical Journal* 10, no. 3 (December 1869), 230–234.

15. Cooke, 13.

16. The restoration of social cohesiveness in the urban environment is usually dependent upon rendering sections of residential parcels high-value, low-density, and high-maintenance with limited potential to generate capital outside resale. The alternative is high-value, high-density, commercial or residential property such as an office or apartment building that generates capital through rent. The object of this allocation of urban space is to contain at the margins those activities that degrade land value, and that do not readily attract investment capital. The symbolic, administrative, and technological institutions at the core are sustained by the long-term economic output of property (including tax value) where geographic expansion always includes a high proportion of desirable property relative

to degraded parcels. Noxious activities, industrial and social, tend to be less disruptive when contained within their own time-geography routines; and the economic value of allowing this type of land usage contributes to the overall economy of the entire urban environment.

17. Geoffrey L. Herrera, "Inventing the Railroad and Rifle Revolution: Information, Military Innovation and the Rise of Germany," *The Journal of Strategic Studies* 27, no. 2 (June 2004), 245.

18. R. R. "Dicky" Davis, "Helmuth von Moltke and the Prussian-German Development of a Decentralised Style of Command: Metz and Sedan 1870," *Defense Studies* 5, no. 1 (March 2005), 87–88.

19. Wilmington & Weldon Rail Road Company, *Proceedings of the Stockholders of the Wilmington & Weldon R.R. Co., at their Special Meeting, August 1st, 1865; together with the Proceedings of the 30th Annual Meeting, held at Wilmington, North Carolina, November 22, 1865, with the Reports of the President and Directors, and the Chief Engineer and Superintendent* (Wilmington, NC: Engelhard & Price, 1866), 9, UNCCH, Cp385.1 W78r 1865.

Chapter VII

1. Wilmington & Weldon Railroad Company, *Annual Reports of the President and Directors, and the Chief Engineer and Superintendent of the Wilmington & Weldon Rail Road Co., with the Proceedings of the General Meeting of Stockholders, November 11th, 1868* (Wilmington, NC: Engelhard & Price, 1868), 5. It is interesting to note that the funded debt of the company approaches the amount of worthless Confederate paper the company possessed at the end of the war.

2. Wilmington & Weldon Rail Road Company, *Annual Reports of the President and Directors, and the Chief Engineer and Superintendent of the Wilmington & Weldon R.R. Co., with the Proceedings of the General Meeting of the Stockholders, November 8th, 1860* (Wilmington, NC: Fulton & Price, 1860), 19, 21; Wilmington & Weldon Railroad Company, 1868, 5–6.

3. Frank D. Smaw, Jr., *Smaw's Wilmington Directory, Comprising a General and City Business Directory, and a Directory of Colored Persons, to Which is Added a Complete Historical and Commercial Sketch of the City* (Wilmington, NC: Smaw, 1867), 76.

4. *Daily Phoenix* (Columbia, SC), October 19, 1865.

5. Ellis Merton Coulter, *The South during Reconstruction, 1865–1877* (Baton Rouge: Louisiana State University Press, 1947), 204–206.

6. T.M. Haddock, *Haddock's Wilmington, N.C., Directory, and General Advertiser, Containing a General and Business Directory of the City, Historical Sketch, State, County, City Government, &c., &c.* (Wilmington, NC: Engelhard, 1871), 5, 62, 66, 85, 113, 123, 130–131, 190, 250.

7. North Carolina, *North Carolina, the Pacemaker in Industry, Agriculture and Substantial Progress* (Raleigh, NC: Department of Conservation and Development, 1929), 31, 33, State Library of North Carolina, C1 Z:P1.

In agriculture the range of products with their values is shown from the reports of the Department of Agriculture for the year 1925. They include cotton, $98,993,800; tobacco, $83,034,600; corn, $47,273,600; wheat, $7,636,860; oats, $3,725,520; cottonseed, $25,737,294; tame hay, $12,093,040; sweet potatoes, $8,448,000; Irish potatoes, $8,143,200; peanuts, $2,815,000; annual legumes, total including all legumes for hay, $6,375,000; cow peas, $1,377,000; soy beans, $1,938,000; grains, cut green for hay, $1,608,000; sorghum for syrup, $1,865,920; rye, $1,281,128; clover, $2,320,000; timothy, $527,000; clover and timothy mixed, $986,000; clover seed, $412,800; barley, $276,000; alfalfa, $162,000; buckwheat, $154,000. In fruits the State has more than five million apple trees that last year yielded a crop worth $4,245,000. During the same season the three million peach trees gave a harvest valued at $2,400,000. Between 1924 and 1925 the number of apple trees of the bearing age increased by more than

25,000 and the number of peach trees by 100,000. There were 250,000 bearing pear trees. These yielded fruit worth $268,000 in 1925, while the grape industry netted $366,300. In truck, North Carolina strawberries last year brought growers in the neighborhood of $2,000,000 and a larger amount the previous year. Each acre planted to strawberries represented an income of $360 — on an average. Other truck crops in 1925 brought growers the following amounts: Snap beans, $641,550; cantaloupes, $268,000; watermelons, $198,000; cabbage, $128,000; sweet corn, $117,000; spinach, $53,000; lettuce, $326,000; cucumbers, $645,000; green peas, $855,000, and peppers, $130,000.

    8. *Ibid.*, 33.

During the season of 1925 North Carolina shipped out of the State 13,405 carloads of fruits and vegetables, including the following: peaches, 1,763; Irish potatoes, 4,031; cucumbers, 1,523; dewberries, 275; sweet potatoes, 498; lettuce, 542; beans, 496; cabbage, 339; corn, 103; strawberries, 1,664; watermelons, 643; cantaloupes, 632; carrots, 13; peppers, 18, and beets, 16.

    9. North Carolina, *North Carolina and Its Resources* (Winston, NC: Stewart, 1896), 60, 179, 183–184, 197, 325, 333, 373, 375, 381, State Library of North Carolina, A1 2:N8.

    10. North Carolina, *A Sketch of North Carolina* (Raleigh, NC: Board of Agriculture, 1902), 88, Library of Congress, F254.N942.

    11. Beverly Wilson Palmer, and Holly Byer Ochos, "'Reconstruction' September 6, 1865," *Pennsylvania History* 60, no. 2 (April 1993), 196–197, 203–205.

    12. Walter L. Fleming, "Forty Acres and a Mule," *The North American Review* 182, no. 594 (May 1906), 733–737.

    13. James S. Fisher, "Negro Farm Ownership in the South," *Annals of the Association of American Geographers* 63, no. 4 (December 1973), 478–479.

    14. Petersburg Rail Road Company, *Annual Report to the Stockholders of the Petersburg Rail Road Comp'y* (Petersburg, VA: Ege & Ellyson, 1866), 3–4, UNCCH, Cp385.1 P48p2 1866.

    15. Seaboard & Roanoke Railroad Company, *Fourteenth Annual Report of the President and Directors to the Stockholders of the Seaboard & Roanoke Railroad Company, with the Report of the General Superintendent, Submitted February 27, 1862* (Portsmouth, VA: Transcript Office, 1862, 8, UNCCH, Cp385.1 S4Sp 1862; Petersburg Rail Road Company, 1866, 7; Raleigh & Gaston Rail Road Company, *Proceeding of the Sixteenth Annual Meeting of the Raleigh & Gaston Rail Road Company, held at Raleigh, July 5, 1866, with the Reports of the President, Treasurer, &c.* (Raleigh, NC: Nichols, Gorman, Neathery, 1866), 4, 8, UNCCH, C385.1 R16s 1853–1868.

    16. Petersburg Rail Road Company, 1866, 3, 5, 9.

    17. Bill Reaves and J. Kenneth Davis, *Bill Reaves Collection*, Ser. 1, Vol. 75 (Wilmington, NC: New Hanover County Library, n.d.), NHCL, NC 929.2 V.75; T. Tuther, Jr., *Kelley's Wilmington Directory, to Which is Added a Business Directory for 1860* (Wilmington, NC: Fulton & Price, 1860), 106,109. NHCL NC917.56K; Smaw, 145, 165; Haddock, 45, 189.

    18. Reaves, *ibid.*

    19. James Sprunt, *Chronicles of the Cape Fear River, 1660–1916* (Raleigh, NC: Edwards & Broughton, 1916), 337.

    20. R. Matthew Poteat, "Part 1: 'A Modest Estimate of His Own Abilities': Governor Henry Toole Clark and the Early Civil War Leadership of North Carolina," *North Carolina Historical Review* 84, no. 1 (January 2007), 20–21.

    21. Reaves, 7.

Bibliography

Ayers, Edward L. *The Promise of the New South: Life after Reconstruction*. Oxford: Oxford University Press, 2007.
Black, Robert C. *Railroads of the Confederacy*. Chapel Hill: University of North Carolina Press, 1952.
Boney, Leslie N., Jr., and James L. Allegood. *The Cape Fear Club*. Wilmington, NC: Wilmington, 1984.
Burke, James C. *The Wilmington & Raleigh Rail Road Company, 1833–1854*. Jefferson, NC: McFarland, 2011.
Burton, E. Milby. *The Siege of Charleston: 1861–1865*. Columbia: University of South Carolina, 1982.
Chittenden, Lucius E. *A Report on the Debates and Proceedings in the Secret Sessions on the Conference Convention, for Proposing Amendments to the Constitution of the United States, held at Washington, D.C. in February, A.D. 1861*. New York: Appleton, 1864.
Confederate States of America. *Journal of the Confederate States of America, 1861–1865*. Washington, DC: Government Printing Office, 1904.
Cooke, Robert J. *Wild, Wicked, Wartime Wilmington: Being an Account of Murder, Mayhem and Other Assorted Malice in North Carolina's Largest City during the Civil War*. Wilmington, NC: Dram Tree Books, 2009.
Coulter, Ellis M. *The South during Reconstruction: 1865–1877*. Baton Rouge: Louisiana State University Press, 1947.
Cross, Jerry L. *Biographical Sketches of Seven State Treasurers*. Raleigh: North Carolina Department of Cultural Resources, 1994.
Daily Phoenix (Columbia, SC).
Davis, Jefferson. *The Rise and Fall of the Confederate Government*. Vol. 1. New York: Appleton, 1881.
Davis, R. R. "Dicky." "Helmuth von Moltke and the Prussian-German Development of a Decentralised Style of Command: Metz and Sedan 1870." *Defense Studies* 5, no. 1 (March 2005): 83–95.
Farmers' Register. "Extracts from the Report of Walter Gwynn, Esq., Engineer, to the President and Directors of the Wilmington and Raleigh Rail Road Company." October 1836: 348–351.
Fisher, James S. "Negro Farm Ownership in the South." *Annals of the Association of American Geographers* 63, no. 4 (December 1973): 478–489.
Fleming, Walter L. "Forty Acres and a Mule." *The North American Review* 182, no. 594 (May 1906): 721–737.

Bibliography 251

Fonvielle, Chris E., Jr. *Fort Fisher 1865: The Photographs of T.H. O'Sullivan*. Carolina Beach, NC: SlapDash, 2011.
Freehling, William W. *The Road to Disunion*. Vol. 1. New York: Oxford University Press, 1990.
_____. *The South vs. The South: How Anti-Confederate Southerners Shaped the Course of the Civil War*. New York: Oxford University Press, 2001.
Georgia. *Journal of the Public and Secret Proceeding of the Convention of the People of Georgia, Held in Milledgeville and Savannah in 1861. Together with the Ordinances Adopted. Published by Order of the Convention*. Milledgeville, GA: Broughton, Nisbet & Barnes, 1861.
Hamilton, J.D. de Roulhac. *History of North Carolina*. Vol. 3. Chicago: Lewis, 1919.
_____. *Reconstruction in North Carolina*. Chicago: Lewis, 1906.
Herrera, Geoffrey L. "Inventing the Railroad and Rifle Revolution: Information, Military Innovation and the Rise of Germany." *The Journal of Strategic Studies* 27, no. 2, (June 2004): 243–271.
Hollowell, J.M. *War-Time Reminiscences and Other Selections*. Goldsboro, NC: Goldsboro Herald, 1939.
Johns, John. "Wilmington During the Blockade." *Harper's New Monthly Magazine* 33, no. 196 (September 1866): 497–503.
Jones, J.B. *A Rebel War Clerk's Diary at the Confederate States Capital*. Vol. 2. Philadelphia: Lippincott, 1866.
Kynett, Harold Havelock, Samuel Worcester Butler, and D. G. Brinton. "News and Miscellany." *The Medical and Surgical Reporter* 9, no. 2 (October 11, 1862): 54.
Lefler, Hugh Talmage, and Albert Ray Newsome. *The History of a Southern State: North Carolina*. Chapel Hill: University of North Carolina Press, 1954.
Murray, Stewart L. *The Reality of War: A Companion to Clausewitz*. London, England: Hodder and Stoughton, 1914.
New York Times.
North Carolina. "Governor's Letter Book." *Governor's Papers, John Willis Ellis*. Raleigh: North Carolina State Archives, 1861. NCSA, GLB 49.
_____. *North Carolina: The Pacemaker in Industry, Agriculture and Substantial Progress*. Raleigh, NC: Department of Conservation and Development, 1929.
_____. *A Sketch of North Carolina*. Raleigh, NC: Board of Agriculture, 1902.
_____. Board of Agriculture. *North Carolina and Its Resources*. Winston: M.I. & J.C. Stewart, public printers and binders, 1896.
North Carolina Railroad Company. *Proceedings of the Twelfth Annual Meeting of the Stockholders of the North Carolina Rail Road Company, held at Salisbury, on Thursday and Friday, July 11th & 12th, 1861*. Raleigh: North Carolina Institute for the Deaf and Dumb and the Blind, 1861.
_____. *Proceedings of the Thirteenth Annual Meeting of the Stockholders of the North Carolina Rail Road Company, held at Hillsboro, Thursday and Friday, July 10th and 11th, 1862*. Raleigh: North Carolina Institute for the Deaf and Dumb and the Blind, 1862.
_____. *Proceedings of the Fourteenth Annual Meeting of the Stockholders of the North Carolina Rail Road Company, held at Greensboro, on Thursday, the 9th day of July, 1863*. Raleigh: North Carolina Institute for the Deaf and Dumb and the Blind, 1863.
_____. *Fifteenth Annual Meeting of the Stockholders of the North Carolina Rail Road Company, Held at Raleigh, Thursday, July 14, 1864*. Raleigh: North Carolina Institute for the Deaf and Dumb and the Blind, 1864.
_____. *Proceeding of the Sixteenth Annual Meeting of the Stockholders of the North Car-

olina Railroad Company, held at Salisbury, July 13, 1865. Raleigh: North Carolina Institute for the Deaf and Dumb and the Blind, 1865.
Oakdale Cemetery Company, Inc. *Burial Database*. Wilmington, NC: Oakdale Cemetery, 2007.
Olsen, Otto H. "Historians and the Extent of Slave Ownership in the Southern United States." *Civil War History* 50, no. 4 (2004): 401–417.
Palmer, Beverly Wilson, and Holly Byer Ochos. " 'Reconstruction' September 6, 1865." *Pennsylvania History* 60, no. 2 (April 1993): 196–212.
Pearson, Reggie L. "There Are Many Sick, Feeble, and Suffering Freedmen": The Freedmen's Bureau's Health Care Activities during Reconstruction in North Carolina, 1865–1868." *North Carolina Historical Review* 79, no. 2 (April 2002): 141–181.
Pendleton, Louis. *Alexander H. Stephens*. Philadelphia: Jacobs, 1908.
Petersburg Rail Road Company. *Annual Report to the Stockholders of the Petersburg Rail Road Comp'y*. Petersburg, VA: Ege & Ellyson, 1866.
Post, Charles. "Plantation Slavery and Economic Development in the Southern United States." *Journal of Agrarian Change* 3, no. 3 (July 2003): 289–332.
Poteat, R. Matthew. "Part 1: 'A Modest Estimate of His Own Abilities': Governor Henry Toole Clark and the Early Civil War Leadership of North Carolina." *North Carolina Historical Review* 84, no. 1 (January 2007): 1–36.
Powell, William S. *Dictionary of North Carolina Biography*. Vol. 2. Chapel Hill: University of North Carolina Press, 1986.
Pred, Allen. "The Choreography of Existence: Comments on Hagerstrand's Time-Geography and Its Usefulness." *Economic Geography* 53, no. 4 (April 1977): 207–221.
Radford, John P. "Testing the Model of the Pre-Industrial City: The Case of Ante-Bellum Charleston, South Carolina." *Transactions of the Institute of British Geographers*, New Series 4, no. 3 (1979): 392–410.
Rains, George W. *History of the Confederate Powder Works*. Newburg, NY: Newburg Daily News Print, n.d.
Raleigh & Gaston Rail Road Company. *Proceedings of the Fifteenth Annual Meeting of the Stockholders of the Raleigh & Gaston Railroad Company, with the Reports of the President, Treasurer, &c*. Raleigh: North Carolina Institute for the Deaf and Dumb and the Blind, 1865.
———. *Proceeding of the Sixteenth Annual Meeting of the Raleigh & Gaston Rail Road Company, held at Raleigh, July 5, 1866, with the Reports of the President, Treasurer, &c*. Raleigh, NC: Nichols, Gorman, Neathery, 1866.
Reaves, Bill, and J. Kenneth Davis. *Bill Reaves Collection*. Ser. 1, Vol. 75. Wilmington, NC: New Hanover County Library, n.d.
Reid, Whitelaw. *After the War: A Southern Tour*. Cincinnati: Moore, Wilstach & Baldwin, 1866.
Russell, William Howard. *My Diary North and South*. Vol. 1. London: Bradbury and Evans, 1863.
Schenck, Nickolas W. *The Diary of Nicholas W. Schenck*. Transcribed by LuAnne Mims. Wilmington: University of North Carolina, William Madison Randall Library, Special Collections, (1905), 2000. http://library.uncw.edu/web/collections/Schenck/schenckintro.html. Accessed on October 7, 2011.
Seaboard & Roanoke Railroad Company. *Fourteenth Annual Report of the President and Directors to the Stockholders of the Seaboard & Roanoke Railroad Company, with the Report of the General Superintendent, Submitted February 27, 1862*. Portsmouth, VA: Printed at the Transcript Office, 1862.
Smaw, Frank D., Jr. *Smaw's Wilmington Directory comprising a General and City Business*

Directory, and a Directory of Colored Persons, to which is added A Complete Historical and Commercial Sketch of the City. Wilmington, NC: Smaw, 1867.

———. *Wilmington Directory, including a General and City Business Directory for 1865–66.* Wilmington, NC: Heinsberger, 1865.

South Carolina. *Journal of the Convention of the People of South Carolina, Held in 1860–61, together with the Reports, Resolutions, &c.* Charleston, SC: Evans & Cogswell, 1861.

———. *Journal of the State Convention of South Carolina; Together with the Resolution and Ordinance.* Columbia, SC: Johnston & Cavis, 1852.

Sprunt, James. *Chronicles of the Cape Fear River, 1660–1916.* Raleigh, NC: Edwards & Broughton, 1916.

———. *Derelicts: An Account of Ships Lost at Sea in General Commercial Traffic and a Brief History of Blockade Runners Stranded Along the North Carolina Coast, 1861–1865.* Wilmington, NC: Sprunt, 1920.

Stephens, Alexander H. *Extract from a Speech by Alexander H. Stephens, Vice-President of the Confederate States, Delivered in the Secession Convention of Georgia, January, 1861.* No publisher. Library of Congress, E440.5 .S83.

The Stranger's Guide and Official Directory for the City of Richmond. Showing the Location of the Public Buildings and Offices of the Confederate, State and City Governments, Residences of the Principal Officers, etc. Richmond, VA: Evans, 1863.

Teal, Harvey S. "Experiencing History: A visit to a Railroad 'Stonehenge.'" *USCS Newsletter.* Columbia: University of South Carolina, University South Caroliniana Society, 1997.

Tetterton, Beverly. *Wilmington: Lost But Not Forgotten.* Wilmington, NC: Dram Tree Books, 2005.

Thomas, William George. "A Review of the 'Report on the Epidemic of Yellow Fever which prevailed at Wilmington, N.C., in the Fall of 1862. By William T. Wragg, M.D., of Charleston, S.C.'" *New York Medical Journal* 10, no. 3 (December 1869): 225–253.

Trowbridge, J.T. *The South: A Tour of Its Battlefields and Ruined Cities, A Journey Through the Desolate States and Talks with the People.* Hartford, CT: Stebbins, 1866.

Turner, L.C. *Plan of Wilmington, North Carolina.* Philadelphia: Duval, 1856.

Tuther, T., Jr. *Kelley's Wilmington Directory, to which is added a Business Directory for 1860.* Wilmington, NC: Fulton & Price, 1860.

United States. Census Office. *Population of the United States in 1860; Compiled from the Original Returns of the Eighth Census, Under the Direction of the Secretary of the Interior, by Joseph C.G. Kennedy.* Washington: Government Printing Office, 1864.

———. ———. *Manufactures of the United States in 1860; Compiled from the Original Returns of the Eighth Census, Under the Direction of the Secretary of the Interior.* Washington, DC: Government Printing Office, 1865.

———. ———. *Statistics of the United States (Including Mortality, Property, &c.,) in 1860; Compiled from the Original Returns and Being the Final Exhibit of the Eighth Census, Under the Direction of the Secretary of the Interior.* Washington, DC: Government Printing Office, 1866.

———. Circuit Courts. *The Federal Reporter, Volume 97, Cases Argued and Determined in Circuit Courts of Appeal and Circuit and District Courts of the United States, Permanent Edition, November, 1899–January, 1900.* St. Paul, MN: West Pub. Co., 1900.

———. Congress. House of Representatives. *Journal of the House of Representatives of the United States, 1849–1850.* Washington, DC: 31st Congress, First Session, 1849–50.

———. ———. ———. *Journal of the House of Representatives of the United States, 1850–51.* Washington, DC: 32nd Congress, First Session, 1851–52.

_____. _____. _____. *Railroads—Atlantic to the Mississippi.* Washington, DC: 23rd Congress, 2nd Session, 1835. Document 177.

_____. National Archive. *Confederate Papers Relating to Citizens or Business Firms, compiled 1874-1899, documenting the period 1861-1865.* Washington, DC: National Archives, 1874–1899, Records Group 109, ARC Identifier 2133274 / MLR Number PI101 180, Roll 1122, Document 261.

_____. Naval War Records Office. *Official Records of the Union and Confederate Navies in the War of the Rebellion.* Ser. 1, Vol. 1. Washington, DC: Government Printing Office, 1894.

_____. _____. _____. Ser. 1, Vol. 6. Washington, DC: Government Printing Office, 1897.

_____. _____. _____. Ser. 1, Vol. 7. Washington, DC: Government Printing Office, 1898.

_____. _____. _____. Ser. 1, Vol. 8. Washington, DC: Government Printing Office, 1899.

_____. _____. _____. Ser. 4, Vol. 3. Washington, DC: Government Printing Office, 1900.

_____. _____. _____. Ser. 1, Vol. 12. Washington, DC: Government Printing Office, 1901.

_____. Sanitary Commission. *Sanitary Memoirs of the War of Rebellion.* Vol. 1. New York: Hurd and Houghton, 1867.

_____. War Department. *Instruction for Heavy Artillery; Prepared by a Board of Officers, for the use of the Army of the United States.* Charleston, NC: Evan & Cogswell, 1861, (reprinted) Richmond, VA: West & Johnston, 1862.

_____. _____. *The War of Rebellion, A Compilation of the Official Records of the Union and Confederate Armies.* Ser. 1, Vol. 1. Washington, DC: Government Printing Office, 1880.

_____. _____. _____. Ser. 1, Vol. 5. Washington, DC: Government Printing Office, 1881.

_____. _____. _____. Ser. 1, Vol. 18. Washington, DC: Government Printing Office, 1887.

_____. _____. _____. Ser. 1, Vol. 27, Pt. 2. Washington, DC: Government Printing Office, 1889.

_____. _____. _____. Ser. 1, Vol. 33. Washington, DC: Government Printing Office, 1891.

_____. _____. _____. Ser. 1, Vol. 42. Washington, DC: Government Printing Office, 1895.

_____. _____. _____. Ser. 1, Vol. 47. Washington, DC: Government Printing Office, 1895.

_____. _____. _____. Ser. 2, Vol. 2. Washington, DC: Government Printing Office, 1897.

_____. _____. _____. Ser. 4, Vol. 2. Washington, DC: Government Printing Office, 1900.

Virginia. *Proceedings of the Virginia State Convention of 1861, February 13-May 1*, George H. Reese, ed. Richmond: Virginia State Library, 1965, 362, University of Richmond, Boatwright Memorial Library, "Monday, April 8, 1861," Virginia Secession Convention, http://collections.richmond.edu/secession/documents/index.html?id=pb.3.372. Accessed on September 25, 2011.

_____. *Regulations for the Commissary's Department of the State of Virginia.* Richmond, VA: Wynne, 1861.

Weidenmier, Marc. "Money and Finance in the Confederate States of America."

EH.Net, Economic History Association, February 1, 2010. http://eh.net/encyclopedia/article/weidenmier.finance.confederacy.us. Accessed on December 2, 2011.
Westwood, Howard C. "Ulysses S. Grant and Benjamin Butler in the Appomattox Campaign." *Illinois Historical Journal* 84, no. 1 (Spring, 1991): 39–54.
Wilde-Ramsing, Mark, and Wilson Angley. *National Register of Historic Places Nomination, Cape Fear Civil War Shipwreck District*. Raleigh: North Carolina Department of Cultural Resources, Archaeology, 1985.
Wilmington & Weldon Rail Road Company. *Proceedings of the Wilmington & Weldon Rail Road Co. at their Twentieth Annual Meeting, held at Wilmington, North Carolina, November 9th 1855*. Wilmington, NC: Loring, 1855.
_____. *Annual Reports of the President and Directors, and the Chief Engineer and Superintendent of the Wilmington & Weldon R.R. Co., with the Proceedings of the General Meeting of the Stockholders, November 8th, 1860*. Wilmington, NC: Fulton & Price, 1860.
_____. *Annual Reports of the President and Directors, and the Chief Engineer and Superintendent of the Wilmington & Weldon R. R. Co., with the Proceedings of the General Meeting of the Stockholders, November 14, 1861*. Wilmington, NC: Fulton & Price, 1861.
_____. *Annual Reports of the President and Directors, and the Chief Engineer and Superintendent of the Wilmington & Weldon R.R. Co., with the Proceedings of the General Meeting of the Stockholders, December 14th, 1862*. Wilmington, NC: Fulton & Price, 1862.
_____. *Annual Reports of the President and Directors, and the Chief Engineer and Superintendent, of the Wilmington & Weldon R.R. Co., with the Proceedings of the General Meeting of Stockholder, November 18th, 1863*. Wilmington, NC: Fulton & Price, 1863.
_____. *Annual Reports of the President and Directors, and the Chief Engineer and Superintendent of the Wilmington & Weldon R.R. Co., with the Proceedings of the General Meeting of the Stockholders, November 23D. 1864*. Wilmington, NC: Fulton & Price, 1864.
_____. *Proceedings of the Stockholders of the Wilmington & Weldon R.R Co., at their Special Meeting, August 1st, 1865; together with the Proceedings of the 30th Annual Meeting, held at Wilmington, North Carolina, November 22, 1865, with the Reports of the President and Directors, and the Chief Engineer and Superintendent*. Wilmington, NC: Engelhard & Price, 1866.
_____. *Annual Reports of the President and Directors, and the Chief Engineer and Superintendent of the Wilmington & Weldon Rail Road Company, with the Proceedings of the General Meeting of Stockholders, November 21st, 1866*. Wilmington, NC: Engelhard & Price, 1866.
_____. *Annual Reports of the President and Directors, and the Chief Engineer and Superintendent of the Wilmington & Weldon Rail Road Co., with the Proceedings of the General Meeting of Stockholders, November 11th, 1868*. Wilmington, NC: Engelhard & Price, 1868.
_____. *Annual Reports of the President and Directors, and the General Superintendent of the Wilmington & Weldon Rail Road Company, with the Proceedings of the General Meeting of the Stockholders, November 19th, 1878*. Wilmington, NC: Morning Star, 1878.
Wilmington, Charlotte & Rutherford Railroad Company. *Proceedings of the Stockholders of the Wilmington, Charlotte & Rutherford Rail Road Company, Wilmington, N.C., October 20th, 1870*. Wilmington, NC: Carolina Farmer & Morning Star, 1870.
Wilmington, Columbia & Augusta Rail Road Company and the Wilmington & Wel-

don Rail Road Company. *Annual Reports of the President and Directors and the General Superintendents of the Wilmington, Columbia & Augusta and the Wilmington & Weldon Rail R.R. Co's., with the Proceedings if the General Meeting of Stockholders, November 19th, 1873.* Wilmington, NC: Englehard & Saunders, 1873.

_____. *Annual Reports of the President and Directors and the General Superintendents of the Wilmington, Columbia & Augusta and the Wilmington & Weldon Rail Road Companies, with the Proceedings if the General Meeting of Stockholders, November 20th, 1877.* Wilmington, NC: Morning Star, 1877.

Wilmington Herald. Microfilm; Raleigh: North Carolina Department of Archives and History, Division of Archives and Manuscripts.

Wilmington Journal. Microfilm; Raleigh: North Carolina Department of Archives and History, Division of Archives and Manuscripts.

Woodward, Joseph Janvier. *Report on Epidemic Cholera and Yellow Fever in the Army of the United States, during the Year 1867.* Washington, DC: Government Printing Office, 1868.

Yale University, Lillian Goldman Library. "Amendments Proposed in Congress by Senator John J. Crittenden: December 18, 1860," *The Avalon Project, Documents in Law, History and Diplomacy* (2008). http://avalon.law.yale.edu/19th_century/critten.asp. Accessed on September 14, 2011.

Index

acid 86–87
Alabama troops 139, 215, 223
Anderson, Maj. Robert 55, 60–61, 64, 235n59, 236n65
Arrington, Dr. B.F. 128
artillery 3, 4, 8, 10, 78–82, 87, 111–112, 148; in battle 113–119, 139; shells 56, 60, 66, 78–82, 121, 140
Ashe, William S. 7, 31, 38, 46, 48–49, 59, 68–69, 98, 99, 109, 155, 156, 164–166, 225n1, 232n11, 237n75
Atlantic & North Carolina Railroad 13, 77, 82, 109, 111, 138, 154
Atlantic Coast Line Railroad 5, 17, 22, 27, 153, 156, 167

bacon 74–75, 77, 83, 89, 110, 118, 205–212
Baker, John A. 54
Baker, Gen. Lawrence S. 131–132
Barnes, Lt. John S. 79
Barringer, Daniel M. 57
Barry, John D. 38
Battle Cotton Mill 120–121
Beauregard, Gen. P.G.T. 64, 66, 113, 114, 126, 239n2
Beaver Creek 111
Beery & Brothers 102, 104
Bell, John 38, 41, 44, 46
Bellamy, Dr. John D. 28, 46, 47, 49, 98
Berry, Robert 17, 32, 177, 195
Bettencourt, William C. 46, 98, 99
Bisset & Birchett (contractors) 13
Bivens, W.J. 160
blockade runners 85–91; *Kate* 99–106; *Modern Greece* 89, 102; *R.E. Lee* 90
bonds 11, 13, 18, 158–159, 162; brokers 23, 159, 229n38; Confederate States 71, 87, 129, 244n66; cotton 87–88; English 129, 143, 158; mortgage 25–26, 129, 143; Negro 30, 129; North Carolina Special Tax Bonds 26–27, 229n38; wartime 26
Bragg, Gen. Braxton 23
Breckinridge, John C. 40, 42, 48, 233n25
Bridgers, Robert Rufus "R.R." 17, 33, 46, 69, 98, 158, 160, 164, 178, 197
Brink, Ed R. 160
Buchanan, James 40–41, 51, 53, 56, 141
Burkeville, VA 125, 243n57
Burnside, Maj. Gen. Ambrose E. 10, 65, 111, 116–117
Butler, Maj. Gen. Benjamin 72, 126

USS *Cambridge* 90, 109
Campbell, Robert 104
Cantwell, Col. John L. 57, 179, 191, 195, 234n45
Cape Fear Light Artillery 57, 234n45
Cape Fear River 3–4, 14, 18–20, 24, 36, 61, 80, 86–87, 89, 138–139, 148, 152; bridges 8, 25, 34, 68–70, 79, 156, 158; defenses 63; railroad accident 230n46
Capps, J.W. 104
Capps, Mrs. Thomas J. 104
Carolina Central Railway Company (Carolina Central Railroad Company) 26–27, 32, 34
Carr, Dr. Thomas B. 102
Cary and Cox 32
Charleston, S.C. 13, 19, 21, 44, 48, 50, 53, 54–55, 60, 64, 66, 78, 79, 84, 86–87, 90, 100, 108, 140, 142, 151–152, 217, 225n1, 233n28, 240n19; *see also* Anderson, Maj. Robert; Fort Sumter

257

Chase, Salmon P. 64, 146
Chew, R.S. 64
Chittenden, Lucius E. 57, 58
Claiborne, Dr. John H. 143–145
Clarendon Iron Works 37, 80–81, 100
Clark, Gov. (N.C.) Henry T. 60, 72, 165
Clark, Mrs. Thomas 104
Clay, Henry 45, 52
Clingman, Thomas L. 64
Compromise of 1850 45, 52
Confederate States of America 60–61, 71, 82, 87–89, 97, 134, 136–137, 139, 235n53, 236n69, 240n19; Army 10, 23, 66, 78, 113, 117, 126–127, 133, 243n58; bonds 71, 129; Confederate Congress 95, 97; Confederate Powder Works, Augusta, GA 85–86, 139, 239n15; Navy 104, 107, 133, 239n15; publications 78, 100
Congaree River 20
Constitutional Union Party 38–45, 100
Cooper, Col. S. 56
copper 86, 239n15; railroad shops 16, 173–175
Cornwallis, Lord Charles 62
cotton 4, 21, 37, 66, 73, 75, 89–91, 102, 107, 110, 118, 120, 133, 136, 139–140, 150, 159–160, 222, 248n7; bonds 87–88; cotton states 50–51, 233n29; mills 120–121; *see also* Battle Cotton Mill
Cowan, Robert 38, 43, 59, 152, 179, 194, 236n69
Crittenden, John J. 54, 57, 60

Danville, VA 9, 125–126, 163, 237n75, 243n57, 243n58, 244n59, 244n66
Daughtry, William T. 32, 231n51
Davis, George 38, 44, 57, 59–60, 234n46, 235n52, 236n69
Davis, Jefferson 65, 84, 85, 86, 126, 140, 220
Dawson John 60, 84, 85, 108, 128, 216, 236n66, 246n1
Democratic Party 26, 38–46, 225n1, 233n14, 246n12
DeRosset, Armand J. 46–47, 48, 98, 171, 146n1
Dickinson, Platt K. 46, 47, 49, 98–99, 152, 169, 170
Dickinson's Shantees 31
Dickson, Dr. James H. 58, 99, 103, 108
Douglas, Stephen A. 39, 41–42, 44, 48, 233n25; (Dr. Keen, Douglas elector) 46

Drane, Henry M. 22, 23, 80, 83, 84, 180, 191, 194, 212
Drane, R.H. 21–22
Dred Scott Case 41–42
Dry, Abby 33
Dry Pond (Wilmington) 60, 105
Dudley, Edward B. 152, 155, 165
Dudley Depot 113–115
Dudley's Mill Pond (Rouse Pond) 3, 36–37, 100, 105–106

Eagles Island 19–21, 34, 62, 104
Ellis, Gov. (N.C.) John W. 24, 54, 56–57, 64, 67–68, 72, 82, 169, 233n25
Elmore, John A. 53
Emigrant Aid Society 52
Endor Furnace 127
Enfield (N.C.) 9, 16, 90, 129, 130–132
Evans, Clarence 131
Evans, Gen. Nathan G. 113
Everett, Edward 38, 41, 44, 46

Fayetteville, N.C. 24, 61–62, 100, 150, 228n33; arsenal 63, 68, 86, 240n17
Fillmore, Millard 41, 45
Fillyaw, Owen L. 37
Fisher, Charles F. 72
Flemming, E.J. 18
Fonvielle, Chris E. 19
Fort Sumter 54–55, 60, 64–66, 87, 141, 235n59, 236n69; *see also* Anderson, Maj. Robert; South Carolina forts
Foster, Maj.-Gen. J.G. 62, 65, 73, 109, 111–120, 123, 139
Fraser, Trenholm & Company (John Fraser & Company and Trenholm Brothers & Company) 87; *see also* Trenholm, William
Free Soil Party 41, 45, 233n14
Fremont, S.L. 9, 16–17, 33, 49–50, 70–73, 93–95, 97–98, 107–109, 117–118, 120, 122, 123, 129, 131, 136–137, 143, 155–156, 163, 171, 181, 191, 194, 197, 238n84
Fulton, James 107, 108, 232n10

Garrett, J.W. 53
Gay, William 31
Georgia, State of 22, 237n75, 237n77, 238n89, 240n18; Convention 52, 60; troops 84–85, 139, 215–216, 222–223
Globe Tavern 125
Goldsboro (N.C.) 8, 9, 10, 13, 16, 31, 32,

62, 65, 71, 73, 75, 77, 80, 82, 84, 85, 111, 113–120, 122, 124–125, 129, 131, 133, 138–139, 162, 212, 214, 217–218, 222–224, 237n77, 243n57
Graham, William Alexander 40–43, 100, 169
Grant, Gen. Ulysses S. 23, 32, 62, 125–126, 244n66
Greeley, Horace 41
Green, James S. 99
Greensville & Roanoke Rail Road 163
Greenville, N.C. 120–121
Gorgas, Col. (later Brig. Gen.) Josiah 86–87, 240n18
Goshen Swamp 114
grid plan 152, 153–154
Guilford (locomotive) 170–171
gunpowder 4, 77–80, 84–87, 89, 119–121, 139–140, 212, 217, 239n15, 240n18
Gwynn, Water 10, 18, 127, 138, 245n7

Hall, E.D. 38
Hall, Edward P. 46, 98, 170–171
Hall, Eli W. 38, 236n69
Hall, Samuel 60
Hall, Dr. William H. 101
Halleck, Gen. H.W. 62, 109
Hamlin, Hannibal 40
Hedrick, Maj. John J. 54, 56–57, 62, 234n45
Heyer, Jonathan C. 99–100
Heyer, Wilhelm A. 103, 106
Hill, Lt. Gen. Daniel H. Hill 118, 123
Hogg, Dr. Thomas D. 142
Holmes, John L. 38, 236n69
Holt, United States Secretary of War Joseph 56
Hooker, C.E. 53
Huse, Caleb 87, 240n19

iron: bridges 20, 25, 132; deposits 127; equipment 16, 78, 80, 136, 173, 174, 175; ironclads 102, 108–109, 112, 122; manufacturers 37, 70, 79–81, 86, 100, 102, 109, 127, 139; metal 9, 37, 78, 86, 89, 94, 102; rails 1, 7, 9, 127, 134, 143, 156, 158, 162, 165, 229n38; ship construction 89, 102, 108, 109, 112, 121–122; smelting 127

Jamison, D.F. 51–52
J.L. Cassidy & Sons 102–105, 242n17
Johnson, Herschel V. 40
Johnston, Gen. Joseph E. 23, 131, 148

Jones, Andrew J. 26
Jones, John Beauchamp 139, 244n66

Kansas-Nebraska Act 41–42; *see also* Emigrant Aid Society
Kennaway, John H. 148–149
Kilkelly, W.G. 32
Kingsville, S.C. 9, 18, 20, 22, 227n27
Kinston (N.C.) 73, 111–114, 123, 131
Knight, James 170–171, 184, 197; *see also Guilford*
Ku Klux Klan 27, 32

Lancaster County (PA) 161
Lane, Joseph 40
Laugherty, Edward 104–105
Laurinburg, N.C. 24, 61
Laspeyre, William H. 46, 115, 230n46
lead 86, 90, 110, 174–175
Lee, Maj. Francis D. 79
Lee, Gen. Robert E. 85, 117–118, 126–127, 140, 143, 156, 223, 244n66; Army of Northern Virginia 5, 8; Daniel's Brigade 113
Lewis, Col. George W. 119–120
Lincoln, Abraham: abolitionists 66; amnesty proclamation 23; call for North Carolina troops 66–68; candidate 40, 246n12; inauguration 64; policy 64, 141; president elect 47, 50, 56
Little Pee Dee River 61
Littlefield, Milton S. 27
Lockwood's Folly, N.C. 89
London, England 87, 129
Love, J.D. 37
Love, Dr. William J. 109
Lumberton, N.C. 24, 61, 228n33

MacLaurin, John 36, 107, 232n5
Macomber, R.S. 37
Magnolia, N.C. 9, 16, 109, 119–120, 129, 130–131
Mahone, Gen. William "Little Billy" 144–145
Margarettsville, N.C. 31–32, 231n51
Marine Hospital 102
Masonboro Inlet 62
McCaleb, Mrs. M.S. 106
McClellan, Gen. George 10, 111, 116
McDugal, George C. 102
McKee, Jim 56
McLean, Archibald 63
McNeill, Duncan 232n10

McRae, Alexander 24, 165, 171, 228*n*33, 230*n*48
McRae, D.K. 80
McRae, Hugh 160
McRae, John C. 24, 38, 46, 54, 228*n*33
McRee, Dr. James 100
Meares, O.P. 38, 42, 44, 58
Meares, T.D. 236*n*69
Meares Bluff 25
mercury fulminate 86–87
Missouri Compromise 41, 45, 51
Mitchell, Dennis 103–104
M.K. Jesup & Company 23
Moore, Gov. (Alabama) A.B. 53
Morehead, John M. 57
Morris, Wilkins 105
Morris Island (Charleston Harbor) 54–55

CSS *Neuse* 112
Neuse River 16, 82, 112–118, 123–133, 158
New Bern, N.C. 10, 65, 73, 82, 84, 109, 111, 113, 115, 120–121, 139, 146, 213
Norfolk, VA 32, 62, 68, 83, 84, 85, 108, 144, 215–219, 221–222
CSS *North Carolina* 104
North Carolina forts: Anderson/Saint Phillip 56, 62–63; Caswell 56, 57, 66, 80, 89, 102; Clark 72, 73; Dixie 82; Ellis 82; Fisher 7, 72, 80–81, 89–90, 102, 128, 131, 136, 146; Hatteras 71–73; Johnston 54–57; Lane 82; Macon 65, 66, 73, 80; Thompson 82
North Carolina General Assembly 13, 25–27, 57, 60, 66–68, 71–72, 125, 149, 162, 233*n*25, 233*n*28, 229*n*38, 243*n*58
North Carolina Railroad 13, 16, 18, 21, 62, 71–72, 75, 77, 87, 117, 126–127, 133, 138–140, 243*n*58
North Carolina troops: Volunteer Artillery and Engineers, 1st Corp 72; 3rd, Company B 116; State Troops, 6th Regiment 72–73; 30th Militia 57; 51st 116; 52nd 116; Ordnance Department 80–81
Northrop, Col. L.B. 242*n*52
Nutt, Henry 44, 152

O'Donohoe, Florence 102–103
Orrell, Ester "Hester" E. 103
Orrell & Hawes 77, 79, 80, 87, 139
Owen, James 44, 152, 165

Parsley, Oscar G. 23, 44, 54
Pee Dee River 18, 23, 25; Little Pee Dee River 61

Perry, Gov. (Florida) Madison S. 53
Person, Samuel J. 38, 236*n*69
Petersburg (VA) 9, 62, 84, 108, 113, 116, 132, 149; siege of 124–127, 139, 162–163, 219, 239*n*15, 244*n*66; *see also* Globe Tavern
Petersburg Railroad (Petersburg & Weldon Railroad) 14, 77, 82, 83, 124, 162, 231*n*51
Pettus, Gov. (Mississippi) John J. 53
Pickrell, John F. 25–26, 229*n*38
Piedmont Railroad 9, 125–127, 163
Plymouth, N.C. 62, 127
Poisson, Fred D. 38, 54
Pontain, Sterling 31
Post, James F. 49, 59
Potter, Brig. Gen. Edward E. 23, 65, 121–122
Potter, Gilbert 46, 98–99, 170–171
Price, George W., Jr. 160

Quincy, W.H. 159

Rains, George W. 63, 85–87
CSS *Raleigh* 104
Raleigh, N.C. 1, 10–11, 27, 33, 62, 84, 111, 126, 131, 133, 222, 229*n*38, 239*n*15
Raleigh & Gaston Railroad 11, 14, 77, 132, 162–163
Randolph, Confederate Secretary of War George W. 125
Rankin, Robert 57, 83–85, 187, 198, 202, 207, 210, 216
Ransom, Jacob 32–33
Reconstruction 1, 4, 5, 16, 17, 35, 58, 144, 146, 154, 155–156, 161, 167
Reid, David S. 57
Reid, Whitelaw 146–149, 160
Reilly, Sgt. James 55
Republican Party 26, 40, 44–45, 47, 50, 161
Richmond, VA 9, 12, 62, 67, 78–80, 83–86, 95, 100, 102, 108, 113–114, 116, 124, 126–127, 133, 139–140, 163, 205–224, 237*n*77, 239*n*15, 244*n*66
Riegelwood, NC 24
Roanoke Island 10, 73, 111, 139
Roanoke River 13, 73, 113, 123, 125, 132, 149–150, 151, 162–163, 171
Robeson County, N.C. 62
Rocky Mount, N.C. 16, 31, 120–123
Ruffin, Thomas, 57

Salisbury, N.C. 133; provisions 75; state convention of "Union Men" 44

salt 83, 110, 118, 205, 207–208, 212
saltpeter 84–87, 89, 139, 215
Schenck, Nicholas W. 37, 99–101, 110, 140, 152, 153
Schofield, Maj. Gen. J.M. 22, 47, 150
Schonwald, Dr. J.T. 100–101, 104
Scott, Winfield 41, 45, 56
Seaboard & Roanoke Railroad 14, 31, 73, 77, 83, 98, 109, 132, 162, 231n51
Seaman's Home Hospital 103, 108
Seddon, James A. 113–114, 116, 125
Seven Springs (N.C.) 111–112
Seward, William 40–41, 45, 47, 67, 240n19
Sherman, Gen. William T. 7, 62, 128, 131, 138, 150
Sjoberg Model 151
slaves 2, 12, 17, 28, 30–33, 50, 52, 102, 118, 125, 227n13, 235n59; emancipated/Freedmen 148–150, 161; and free person of color 31, 227n13, 232n5
Sloan, William 26
Smith, D.A. 37
Smith, Gen. Gustavus W. 112–114, 116, 118, 122
Smith, Harry 104–105, 107
Smith, William 129, 131, 167
Smith's Creek 73, 110
Smithville (Southport, N.C.) 19, 54, 55, 57, 100, 102
South Carolina: legislature 50, 53, 233n29; troops 79
South Carolina forts: Beauregard 79; Moultrie 54–55; Walker 79; *see also* Fort Sumter
Southside Railroad 125
Spicer, Isaac 17, 32, 188, 196
Sprunt, James 57, 58, 89–90, 99, 235n52
steamboats 13, 19, 20, 225n1; steam ferry 66; at Tarboro 121–122
Stephens, Alexander H. 52, 60
Stevens, Thaddeus 161
Strange, Robert 38, 45
Swartzman, Louis 100, 105–106
Swepson, George W. 26, 27

Tarboro (N.C.) 120–122, 131
Tarboro Branch Line 13, 46, 69, 73, 77, 119, 131, 171
Taylor, John A. 39, 147, 246n1
Taylor, John D. 46
Taylor, Zachary 41, 233n14
Teachey's Depot 31

Thomas, Dr. William G. 37, 99–101, 103–107, 242n17
time geography 152–153
Toisnot Creek 73
Tredegar Iron Works 79, 81, 86, 139
Trenholm, William (CSA Secretary of the Treasury) 19
Trimble, John M. 59
truck farms 4, 158–162, 248n7
Twelfth Virginia Infantry 143; *see also* Mahone, Gen. William "Little Billy"

Union Forces: 1st North Carolina Colored Regiment 119–120; 3rd New York Artillery 114; 3rd New York Cavalry 111, 119, 121–122; 5th Rhode Island 113; 9th New Jersey 113; 10th Connecticut 113; 17th Massachusetts 113, 116; 23rd Massachusetts 112, 115; 23rd New York Battery 115, 117; 44th Massachusetts 113; 85th Pennsylvania 112; 96th Regiment New York Volunteers 113
United States: Army 10, 16, 22, 54, 63–64, 82, 91, 108, 117, 126–127, 133, 138, 150, 244n66; Congress 42, 45, 47, 51–53, 56–58, 69; Navy 10, 41, 79; *see also* Union Forces

Van Buren, Martin 41
Vance, Gov. (N.C.) Zebulon B. 113, 125, 126, 170, 243n52
USS *Victoria* 102
Vine Swamp 111
Virginia, State of 4, 7, 9, 11–12, 15, 53, 61–62, 67, 76, 82, 84–87, 113, 125–126, 138–141, 145, 156, 161–162, 166, 237n76, 238n89, 243n58; Commissary 83; Convention 64, 67; General Assembly 57
Virginia Central Railroad 69, 83
von Clausewitz, Karl 137
von Moltke, Helmuth (the Elder) 157

Waddell, Alfred M. 38, 100, 232n10; *see also Wilmington Herald*
Walker, Agnes 33
Wall Street (New York) 159, 229n38, 240n19
Wallace, Stephen D. 38, 90, 97, 98, 99, 109, 110, 124, 129, 155, 157, 163, 164, 165, 166, 171, 236n66
Wateree River 20
Webb, Thomas 71, 126
Weed, Thurlow 41

Weeks, Georgia 101, 103, 105, 242n17
Weldon (N.C.) 1, 6, 10, 13, 18, 24, 31, 62, 74–75, 77, 78, 80, 81, 82, 84, 85, 87, 90, 108, 110, 113, 118, 119, 120, 122, 124, 125, 131; Weldon Toll Bridge/Seaboard & Roanoke Bridge 73, 132
Wheeler, Lt. Gen. Joseph "Fightin' Joe" 113
Whig Party 41, 42, 44, 45, 57, 225n1, 232n14, 246n12
Whitcomb, H.D. 69
White, Pvt. George A. 122
Whitehall: Bladen County, Northwest Cape Fear River 24; White Hall, Wayne County, Neuse River 73, 111–114; *see also* Seven Springs
Whiteville, N.C. 24
Whiting, Gen. William H.C. 62, 66, 68, 80, 81, 114, 120, 236n68
Wilkinson, Captain John 107
Wilmington, N.C.: Cape Fear Light Artillery 57; Cape Fear Minute Men 57; Committee of Safety 57, 66; Oakdale Cemetery 37, 108, 164, 242n17; Oaks 3, 36, 38, 46, 54, 60; streets 19–22, 28, 33–34, 36–41, 43, 47–49, 53, 58–59, 100, 102–104, 106, 110, 147, 149–155, 192–203, 232n5, 232n10, 236n69, 246n1; yellow fever 3, 7, 10, 93, 99–110, 146, 166, 231n51, 242n17, 246n1
Wilmington & Manchester Railroad 1, 11–12, 14, 16, 18–25, 30, 34, 62, 69, 77–82, 86–87, 90, 138, 148, 225n1, 232n10; accidents 30–32, 230n44; bonds 23, 25; Confederate troops 8; employees 177–196; food 4, 84, 139, 156, 205–224; freight 10, 205–224, 240n18; gauge 14, 25, 61; shares 18, 46; South Carolina 13, 23, 61, 63; Union attacks 23, 128; Wilmington depot 19–22, 77–80, 90, 139; *W.W. Harlee* 18
Wilmington & Raleigh Rail Road 1, 5, 7, 11, 13, 19, 21, 24, 44, 47, 127, 138, 155–165, 224n1, 230n44, 230n46, 230n48, 234n46; accidents 30–31; change of corporate name 15; directors 44, 47–48, 69, 99, 152, 155; shares 18; steamboat line 19–21
Wilmington & Weldon Railroad 1–12, 15–18, 24–32, 61–62, 65, 71, 73, 108, 127, 131–135, 137–138, 143, 150–151, 156–157, 160, 162–163, 226n12, 227n13, 232n10, 237n75, 248n1; accidents 31, 230n44, 230n46; accounts 72, 77, 136, 138; annual reports 15, 46, 48–50, 68–70, 73–75, 90, 98, 109–110, 118, 123, 127, 142, 158, 225n1; Dudley Depot 31, 113–115; early history 13; employees 32, 34, 176–203, 231n58, 234n46, 236n66; freight 73–76, 77–87, 90, 97–98, 110, 139, 204–225, 242n31; hospital 30, 101, 109–110; Joyner's Depot 31; officers 17, 38, 46, 48–50, 59, 68–70, 90, 97–99, 117–118, 120, 122, 136, 143, 152, 155–157, 163–167; shares 30, 46, 226n9; shops and equipment 15–16, 70–71, 150, 169–175; Tarboro Branch 13, 16, 46, 69; Union attacks 16, 65, 73, 111–124, 139; Wilmington depot 14, 77–87, 139
Wilmington, Charlotte & Rutherford Railroad 1, 13–14, 16, 23–27, 43, 77, 133, 139; bonds 25–26, 229n38; construction 25; employees 177–203; gauge 24; Riverside Landing 24–25, 34
Wilmington Herald 25, 38, 42, 44, 50–51, 54, 59–61, 64, 232n10, 233n29, 235n59, 236n68; *see also* Waddell, Alfred M.
Wilmington Journal 20–21, 30, 32, 38–39, 41–46, 47, 50–51, 66, 68, 107–108, 110, 232n10
Winslow, Warren 56, 232n11
Wood, Dr. Thomas F. 100
Wragg, Dr. William T. 100–101, 104, 108
Wright, Julius 38, 46
Wright, William A. 46, 47, 60, 98

Yancey, William 42

www.ingramcontent.com/pod-product-compliance
Lightning Source LLC
Chambersburg PA
CBHW051214300426
44116CB00006B/568